Here is an epic memoir that reads like a best-selling thriller. This fast-paced page turner has it all: Russian intrigue, spies, narrow escapes, adventure, political hijinx, mavericks, monsters, the birth of Alaskan statehood, and an ongoing love affair that spans the roller-coaster history of the Last Frontier

R. J. Rubadeau, award-winning author of *The Fat Man*

Vic Fischer's life story reads like a real-life Forrest Gump, with appearances by Lenin, Stalin, Eleanor Roosevelt, Winston Churchill, Saul Alinsky and many more, together with everyone in the whole history of Alaska from statehood to the present day. A great read by a great Alaskan.

—Brian Rogers, Chancellor, University of Alaska Fairbanks

Vic Fischer is Alaska's leading elder statesman and a leader in the Arctic. The lives he has touched span continents. It is no exaggeration to say his analytical skills and big heart changed the future for Alaska Native people in very positive ways. I enjoyed his book so much I read it twice.

—Julie Kitka, President, Alaska Federation of Natives

From a childhood marred by Stalin's rule to become a leader of Alaska, connecting Russia and America across the Bering Strait, and helping draft the state's constitution, Vic Fischer's life has been full of colorful incidents, remarkable coincidences, and historical echoes. This brilliant account of that extraordinary tale is enjoyable and powerful.

—Thom Hartmann, author, *The Last Hours of Ancient Sunlight*

T0345071

To Russia with Love

To Russia with Love

An Alaskan's Journey

Victor Fischer
with Charles Wohlforth

UNIVERSITY OF ALASKA PRESS
FAIRBANKS, ALASKA

© 2012 Victor Fischer
All rights reserved

University of Alaska Press
P.O. Box 756240
Fairbanks, AK 99775-6240

Library of Congress Cataloging-in-Publication Data
Fischer, Victor.
 To Russia with love : an Alaskan's journey / Victor Fischer ; with Charles Wohlforth.
   p. cm.
 ISBN 978-1-60223-140-5 (pbk. : alk. paper)—ISBN 978-1-60223-139-9 (cloth : alk. paper)—
 ISBN 978-1-60223-141-2 (e-book)
 1. Fischer, Victor. 2. Russian Americans—Alaska—Biography. 3. Jews, Russian—Biography.
 4. Soviet Union—History. 5. Alaska—Politics and government—1959– 6. Alaska—
 Biography. 7. Soviet Union—Biography. I. Wohlforth, Charles P. II. Title.
 F915.R9F47 2012
 979.8'05092—dc23
 [B]
                           2012006400

Cover design by Dixon Jones, Rasmuson Library Graphics
Cover illustration: Victor Fischer in Red Square in Moscow, 1989
Text design and layout by Paula Elmes

Support for this book was generously provided by the University of Alaska Anchorage. This
publication was printed on acid-free paper that meets the minimum requirements for ANSI /
NISO Z39.48–1992 (R2002) (Permanence of Paper for Printed Library Materials).

Printed in the United States

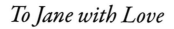

To Jane with Love

Contents

Introduction

A book can be a time machine. My father's autobiography returns me to a backyard fight in Berlin, Communists versus Nazis. Through my mother's memoir, I see my own big eyes as a teenager in Moscow, suggesting a trip to the circus to cheer her up as she faced the threat of liquidation by Stalin's secret police. Fifty years later, in Alaska, a book changed my life, bringing back the times and places of my youth and reconnecting me to those I knew when we lived our brightest days through the darkest hours of history.

The book that so influenced me was published in German in 1989 as *The Troika: The Story of an Unmade Film.* The author was the legendary head of the East German intelligence service, the "man without a face," my old friend Markus Wolf. The subject was my own childhood and that of my two closest friends, Lothar Wloch and Koni Wolf, Markus's brother, as we grew up in the shadow of Josef Stalin's Great Purge in 1930s Moscow.

World War II put us three friends on opposing sides as soldiers in three different uniforms—a Soviet, a German, and an American. But although we lived in different worlds, we never lost our connection, a link beyond brotherhood.

A 1990 Russian translation of Wolf's book reunited others from our teen days in Moscow. By then, I had reconnected my life to Russia, making links from my home in Alaska to help those in eastern regions who were experiencing freedom for the first time. After it was published, I met up with friends I hadn't heard from in fifty years.

Despite the passage of time, the ties to my classmates remained powerful. We had shared a tumultuous, joyous, terrible period of our lives, growing toward adulthood amid the constant fear of a knock late at night that would mean the political arrest of our parents. Three-quarters of our families were victims of Stalin. My mother escaped only with the help of Eleanor Roosevelt.

That experience didn't teach me to hate Russia. Not withstanding frequent abhorrent policies and politics, Russia has remained a second home for me, powerfully linked through family, friends, and deep memories. I have traveled a long journey to arrive as a senior statesman in Alaska, but have never left behind Russia or the love it gave me.

Born a US citizen, I learned English and started the personal process of becoming an American only after arriving in New York City in 1939. Then, as a GI on a troopship bound for France in 1945, I used library books to set two goals: to become a community planner and to go to Alaska. By 1950, I had finished graduate school in planning and made it to Alaska, finding a brand-new society with open arms for newcomers.

I joined the fight for statehood and, only five years later, was elected as a delegate to Alaska's constitutional convention, the most rewarding experience of my life. Also elected to the last territorial legislature, I cosponsored the abolition of the death penalty.

After statehood came in 1959, I worked in the Kennedy and Johnson administrations in Washington, DC, overseeing metropolitan planning programs nationally and assisting the reconstruction of my hometown of Anchorage and other Alaska cities after the massive 1964 earthquake.

Returning home, I helped found a social and economic policy institute at the University of Alaska that influenced many of the state's formative decisions. I also served in the Alaska state senate in the 1980s.

In 1989, when the Iron Curtain collapsed between Russia and the West, the Ice Curtain also thawed between Alaska and the Russian Far East. I leapt into the work of exporting Alaska experience and assistance to the gulag provinces of Siberia. Already in my sixties, I embarked on a new phase of my life, which became as rich and as full as any I had known. At seventy-five, I was recruited to be the governor of a province in eastern Russia. I declined.

The constant fact of my life is that I've kept hungrily diving into every opportunity to learn and do something new, to meet interesting people, or to go somewhere different. And I've been lucky. While the Soviet system constricted the lives of my classmates, the freedom of America burst boundaries and made anything seem possible for me. Transplanted from Russia's poisoned garden to the fertile land of Alaska, I gained everything that my friends lost to decades of repression. I've outlived most who remember the shadows cast by Hitler and

Stalin or the bright miracle of the writing of Alaska's Constitution and the dawn of Alaska statehood. Even many of the Russian friends with whom I reunited in the 1990s are gone.

Yet I don't feel that old. I have more energy for the future than for the past. The urging to write a book has come from others. I relish the invitations to speak and share my memories, because I enjoy connecting with people—especially young people—and talking about shared interests. But I am not a philosopher. I've always preferred action to introspection. When I try to write, I often find my mind too full and my interest too easily distracted into the moment and its possibilities.

My failure to write an autobiography until now makes me the black sheep among my family and oldest friends. My father, Louis Fischer, an American journalist and author of twenty-five books, published his autobiography in 1942, when he was only forty-five years old. *Men and Politics* was an influential book that traced the causes of World War II and covered his years in Russia and the Spanish Civil War.

My Lives in Russia, the autobiography of my mother, Markoosha Fischer, was a bestseller in 1944. She recounted her excitement at the overthrow of the tsars in 1917, her hopes for a new Russia, and her eventual disappointment with the Soviet Union, although it was too soon to reveal in that book the intense pressure Stalin's secret service applied to make her a spy.

Family friends who helped raise me, Paul and Hede Massing, also wrote books. Paul exposed Hitler after his early imprisonment in a concentration camp. Hede spied for the Soviets, but switched sides and testified against Alger Hiss in the biggest espionage case of the century. She wrote a book about that, too, although how much of her story is true is beyond anyone's ability to know.

My own generation followed with numerous books and films about our classmates, friends, and family. My brother George, besides his many academic books, wrote a series of unpublished autobiographies to assist his own self-examination and exploration of the world.

Now my accumulated experience impels me to write a book. My life is that full and my time that long. I've lived under fascism, communism, and democracy. I've spoken three primary languages. In addition to the greatest gift, to love and be loved, I have been privileged to write my values into documents guiding generations of people, including Alaska's constitution.

In writing this book I mainly relied on my memory, but I have also drawn on those old books and the thousands of long letters my family exchanged over five decades, as well as other massive archives. Those words allowed me to understand events that I couldn't have grasped as a child and to examine them from many perspectives. After so much time, I could see the motivations and hidden intrigues of people who are no longer living. Through this research, many facts that I misremembered were clarified. I have sought to make the book strictly accurate. With that aim, I've also employed a professional writer, Charles Wohlforth, with whom I spent several hundred hours engaged in lively and illuminating interviews. Charles overcame my nemesis, the blank page.

As I have looked to others to shed light on my life, I now understand that my accumulated experience perhaps teaches something useful.

Preparing a commencement address for 2009 graduates at the University of Alaska Fairbanks forced me to clarify my thoughts. Conscious not to bore a restive young audience and intimidated by an immovable deadline, I whittled away for days in search of the essential kernels of my beliefs. Many pages went by the wayside before I arrived at a simple, three-page statement that I could deliver in a matter of minutes.

In the end, I found I had two essential things to say. I encouraged the graduates to find, evolve, and strengthen their values, and to live by them. And I *demanded* of them generous participation in their state and their community, with responsibility to their fellow citizens. I told them of my deepest values. Respect for individual rights. Abhorrence of the state's power to kill its citizens. Opposition to all forms of insidious discrimination due to race, gender, sexual orientation, or any other such characteristic. I am dedicated to those without power—the poor, the underdog. I believe in fairness and equality.

These are basic humanistic beliefs and may seem self-evident in this first part of the twenty-first century. But for most of the twentieth century, they were matters of deep and terrible conflict. As bleak as the world often seems today, it has improved. We are making progress.

My personality makes me a full participant in life, but my sense of obligation to others, and the values that define that obligation, clearly came from the formative people and events of my life. What I am, and whatever I may have achieved, is the collective product of my parents and family, of my friends, classmates, and teachers, of all the people I have worked with and known. I am the product of all the opportunities I've had, and of the world around me. Of the books I read and all that's gone through my head.

As a kid, I saw the ennobling hope and common cause of those who believed communism could serve all of humanity and defeat fascism. My parents were among those believers. And I saw their dreams for the new Soviet Union become the nightmare of Stalin's repressive police state.

As an American, I lived the miracle of freedom and opportunity. I felt the positive power of democracy in ordinary people's hands. I saw how a single person can help shape the future.

My story *follows* the milestones of humanity's journey. I lived through the Reichstag fire that brought Hitler to power—and the fall of the Berlin Wall that reunited Germany. I felt the fear of Stalin's terror—and the joy of the first flights between Alaska and his former death-camp territories in Magadan.

My motivation for writing is as a witness to these events, as a participant in many, and as a product of the rise from repression to freedom. As an Alaskan, I am among those who have traveled farthest in space and time toward the better, more just society our state embodies, and which our constitution assures.

The book that follows contains the stories of my own life and only a little, if any, philosophy or theory about the meaning of the events that shaped me. Ultimately, good stories stand on their own. I relate them not to resuscitate the past, but to confirm my enthusiasm for the future.

The book is for my many wonderful friends, virtually all younger than I am, who keep asking around the campfire or dinner table for the stories it includes. It is for the young people in whose hands we leave the future. And, yes, it is for my children and grandchildren and their children yet to come.

I write with the same simple purpose I expressed to the UAF graduates: to live and strengthen my humanistic values as an eager participant in my state and my world.

Formative Years

1

The Reichstag Fire

It was 1931. Berlin, Germany. I was seven. Almost every balcony in our apartment building flew a party flag. Ours was red. We were the good guys. The bad guys had the swastika flag. There were others, but they are not in my memory.

Politics dominated even the life of this seven-year-old, as communists and fascists vied for power on the playgrounds as well as in Germany's parliament, the Reichstag. My brother George and I joined other kids from leftist families to face off with Nazi children, shoving and taunting, copying the political toughs who fought with sticks and brass knuckles in the streets.

When we saw children on another balcony in our L-shaped building flying their swastika Nazi flag, we screamed insults at them and they back at us. We had become conscious of the world around us back home in Moscow, where all of life was colored red. We had learned from our parents and from others around us the importance of the struggle for which everyone there was sacrificing.

Besides fighting for our side, we were raised in the cause of equality and economic justice. It motivated all the adults in my world to dedicate their lives to their ideals. At that time, many of them believed the communists were more likely to take over Germany than the fascists, as Marxism and Leninism spread worldwide. The idealism of those heady, chaotic times sank deep into my sense of myself, not as a communist, but as an optimist for humanity.

My mother, Markoosha Fischer, who was born in tsarist Russia, had bundled George and me off to Berlin to live with family friends, Paul and Hede Massing, whom she first met in the Soviet Union during the 1920s. Living conditions in

1

Moscow drove her to the decision. We had reached the point of near starvation under Josef Stalin's First Five-Year Plan for industrialization. Markoosha had struggled through the bitter Russian winter of 1930–1931 raising us on her own, supporting us with her scant earnings as a translator and with loans from friends. We had lived in a room in a filthy, dilapidated communal apartment.

Writing years later in her memoirs, she glossed over her hardships during that winter of the Five-Year Plan, but I've recently excavated her private letters written to my father, Louis Fischer, an American born in Philadelphia. He constantly traveled as a foreign correspondent and lent her no financial support.

She had sewn our winter clothes from his old pajamas. Unable to obtain butter, cream, meat, or chicken for weeks on end, she gave the best food she could find to George and me, while she and the maid ate boiled potatoes for every meal. Nonetheless, we boys grew thin and pale and were constantly ill from malnutrition and inadequately treated malaria.

Despite her sacrifices, Markoosha felt the need to apologize for complaining in her letters:

> To me Russia is the goal of everything. I arrived here as to the last escape from a world which I hate. And I, just as everybody else, must have an aim, a goal, a high idea. You may think that I pay too much attention to little things.... But when I see the children, the adults, pale and weak from *nagruzka* [burden] which no young organism can stand, narrow and one sided—I don't know where to look for hope.

Besides the physical privations, our mother worried about my brother's social development. The children in our Moscow neighborhood were tough; stealing and fighting were common. George became defiant of adult authority, a little revolutionary in his own right. The adults praised him for his fiery zeal for the Red cause when he organized the other children to march in front of the house chanting slogans, but his open challenges to his teachers got him in serious trouble.

George was Yuri when we were in Russia and Jura in Germany (I'll use George to keep things clear). The swirling emotions of our unsettled life tortured him. He idolized our important American father, but Louis had no interest in family life and treated us coldly when he did live with us. Louis preferred to stay in hotels and hobnob with the powerful rather than huddle in our one room in Moscow, harried by two boys, a wife, and a maid. He would not return as long as we lodged there. Markoosha needed to be free of us to be reunited with Louis, whom she adored.

George suffered from Louis's neglect and Markoosha's abandonment when she left to travel with him after installing us in Berlin. The banishment affected George as a rejection and he worried over it for the rest of his life, compulsively researching in his old age our parents' motivations through their archived letters. Among the discoveries from the archives: Markoosha hoped the Massings' German discipline and Hede's training in child development would straighten him out.

These issues barely affected me. A year younger than George, I was the infinitely adaptable child. Rather than being traumatized by the change, I remember being astonished by the size and cleanliness of the Massings' working-class apartment in Berlin, and the beauty and open space of the housing complex, called Friedrich Ebert Siedlung. The Social Democrats had recently built it as an enactment of their progressive policies to provide decent housing to the masses. Compared to Moscow, Depression-era Berlin was paradise.

Despite the political chaos in the streets, the Massings brought order to our lives and, for the first time, a loving father figure. Like all our parents' friends, Paul Massing was a leftist intellectual. He had earned a PhD in agronomy and had lived in Russia and written about the new communal agriculture. He also was a caring and charismatic young man who loved George and me and treated us as if we were his own sons. We came to treat him as our true father.

Paul was strict in the German style of raising children, but his warmth and humanity always predominated. He gave us a sense of security and value, which are critical to the happiness of a child. He also knew how to relate to our friends, becoming an adult member of whatever group might form around us. I spent many hours stamp collecting and playing chess with Paul in the apartment and hiking with him in suburban parks. We developed a connection that would support me many times throughout my childhood, teens, and adulthood.

In Berlin, Paul was a popular speaker, under an assumed name, working within the Communist Party. He and his comrades were convinced that their efforts, combined with a popular reaction against the rise of Adolf Hitler, would bring about a proletarian revolution in the streets. With this belief, they pursued a disastrous policy of fighting the moderate-left Social Democrats almost as avidly as they resisted the fascists, working to eliminate the middle rather than uniting with their natural allies against the Nazi Party.

Our elders analyzed these issues long afterward. German Communist Party members at the time probably could not have adopted a more reasonable strategy. They were controlled by the party in Russia under Stalin, which veered from one policy to another. Members learned to instantly agree with the latest dictate, as the party denounced and punished those who adhered to its former views as soon as they were officially discarded.

My mother described German party meetings as weird and unpleasant. Members tried to parrot the lines they thought they were supposed to be repeating from the Soviet Union and attacked anyone who diverged from that day's party line. The strongest reason to remain involved, for my parents as well as the Massings, was staunch resistance to fascism, which only the Soviets and communists wholeheartedly maintained.

Paul's wife, Hede, participated in the party much less, because she had been recruited, as I learned later, as a Soviet spy. After an unhappy childhood, Hede had fallen in with a set of German communist intellectuals, spending her days listening to their debates in the cafes and practicing their free-love philosophy. Paul was her third husband. Her second had been an American, and while with him, teaching in an orphanage in Massachusetts, she had obtained US citizenship. That US passport became her most important asset as a Soviet courier.

Ultimately, her passport brought Hede to safety in America before World War II. Her espionage work continued there until, in the late 1940s, she betrayed her old comrades and gave key testimony in court against Alger Hiss in one of the most famous spy cases in US history.

As children, all we knew about the Massings was that we liked Paul far better. Hede didn't connect with us, and George positively hated her for her discipline. The icky feeling she gave me, of course, had to do with her personality and psychology rather than her unknown life as a Soviet agent.

Political meetings frequently convened in the apartment. On one occasion, I was sent to a nearby store for a couple of pitchers of beer for the thirsty party members only to be found an hour later sleeping in a doorway with half a pitcher gone. Apparently I had gotten thirsty on the way home.

Paul enrolled George and me in the Berlin workers' sports club Fichte (Spruce) for swimming lessons. Even learning to swim was political. The international workers' sport movement, begun in the 1920s, emphasized fitness and cooperative activities as a counter to competitive capitalist sports. Millions participated, including some ten thousand in the Fichte club.

Getting to our evening swimming class required a scary walk in a downtown industrial area, crossing many blocks in pitch darkness from the trolley stop to the pool and back. But I loved the swimming and quickly learned to cross the pool underwater. When the instructor pushed me into the deep end of the pool without warning, I didn't drown.

Just as swimming has remained a great joy to me ever since, my Fichte membership card, dated 5 December 1932, has survived all this time in my possession, my oldest document except the birth certificate that I obtained later. It shows that I was known in Berlin as Vitja, the German spelling of Vitya, my

Russian name. The card was paid up for January and February 1933. March dues were not paid: Hitler had taken absolute power and we left Germany.

I sometimes resented the obsessive focus on politics around us, especially on one terrible day that is etched into my mind. A dear classmate, my only close friend at the time, came to our apartment to celebrate his birthday. On the return home, he had to cross the Müller Strasse, a wide boulevard with a park strip down the center and two streetcar tracks. His older sister went ahead by herself. As he followed her across, my friend ran in front of a car and was killed.

At the funeral, as I grieved, the adults around me wouldn't stop talking about Red politics. On one side of the room, a small window gave a view into the crematorium, and I could see the flames rising that were consuming my friend's body. Beside this horror, the adults kept chattering on. My fury returns vividly today as I recollect that moment.

Another powerful image from that period sticks with me more positively. We were invited to a town in the country for Christmas in 1932 to visit friends of the Massings. A boy in that family, Vikki, received a new electric train. I got his old wind-up train. The magic of the electric train fascinated me; and from that time forward, I became focused on electricity and how to make things work.

Ultimately, I would learn to build ingenious electrical toys from ordinary materials I could obtain. This mechanical outlet, along with my generally easygoing personality, may have protected me through difficult years that had more impact on my brother. I became enamored with the idea of being an electrical engineer, wherever I might end up in the world.

But one could never forget politics for long in Berlin. I remember a strike at the Müller Strasse streetcar barn, which we could see from our apartment. Most people in the neighborhood supported the strikers. For its leftist leanings, the district was called Red Wedding.

Nazi Party brownshirts arrived en masse to attack the strikers. A huge melee erupted with vicious, bloody fighting between the two sides. We watched from our window as the Nazis and the streetcar workers beat one another with clubs and any other weapon at hand. After that fight, and many others, we saw blood in the streets, both fresh and dried.

We boys did our part, fighting fascist children with slingshots and whatever other forces our skinny, little bodies could manage. I don't remember anyone getting seriously hurt. Some boys called George a "dirty Jew," the first time he had ever realized he was Jewish, prompting him to come to ask Hede what being

a Jew meant. But on the whole, the Jews didn't take Hitler's anti-Semitism seriously at that point. Few took the opportunity to get out of Germany.

The conditions that could create such political conflict are difficult to
imagine from the perspective of our affluent American society. My father
was one of the first and most perceptive writers on the subject. He was a
regular correspondent for the then influential liberal weekly, the *Nation*.
Louis also wrote for many other publications and wrote books, always as an
independent freelancer.

As Louis explained, the economic chaos and social despair imposed upon
Germany by the victors of World War I created an atmosphere of emergency
in which extremists could win supporters for their side. Moderates within the
country, and outsiders who could have helped, repeatedly failed to take decisive
action to reduce the German peoples' suffering or to resolve their grievances.
International policy focused on sham arms-control talks.

Big business funded the Nazis to beat back labor unions and strengthen capitalism. The industrialists foolishly believed they would always be able to control Hitler. The communists indirectly contributed to his rise, too, by creating a
frightening alternative to fascism. Fear of communism helped drive the middle
class toward the Nazis.

Two rounds of elections in 1932 brought Berlin to a frenzy of marches and
demonstrations. I well remember our hope that the left would make advances
and our fear that a Nazi victory would bring our annihilation. Scores of Germans
on both sides died in election violence.

The fascists did well in the voting, but not as well as the moderates. The
communists and moderates could have heavily overbalanced the Nazis, but
they were unable to work out their differences. After a period of stalemate and
uncertainty, President Paul von Hindenburg unexpectedly named Hitler as
Germany's chancellor on January 30, 1933.

In his book *Men and Politics*, my father documented the meeting with the
industrialists when Hitler won Hindenburg's support. Hitler's mediocrity and
extremism convinced them he could be handled as a puppet.

Four weeks later, on the night of February 27, 1933, explosive news came
that the Reichstag—the home of the German parliament—was burning. Only
a shell was left of the grand stone building. The government accused a deranged
communist of setting the fire. Using this as a pretext, Hitler declared a state of
emergency and suspended civil rights, outlawing communists and making massive arrests. Within a month, he had taken total control of Germany.

Until the Reichstag fire, Communist Party members such as Paul Massing
still believed events were playing into their hands. They expected Hitler to over-
reach, motivating the mass populace to take to the streets in revolution. Now,

suddenly, all communists were in grave danger. They began to scatter or go underground as quickly as they could.

My father was in New York. He called Paul Massing and demanded his boys be moved out of the country immediately. Paul countered that Hitler would not last ninety days. But Louis insisted, saying his sons would never live under fascism. Finally they agreed we would be out of Germany within forty-eight hours. A mad rush began to prepare for our departure. Hede herded us around, urging us to speed our packing, making arrangements for a long trip. She took charge of Vikki as well. In a brief, anguished telephone conversation, Hede told Markoosha she would try to get us to Czechoslovakia as Louis demanded, but then she dropped from contact.

Markoosha, in a comfortable new apartment in Moscow, heard news of arrests in Berlin and rumors of horrors, but couldn't find out what was going on with her children. After a couple of frustrating attempts, she stopped trying to call Berlin out of fear that anyone she contacted in Germany could be arrested and executed as a traitor. Meanwhile, unknown to her, we had left for Czechoslovakia under the guise of a skiing vacation under the charge of Hede's domestic helper. Eventually Markoosha learned of our whereabouts through the assistance of a friend.

After the trauma of the fascists' rise, fear for our friends, and our hurried departure, I remember arriving at a large building in the mountains, in the dark. And I remember my amazement when light returned in the morning and I found we were at a mountainside lodge in a mostly treeless alpine faerie land. The setting was extraordinarily attractive to a boy like me, who loved the outdoors but had mostly been confined to cities. Whatever else was happening in the world, I suddenly found myself in paradise.

The resort was in the Isar Mountains in the Sudetenland of Czechoslovakia, which Hitler later would annex to Germany by force. George and I arrived in late winter and stayed six months. We immediately got skis and took off to explore. We studied with a private tutor, enjoying occasional visits from my mother and Hede.

I remember one visit when Markoosha came with a rich American friend who took us out to dinner and said we could order anything we wanted. I had fried eggs and spinach. Another visitor gave us all the ice cream we wanted.

A local boy who met us that summer, Günther Rücker, remembered our appearance with more drama. He was introduced to us with instructions not to ask us too many questions. The air of mystery made a deep impression on him and he came to admire us out of all proportion to our importance.

Rücker later recorded the experience in a letter: "They had black hair, spoke the Berlin dialect, had no respect of anybody, and everything associated with them was surrounded by secrecy. Even their family name was never called out.... I felt more than I knew that the dangerous world came closer, and so did the images of nearby Germany or the far away world of the Soviet's five year plans."

Meanwhile, in Germany, Hitler had total control. The Nazis rounded up known communists. Paul and Hede at first believed they could survive by moving to a bourgeois area of Berlin and assuming a new identity.

When Hede cleaned out their old apartment, she took as many precautions as possible to avoid detection as a communist. She hired movers from a firm without party connections and refused to give them either address until the last minute. To her horror, one of the movers found a red flag in the closet of the bedroom George and I had used.

Hede pretended she didn't know why the flag had been in the apartment and told the mover to throw it away. He lowered his voice and said she shouldn't get rid of the flag, because she might be needing it again soon. Hede repeated the story many times to friends in her movement as evidence that the common working man in Germany was ready for revolution.

Feeling more secure and optimistic, Hede even wrote to Markoosha suggesting that George and I return to them in Berlin. But as the crackdown continued, Paul went deeper underground, refusing to flee despite his reputation as a public speaker against fascism, which made it likely he would be arrested. He worked to organize professors and scientists to produce a student uprising.

No uprising materialized. The Nazis' massive security apparatus made organizing nearly impossible. Communist Party members disappeared into prisons and labor camps and were tortured for the names of their comrades, sometimes tortured to death. For all the risk, they accomplished little. They produced illegally mimeographed leaflets on illicitly obtained paper—leaflets no one could read without putting themselves in grave danger.

Working in Berlin, Paul tried to become invisible, burning all his political books and papers, slipping out back doors and moving in crowds, and always looking for who might be following him. But despite these pressures, he didn't forget us. One morning I woke at the ski lodge in Czechoslovakia and told Hede I'd had a dream that Paul came to my bed during the night and kissed me while I slept. And then I discovered, to my great joy, that it was not a dream. Paul had slipped over the border through the forest and was there to visit us. A few days of hiking in the mountains and playing chess, and he was gone again.

A few months later, Paul was arrested in his new apartment and taken by Nazi storm troopers to the notorious Columbia House prison in Berlin to be locked alone in a tiny, unlit cell. The brand-new Hitler regime had already perfected its brutal institutional sadism. Prisoners were tortured in the cellar, their screams ringing through the prison. Part of each victim's mental torture was to be informed of the exact date and time of his next torture session so he could anticipate it.

Paul withstood lashing that left him unable to stand, yet never gave up the names of any of his comrades. After more than two weeks, he and some other prisoners were transferred to the Oranienburg concentration camp, where they were welcomed by another round of beatings. Hundreds of political prisoners slept on straw pallets in a damp, converted wine cellar. They marched two hours a day to pile dirt on dykes and marched two hours back, subsisting on thin potato gruel.

In his months at the camp, Paul got to know the prisoners and the workings of the system. Some fellow inmates were communists, while others were members of the center-left Social Democrat Party, or were pacifists, or, receiving the worst treatment of all, were Jews. Formerly important people, such as former Reichstag delegates, slept in the cellar and ate the gruel along with the others.

Some prisoners suffered in the camp for no reason at all, perhaps turned in because of someone's grudge. Failure to confess brought beatings and confinement for days at a time in chambers that were too small to sit down, with floors slanted too steeply for standing.

Hede went to Paris, where her Soviet spy network supported her and offered help to get Paul out. Under her colleagues' care, she secretly returned to Germany. They managed to pass a message to Paul. Hede was able to watch from a cafe as he marched back to the camp each day from his work detail, pale and limping after months of beatings.

In the end, Paul's older brother got him out of the camp. The brother held a high position in a regional branch of the Nazi Party. Paul came back to Berlin briefly and was hustled out of Germany. Thanks to Hede's American citizenship, he was able to go to the United States, where they settled in New York.

Safe in America, Paul wrote an influential book describing his experiences, *Fatherland,* which the *New York Times* called, five years later, in 1940, the most important early book to reveal the cruelty of the Nazi state from the inside. To protect his brother, he wrote under the pseudonym Karl Billinger and made the book a novel, although he changed little from his own personal experiences.

Looking back on my childhood, it is tempting to focus on my parents' problems. My brother did so when he dredged their hidden needs in the papers stored in the Princeton University library. Likewise, one can second-guess the sacrifices made to protect and spread a communist political system that, as my father later wrote, evolved from the world's greatest hope to its greatest threat. But judging political decisions out of context is unfair. At the time, Paul's heart connected with mine and his courage inspired me. I still feel that way.

Long before Paul and my parents broke with communism, they saw its intellectual tyranny and bureaucratic stupidity. They experienced the beginnings of the Soviet police state while still supporting it with sacrifices large and small. Paul recognized some of these faults even before his heroic decision to go underground in Germany with the constant threat of capture. But his sense of responsibility gave him no alternative.

As journalist Lincoln Steffens wrote in the foreword to Paul's book *Fatherland,* the world had only two choices in the 1930s: fascism or communism. "Communists are the worst hated of all men by the Nazis," Steffens wrote. "You can see here [in Paul's book] the reason for this. Communism is the opposite of the Fascists' way; the Communists are the most dangerous of all people to the Fascists; and the Communists are the hardest to conquer."

Paul answered the call as one of the earliest resisters to the worst regime in human history. Likewise, my father's writings were prescient. If Western leaders had listened, Hitler would have had no chance. The ultimate motivation behind Paul and my parents' work was simply the good of humankind. They believed in social justice and the equality of all people. Amid the great, convulsive world events of their time, they did their best.

My parents both developed belief in liberalism and the improvement of humanity from the circumstances in which they were raised, as witnesses to poverty and injustice. But even as mates they remained opposites, one warm and one cold, one personal and one analytical. Their beliefs and their strange marriage shaped me in many ways, some I'm still discovering.

⇥ 2 ⇤

Markoosha and Louis

I begin with Markoosha, because I was my mother's son. From her I inherited my open, affectionate spirit; my ability to accept change and adapt to new experiences; and my need for love, intimacy, and deep connection with my family and friends. She was often uncertain or sad, as I have learned in detail from her private letters, read forty years after her death. But as my mother, and as a friend to many, she always offered strength and comfort.

Markoosha got the name she would use throughout her life in young adulthood. She was born Bertha Mark in 1888 in Libau, Latvia, when that country was still part of tsarist Russia. Her childhood was difficult. As a fun-loving and rebellious girl, she was constantly in trouble.

Her father, Jakob Mark, emerges in her writings as a wise and kindly man and a friend to his children and everyone else, but he had little hand in her upbringing. Instead, his strict and humorless second wife oversaw Markoosha. It's easy to imagine how this home life led my mother to idolize and emulate her father, especially after she learned, at age twelve, that her stepmother was not her biological mother. Her real mother had died shortly after her birth. Accidentally receiving this information redoubled her resentment against her stepmother, although she never revealed why.

While Markoosha felt hostile toward the parent who had time for her, she adored her father, who was too busy to get involved. He was a learned man and active social reformer and a helper to every unfortunate who came to him. Admiring him, Markoosha developed the same qualities.

Jakob, whom I never met, came from six generations of Jewish rabbinical teachers. He was a synagogue elder and advocate for a Jewish state, yet also a liberal and lover of high culture who devoured German books and newspapers. His ethnicity as a Russian Jew evidently accorded higher status than that of the native Latvians among whom they lived.

As a young man, he invented a correspondence course to teach double-entry bookkeeping in Hebrew and later in Russian, selling the service with small newspaper advertisements. Through persistence and careful attention to his pupils, he turned the course into a business that supported the family amply for thirty years and helped tens of thousands of young men learn a career.

Much of what I know about my mother's younger years comes from her auto-biography, *My Lives in Russia,* especially chapters that were deleted from the published version but turned up recently when I was researching her papers. She describes her outrage and increasing resistance against her teachers and her mother as she saw the unfair treatment of poor and non-Russian children at school. Even with superior ability, their class or ethnic status denied them good grades or chances to attend university.

She blamed the tsar. She once saw him and the tsarina at a ceremony at the Libau port. He seemed to her weak and pale, appearing scared of the burly local men who presented him with bread and salt, the traditional offering to a visiting dignitary. In 1905, during an unsuccessful revolution, police raided the family apartment in the middle of the night and took away her older sister, Tatyana, who had been working with a group opposed to the tsar. Markoosha had already developed a taste for the Russian and French literature of rebellion. She joined a secret study circle of girls to learn about Marxism led by a romantic young man. Her stepmother, hoping to keep her from the path that had led to Tatyana's arrest, sent her first to music conservatory in St. Petersburg and then to a girls' finishing school in Switzerland.

A Swiss headmistress finally discharged Markoosha to prevent the spread of her free-spirited resistance to the school's strict lessons on propriety and for-mality in all aspects of life. The school was also eager to excise the spreading germ of her ideas about love and feminism (which did catch on and change the lives of some of her friends anyway).

She then attended Lausanne University in Switzerland and subsequently went to Berlin to be near her sister. Tatyana had been released after two years as a political prisoner in St. Petersburg and had moved to Berlin with her husband, whom she met by tapping messages in Morse code on the wall of her cell.

In Switzerland and Berlin, Markoosha found herself amid the leaders of the coming Russian revolution, who argued and refined their theories in lectures, debating clubs, and publications. Vladimir Lenin stood above all—Markoosha encountered him and his wife once at a bookstore in Geneva—and she also knew the Russian writer Maxim Gorky, for whom she worked in a Berlin publishing house. Through Tatyana, Markoosha made friends with Karl Radek, who became Lenin's close collaborator, and with Georgi Chicherin, who would become Lenin's first foreign commissar, the Soviet equivalent of foreign minister.

She learned most from the glamorous Alexandra Kollontai, a future Soviet ambassador. In a passage deleted from her autobiography, Markoosha wrote,

> [Kollontai] believed in a woman's right to free love. She preached it and lived it. Until I heard her speak for the first time in Lausanne, it bothered me greatly that the word "freedom" was applied only to political and economic systems. Only pornographic novels and modernistic poems talked of freedom of the body and free love. But they hardly gave me the answer to tormenting questions. Alexandra Kollontai spoke clearly and plainly of the new human being, free from political, economic and personal chains. She spoke of the new family based on economic independence of man and woman.

Although committed to freedom and other left-wing causes, Markoosha never joined a party. Tatyana belonged to the Mensheviks, a group that had splintered from Lenin and his Bolshevik comrades over issues of revolutionary policy and strategy. Many other varieties of radical wanted to overthrow the tsar as well. Markoosha agreed with them all and, despite earnest study, could not choose which to join. Instead, she contributed by playing the piano and selling sandwiches and programs at events put on by all of the groups.

With the outbreak of World War I, Markoosha returned to Russia, hoping to assist with humanitarian work. But she became disgusted once again with the tsarist government, which continued to exploit workers and peasants and to repress all political dissent. So she left for Copenhagen to work with the Danish Red Cross, while also carrying messages, on tiny slips of paper and in her memory, for the revolutionary movement around Europe. Among her friends in Denmark was Nikolai Bukharin, soon to be a key figure in the revolution.

While in Copenhagen, she received an offer to travel to America as a pianist for a traveling group of Russian classical musicians, which she accepted on a whim. She arrived in New York in 1916.

After the American performances, the United States' entry into the war interfered with Markoosha's planned return to Europe. So she stayed on in New York and worked as an interpreter and translator, thanks to her fluency in English, Russian, German, and French.

She became a close friend of Jewish writer Sholem Asch and easily fell in with a bohemian set of young intellectuals in Greenwich Village, including Emma Goldman and journalist John Reed. In her later life, she enjoyed telling young people that the sex and drugs in the Village during World War I surpassed anything imagined by the beat or hippie generations decades later.

In March 1917, when the tsar fell in Russia, celebrations lasted days in the Jewish community in New York. At first, Markoosha wanted nothing more; she was happy for Russia's freedom under the democratic Kerensky government. But one night when she went to hear her friend Bukharin speak, she was transformed by an oration by Leon Trotsky, Lenin's Bolshevik partner.

While Trotsky was in New York, she traveled to the far reaches of the city to hear him several times each night, as she related in the excised chapters of her memoir.

> He said that the banks, railroads, land, mines, factories must belong to the people. He said that the war must end. That there must be no rich and poor. He spoke of the abolition of money, of new women's rights and of universal education. I transferred his political slogans into everyday life and it became just what I always dreamt about without being able to put it into words.

Still, she didn't join the Bolsheviks. But she worked in an office that they soon took over, under a railroad expert assigned to acquire equipment for the obsolete and war-ruined Russian rail lines. Through the office flowed the drama of the Russian Civil War and the genocidal pogroms against Jews in Ukraine, as visitors and huge stacks of mail brought horrible news of slaughters and upheavals.

My father was an aspiring journalist when he met Markoosha in New York in 1920. Louis Fischer's early life had been much harder than Markoosha's. His father, David, an illiterate fishmonger from a poor village in Ukraine, adopted the name Fischer in America because his traditional name, Khmelnitski, was too difficult to spell. In Philadelphia he worked in a factory or sold fish and fruit from a pushcart. He abandoned the family when Louis was young, adopting a squalid life of alcoholism. Without him, the family struggled on the edge of survival in the city's worst slums.

Louis's mother, Shifrah, worked herself to exhaustion taking in laundry and cleaning houses to support him and his older sister, Ida. Frequently unable to afford rent, the family moved with each new eviction. Louis possessed only one suit, which had to be washed at home before he could venture back to school the next day. Until he was sixteen he never lived in a home with electricity, central heat, running water, or an indoor toilet.

But Louis was bright, precocious, and a constant reader. He devoured Tolstoy, Dostoevsky, Turgenev, and Gogol in translation. His mother and his sister Ida doted on him and made every possible sacrifice for his education. Ida herself quit school so she could earn money to help Louis attend a two-year teachers' college.

I never met any of my father's family until I was a teen and Louis was already a famous journalist. His mother had died, but Ida lived happily in Philadelphia with children of her own. Her adoration of Louis continued. She seemed to love him better than her kind and gentle husband, Harry Sigmond. Louis's success repaid her every sacrifice with pride and status in their community.

Louis taught only briefly. Instead, he volunteered near the end of World War I, in 1917, to fight with the Jewish Legion, a unit of the British Army, which took him to the Middle East. He already had developed remarkable skill as a writer, sending home vivid letters, carefully typed with double-spaced lines. After an adventure driving for days through the deserts of Palestine and trying to ford the Jordan River on foot, he wrote to Shifrah and Ida:

> What say you? You will probably say I am a fool, and worry because I risk things. Don't worry. I have confidence. I have confidence now sitting in my car, the only non-Arab for miles around. Firing is regular business in these parts. Every once in a while the encircling hills re-echo and again re-echo a shot from a Bedouin's rifle. They do it for sport. Then the caves, the mouths of which I see now, give the sound back after a strange silence.

Louis adventured and romanticized his travels, but also thoroughly analyzed the news and events around him. When the war ended and the ALLIES negotiated the Treaty of Versailles, he spread a map on the Egyptian sand to interpret its provisions, studying each of the 440 articles. Both habits served him well as a journalist when he left the military.

From the British Army Louis went to New York to work for a news agency and met my mother among the fast, bright, leftist crowd in Greenwich Village. She was eight years older (although she always shaved two years from her age) and far better connected than he was at the time. Her important international friends must have added to her allure. He wanted to be a foreign correspondent.

In 1921, when Markoosha moved to Berlin to continue the railroad work there, Louis followed her, hoping to contribute as a low-level stringer to the *New York Evening Post*. Her sister was there, and she quickly joined the community of Russians and leftists. By contrast, when Louis arrived, he was a beginner. He got off the train in Berlin at the wrong station and wandered in the new city until finding someone to take him to her.

Markoosha provided Louis with a linguistic, cultural, and personal base from which to build his writing career. And they had a passionate relationship. She was a spirited woman, lovely and slender, freethinking, and outwardly adventurous. Her interest in him began with the physical as well. Louis was tall and athletic. He exuded masculine intensity that impressed men and women, and he knew how to sweep a potential lover off her feet.

The exact terms of their relationship were known only to them, but both had affairs over the years. Louis's were frequent and eventually became legendary, as did the brutal way he discarded women when he was done with them. Near the end of his life, *Time* magazine even took note of this practice, after Louis dumped Josef Stalin's daughter and she came unglued on the doorstep of his Princeton house and had to be removed by the police.

Louis's personality contributed to great journalism, some of which sells well to this day. His 1964 biography of Lenin won the National Book Award. Scholars study his books from the early years of the Soviet Union because he talked extensively with the men making history, he read their papers in their own offices and hotel suites, and he solicited and incorporated their comments on his manuscripts. He was the historian's surrogate as history happened.

The texts themselves show why these busy, important men spent so many hours with him. Besides recording events in clear, assertive prose, Louis synthesized what he learned into powerful, overarching ideas. From amid a complex political situation, he could sum up lasting meaning.

Undergraduates continue to read his 1950 biography, *The Life of Mahatma Gandhi*, upon which Sir Richard Attenborough based the film *Gandhi*, which won eight Academy Awards in 1982. Louis visited Gandhi's ashram in India in 1942 and they talked day after day. His verbatim diaries about the meetings, published as *A Week with Gandhi*, show their developing rapport, which led to Gandhi asking Louis to stay even longer. Gandhi appreciated my father's contributions to the conversations. He asked big questions, he challenged assumptions, and he shared his own deep, inside knowledge of politics and world events.

But at the beginning, his relationship with Markoosha helped Louis to his first big break. In spring of 1922, a delegation came to Berlin from Moscow to prepare for an international conference in Genoa, Italy, intended to set up a new world economic system for recovery from World War I. For the first time, the Soviets would face their Western adversaries and try to gain entry into the world economy.

While preparing, the leader of the delegation, Maxim Litvinov, dined with Markoosha's employer and learned that she could type and was fluent in four languages. They agreed to a loan. Markoosha went to the embassy for an interview with Litvinov. They had hardly begun when her old friend Karl Radek, now a top Soviet official, threw his arms around her in greeting. She became a member of the delegation without further questions.

Markoosha attended secret, unrecorded discussions in which the most critical interactions of the conference occurred, and typed the Treaty of Rapallo between Germany and the Soviet Union, which normalized relations and opened trade between the two countries. She also joined in the Russian delegation's fun evening gatherings, as Chicherin played Mozart on the piano and other important Soviet leaders demonstrated their folk dancing skill.

Louis got access to these men through Markoosha and gained a close view of the workings of international power politics. Among the key issues at play in Genoa was the control of oil in the Caucasus region, which became the subject of his first book.

During World War I, away from the trenches in Central Europe, armies had grappled in the Middle East and in the Caucasus, which is bounded by the Black Sea to the west and the Caspian Sea to the east, by Russia proper to the north and by Turkey and Iraq to the south, and which includes Azerbaijan, Georgia, and Armenia. British forces had captured Baghdad with its rich oil lands and, at the end of the war, occupied Baku, the capital of Azerbaijan, lying amid the largest oil fields in the world.

Before going home, the British installed and armed friendly local forces to oppose the Bolsheviks in the Russian Civil War. Major international oil companies bought into the oil fields. But in 1921, the Red Army conquered Baku and nationalized the oil industry there.

When the Genoa Conference convened in 1922, civil war still continued in the Russian Far East. The Soviet Union, unrecognized internationally and economically desperate, was ready to make a deal over the oil at Baku in order to improve ties to the West. None of these discussions happened in public, but Markoosha certainly would have heard them. (She later claimed not to have understood, but I do not believe that.)

Standard Oil, Shell, and other oil companies worked through their national delegations to maneuver for a larger piece of the prize. Then the Americans torpedoed the conference rather than let Baku's oil fall into competitors' hands.

Louis picked up this journalistic lead and followed it like a detective. He had served under the British in the Middle East until only two years earlier. Now he played one oil company against another for evidence and cultivated new friendships with Markoosha's contacts. Foreign commissar Chicherin became a particular confidant and helper.

Later that year, in September, Louis went to Moscow, bunking with a reporter from the Associated Press in the rat-infested Savoy Hotel, the only place open to journalists. He rapidly joined the fraternity of the foreign press corps, playing poker, drinking, and watching the birthing of the great Soviet experiment.

Louis already admired the Soviet leaders he knew, especially Chicherin, whom he described as speaking "with piercing honesty, humor and brilliance" (though Markoosha found him "fussy and tyrannical"). Now Louis also rejoiced in the spirit of the new nation itself. Although crushed by poverty and with an economy that didn't function, the people believed.

For Louis, a child of the slums, the Russians' dreams had special meaning, as he wrote in *Men and Politics*:

> Especially did I feel that society has an obligation to help us overcome the accident of birth. Soviet Russia... was conceived by its creators as the kingdom of the underdog. Evolution is the survival of the fittest; civilization is the survival of the unfittest. The Bolsheviks undertook to serve civilization by aiding those handicapped by poor parents, inadequate education, bad health, and slave psychology.

Louis interviewed ordinary Russian people in the streets of Moscow and in the countryside. He attended historic political meetings. At one, in the tsar's former throne room, Lenin entered and quietly sat down in a folding chair not far from my father. Lenin had been absent, recovering for six months from a stroke. When others began to notice him, cheers rose and he was ushered forward to speak.

Lenin talked for fifteen minutes, the time allowed by his doctors. Louis didn't understand much of the speech, but managed to squeeze close to Lenin for the group photo taken afterward in an anteroom to the tsarina's bedroom. After a brief time as a reporter and with only casual freelance outlets for his work, Louis had found his way into the most exciting events of his day.

Markoosha finally got to Russia at the same time by other means. Her employer in Berlin included her in a journey to test new locomotives. She rode through the poverty-stricken Russian countryside in the tsars' opulent railcars, feeling distaste at the silk brocade and painted cupids in her own compartment, which had belonged to a princess.

Snowy plains and frozen lakes passed by outside the train, and hungry Russian people, ragged and grim, on muddy roads and atop filthy station platforms. By late October she was reunited with Louis at the Savoy Hotel in Moscow. The rest of her delegation returned to Germany without her.

In Moscow, Markoosha was thrilled, like Louis, by Trotsky's inspiring speeches and Lenin's humanity. Food was scarce, but theater tickets plentiful. She avidly absorbed an explosion of experimental art, drama, books, and ways of organizing society. Everyone was involved. In her memoir she wrote:

> Around the theaters, as well as around music, movies, paint-
> ing, or any other expression of art, raged endless public dis-
> cussions. The new and the old fought fiercely with each
> other. These discussions, as well as all other public debates
> or lectures, invariably attracted large crowds. The thirst for
> knowledge and intelligent entertainment was immense. These
> gatherings frequently lasted until well after midnight. It was
> not out of love for late hours. In these heated debates Russians
> were struggling to see their way clear through the multitude
> of new ideas and situations which the revolution had created.

When she arrived in Moscow, Markoosha already was pregnant with my brother, George. Louis and Markoosha went to a government office to fill out the necessary papers to be married. The revolution had changed sexual relations, too: divorce could be effected by mailing a postcard to a registrar. At first, they accidentally went to the wrong window, the one for divorces.

In his *Men and Politics*, Louis passed off his wedding with a single cold phrase: "We were married so that Markoosha could have a baby without too much social inconvenience." In that book of almost seven hundred pages, full of the names of famous politicians and journalists he knew, and their tennis and poker games, he mentioned his family only for a few brief sentences.

The truth, which Louis readily acknowledged, was that he never had any intention of being a good husband or father. He wrote, "I am essentially a liber-tarian and resent shackles, even personal ones. I can impose discipline on myself but I would fight its imposition on me by others." He offered Markoosha no financial support and scant emotional support, nor did he live with her, for the next six years.

Chicherin persuaded Markoosha to accompany him from Moscow to a diplomatic conference in Lausanne, Switzerland. She departed sadly, within weeks of the wedding, and afterward could not return. She couldn't have a baby in Moscow's Savoy Hotel. She settled again in Berlin. George was born there on May 5, 1923, propitiously the birthday of Karl Marx.

Louis reappeared that summer and took Markoosha, the baby, and a nurse for a Baltic seaside vacation at a good hotel. The German currency was so weak he could afford all that on his meager dollar-denominated earnings from selling newspaper articles. I must have been conceived on that trip. I was born a day before my brother's first birthday, although my mother always celebrated both our birthdays on May 5.

After the German vacation, Louis went to New York with a set of articles on Russia to sell to the *Nation,* the liberal weekly he had dreamed of writing for since childhood. He had no idea how to accomplish it and, after being turned away by a receptionist, spent months idly hoping for something to turn up.

Friends encouraged him to try again. When he did, the managing editor, Ernest Gruening, read his work and liked it. (Gruening later was governor of Alaska.) Louis became a regular foreign correspondent for the *Nation.* Although he sold his articles to the magazine one at a time and without an expense account, the relationship gave him a steady market for his work and the prestige of representing an important publication.

In 1926 he published his first book, *Oil Imperialism,* which investigated the connivance of Western governments and the oil industry to access the Soviet Union's Baku petroleum reserves, beginning with the Genoa Conference. The book also documented Japanese and Western attempts to gain control of the Sakhalin oil fields located in the Russian Far East north of Japan.

Louis's brisk, assertive writing style had matured. His reporting skills brought together a complex story with clarity and new revelations. The book established his international reputation and started his lecture career in the United States, which often earned more money than writing. He didn't mention Markoosha's role in the acknowledgments or elsewhere in the book.

A pattern became established in my parents' odd marriage. My mother earned money from translation, or whatever else she could manage, and created a warm, secure home for George and me. She helped friends and strangers in trouble with a generosity bordering on sainthood, or perhaps mania, for her private writings reveal that behind her outward strength she hid sadness and need.

At times she couldn't keep it up any longer and sought psychological help. Her long, complex letters to my father attempted to attach him to her, with guilt, with seduction, and with the truth that she longed for his love and support. He lived in hotels and traveled the world. Her home in Berlin was a pit stop. She knew he wasn't faithful to her, but she still wanted him.

But I can't blame my father. I don't know that he broke any promise to Markoosha. He expressed regret in his own letters that he was incapable of showing affection to those who were closest to him. He once noted in a book on Stalin, "He does not give emotionally. What he cannot give he does not receive." Yet that wasn't true in Louis's case, as his coldness was met by love from his family.

At this date it's too late to divine Louis's motivations or understand why he could not show real warmth. His inner life is opaque in his writing. As an adult, I received letters from him that began with long recitations of his daily activities, which I realized at the time were written for his own benefit as a record for future reference. He gave few clues of what was in his heart. But he kept in touch with me in later years and always kept an interest in what I was doing.

A set of letters from 1931 gives some insight into my father's upbringing and how he developed his hard shell. He was staying at the Hotel Lafayette in Washington when he received word from a cousin in Pennsylvania that his father was dying in the incurables ward of a hospital from the effects of his dissipated life, and was asking constantly for his son.

The cousin, Ethel Berman, wrote, "Can you picture anything more desolate than a poor, broken (spiritually and physically) old man, living his last days in the squalor of the Philadelphia General Hospital, without so much as the comfort of seeing someone who is dear to him, despite everything?"

Louis refused to go. He wrote back,

> My life of recent years has been rich and full, and I rarely linger on the distant past. My father long ago ceased to exist for me. Why should I not say it when it is true?...Under these circumstances, what would be the sense of my seeing him? I would be ready to accept the trial of an embarrassing half-hour, but to what end?...I could not be affectionate to him: I sometimes experience difficulty in manifesting my emotions even to persons who are dear to me.

Ethel Berman responded with even more passion: "You paint a picture of your mental attitude, and while not anxious to philosophize nor moralize, [I] wish you would destroy that heritage of your father's before it destroys you, for in his life he would go to all lengths rather than show what seemed to him a weakness."

Louis's father died alone and Louis never did overcome his heritage of coldness. He was a frowning presence in my childhood memories. At those times
when he did live with us, George and I were frequently told to keep quiet so he
could work, and we did. I fortunately didn't inherit that from him, nor did I suffer much from it. I had my mother and Paul Massing as models for how to feel.

In the end, I was proud of my father's work and his ideals, and of being the
famous Louis Fischer's son.

⇥ 3 ⇤

Early Soviet Years

When asked about my first language, I cannot give a simple answer. During our early days in Berlin, my mother continued working for the Soviet Railroad Mission, leaving George and me with a nurse or housekeeper. When I was a baby, a Russian émigré cared for me, speaking Russian. Next came a caregiver I remember only as Frau Schröder, who spoke German, which then became my language. My mother could speak Russian or German equally well, and did.

I was three when we moved to the Ukraine for Markoosha to do social work, and my brother and I switched to Russian again. By then we were bilingual, in a sketchy way. According to family lore, I was an early speaker, but George did not talk until he was three; however, when he began to speak he started right off in full sentences and never stopped talking thereafter.

Markoosha had wanted to return to the Soviet Union ever since her exciting days in 1922, when Lenin was still in charge. She began trying to get there as soon as I was out of infancy but couldn't find housing for the family in Moscow. Finally, in 1927, she at least got closer when she accepted a job offer to help dispossessed Jews in the Ukraine.

Under the tsar, Russian Jews could not own land and, in most cases, lived confined to crowded towns, mostly in Ukraine, a region that had long been part of Russia. During the nineteenth and the early twentieth centuries they suffered terrible violence and displacement in pogroms, anti-Jewish riots that killed thousands during the last years of the tsars and during the civil war.

After the Soviets took power in 1917 their policies officially erased racial and ethnic differences, but the changes of communism fell hard on the Jews anyway. The new government did away with private property and declared war on the middle class, which was defined to include business people of all sorts, right down to individuals such as vegetable peddlers. In the villages of Ukraine and through much of Russia, millions of Jews were part of this outlawed middle class, working as artisans or traders. Now classified among the Soviets' "class enemies," they lost the privileges of citizenship—they could not vote, work, receive housing or ration cards, or send their children to school.

Some Jewish communists supported the policy but worked for a solution. If the Jews became peasants, members of the working class, they would no longer be class enemies. My mother recounted how George and I used the same reasoning when we were little. We begged her to make our father stop being a journalist and become a factory worker so he could be a hero like other children's fathers.

Dr. Joseph Rosen worked toward such a solution. An agronomist and revolutionary, he was exiled by the tsar and went to the United States in 1903. In the early 1920s, he moved to the Ukraine with the backing of wealthy Jewish-American sponsors to alleviate the suffering of Jews who had fallen to the lowest level of a starving society. He won the support of the Soviets thanks to the scores of tractors he imported and his powerful personality and sincere socialism. He began setting up large agricultural colonies to convert city Jews into rural peasants.

Dr. Rosen hired my mother to work on the project. He became a longtime family friend and later a frequent guest in Moscow and helper to my mother. He eventually hired me as a gardener when I was a teenager in the United States.

His accomplishments in Russia were extraordinary. His organization, called Agrojoint, received many millions of dollars in funding through the Jewish Joint Distribution Committee and established thousands of families in communal farming settlements in the Ukraine.

My mother took the job without specific duties, choosing her task after arriving on the treeless steppes and seeing the misery of the women on the new farms. They cried with fatigue and shame as they milked the cows. As townspeople, they had looked down on the peasantry, but now they had to adopt that role and its hard physical labor, doing work that at first was totally unfamiliar to them. Markoosha decided to set up kindergartens to lighten the women's load and win them over to the project.

I recall our home only vaguely, but my mother's writings confirm that my memory fragments are accurate. We lived in a whitewashed clay hut with a dirt floor. Besides the beds and a wardrobe, our furniture was made of cast-off boxes from the cooperative store. Heat came from a huge kitchen stove that burned bamboo. Light came from kerosene lanterns.

George and I learned to carry water from a communal well and to eat coarse rural food. At first we became seriously ill, which our mother attributed to the loss of our carefully balanced Berlin diet. Eventually, we became accustomed to eating local foods, mainly coarse grains, root vegetables and cabbage, and a lot of potatoes.

I've always remembered the good more than the bad. Among my earliest memories is that of a thrilling ride on horseback in the Ukraine, although I suppose, because I was very young, the horse was probably led around by the nose. My mother described the Ukraine as a desolate, treeless plain, frigid in winter and mercilessly hot in summer. I do recollect the endless, flat world around us and the total absence of trees, but I did like the horse rides.

The dozen kindergartens Markoosha started were in colonies separated by as much as thirty-five miles, distances she traveled in horse carts over rough, muddy roads. But her work succeeded. The programs provided hungry children with food and a happy, healthy place to spend their days. That improved their mothers' morale, too. In addition, teachers gave the students new standards of hygiene, which they passed on to their parents. Her only criterion for hiring her assistants had been the order and cleanliness of their own homes.

The Agrojoint collective farms worked well, at least while political and social conditions allowed. However, the Soviets' agricultural policy soon resulted in famine and starvation, even in the rich farming country of Ukraine. The policy unleashed local peasant committees to dispossess the kulaks. The word *kulak* literally referred to rural bosses long resented by the peasantry, but in practice, any particularly prosperous peasant could be called a kulak.

All across Russia any family that had accumulated a little more than their neighbors could be robbed of everything and left destitute, without even food to eat. Only the least productive farmers were safe. Hard-working peasants learned to emulate the lazy ones.

Markoosha was present one rainy night when a peasant committee descended in chaos on a supposed kulak family, stripping their belongings while children wailed and animals brayed and panicked. The attackers ransacked the farm. They snatched farming implements, livestock, even sheets from the beds, saucepans from the kitchen, the mother's skirts, and the baby's toys.

Moscow's order for forced collectivization of farms made the situation much worse. Peasant farms were generally too small to afford mechanization that could increase productivity. The regime believed new farming equipment could create a surplus of grain it could sell overseas to raise money for industrialization. The word came down to merge individual peasants' possessions into large collective farms with tractors and new equipment.

Markoosha told the story of a friend who was the only party official in his rural district. He didn't think forced collectivization would work. Instead, he

formed a collective with as many families as he could persuade to join volun-
tarily—twelve—believing their example of success would bring in more people
over the next year. But Moscow had given his superiors a quota of one hundred
collectivized peasant families in his area, and he was told he must comply.

Markoosha's friend gave the villagers the order that if they didn't join the
collective they would be exiled. The farmers signed a paper to join, but then
slaughtered and ate their livestock to avoid giving up their wealth. Once in the
collective, they refused to work. The same pattern repeated across the Soviet
Union, causing a collapse of agricultural production. Finally, Stalin wrote an
editorial in *Pravda* saying collectivization should be voluntary. The peasants
dispersed back to their own farms.

The blame for the error of forced collectivization in the district of Markoosha's
friend fell on him personally. "I wanted to go away and never return," he said.
"But the committee wouldn't let me go. 'No,' they said, 'you carry on, but do
it right this time.' As if they didn't know that I had been right all the time and
that I was made to pay for other people's mistakes. They made me spit in my
own face. And here we are now, the same twelve families working together as we
had started, only with our livestock gone, our minds confused, and the villagers
laughing into my face."

Markoosha herself came under attack by village communists. She stood
accused of "patronizing hostile elements" and supporting "class enemies" by hiring former capitalists in kindergartens. These were the women she had employed
because they kept their houses clean. She endured rehearsed denunciations at
a public meeting. Her defense made no impression with party members, who
repeated their lines like automatons. As an employee of Agrojoint she escaped
punishment. But with the kindergartens running smoothly and no funding to
start more, she resigned and left with us kids for Moscow in 1928.

Lenin had died in 1924. By 1928 Stalin had consolidated power, exiling his
main rival, Leon Trotsky. My father followed these events in person, watching Trotsky's last, unsuccessful speech in Moscow, and his flight from an
unfriendly crowd.

Markoosha noticed how differently people now behaved and how the art
and theater they consumed had changed. The freewheeling debate she had reveled in was gone. Pressure came, at first subtly and then with a heavy hand, to
stifle books, plays, or opinions that didn't explicitly support Stalin's policies.

For the first time we lived together with my father. In the beginning, we
stayed in a series of temporary quarters, including someone's airy apartment,
where I remember my parakeet flying away through an open window.

Our first home, which I remember well, was a pair of rooms in the official compound of the Soviet foreign commissar. I'm sure Louis's friendship with Chicherin helped land us there. Maxim Litvinov, who also lived in the building at the time, was very close to my parents. I remember him as an affectionate visitor in our rooms, where he would cuddle me in his lap. He succeeded Chicherin as foreign minister in 1930 and served through that decade.

The compound of buildings had been the estate of a sugar merchant, one of Russia's richest men in tsarist times. Known today as the British ambassador's residence, it stood among beautiful gardens on an island right across the Moscow River from the Kremlin, with an unequalled view of its domed churches and towers.

Our location was great. There was always something to do. We walked along the river embankment, watching passenger boats moving between different parts of the city. We crossed over the bridges to nearby Red Square and other central places. In winter, we saw the river freeze. One spring it flooded, bringing water and ice floes to the foot of our building. We had space to play ball and to skate. It was a wonderful home for a young boy. (However, one of my sharpest painful memories is there, too: I remember falling on my tailbone on the frozen street in front of the palace.)

Our time living in the foreign commissariat may have been our closest as a complete family. Louis worked on his landmark two-volume work, *The Soviets in World Affairs.* Using the records of the foreign commissariat and the personal papers and recollections of top Soviet diplomats, the book told the detailed, inside story of the Soviet Union's first decade of foreign relations. Litvinov himself kept it as a desk reference.

Markoosha researched for Louis in the commissariat library and worked on translation. Ever the social activist, she also volunteered in a kindergarten housed in the building, which took in children of parents in the Soviet foreign service and in the secret police. Thanks to our father's foreign correspondent status, George and I were also there.

As president of the parents' council, Markoosha kept other parents updated on their children's progress. These conferences usually took place in our rooms, where Louis would then interview the parents to keep current on public opinion for his articles.

Louis wrote prolifically in those days for the *Nation* and top publications in Germany and England. He wrote clear, well-informed articles that consistently sympathized with Soviet aims. Louis never joined the communists, but he wanted them to succeed and took their side, sometimes to an extent that would become embarrassing later. Looking back on the period, *Time* magazine in 1941 called Louis "the favorite Russian author of wishful-thinking US intellectuals."

We had only two rooms in the palace, one of which Louis used as his study. The rest of us lived in the other, larger room with our domestic worker, a young rural woman named Frossya, whose bed was divided off by a curtain. The kitchen and bathroom were elsewhere in the building.

Frossya was like a member of the family. My mother needed her. Busy with translating, research, and the kindergarten, she did not have time for the daily struggle of gathering food in Moscow, which often entailed endless trips to many different shops with long lines just to make an evening meal.

The availability of food and other everyday needs became progressively worse. As poor as the standard of living was in 1928, that year marked a peak of abundance in the Soviet Union not to be reached again for years. Stalin's First Five-Year Plan began that October. It decreed an all-out push for industrialization. Everything would be sacrificed for heavy industry, with extraordinary goals for new factories, power plants, railroads, and mines. All economic resources went into concrete and steel rather than food or soap.

Despite shortages and hardship, Markoosha said the people around her supported the Five-Year Plan. Hope for the fruits of industrialization in the future made bearable the privations of the present. Russians in her circle of friends still believed in the Soviet dream. After ten years under communism without much material gain to show for it, the Five-Year Plan rekindled idealism for building a better world.

In her private letters written during the dark, cold winter months, Markoosha sometimes questioned Stalin's policies. She described starvation gnawing at skinny, pale Russians in ragged, patched clothes. They were forced to give up their health and, increasingly, their ability to think freely for an abstract state industrial goal. But she knew these thoughts were unacceptable and hid them. Even in her memoir about those times, *My Lives in Russia,* my mother primarily recalled a real sense of comradeship among Soviet citizens.

She reported that Russians, lacking all material comforts, unable to buy adequate food, clothing, medicine, or much of anything else, nonetheless knew their sacrifices were for a greater good. She wrote that friends talked late into the night about industrial statistics, believing the success of the plan would translate into transformation for humankind.

Production figures represented the hope for schools, theaters, books, and hospitals. They meant plenty and contentment for all, with limitless work and educational opportunities. They promised that the Soviet Union could become the first country where everyone, without exception, would enjoy the best life can give to a human being. And after that, of course, the rest of the world would follow the Soviet example. With this aim in view, no sacrifice seemed too big.

I remember the enthusiasm for the plan even in kindergarten. We learned about it every day. Older children were instructed about production goals. The three-year-olds were shown the benefits of working together in the sandbox as a step toward understanding the benefits of agricultural collectives. Fairy tales and picture books were declared harmful for children and replaced by books that extolled industrial production. Posters were everywhere. A phrase first appeared in that era and continued for decades: "Dognat' i Peregnat' Ameriku!" which in English means "Catch Up to and Overtake America!"

In 1930, the same year my father published *The Soviets in World Affairs,* the British government, having established full diplomatic relations with the Soviet Union, moved its embassy into the compound where we had been living. And we moved into a communal apartment, the miserable place I mentioned in the first chapter. Our life could not have become more different.

The two-story house had been condemned for demolition. The ten rooms on our upper floor housed seven families with twenty-three people. All shared a tiny, dark kitchen without water, icebox, gas, or shelving. Each family had a small table for a kerosene stove in the kitchen, but had to remove the burner when not in use for fear it would be stolen. Anyway, the kitchen was so filthy and sooty that Markoosha avoided cooking there.

Markoosha and Frossya kept our own rooms scrupulously clean, but the cracked paint and worn wood couldn't be made to *look* clean. Foreign visitors constantly streamed through, many of them American tourists curious about Russia sent to see my famous father. Markoosha felt ashamed, but she wouldn't tell them why the place looked so bad. She preferred that they think she was a bad housekeeper rather than learn the Soviet Union was so poor that paint was unavailable.

The communal nature of our housing meant, in practice, too many people in too small a space, without privacy or quiet, in conflict, and unable to maintain decent living conditions in a dilapidated building. No one had a choice. One of our communal neighbors lived in one room with her third husband, and her divorced second husband, and her son by the first husband. Housing was so tight in the Soviet Union that bitterly divorced couples commonly had to continue living together for years after splitting.

Markoosha made friends of the neighbors and learned their stories. According to *My Lives in Russia,* most were better off in that dreadful apartment under the Soviet government than they had been under the tsar. A peasant woman was able to get medical care so her baby could survive, after losing her previous six in the village. Grandparents who never had the opportunity to learn to read were caring for a granddaughter studying to become a doctor. A large Jewish family's children were involved in work and activities of all kinds; little more than a decade earlier, they would have been pariahs without rights, unable to live in the city, and subjected to pogroms.

Markoosha became the leader of the floor but couldn't force the neighbors to do their chores or pay their full electric bills, so she often paid extra and, with Frossya, took others' turns scrubbing the common areas. Some of the residents were new to indoor plumbing and clogged the apartment toilet frequently. It was often broken for days on end.

I still remember the disgusting toilet cubicle; it reeked so badly that the smell is still with me. My mother wouldn't consider bathing us in the filthy tub. Instead, she scheduled dates to take baths in the hotel rooms of our foreign friends, or we took sponge baths in a washtub in our own room.

Food became ever scarcer as the Five-Year Plan progressed. My mother and Frossya could spend the entire day going from shop to shop without finding anything for us to eat. Shops displayed wooden models of meat and cheese, since they didn't have the real thing for weeks on end. Frossya's peasant family helped keep us going, occasionally bringing their homegrown potatoes and fresh vegetables from the countryside. On one joyous occasion, her mother sent a giant jar of sweet cherry preserves, a marvelous treat that still makes my mouth water when I think of it.

Our mother couldn't find lemons or other citrus she believed essential for our health, and George and I were sick much of the time. We came down with every children's disease: mumps, scarlet fever, and the rest. Perhaps having picked it up in the Ukraine, I became gravely ill with malaria, which can cause many months of fevers, headaches, fatigue, and nausea.

My mother sought the only medicine available to deal with the fever: quinine. It was not available in pill form, but she found powdered quinine. Straight quinine is unbelievably bitter. When I tried to swallow the powder, it coated my mouth and throat and gave me a terrible burning and choking sensation. She tried to mold it inside a ball of bread, but that simply disintegrated before I could gulp it down. The same happened when the powder was put inside some chocolate she had somehow obtained. So I just had to tough it out, taking the quinine powder until the malaria receded, fortunately forever.

Despite all the hardships, I remember happy times at that house. It was located on the Garden Ring, one of Moscow's circumferential boulevards, with big trees and open space and a pond where we could skate in the winter. Our friends were a mixed bunch, and we were free to roam. On one occasion, one of them hit me on the back of the head with a brick as we were chasing each other around a yard. I returned home with blood streaming down my head. But even that memory brings back only a sense of the rough, physical nature of our play, which I enjoyed.

My mother saw our friends differently. She believed our behavior was deteriorating because we were in contact with children who stole, smoked, and used bad language. Without decent food or housing, she feared my health could not improve.

George had become unmanageable. He got in trouble for speaking defiantly to teachers. On an occasion when Markoosha slapped my hand, he reminded her that no law permitted corporal punishment in the Soviet Union and that he could turn her in to the police.

We probably also created a problem for Markoosha's tenuous relationship with our father. Louis's rising career brought him international acclaim and frequent meetings with important men and colleagues in grand buildings and luxurious hotels. The contrast to the home life he had never really wanted must have been striking.

While traveling, he could play poker and tennis with friends, talk to world leaders, and make love to a variety of women. At home, he worked in a squalid room with a pair of little boys underfoot and a peasant maid whose quarters consisted of a corner segregated from the rest of the space by a wardrobe and strategically hung gypsy shawls.

Markoosha reached a breaking point. In 1931, she took us to Latvia for the summer, and then to Berlin, to live in the Wedding District with Paul and Hede Massing. My parents had first known them when Paul came to Moscow in 1928 for a year's study of the economics of Russian agriculture. Now we became ensconced in a clean, orderly home, went to a local school, learned to swim, and found a warm father figure in Paul.

George and I were true believers in the Soviet Union. My mother noted our efforts to hide our surprise and delight at seeing toys and other goods in store windows—we didn't want anyone to know how poor our lives were in Moscow. In Berlin, we waved the red flag and confronted the children of Nazis, for the first time encountering people from different political viewpoints. And we adapted again to speak German as our primary language.

I was nine years old when we returned to Moscow by way of Czechoslovakia late in 1933. The Soviet Union had changed dramatically, even in our juvenile perception. The First Five-Year Plan had been completed in four years. Although not all of Stalin's impossible production goals had been attained, the country had made extraordinary progress in industrialization, doubling in some categories. A rate of economic growth rarely seen anywhere changed an agrarian society into an industrial one almost overnight.

With the completion of the first plan, the regime relaxed the austerity it had imposed. Urban dwellers like my mother rejoiced with the new availability of food and consumer products. The Great Depression had hit its nadir in the West. The energy and progress of Soviet industry inspired leftists in the United States and other capitalist countries around the world. Visitors kept coming to admire our socialist country.

Stalin's policies get credit for wrenching a huge, backward nation forward to become one of the world's leading industrial powers. But the First Five-Year Plan, and the others that followed, also concentrated political power in a way never before seen on earth. Modern technology allowed the state to suppress local and individual self-determination in a new, comprehensive way.

Louis Fischer later wrote about Stalin's innovation in human control, although not at the time it was happening. The centralized planning of every detail of the economy eliminated the authority of local councils, factory committees, labor unions, and the Communist Party itself, Louis observed. The Five-Year Plan not only set goals for factories and regions, it also replaced local leadership with engineers and technocrats who reported only to the Kremlin. Every worker had a job, but none could choose a job. The state assigned each to where he or she would live and work, and required government permits to travel from place to place inside the country.

Under the Five-Year Plan, all power flowed from one man, Josef Stalin. The economic system became feudal, not communist. But Louis didn't fully recognize that until later, after Stalin began using his power to impose his paranoia and brutality on generations of Russians.

⇥ 4 ⇤

The Troika

Our return to Moscow in 1933, when I was nine, began one of the happiest periods of my early life. New friendships developed into my deepest and most durable, surviving across decades and the boundaries created by war and political repression. Three of us, particularly, became fast friends, inseparable for years—three boys having the time of our lives, growing up together, joyously sharing everything, and supporting one another through tough times. We were the "troika," a threesome of permanent connection: Lothar "Lotka" Wloch, Konrad "Koni" Wolf, and Victor "Vitya" Fischer.

While living in Berlin, George and I had quickly become German again. We returned to Moscow as outsiders. Our once-fluent Russian was rusty and our early friendships forgotten. Our mother decided to stop our switching from one primary language to another by making us fully bilingual. While living in Russia, we would retain our German by speaking it at home and enrolling in a German school. Our Russian would come back naturally because that language was all around us.

The school was named for Karl Liebknecht, hero of an abortive 1918 communist uprising in Germany. It existed to teach the children of German families in Moscow and for the children of Russians who wanted them to become thoroughly conversant in German. After the Nazis took control in Berlin, many communists escaped Germany to the Soviet Union and placed their children there.

The school grew rapidly, offering elite students lessons in Leninism and advanced math and science, all taught in German. The curriculum emphasized art, choir, and marksmanship training, and taught Russian as a second language. Tough exams kept academic standards high. Behavioral standards were strictly enforced to create self-discipline in service to the cause of the Soviet Union.

I never liked the Karl Liebknecht School. I was still enough of a Russian to feel it was a foreign creature. Besides, to get there from our apartment in the Arbat district required a long trip on two trolleys. While I enjoyed the independence of riding on my own across Moscow, I had few opportunities to make friends with other children in our neighborhood, since the school served the entire city. Yet I was born adaptable. I found a way to fit in at the German school as I had in the various new situations before.

Lothar Wloch came to the school some months after I did. He became my first real friend among the strangers. He showed up in my class, brand new to Moscow, obviously lost. I reached out to him, and since I had not become close to any other kid, our relationship grew rapidly.

Adjustment was far easier for me than Lothar since I had already lived in Russia and knew the language. German children in short pants such as my new friend stuck out in Moscow, where even the smallest boys wore long trousers. Russian children made fun of him. I was there for Lothar's transition.

I later wondered why Lothar and I hit it off as we did, with our dissimilar backgrounds and personalities. He was solid and grounded, a leader, not pushy but confident. I never put myself forward. I had plenty of energy for swimming, skiing, and building, but, like my mother, I was always concerned about others' feelings. I was known for my calmness, soft face and big eyes, and how easily I got along with adults. While I was taller and thinner, Lothar, almost a year older, was more solid, stronger, and rougher-edged.

One evening in Moscow, Markoosha came home from a parent meeting at the school and told me about a woman she had met whom she liked and wanted to know better. She suggested I seek out her son. Her new acquaintance was Erna Wloch, and my mother was pleased to learn that her son Lothar and I were friends already. When we boys started hanging out together all the time, my mother at first worried about having him around the apartment so much, concerned that I might become too dependent. However, she soon got over that and took him on as almost another son.

Lothar's father, Wilhelm Wloch, had been a construction and industrial worker in Germany and was a Communist Party member. After a stint in the underground resistance, he immigrated to Russia with Erna, who had been a shop girl and political worker, and their children: Lothar and his younger sister,

Margot. In Russia, Wilhelm worked for the Comintern, the international arm of the Communist Party responsible for spreading world revolution under Moscow's control. He was often absent due to assignments that took him around the globe, and I never got to know him well.

Lothar and I next befriended Konrad Wolf, called Koni, another new boy from Germany at the Karl Liebknecht School. He was unlike either of us in personality. Somewhat younger and taller than I, Koni was a dreamer and an artist, more delicate, often lost in creative thought or making drawings that were a chronicle of our lives and his fantasies.

Lothar's harder experience of the world had toughened him. When his father was underground, Lothar had been forced to watch Nazi police beat his mother to find out Wilhelm's whereabouts, destroying her hearing in one ear. I was a gentle soul, but had seen more than most ten-year-olds. Koni's parents had protected him, and he seemed innocent.

Despite our differences, we made a good team. As Koni's older brother observed, if a boat were to be built, Lothar would direct the project, I would figure out how to do it, and Koni would consider the decoration.

Koni's father, Friedrich Wolf, led an extraordinary life as a flawed visionary. Trained as a medical doctor in Germany in the 1920s, he adopted homeopathy and became a vegetarian, fitness fanatic, and nudist. He published a book espousing this lifestyle and its health benefits, illustrated with photographs of himself and his two sons engaged in nude calisthenics. It was a hit and set up the family financially.

Wolf also began writing plays in Germany. They were generally family dramas on social themes and were popular and critically praised. A play on abortion got him arrested. As both a Jew and a communist, Wolf fled Germany after the Reichstag fire and wrote an early play about Nazi oppression of the Jews, *Professor Mamlock*, that was performed around the world, including America, and was twice made into a movie.

Having lost all their property to the Nazis, the Wolf family came to the USSR at the invitation of the Soviet Writer's Union. Friedrich Wolf had much in common with my father and became Louis's good friend. The working-class Wilhelm Wloch, on the other hand, was a busy Communist Party functionary in Russia and very rarely figured in our family gatherings.

Louis and Friedrich shared the habit of long absences from family for international travel and a penchant for extramarital affairs. Wolf was worse in that regard, even worse than Louis. He fathered children in Russia, Europe, and America. His beautiful second wife, Else, who had met Friedrich in a German artists' commune, accepted and befriended the many extra children who would appear from time to time.

Koni had a brother who was a year older, Markus. The brothers' ages closely matched George's and mine. Like the three younger boys and the three mothers, the two older boys quickly became close friends. George dubbed Markus with the Russian nickname Mischa, a name he kept through his life. George was known as Yura and I was Vitya.

The older boys were achievers. They strived for political positions in the communist youth organization, the Komsomol, of which most aspiring activists were members. George hoped to one day be a high government official like those who held our father's attention. In his later self-analysis, he believed his desire for Louis's approval motivated his ambition.

George did get approval. Adults noted his precocious political skill. Early on, my parents transferred him to an elite Russian school. But I don't believe the desire to please Louis drove George entirely. He always had been the aggressive one, always stepping forward, full of certainty. Markus likewise pushed ahead, trying to rise to the top of the class and become a leader. In their zeal, both boys developed blind devotion to Stalin's regime.

Our troika, on the other hand, didn't care about political advancement or official goings-on, even though we studied world affairs and were steeped in antifascism. Of course we knew about Hitler's ranting against democracies and the Soviet Union, his dreams of world domination, his annexation of Austria, his Aryan nationalism and anti-Semitism. We followed the crushing of Abyssinia, the Ethiopian kingdom, by Benito Mussolini, Italy's fascist dictator. We were enthusiastic about every Soviet military improvement to strengthen defenses against any fascist aggressors.

But we lived largely in our own world, for each other, concentrating on imagination and fun. We read as much as the older boys, or more, but our books were about inspiring adventures, the wars of Rome and Carthage, Arctic exploration, and technological achievements.

One of our favorite authors was Karl May, although our school prohibited the reading of his books. He wrote a seemingly endless series of exciting volumes about riding camels across the Arabian desert, exploring the wilds of Venezuela's Orinoco River, fighting through swamps with American Indians, chasing crooks on European trains, and dozens of other adventures. May obviously had a great imagination, for he never left Germany. Unfortunately, Hitler liked his books too, so Soviet students had to pass copies surreptitiously to avoid confiscation by teachers.

We followed real-life adventures closer to home with fascination. In the mid-1930s, Soviet pilots made the first airplane landings at the North Pole. Russian fighter planes achieved all sorts of other speed and distance records. A high-altitude balloon ascended to the stratosphere, higher than had ever been achieved by man. Icebreakers were smashing through the Arctic Ocean. And you could take parachute jumps from a tower in Moscow's Gorky Park.

While I was fascinated with making and fixing things, Lothar planned to become a pilot like the heroes we read about in the Soviet press. He made model airplanes that hung in the one room his family occupied in the Hotel Lux, a large housing complex where many German political immigrants lived in Moscow. I dreamed, as well, of being a pioneer exploring Arctic Siberia.

Another book is worth mentioning: *The Three Musketeers*. We read it and read it together. The book was about us. It appealed to our feisty, adventuresome spirits. Our threesome roamed the streets of Moscow as if the city were our private property. When it rained, we made boats to float down the gutters. On the Arbat, the major street where Stalin would ride by in his limousine on the way to his country house, his dacha, policemen in white uniforms would stand along the sidewalk keeping perfect order. We delighted in jaywalking across the road between crosswalks to provoke them into blowing their whistles while we took off into side streets and courtyards that we knew better than they.

Once I grabbed a watermelon from a vegetable stand and we ran while a screaming farmwoman chased us down the street. We got away, although I have forever felt guilty about that theft. If ever the police did stop us for some infraction, we would speak German, pretending not to understand Russian, and invariably got off without consequences.

Moscow was much smaller then and still had vestiges as a center of rural life, with horse-drawn carts clattering down the cobbled streets. But during our teenage years the Soviets transformed Moscow, to our fascination. We watched the subway being constructed and explored the underground vaults to hear our voices echo. The piles of sand excavated from the tunnels became our playgrounds. Occasionally, we would take shovels and help the workers, as much of their effort involved manual labor.

Around this time, the Soviets printed a new plan for the city as it would appear in a decade, in 1945. Existing maps were already out of date, but rather than produce a corrected version, authorities made the 1945 plan the only map of the city. Newcomers were bewildered when they tried to use it to navigate, but we boys delighted in seeing aspects of the redesigned city become reality, as modern buildings and apartment blocks took the place of structures from earlier centuries.

We observed in wonderment the widening of Moscow's main avenue, Gorki Street (now known, as it was under the tsars, as Tverskaya). Block-long, multistory buildings were carefully jacked up, put on rollers, and ever so slowly pulled and pushed back to create a wide thoroughfare consonant with dreams for Moscow's future.

On the edges of the city, we roamed the woods, picking wild strawberries and mushrooms that we brought back by the pail. That land has since been converted into residential districts, wide avenues, and the buildings of the University of Moscow. Or we would just walk in the woods. It was a sunny time, even when the rain fell.

In the depths of winter, we were immune to the cold. Once, when the outdoor temperature was minus forty degrees (the temperature at which Celsius and Fahrenheit coincide), my mother chided me for coming home with my coat unbuttoned after one of our active outings. We didn't care.

Markoosha arranged to send the three of us to a collective farm for the summer when I was eleven. We stayed in the house of the collective's chairman, slept above the traditional brick oven, and ate at a big table with all the others. We tramped through the fields and woods all day, sometimes making a fire and roasting potatoes that we dug up.

We swam in a hole in a creekbed. With our usual mischief, we cleared out the village children who crowded our swimming area by posting a formal-looking notice that said NO SWIMMING ALLOWED; CLOSED UNTIL FURTHER NOTICE, having stamped it with the chairman's purloined official seal. We had a fabulous time.

My mother had moved from the dreadful communal apartment into a newly built eight-story building in the Arbat, just a block off the street of the same name. The historic district of narrow, twisting streets was famous for its literary and intellectual history. Pushkin had lived there. Now it was the neighborhood for "specialists," the elite members of Soviet society with managerial or technical skills, and full of interesting people.

Our modern building, not entirely finished when we moved in, stood among gracious old houses, some of which became embassies. Our rooms were light and well designed, with exposure on two sides. We finally had enough space.

The living room housed a dining table, my mother's large desk and her bed, which in daytime also served as a couch, and a wardrobe with a full-length mirror. Connected to this room by French doors was Louis's study, with extensive bookshelves, a large desk, and a bed. A balcony off the main room looked out over the playground in the back yard and the neighborhood beyond, including the French embassy. We now even had our own private bathroom and toilet, as well as a comfortable spot for our Russian maid, Nyura, who slept in the long, narrow kitchen.

I later learned that the apartment had been assigned through the foreign ministry. There were several other foreign journalists living in the apartment complex. Combined with the new availability of food and goods that came after the First Five-Year Plan, the living situation now seemed nothing short of paradise.

George and I explicitly divided our bedroom into two sides, just as we separated our lives into our different interests and attitudes. We each had a desk, bed, and dresser. On his side, politics and party were always most important. On my side, there were books and gadgets. I built electrical devices out of any parts I could scrounge, using the full 210-volt house current. To keep my brother from getting into my desk, I equipped it with a secretly activated magnetic latch that would give him an electric shock should he come across our invisible dividing line and try to rummage through my treasures.

My proudest creation was a bulletlike metal car that raced around an oval track through a series of induction coils that I built. As the projectile moved forward, it would briefly close the electric circuit to the next coil, producing a strong magnetic field that accelerated it onward. The circuit immediately disconnected, killing the magnetic force, and the car flew toward the next coil. The car would keep speeding up as it went from coil to coil until either it hurtled off the track or I cut the electricity.

This project more than made up for not having an electric train when I was eight. It was probably also an underpinning of my later decision to become an electrical engineer.

Markoosha was an avid photographer. Her 35mm Leica camera was constantly in use for pictures of family, friends, and occasionally our cat. I helped her set up a darkroom in our bathroom, where she would develop film and print the photos. I did not recall, but learned recently from family letters, that I also built her an enlarger and constructed a movie projector for the amusement of our troika.

Our apartment always had visitors, both Russians and intellectuals from around the world. I enjoyed listening quietly to the adult conversations. I especially remember my father's "ninth birthday" in 1936. Louis was born on leap day in 1896, so he was actually forty in 1936 (1900 was not a leap year, as is the case in three centuries out of four).

Guests came as nine-year-olds, bringing age-appropriate gifts. It was fun. George and I met each guest at the door, blowing toy horns. On each guest we pinned a card with an image representing his or her identity, which Louis and Markoosha had carefully chosen as part of an ice-breaking system for people from different social circles and nationalities. Thus, upon Constantine Oumansky, then press officer at the foreign office, we bestowed a picture of a telephone, since he had several on his desk and often talked on at least two at a time.

Markoosha remembered the evening as the peak of good life in the Soviet Union. Within a few years, many of the guests at that party would be dead in Stalin's purges. Oumansky would become Soviet ambassador to the United States, with our lives in his hands as we sought to leave the country. At the time, as the party lasted through the night and into the morning, I felt nothing but amazement and delight to see important adults behaving like silly children, even as they debated modern art, film, and politics.

There were many other parties that lasted just as long, though they were rarely very wild, as my father never drank or smoked and my mother just sipped a bit. The quality all the gatherings had in common was the conversation of fascinating, creative people.

Singer Paul Robeson visited us, the first black man I was ever aware of seeing. He sang memorably at one of my parents' parties. The filmmaker Sergei Eisenstein was a good family friend, and we frequently exchanged visits. I particularly remember the apartment of his cinematographer Eduard Tisse, which had bookcases that could be raised up out of the way to the high ceiling.

I listened in on adult discussions, but intellectuals didn't impress me. Lothar, Koni, and I saved our real interest for a different type of celebrity. We idolized the heroes of the Russian Civil War. We knew the names of the marshals at the head of the Red Army and had our favorites, discussing them as boys in America would their favorite baseball players.

In 1934, we keenly followed the heroic rescue of the polar vessel *Chelyuskin*. The ship was frozen in and went down in the Chukchi Sea. The crew and passengers, including women and children and a baby born on the trip, were all evacuated onto the ice together with critical supplies. A massive rescue operation was organized and everyone eventually was brought to safety by pilots who landed on runways chipped out on the sea ice. When they returned triumphantly to Moscow and came to Red Square to be awarded medals, we were on hand and cheering with the throngs.

My father's journalistic status assured us the best seats for the enormous parades held twice a year in Red Square, on May Day and on the anniversary of the October revolution. We were right near Stalin and the other top officials reviewing the troops.

Thousands of soldiers marched in. Marshall Voroshilov, the commissar of the army and navy, rode in on a horse, received the salute of the troops, and reported to Stalin that all were in order. Then came the tanks, aircraft, thousands more soldiers, masses of gymnasts, veterans of the civil war, schoolchildren, factory workers, and other marchers. The parade lasted almost the whole day and eventually became boring.

We loved being there for the early parts of the parade and marching ourselves with our school. Our excitement for the glory was real. We believed in the Soviet Union. The evidence of its superiority was all around us: In the new buildings and prosperity, in the education system, and in the equality enjoyed by all. All this contrasted to the stories we heard of the Depression in the United States, where the parks were full of the homeless, unemployed workers and where blacks could be lynched.

But we dreamed of America, too. I wanted to see New York, with its skyscrapers and high technology. Unlike Markus and George, we three boys never bought all the dogma that our teachers and the media fed us. We gloried in Soviet successes because they matched our own enthusiasm for aviation, the Arctic, the construction of the subway, and the grand, new buildings. But the feats of American society and the broad span of the world for adventures carried equal weight in our imagination. We three lived in our own world.

Our best times of all happened in the country, at a place called Peredelkino. For his literary success, Friedrich Wolf received land in a writer's colony there with an unfinished country home, known as a dacha. We members of the troika helped finish the house and worked in the vegetable garden, the beginning of my lifelong love for that kind of outdoor work. And we explored the countryside and made friends among the children of other famous intellectuals.

The dacha stood half an hour outside Moscow by rail and a long walk through fields, across a creek leading to a pond, and by a cemetery and country church. In the summer we swam and in the winter we skied over the rolling hills. I wore Friedrich Wolf's far too heavy telemark skis. The other teens in Peredelkino, boys and girls, joined us for volleyball games. Popular Russian poet Boris Pasternak, author of *Doctor Zhivago*, watched us play; decades later, I would visit his grave on a hill out there. On warm summer evenings, the girls taught us to dance by the gramophone.

This was the happy life of our group when the dark cloud of Stalin's terror descended.

⊰ 5 ⊱

The Purge

One day in June 1937 it fully hit us that something was terribly wrong in our world. Koni, Lothar, and I were riding on a trolley and reading *Izvestia,* the government newspaper, looking for football scores and international news. I found an article reporting that Marshal Mikhail Tukhachevsky had been charged with treason and demanding that he be executed. The next day, or maybe that same day, he was shot.

Tukhachevsky was one of our favorite heroes. In his twenties, he had risen to leadership of armies in Russia's Civil War, winning some of the Soviets' greatest victories. His daring and brilliance were famous. After the war, he became the Red Army's top commander and masterminded its modernization and strategy.

We were aware of the political turbulence churning in Moscow, but the news of Tukhachevsky's execution, and that of seven other accused generals, came as a complete shock. It was unbelievable. We boys simply could not believe our hero, the chief of staff of the Red Army and deputy commissar of defense, was a traitor, an agent of Hitler and the German military establishment.

We were correct: The charges were invented by Stalin, and the generals' false confessions were extracted by torture. He planned their deaths and the subsequent deaths of the great majority of all the military's high officers—three of five marshals, thirteen of fifteen army commanders, eight of nine fleet admirals, and tens of thousands of lower officers. And to maintain the terror, he also executed the inexperienced officers promoted to replace those he first killed.

To Stalin's mind, the military presented a potential barrier to absolute power. Killing its best leaders and keeping the survivors in mortal fear gravely weakened the Soviet Union in the coming war. But it gave Stalin the power he sought, as well as a free hand to kill many others.

We three boys had already seen the beginnings of Stalin's purge at work in newspaper headlines and radio news reports and in our own experiences at school, among our teachers. But at first this political stuff did not affect us directly; it did not strike close to home. Besides, while we weren't focused on communist politics, the suppression of dissent was nothing new in our young lives.

Among Stalin's shrewd tactics, as documented in Robert Conquest's *The Great Terror,* he calibrated his destruction of opponents in the beginning to a level that would not produce too much shock in a population accustomed to political thought control. Only when he had eliminated all those, such as the generals, who could potentially oppose him, did he unleash the full frenzy of mass arrests and executions that ultimately claimed millions of lives.

The seeds of the terror lay in the form of government. Lenin himself had used political executions to enforce control by the Communist Party in the aftermath of the 1917 Bolshevik revolution. He did not tolerate opposition even from other leftists, such as those who shared many of his goals but did not support creation of an undemocratic, single-party dictatorship. Lenin also recognized that the Russian masses didn't yet back the party leadership and would have to be prepared for the better world he had in mind for them, by force if necessary.

In 1921, Lenin dispatched Tukhachevsky at the head of an army to suppress a rebellion at the Baltic naval base at Kronstadt. Sailors were demanding free expression for non-Bolshevik leftists. The fierce battle and following mass executions killed thousands.

An American, Alexander Berkman, had come to Russia from the United States after the revolution as a supporter of Lenin. Although he believed that dissent should be permitted, he was at first willing to quiet his criticism of communist tactics, because the goal of world revolution was so important. But he found the bloodbath at Kronstadt inexcusable. Berkman broke with the Soviets; he could no longer keep silent.

As kids we, of course, knew nothing about the Kronstadt massacre, nor is it likely my parents knew at the time. However, Berkman later wrote that Louis Fischer's work in Russia put him in a similar, "pre-Kronstadt" position of excusing the communists. Louis, like many other liberal intellectuals through the 1920s, opposed political repression but tolerated it because "the aim of the Bolsheviks was a new society," and the tsar had been even worse. Louis later admitted, regretfully, "I had no Kronstadt for many years." For him, the final break came only after the 1939 Soviet–Nazi pact.

Louis and Markoosha were aware, at least to some extent, of the Stalin government's attack on the Soviet Union's recalcitrant peasantry from 1929 to 1933, as Louis traveled widely and Markoosha had seen a supposed rich peasant family dispossessed in the Ukraine. But they likely did not understand the full scale of the suffering or the death of millions displaced or starved in the countryside during that period. Despite their awareness of events in the countryside, they would not have known that Stalin personally masterminded the strategy.

In any case, like the brutal Five-Year Plan, the policy worked, and by the end of the period agricultural collectivization was virtually accomplished. Louis's subsequent writings praised the completed system for its efficiency and improvement of human conditions.

As children, we knew our place politically. From kindergarten on teachers drilled all students with the party line. We were taught to worship Lenin and to revile Trotsky, whom Stalin had exiled after they struggled for power, and then to worship Stalin. At the beginning of the school day, each class recited, "Thank you, Comrade Stalin, for our happy childhood."

My classmate, Lena Kostyakova, recalled a day in 1934, before the extensive purges started, when a social studies teacher scolding an impertinent boy inadvertently said, "Now, our leaders, such as Lenin and Trotsky, taught us to be modest." Pandemonium erupted as students rushed to the teacher's desk, shouting, "Trotsky a leader? How dare you say such a thing?" The teacher flushed with red spots on her face and hurried out of the room, never to be seen at the school again. Lena and her friends never knew what happened to her.

Fathers or uncles sometimes disappeared to prison or exile even before what became known as the Great Purge. People accepted that as part of a life controlled by the government. Several of my classmates had lost family before I met them—some temporarily—during the wave of repression associated with the First Five-Year Plan and collectivization.

Another classmate, Rosa Aronova, remembered many details from her father's arrest in 1929, when she was only five years old. Agents ransacking their poor apartment spread his papers over the floor thirty centimeters (one foot) deep. He was a librarian and had gathered files for a book on rural libraries.

Rosa's father was imprisoned, hung by ropes from the ceiling, and sprayed with ice water all night. The only time Rosa saw him after the arrest, on a brief prison visit, his hands were all twisted. She didn't recognize him and she never saw him again. Having a father who was a political prisoner was a dark shame, and Rosa learned to keep quiet about it. She never did find out why her father was arrested. Even after secret service records were opened in the 1980s, still no one knew.

The Communist Party adopted a new level of inhumanity to obtain obedience for the mass dislocations of people during the industrialization and collectivization of the First Five-Year Plan, 1928 to 1933. Nikolai Bukharin, who had fought beside Lenin in the civil war following the revolution, wrote privately of how the killing had changed: "In 1919 we were fighting for our lives. We executed people, but we also risked our lives in the process. In the later period, however, we were conducting a mass annihilation of completely defenseless men, together with their wives and children."

When that phase of arrests ended, some of Lenin's former colleagues, the old Bolsheviks, tried to resist Stalin's attacks on his opponents within the party and to ease him out of power. Sergei Kirov, a member of the all-powerful Politburo, in charge in Leningrad, was popular as a potential replacement. He received some votes instead of Stalin in a secret meeting.

Kirov was well known as a bright star of the new generation. I remember how shocked we all were in December 1934 at the news that Kirov had been assassinated. Rosa recalled that her mother, having lived through a previous period of repression, kept saying, "It's starting again...starting again...."

The nation exploded in anger and grief, spurred by the newspapers and by demonstrations and meetings. Stalin declared great sorrow and rushed to Leningrad to oversee the investigation. We now know he had organized the assassination himself.

With a broad attack on his enemies already carefully planned, Stalin immediately issued a decree to allow hasty arrests and snap executions. Many of the party members who had earlier resisted him were soon dead.

As the historian Richard Conquest wrote, "Over the next four years, hundreds of Soviet citizens, including the most prominent political leaders of the Revolution, were shot for direct responsibility for the assassination, and literally millions of others went to their deaths for complicity in one or another part of the vast conspiracy that allegedly lay behind it."

My friends and I knew about the Kirov assassination and the hysterical cries for revenge, but felt it only as news from the distant adult world. We were not exceptional. My mother recalled 1935 as a particularly happy time when life in Moscow was relatively easy.

Stalin announced in November, "Life has become better, life has become more joyous." Shops carried evening clothes and fine food and wine. Festive activities were officially encouraged, probably to divert attention from the darker forces encroaching on our lives.

Thus, one of Stalin's lieutenants, Pavel Postyshev (later himself liquidated), wrote a letter, published in *Pravda* on December 28, 1935, denouncing the "left deviationist" prohibition of Christmas trees, which he called New Year's fir trees. I remember the excitement and gaiety of Moscow as the dreary policy prohibiting the traditional holiday celebration was reversed in a single day. Fir trees flooded into the city and long-hidden decorations emerged into bright displays.

Since we did not possess any such trinkets to hang on our tree, we set about creating them. We made chains from colored paper, popcorn having not yet reached us, and used foil from chocolate candy wrappers to provide variety. I bent various wires into stars and other shapes, immersed them in different chemical solutions to build up colorful crystals, and hung the sparkly decorations on our tree. There being no small electric lights, we burned live candles on the tree, very carefully. The tradition of decorating fir trees for New Year's continues in Russia today.

Markoosha's autobiography describes the process of mental accommodation to Stalinism that still went on in 1936. She was discouraged by the sudden abolition of abortion rights, which went against widely held public opinion, and by Russia's general lack of freedom. But then some positive changes would give new life to her hopes.

That summer she traveled to Yalta in the Crimea, on the Black Sea, where George had become seriously ill while attending a summer camp. The camp, once reserved for the rich, now served the children of peasants as well as professionals, from all races and from all regions of the country. Two peasant children sharing George's hospital room were bright, ambitious, well spoken, and equal to him in educational attainment. Markoosha wrote,

> They were just ordinary peasant boys like millions of others, and every year new millions like them were graduated from schools and entered life as educated human beings instead of the ignorant, downtrodden peasants of less than twenty years earlier. This always happened to me in the Soviet Union. Something like the anti-abortion law would arouse my indignation and opposition; I would be miserable and skeptical. Then two small peasant boys would cross my path and give me an object lesson which moderated my disapproval.

That same year of 1936, when I was twelve, I received treatment for horrendous pain in my joints that had lasted for more than a year. I did not sleep whole nights and often missed school. During the spring, my doctor, Friedrich

Wolf, Koni's father, put me in a hospital for weeks of total rest to prevent the rheumatism from affecting my heart. To my disgust, I kept getting fatter as a result of inactivity.

On Wolf's further recommendation, my mother took me to Czechoslovakia for sulfur baths at a mountain spa in the Slovakian part of the country. Somehow, the cure worked, the pains abated, my heart was not affected, and I went back to my thin self.

To my great joy, Paul Massing, who was then living in America, came to visit us at the resort, as did my father and cousin Nina. Paul and I spent days together walking, talking, and playing chess. Another high point was the cast that a doctor put on my arm. I had broken the arm tripping over a root during a hike in the woods. Among my friends, our troika, that was a great badge of honor.

On this trip I was first told I was Jewish. It happened on a bus tour of Prague. As the group walked into an ancient Jewish cemetery, I fell behind. A huge man standing at the entrance, all in black and with a large black hat, stopped me and demanded to know, in German, "Are you Jewish?" Having no idea what he was asking, I hesitated, and then said, "No."

Back on the bus, I asked my mother what that incident had been about, and she explained that male Jews had to cover their heads in religious places, such as this cemetery. She told me that because of my parents, I, too, was Jewish. Although we were not religious, we were Jews by birth.

None of that made much sense to me. The information that had been so important to George when he learned of it in the streets of Berlin years before was simply filed in the back of my mind as another irrelevant fact. At our school, no one cared about ethnicity or nationality. It was one of my surprises after I came to America that in capitalist countries people were treated differently according to religion, race, and background.

———

An enormous event happened in Moscow while we were away in 1936: the trial of Grigory Zinoviev and fifteen other prominent Soviet leaders. This was the first major show trial of the Great Purge. Zinoviev had been a Bolshevik since the movement's founding in 1903, Lenin's right hand until the revolution and, after Lenin died, a co-ruler of the Soviet Union with Stalin. At trial, he and the others confessed to a far-reaching conspiracy that included the Kirov assassination and a plan to assassinate Stalin, heaping denunciations on themselves. Zinoviev branded himself a fascist.

The statements were incredible. Markoosha couldn't comprehend how the founders of the Soviet Union could now be declaring themselves its secret enemies. Close observers saw the confessions were factually incredible as well. A hotel where a meeting with Trotsky supposedly occurred had been torn down years earlier. Also, Zinoviev and several other defendants had been in prison or exiled during much of the supposed conspiracy. Nonetheless, some Western journalists and legal analysts vouched for the fairness of the trial.

Reading about the trial and confessions in the European press, Markoosha was shocked and confused. She simply didn't know what to think. Some of the Czechs she met daily began to treat her differently. To them the trial was a grotesque farce.

Louis arrived in Czechoslovakia after a summer spent touring the countryside in the Soviet Union, writing about the success of collectivization and plenitude of the harvest. He knew little about the trial and chose not to write about it even after reading the transcripts. He later wrote, "I did not condone the trials, nor did I undertake to explain them. Neither did I condemn them. I suspended judgment because I was not sure in my own mind what they were."

Louis was becoming disillusioned with the communists. He recognized that the rights promised in Stalin's new constitution meant nothing so long as the secret police, then called the GPU, could snatch and kill anyone with impunity. His journalistic sources in Russia had lost their candor in Stalin's climate of fear.[1]

Louis personally knew well several of those being tried, and he could not believe they were guilty of the charges against them. But he hadn't reached his "Kronstadt" watershed just yet. The Soviet Union still opposed fascism, and at that moment he believed fascism presented a far more pressing threat. Already, Hitler's Germany was building a war machine, and a fascist rebellion was threatening the elected liberal government in Spain.

After a series of trips and articles, Louis had fallen in love with Spain. He met the idealistic leaders of the new republic and deeply admired the dignity and courage of the common people. His passionate affairs with a beautiful Norwegian journalist and a lovely Spanish woman were well known, even making it into a history book.

When my mother and I left Czechoslovakia to return to Moscow, Louis left us to fly directly to Madrid. He never lived in the Soviet Union again and rarely wrote about it. For two years, the worst years of the terror, we saw him for only two one-week visits, when his work in Spain brought him to Moscow to talk to important men.

Later, when his time to denounce Stalin finally came in 1939—his Kronstadt moment—Louis correctly surmised the reason for the old Bolsheviks'

---

1. The GPU, Gosudarstvennoe Politicheskoe Upravlenie, or State Political Administration, was later known under various other names, including NKVD and KGB. For simplicity, I'll use only GPU here.

confessions at the show trials and the improbable confessions of many others accused. In the basement torture rooms of Stalin's security apparatus, victims were subjected to pain and psychological pressure that only a tiny percentage of human beings can ever withstand.

For those few who would not confess, the torture ended with a bullet to the back of the head and secret disposal of the body. But while the torture continued, agents dangled the tantalizing promise of survival for the accused and his family in return for confessing. These promises had faint hope of being fulfilled, but even faint hope could look bright in those dark dungeons.

We now know that Zinoviev insisted on receiving his promise of life directly from Stalin with other witnesses present. With the bargain in hand, he made the confession and exaggerated self-denunciations in open court that so confused Louis and Markoosha. He was convicted and executed within twenty-four hours, along with his codefendants, while crying out for Stalin to keep his word. The prisoners' families were shot as well, or exiled. In Zinoviev's case, the GPU executed his son, three brothers, and a sister, while three other sisters, two nephews, a niece, a brother-in-law, and a cousin were sent to labor camps.

That Stalin's obvious ruse worked again and again is a testament to human hope under unbearable duress. It even worked on the GPU chief Genrikh Yagoda, who had inflicted it on so many others as he carried out Stalin's orders to kill Kirov and frame thousands for the crime. Yagoda himself was arrested, confessed in court, and was shot.

And it worked a couple of years later on the bloodthirsty secret police chief Nikolai Yezhov, who had destroyed and succeeded Yagoda. He also was subsequently arrested on Stalin's order, confessed, and was shot by the apparatus he himself had run. And presumably it worked on the innumerable agents who carried out millions of killing orders and were regularly purged.

Stalin's terror gave him power to make people do almost anything, and not only high political figures. As Louis later wrote, in 1940,

> The Moscow trials and confessions were merely the sensational, highly-silhouetted shape of an everyday Soviet phenomenon, and it is only against the background of this phenomenon that the confessions can be understood. Millions of Soviet citizens live lies every day to save their lives and their jobs. They make false confessions day in and day out.

When our train arrived in Moscow from Czechoslovakia, Markoosha was surprised to be met by a close German friend speaking to us in horribly accented Russian. Markoosha laughed and talked back in German, but the friend said,

"I implore you, for your sake, for your children's sake, don't speak German in public."

The German communists who had come to help Russia or to escape Hitler were disappearing, as were party insiders we knew. A week after the Zinoviev trial, Stalin had ordered five thousand political opponents in camps killed. The process continued in the background night by night as agents arrived after midnight to take people from their apartments.

The German school we attended lost teachers to the purge. I remember people disappearing from school and students talking about it. But Lothar, Koni, and I didn't focus on that as a major event in our lives. We were more concerned, like the rest of Moscow, with the events happening in Spain.

The newspapers reported extensively on the heavy fighting between the fascist rebels under General Francisco Franco and the elected government, a real battle between the world's common people and Europe's voracious forces of fascism. Contributions were raised to help the Spanish Republic. Muscovites welcomed Spanish visitors as heroes, listening raptly to speeches they could not understand.

George and I felt immense pride at our father's important role in Spain. We waited for his letters and gifts and posted maps in our room to track the battlefronts and the positions of the armies.

Louis's charm, brilliance, and international reputation quickly made him a key figure in the Spanish Republic. He gathered and shared valuable information, and got more in return. He drove to the front lines, using his connections to get into the fighting, and even reported from the middle of secret operations known to only a few top officials. On one occasion his car was strafed and bombed as he sped back to the capital.

Louis became a close friend of Juan Negrín, the prime minister, frequently meeting him in the morning in the bathroom while Negrín bathed or shaved and Louis sat on the toilet seat. A photograph taken at a League of Nations meeting in December 1936 shows him deep in conversation with Soviet Foreign Minister Maxim Litvinov and his Spanish counterpart, Álvarez del Vayo, both of whom were Louis's close friends. He had lengthy private interviews with the Spanish president. Frequently, his interviews involved giving advice as much as receiving information.

My father believed—correctly, as it turned out—that the Spanish Civil War was the dress rehearsal for the world war that he had been predicting for years. The fascist governments in Germany and Italy intervened freely on the rebels' side. They bombed Spanish cities mercilessly, creating some of the first images of modern mass violence against civilians. Their motivation, besides supporting installation of another fascist dictator in Europe, was to control a long coastline and a border with France. Hitler and Mussolini also valued Spain as practice for their bomber pilots and military tacticians.

Meanwhile, Western democracies observed a policy of nonintervention that effectively amounted to a blockade, denying the republic the weapons and food it needed to fight back. In the United States the mood was overwhelmingly isolationistic, with no desire to get involved in European conflicts. France and Britain did not want to confront Germany, so they sat on their hands diplomatically, as they had in appeasing Hitler before. Only the Soviet Union supported the antifascist side in the Spanish Civil War, and even that was less than Louis believed was justified.

In November 1936, Louis joined the International Brigade, which consisted of volunteers who came from other countries to fight on behalf of the Spanish Republic. He was the first American to do so and became quartermaster, managing acquisition and distribution of equipment and supplies. But he lasted only two months in the job because of conflict with a Stalinist commander. He had never donned a uniform, preferring to wear his corduroy jacket, and ultimately felt he could do more working internationally to bring aid to the Spanish cause.

In addition to his work as a journalist, Louis essentially was a freelance diplomat for Spain, running as an intermediary and publicist between Washington, London, Paris, Moscow, and Madrid. He traveled all over Europe and to the United States to speak to large audiences and write articles, and he published a short book, *Why Spain Fights On*.

He focused on ending the embargo that kept Spain from obtaining money and arms. He met top international politicians, writers, and celebrities, including British Prime Minister Lloyd George, French Premier Leon Blum, and US Secretary of State Cordell Hull.

Louis spent a private hour with Eleanor Roosevelt at the White House to explain the effects of the embargo on the Spanish Republic. With the Spanish inadequately armed, German and Italian forces slaughtered civilians with impunity. She promised to give Louis's message to the president. Four days later, she wrote that the president agreed with Louis, "but feels that it would be absolutely impossible to repeal the Neutrality Act, because the people of this country feel that it was designed to keep us out of war."

Louis wrote to his editor at the *Nation*, Freda Kirchwey, "We need men and women—nurses—and money and materials. You mustn't allow America to get away with passivity in this great fight. Spain will suffer, but America, too."

Historians and political opponents have written that Louis was a Soviet spy, which he clearly was not, but it may be true that he was involved in managing secret arms deals for Spain. I remember his two brief visits to Moscow, in 1937 and 1938, when the curtains would be constantly drawn and few could be told of his presence. He would disappear in a car to the Kremlin for mysterious meetings. He was in a unique position to coordinate dealings for arms and other support.

But on those visits, Louis's friends could not have met with him anyway. Many were already dead. Others would never dare be seen with a foreigner, lest they be denounced and liquidated. My socially outgoing mother became isolated. She couldn't even speak openly at home.

My troika of friends may have recognized the signs slowly, but after the arrest and execution of our Russian revolutionary heroes in June 1937, Lothar, Koni, and I knew something was terribly wrong in the Soviet Union. Soon it affected us personally.

We kept our former interests. We still followed Soviet achievements with excitement. On top of other flight records, that was the same month that Valery Chkalov flew sixty-three hours nonstop from Moscow over the North Pole to Vancouver, Washington. For a time, Lothar, with his aeronautical enthusiasm, adopted the pilot's surname as his nickname.

That summer, Lothar and his sister, Margot, went to a summer camp, while Koni and I again visited a collective farm. To my surprise, when I returned to Moscow in the fall and called Lothar, he was strangely distant and made excuses rather than agreeing to meet. It was very odd, and I was upset by it.

One day while I was out of the apartment, Lothar came to visit my mother with a note from his mother, Erna. It said that his father had been arrested a month earlier and most of their friends had broken off connections with them. Erna assumed Markoosha would want me to stop seeing Lothar.

Markoosha tore up the note and told Lothar that nothing had changed. But for reasons I never understood, they decided to keep the arrest a secret from me. Only when Markoosha left for a trip to England in October did she break the news to me.

After taking away Lothar's father, the GPU had cast the Wloch family out of their room in the Lux Hotel. They found shelter in a cramped and increasingly crowded barracks with the families of other Germans hit by the Great Purge. Lothar, taking on the premature role of the man of the family, spent days outside the prison, dropping off care packages for his father and waiting for any word of him.

Families of the arrested believed that if the GPU accepted packages that meant their loved ones were still alive. However, Wilhelm Wloch, like others, was probably killed soon after his arrest. The family never learned much about his fate. (After the fall of the Soviet Union in 1991, the Russian government opened detailed records on victims of Stalin's regime, but as non-Russians, the Wloch family did not have access.)

We now know that execution usually came quickly for those arrested during the ongoing purges. The pace of the arrests overwhelmed even the Soviet Union's vast system of prisons and labor camps. In the rush, GPU agents decided whom to kill without any meaningful judicial process.

Often, agents and regional offices were given quotas of arrests. For example, Yezhov sent a cable to provincial GPU chiefs with the order, "You are charged with the task of exterminating ten thousand enemies of the people. Report results by signal." Officials competed to beat their quotas, receiving promotions when they did so. Those who failed could be executed themselves.

Agents couldn't possibly produce enough executions by snatching real or perceived enemies, even including friends and families. They needed more names. One of my classmates lost an uncle who was a tough manager at work when an employee he had disciplined reported him as a traitor. Anyone could settle a grudge with a word to the GPU. When that didn't produce enough victims, GPU agents flipped through telephone books to pick out names at random.

To keep up with the arrests, huge execution grounds were established in the countryside behind fences where local people could hear but not see the pleading of the condemned. All night long, lines of men and women would receive one gunshot each to the back of the head. Mass graves spread year by year. A set of graves near Minsk ultimately contained a quarter million corpses.

As in the case of the collectivization program of 1928 to 1933, historical documents verify that Stalin closely oversaw the process.

The fear of the GPU vans that crossed the Moscow every night kept people silent and separate. Friends stopped visiting or calling each other. No one dared to associate with anyone who might be arrested. That meant almost anyone.

But Koni and I never questioned our relationship with Lothar or doubted his father's honesty. Wilhelm had devoted his life to the party, working undercover for years in Europe and China for the Comintern, the Soviet agency devoted to spreading communism internationally. He reportedly worked undercover as well in Nazi Germany, at great personal risk. We no more believed he could be a traitor than the civil war generals, our teachers at school, or our many neighbors who disappeared.

Our troika of boys had never worshiped Stalin. To us, he was a cold, unpleasant-looking person, not our type of hero. We didn't know exactly what was happening or why, but we didn't trust him. We realized that his party and state had brought down the dark cloud of injustice that affected the world about us.

The Wloch family—Lothar, Margot, and Erna—was eventually evicted even from the barracks in the Lux Hotel courtyard. Koni's mother, Else, invited them to move into the Wolfs' small one-bedroom apartment with Koni, Mischa, and the usually absent Friedrich. To escape the crush there, Lothar spent most nights sleeping at our apartment on a pad on the floor next to my bed. We lived as brothers. The terror and sadness drew us closer as we did our best to support one another.

⇥ 6 ⇤

Escape to America

Late 1937 brought happy news: Paul and Hede Massing had come to Moscow from America for the first time in years, since long before the purges. They stayed in the grand Hotel Metropole with other foreign tourists and did not contact their old Russian friends, worried that associating with foreigners might cause them problems. George found them there accidentally, and we visited often.

I was delighted to introduce my buddies to Paul. He told us about America and Arizona. After his release from the German prison camps, he had lived in the United States under the protection of Hede's passport, although he was not yet an American citizen.

We boys of the troika sat on the floor with Paul for hours, listening to his stories and trying to visualize everything. We started planning to build a hacienda in the Arizona desert. Koni sketched our fantasies with the scenery, flat-roofed haciendas, and ponies.

We played long games of chess and talked. None of our fathers spent time with us. Paul was our fourth musketeer, and we devoted every spare hour to him. On the rare occasions when we strayed close to a political subject, such as mentioning someone who had been arrested, Paul would point at the ceiling. We knew enough to understand that the hotel room was bugged.

My mother returned from a visit to my father in England in early December with a new radio, clothing, food, and various gifts bought at Woolworth's, a store whose opulence was unimaginable to us. Having spent everything on the otherwise unobtainable goods, she had gone hungry on the sea journey and train ride home.

George and I joyously met her at the station. I whispered into her ear that we had better not bring anyone else home because a big surprise was waiting for her there. "Something bad?" she worried; no, I assured her, "something very good."

She got a clue when she saw unfamiliar adult overcoats and hats in the entry, but was still surprised to find Paul and Hede sitting on the couch to welcome her. She hadn't known they were in Moscow. The packages were unwrapped with excitement. Paul and I got to work setting up the radio, which could pick up international news from beyond Russia. I had already become famous among our neighbors for my ability to fix anything electrical, and I loved the attention that work brought me.

Markoosha and Nyura, our maid, who was like a member of the family, prepared the delicacies Louis had sent from England, a rare feast. Around the table everyone talked at once, updating one another after our long separation.

But for all the talk and laughter, many things could not be said. Markoosha knew Nyura was probably reporting to the secret police on our conversations and visitors. Usually sunny and open with every aspect of her life, Nyura would now sometimes go away mysteriously and come back crying, without explanation. Many years later, Nyura told George that she had no choice but to cooperate—as we all knew.

One couldn't say no to the agents, who could arrest and execute anyone without evidence or provocation. As an intellectual, an international traveler, and the wife of an American, Markoosha was dangerous to any Russian she might speak to in the street. Many were killed for less than that.

Paul and Hede's presence in Moscow was a deep secret. It was many years before I learned the reason for their visit.

Since the days when Paul was in the German prison camp, Hede had continued as a Soviet agent in America, delivering money and performing other courier jobs there and in Europe. But the Massings were disillusioned by the news they received of the purges, and she wanted to quit the work.

Hede's handler, Ignace Reiss, also a friend of my father, was a top Soviet intelligence official in Western Europe. The purge drove him to separate from the Moscow regime. In September 1937, he was gunned down by the GPU on a road in Switzerland. The Massings knew they were in danger after Reiss's murder.

Hede's Soviet handler in the United States convinced them that the American police were also a threat and told the couple to go to Moscow to talk to higher Soviet officials before resigning. The trip was a crazy risk, as many Americans disappeared in Stalin's prisons and execution cells during those years. Their decision to go was a sign of the depth of their residual commitment to the cause. The

Massings traveled as American tourists, hoping that would make them more difficult for the GPU to snatch.

Not long after the Massings arrived in Moscow, Paul and George went walking in a park and got into a conversation about the purge. Apparently Paul did not yet know that Russian children and adults never talked about the subject.

George didn't seem to understand Paul's criticism of the arrests. Paul explained by pointing out that some of those who were now branded traitors, including on posters around the city, were much like Paul himself, former German revolutionaries and prison camp victims. As Hede later recounted the conversation, Paul asked, "Do you believe that I'm honest? Do you believe I would do something against the revolution?"

"Don't be silly, Paul, of course I believe in you!" George said. "I know how honest you are. Why do you ask that? I know you could never do anything wrong. You are our hero—Vitya's and mine; we love you as much as our father."

"All right," Paul said. "What would you say, Yuri, if you were to come tomorrow to our rooms and find that I had been arrested? You would be told that I am a traitor to the revolution. What would you think, Yuri?"

After a pause, George said, "Paul, if you are arrested, you are guilty."

Children usually believe what they are taught and we had been raised from the earliest childhood to absorb Soviet brainwashing in school and clubs, in the newspapers we read, and in the celebrations we attended. Our parents had done their best to keep us safe from the political undercurrents of the times. They had never joined the Communist Party and privately were skeptical of the regime, but they never expressed their concerns to us.

Decades later, George painfully analyzed how he became a deeply committed believer, a one hundred percenter for the communists, despite living through the worst of the purge. Of our parents he wrote, "They took care to hide the doubts they did feel or voice to friends. Vic and I could not do well, my folks held, if we did hear such doubts—or voice them outside the home. We could not do well in school or with friends or the state. In this way my pink parents backed the Red state. They covered up for it. They helped me love it all the more."

That encouragement continued through our childhood. It was especially strong for George, who had been precocious in his interest in politics from as young as age six. Always driven by a need to please our cold and disengaged father, George's successes as a youthful communist brought him the greatest praise he ever received from Louis.

In the midst of the purge, on May Day of 1937, Louis submitted to the *Nation* a letter George wrote, which it printed in full. The letter shines with a fourteen-year-old's innocent enthusiasm about his day spent at the parades with three young Spaniards, including the son of Spain's prime minister, which culminated in handshakes in Red Square with the warm and spontaneous Josef Stalin and top members of his government.

All children were taught to inform against adults if they heard anything said or done against the regime. The ideal example was Pavlik Morozov, a thirteen-year-old boy who informed the authorities on his peasant father for hoarding grain. For this act the boy was murdered by his family. It now appears the story was propaganda fiction, but Pavlik was lauded as a model for all of us kids.

Other examples of youthful informers were presented as examples to make us ever vigilant. It is no wonder that most parents lived in mortal fear of their children. They feared for us, as well, as we did for them. But we knew better than to bring up political doubts with our parents.

As adults, my classmates from those days have told me of their anguish at being unable to share the terrifying events of the times with their mothers and fathers. The feelings persisted through their lives into old age. My friend Vadya Popov lost his father to arrest yet could talk to no one about it. My friend Enya Levin recalled his mother's constant fear as their apartment building was emptied by arrests. When Enya asked about a friend whose father had disappeared, his mother told him, "Hold on. There's nothing we can do. We just have to hang on."

Children commonly were told stories about where their arrested parents had gone—that they were in the hospital or off on a work assignment—or they simply never received a good explanation, adding to their grief and confusion. Eventually so many fathers were missing that a child who still had one, such as my classmate Lena Kostyakova, would avoid talking about him to her friends.

I did talk about the purges with my closest friends, Lothar and Koni. We shared our recognition that what was happening was horribly wrong and we gave one another what support was needed. But the subject did not dominate our conversations. We were essentially happy kids sharing some of the best years of our lives with the most intimate friendship and days full of fun. My mother hardly saw me that winter as I spent whole days skiing at the Wolfs' dacha—often with Paul Massing along—or roaming the city with my friends.

The silence between parents and children led Markoosha to believe, as she later wrote in her memoir, that I, like George, sympathized with the communists. Yet the one time she spoke to me directly about the danger around us, she knew she could trust me.

We were alone in our apartment when my mother told me that Paul and Hede had entrusted her with their US passport and travel documents, which they hoped would bring American assistance if they were arrested. She showed me where she had hidden them in Louis's study, in volume 22 of Lenin's *Collected Works*. She wanted me to know this in case the GPU came and took her away.

If Markoosha was gone and I heard that something had happened to the Massings, I was instructed to take their papers to the US ambassador or his wife at their residence, not many blocks from where we lived. As the son of an American, I had been included in screenings of American movies, such as Charlie Chaplin films, so the Soviet police outside the door knew me and would let me in. She cautioned me not to go to the US embassy downtown, as I might be detained before getting to the door.

Mother also made me promise not to tell George about the Massings' documents. He would probably tell the authorities. He had just been proudly admitted to the communist youth organization, the Komsomol, on the first day he was eligible, his fifteenth birthday. We both knew he was a zealot, even though we weren't then aware of his discussion about the purge with Paul.

The purges went on all around us, frequently striking close.

George's best friend from school, Volik Bauman, had already lost his father, Karl, to the purge. George attended an elite Russian school and many of his classmates' parents were top officials who had rapidly disappeared that year, 1937. Karl Bauman had been the head of the science department for the Communist Party's Central Committee, and was a warm man who often took the boys swimming.

George grieved with his friend for the loss of his father. Volik was thrown out of school, then disappeared along with his mother. George took it hard, standing for many hours outside Volik's house, hoping for word of where the family had gone. New people moved in who knew nothing about the previous occupants. He later learned his friend was somewhere in Siberia, but even that contact was soon lost.

But George never doubted the system. He maintained faith in the Communist Party and continued striving as a member of the Komsomol. He made a game of following the arrests, watching the portraits of leaders disappear from shop inventories and the walls of buildings. It was his way of tracking the fall of men whose deaths often were announced in no other way.

George was not unique in dissociating tragedy from the state that caused it. Many true believers explained unjust arrests as errors of the bureaucracy, not flaws in the Soviet system or its great leader. So believed Lothar's father, Wilhelm Wloch, who reputedly told his wife, while agents arrested him and took him away, "Comrade Stalin knows nothing about this!"

Koni's father, Friedrich Wolf, also remained faithful to Stalin, even though every nighttime knock on the door terrified the family during the purge. He got away by volunteering to fight in the Spanish Civil War, leaving at the start of 1938. But he never made it to Spain. As part of their neutrality policy, the French would not let fighters cross its borders and detained Friedrich in the Le Vernet prison camp. Being interned there probably saved his life, as virtually all other German intellectuals in Moscow disappeared.

On New Year's Eve 1938, Markoosha decorated our second tree alone, using baubles sold in shops rather than ones we made. I was off skiing and having fun at the dacha with Paul, Lothar, and Koni. A terrible year of isolation and fear was beginning for Markoosha, under surveillance and in constant fear of arrest.

Neighbors disappeared from our building nightly—the agents always did their work after midnight—until the majority were gone, their apartments sealed until new occupants moved in. When both parents in a family disappeared, the GPU outlawed anyone from assisting the orphaned children without risking arrest themselves. Some children were placed in miserable GPU homes while others were cast into the street like the pathetic heaps of belongings of those who had been arrested and disappeared.

Markoosha couldn't work due to her pariah status as a foreigner's wife. She became desperately short of money, sometimes too poor to respond to a telegram from Louis. The hours hung heavy on her, without work or company, waiting up late for arrest and rising early in hopes of a phone call from Louis. Other than Erna Wloch and Else Wolf, and Hede and Paul Massing, who all had their own problems, she contacted friends only with surreptitious phone calls from pay booths to verify they were still among the living.

With the new year, 1938, all foreign-language schools were suddenly closed, including the German school I attended, which anyway had trouble operating because so many of its staff had been arrested. Markoosha got me into an elite Russian school in our Arbat district, Moscow school number 110, named for the famous Arctic explorer and Nobel Peace Prize laureate Fridtjof Nansen. Else Wolf placed Koni and Mischa there too. The school had been started many years earlier by a gifted principal and offered excellent academics, a handpicked student body of bright, interesting students, and, new for me, an atmosphere that also nurtured children as human beings.

I was thirteen years old on my first day at the Nansen school. It was strange at first, but that didn't last long. When I came, the children expected a foreigner and inspected me with interest.

Several of my old classmates remembered that day and have related their perspective to me. They had been informed that an American student was coming and they wondered which Pioneer unit I would join. (The Pioneers were like a co-ed Boy Scout or Girl Scout group to which everyone belonged.) Upon hearing the quality of my Russian, as good as theirs, I was invited into the best of the Pioneer groups. Its members became my long-lasting friends.[2]

Before the Nansen school, I had never been a group joiner. At the German school, Lothar and Koni had been my only friends. But I blossomed at the Nansen school as a devoted member of a circle of friends studying very hard, engaging in extracurricular activities such as chess, and having fun like any children, while also helping each other through a terrible time. During those years, three-quarters of the families in our class and two-thirds of all students in the school lost at least one parent to the purges.

The school treated children suffering these tragic and disorienting losses with unique gentleness, at great risk to the principal and staff. Among my most vivid memories is that of our principal, Ivan Kuzmich Novikov, coming into class to say that the father of one of our classmates, Svetlana, was going on trial but that the students should treat her as if nothing had happened. He ordered that articles about the trial would not be posted in the wall newspapers we normally read. He explained that until the trial was over, the guilt of Svetlana's father was unknown, and in any event it could not be her fault.

Svetlana's father was Nikolai Bukharin, a leader of the revolution and a close friend of Lenin who had been among the most likely to succeed him if Stalin had not taken control. He was also my mother's friend from her time in Denmark and New York. Stalin placed Bukharin next to Trotsky as an object of hatred. Bukharin's trial in spring 1938, with a number of other leading old Bolsheviks, became known as The Great Trial, the most infamous of the purges.

Markoosha knew Bukharin for his dazzling brilliance and wit, which he also displayed during his trial. He confessed in prison under torture and threats to his family, so he was assured to be tried rather than secretly executed. But once on the witness stand, he made a farce of the charges, brilliantly denying and disproving all specific acts, and even the existence of a conspiratorial group, while upholding his confession by accepting full responsibility for the supposed plot.

---

2. Several levels of membership organizations existed in the Soviet Union. Kindergartners were members of the Oktyabryaty, or October kids. Their symbol was a pin with a picture of Lenin as a child. All schoolchildren were Pioneers, with a red triangular kerchief with a ring on the front decorated with a campfire, similar to Boy Scouts or Girl Scouts. They were organized into squads, units, and troops and participated in organized activities. The Komsomol (literally, "communist youth") were older teens and young adults on a path to the elite and had to pass a rigorous process for membership. Members could go to university, become a teacher, doctor, or Communist Party member. Full party membership was a prerequisite to a high position in any field.

He was found guilty and executed, as he knew he would be, but left a memorized letter containing the truth vouchsafed in the mind of his third wife, who survived prison long enough to save the words. The letter was finally published in 1988.

All of Bukharin's family paid for his courage. His first wife was tortured and executed along with her extended family. Years later, the GPU came in the night and took away Svetlana's mother, Bukharin's second wife. A few hours later, they came back and arrested Svetlana. Both separately sat in prison and were then sent to Siberia. Svetlana told me many decades later of her release after Stalin's death in 1953, and of the long struggle to find her mother in a camp in Siberia and eventually bringing her back to Moscow, a broken woman.

But while in school, her classmates and teachers stuck by her. The principal, Novikov, refused to hold a school assembly denouncing the Trotsky-Bukharin traitors. When a political commissar came to our class for a lesson on the subject, Svetlana was quietly pulled out to copy some papers in the teachers' room.

It may seem odd that this year could have been among the happiest of my childhood. The explanation is that the friendships and fun of that energetic time of our youth filled the foreground of our view of the world. There were a lot of school activities, including chess matches, ski expeditions, and civil defense exercises. We bonded as budding adults at school and in the country at Peredelkino, spending long days outdoors enjoying the capabilities of our strong, young bodies and competing for the affections of the bright, attractive girls in our group.

Of course, we were aware of the purge. We couldn't avoid it, with adults disappearing from around us, or living in silent fear of arrest. For me, the pain came closest as I watched my mother decline into isolation and depression. This outgoing woman, whose warmth supported so many, pined away like a captive animal. Although we couldn't talk about the situation, I sensed her sadness and showed my affection with hugs, bright conversation, and activities we could do together. Only many years later could I know the true depth of Markoosha's desperation by reading her memoirs and letters, some of which remained secret until after her death. Her one link to the outside world, my father, became more distant as her troubles deepened. His mind was on his work for Spain and his friends, comrades, and lovers there.

Telephone calls were brief and sometimes completely inaudible. Since everything was censored, letters had to be written with code and subtle suggestions, which Louis often misunderstood. He didn't grasp what was happening in Moscow. He refused to return for a visit and he frustrated Markoosha by being obtuse and naive in failing to read between the lines in her letters.

But her marriage to this famous American journalist was keeping Markoosha alive during the tumult in Russia. Her letters ached with the conflicting emotions created by the situation. Her anger at his lack of sympathy conflicted with the necessity to attach him more closely to her. Her knowledge that he was making love to other women conflicted with the hope of seducing him back to her and her own sexual desire. Her desperate need for food and clothing conflicted with her knowledge that he was driven away by her expressions of neediness.

In May 1938, Louis finally came for a brief visit, during which he conducted Spain-related business with the Kremlin. Markoosha used much of the week together to discuss her urgent desire to leave the Soviet Union for good. In June, she made the dangerous and final decision to submit her application for an exit visa to the GPU.

I didn't want to leave my friends, but I was fascinated by the technology of the West, excited by the easy availability of parts for my inventions, and drawn to the prospect of seeing the skyscrapers of New York. Besides, I expected Paul would be there.

George, however, flatly refused to go. He loved the Soviet Union; to leave would be to abandon his future as a leader of the great revolution. These dreams were beyond challenge. To disillusion George by telling him why Louis wouldn't come back to live in Moscow could put our lives at risk.

Markoosha ultimately overcame George's obstinate refusal with a deal and some skillful subterfuge. She promised that he could return to Moscow if he didn't like living in America. She found a family in our building willing to take him in if he did come back. And she arranged for a friend, the press chief of the Soviet Foreign Ministry, to call George in for an official meeting to inform him the Soviet state needed him in America. (Soon this good man was also purged.) George was also told by the Komsomol how to contact a youth cell in New York City.

But permission to exit Russia did not come. Paul and Hede Massing finally were able to leave in June, when Hede made a daring threat to the GPU that she would throw herself on the American embassy if not released from Russia. Markoosha lacked even the Massings' company when the glorious summer ended in Peredelkino and we returned to Moscow, where she had nothing to occupy her but waiting for a visa.

During Louis's visit, Markoosha had typed a letter in Russian from him to Nikolai Yezhov, then the head of the GPU, requesting permission for her to leave. No answer. In September, Louis met his old friend Litvinov, the Soviet foreign commissar, at a conference in Geneva. Litvinov said he couldn't do anything and told Louis to write directly to Stalin. In November he did, but again received no response.

He didn't know that Markoosha was by then fast in the grip of the secret police. It began in June with mysterious midnight phone calls telling her to go to a hotel, which she ignored. Next came a call directing her to the visa office. She sat in the office's waiting room for hours until everyone else was gone. Then a man led her down staircases into a second basement below, an office of the GPU. She believed she was being arrested.

She described the moment thirty years later in a private memoir:

> We walked through room after room filled with huge boxes, most of them open. They were filled with furniture, toys, kitchen utensils, books. They were the kind of boxes which one saw now in the commission shops. They were the belongings of those arrested, shot, exiled…Hundreds of boxes. Heartbreaking it all was, remains of once happy lives, but nothing as much as a schoolbook sticking out or a doll or toy train…My hands frozen, my heart pounding I walked on, and I could see our furniture, our books and the children's trains and drawings join the piles. There was not the shred of a doubt in my mind that I was being arrested. All the horror tales of the last two years passed through my mind. But nothing, nothing was as terrifying as the thought of what will happen to the children. They might at this very moment have been taken out of school already and brought to prison or police station or children's home—wherever they take children right after a parent is arrested. Would Yura (George) remain true to his belief in the righteousness of the Communist Party and instantly relegate me into the camp of traitors? No, fifteen is young enough to be crying out (if not outwardly) for his mother. Vitya (Victor) would probably be sure that the whole thing was an error and that in no time he will be back in school and at home with me.

But she wasn't arrested.

Instead, a pair of GPU agents began asking questions about everyone Markoosha saw, with whom she talked, where she went. She knew she couldn't lie, as our phone had long been tapped, they were obviously watching her, and they had many other sources of information, including Nyura and many friends. Any omission, even an inadvertent slip, could be enough to prove her a spy and send her to the executioner.

Finally one of the agents said, "You want to go abroad, don't you? You can if you will work with us. Will you?"

Without a moment's thought, Markoosha said, "No."

The agents didn't give up. They told Markoosha to expect a call each morning at eleven in case they wanted to see her that night. If there was no call, she was free for the day. Every morning she suffered the tension of waiting for the phone to ring with a summons.

About twice a week the call would come, sometimes just seconds before eleven, saying that a car would pick her up at midnight. Then she'd be taken to a hotel, where she would go through another lengthy round of questioning about everyone she talked to, everything she saw, and whatever she did. She began restricting her contact only to Else Wolf, who could talk about personal matters and who she assumed was similarly questioned by the GPU. The agents also asked many times why she wanted to leave the Soviet Union, probed her political beliefs, and suggested Louis should write again about Russia. Markoosha's stock answer, that Louis was interested in writing about Spain now, didn't resolve the issue. It had been more than two years since he had published one of his positive portrayals of Stalin's Russia. Their hope that he would resume may be what kept her alive as the sessions of questioning continued all year.

The pressure of the questioning, her isolation and fear of arrest weighed on Markoosha, as did her sense that Louis, her only hope, had abandoned her. By December 1938 her letters to him had taken on a suicidal tone.

> This is the third letter I am starting to write to you today. I will try to be short otherwise it will, like the others, become a tragic black thing which I wouldn't want to send to you. I have all reasons for it but no use telling you anything, you don't want to realize or to understand anything. Maybe someday—but I am afraid it will be too late then...Don't make me feel that with the exception of an occasional letter to me or to higher ones you left me completely to my fate. That wouldn't be decent of you, you know for whom I am paying...But nothing matters really. Goodbye.

That New Year's, 1939, George went to his first grown-up party, with champagne. I was away at the dacha in Peredelkino with Koni and Lothar and with Else Wolf. On New Year's Eve, we skied in the moonlight, waving sparklers in our hands as we sped down the hills. Even Nyura was away at a party. Markoosha, with her New Year's tree and radio, was more alone than ever.

A few days later, the visa office called her in for a meeting. One of the GPU agents had said her application would soon be approved, so she went hopefully, taking me with her. I had been on these visits to the visa office several times before. I always tried to support her when she came out of the office. She would be drained and often sobbed on the sidewalk, having once more been put off.

This time she finally received a direct answer: A clear refusal. I was waiting outside when she came out and immediately realized her utter despair. Trying to cheer her, I suggested we walk to a nearby office to buy tickets for the circus that evening. Markoosha later wrote that my comment kept her from throwing herself in front of a truck.

She wrote Louis a coded telegram and followed it with a letter, abandoning caution with the censors, who she knew would read her words:

> If you will try to evade under any pretext your responsibilities towards us now you will never see me alive in your life again. I have one glimpse of hope now: that together we may find a way out. If you betray me in this there is nothing in this world to keep me in it. And I suppose this will shake you up enough then to care for the boys. I understand everything, Lou, I know all your feelings and reactions now… (I wish you would have one hundredth of the same understanding for me) and still I insist on the only thing which you as an honest man must do at present. I feel quiet now and possess strength enough to go on for a while because there is this one hope. If you take it away—it is the end.

By the time he received that letter, in January 1939, Louis had already written to Eleanor Roosevelt. A year had passed since their meeting to discuss the Spanish embargo. Now Louis asked Mrs. Roosevelt to receive him "on a purely private matter which is urgent and important to me." They met at the White House three days later.

Mrs. Roosevelt immediately understood the situation. Louis asked her not to have the State Department contact the Soviet embassy in Washington or instruct the US embassy in Moscow to approach the Soviet authorities, because if Markoosha were refused, her plight would be worse. He explained that the request to allow the Fischer family to come to America had to be made in such a way as to preclude any rejection. Understanding that too, Eleanor said, "I shall talk to Franklin at dinner and let you know tomorrow morning."

The next morning Louis picked up his telephone at the Mayflower Hotel to find the first lady on the line.

"I spoke to Franklin yesterday," she said. "He is ready to do what is necessary, but he doesn't like (Soviet Ambassador) Oumansky. He will see Oumansky if you think it is necessary, but he would prefer not to, and I suggested that I might see Mrs. Oumansky."

Louis said, "You are very sweet. Could you tell Mrs. Oumansky that you are making the request in behalf of the president?"

She said yes, and Louis agreed to the plan. And the first lady had tea with Mrs. Oumansky a few days later.

Within a week after that get-together, Louis received an urgent call to meet with Ambassador Oumansky at the Soviet consulate in New York. They had known each other for years in Moscow, when Oumansky was head of the press department in the foreign ministry; he was the same man who had dressed as a nine-year-old in our apartment in Moscow a few years earlier.

After more than an hour of parrying, Oumansky tried the same blackmail threat that had been imposed on Markoosha, urging Louis to write about Soviet affairs. Louis told him that he had no intention of writing about the Soviet Union. Oumansky said, "Moscow will be very interested to learn that Louis Fischer refuses to write about Soviet affairs."

Louis said, "You can report anything you like."

By chance, however, within days of that exchange Eleanor Roosevelt met Oumansky on a rough airplane flight from New York to Washington. The flight was too scary to talk while they were in the air, but as they parted in the airport he told her, "The people you are interested in will soon arrive in this country."

The next day, January 21, Mrs. Roosevelt sent Louis a handwritten note that said, "Just back on the plane with Oumansky who told me he thought your 'little matter' was arranged. Have you heard anything definite?"

The same day in Moscow, Markoosha received permission to leave. She rushed to get ready for departure, obtaining her passport and exit visa, taking care of other paperwork and disposing of property that she couldn't take along. My father's accumulated papers were full of names of Russian leaders who had since been purged. Markoosha had to burn many of his most precious letters and notes, along with many cherished photographs that showed people either of them had worked with who had been eliminated.

The precautions were wise, as agents examined every piece of paper we left with, including my schoolbooks. We carried little. The only personal items I took from Russia were my notebook of addresses and a couple of gifts from my father, a map measurer and a multicolored pen.

I spent the last weeks in Moscow mostly with Koni and Lothar. We didn't part at all for the last twenty-four hours. George roamed through the city alone until train time, committing his favorite streets and metro stations to memory.

Many of Markoosha's friends bravely attended a goodbye party at our apartment on the eve of our departure, sharing laughter and tears, knowing they probably would not meet again.

Then, at midnight, the phone rang. A GPU officer told Markoosha he would pick her up in a half hour. "Only people who were ever faced with catastrophe in the midst of joy could know what I felt," she later wrote. Making up an excuse, she slipped out of the party and got in the GPU's black car. It drove to the most dreaded building in Russia: the Lubyanka, GPU headquarters.

But instead of descending into the sub-basements of torture and execution rooms, Markoosha was taken through a series of big, grand rooms, busy with workers rushing in with written and oral reports, no doubt carrying news of the night's torture sessions. In trepidation, she spent many hours waiting in a series of ornate offices.

Finally, she was shown into the huge office of a high secret service official, the right-hand man of Lavrenti Beria, the director of the purge who had taken over the GPU from the purged Yezhov. For whatever reason, this man delivered to Markoosha a long speech about her expected work as a spy in America. She had already refused to be a spy, but she said nothing and the subject never came up again. After a while he let her go.

She was returned to the apartment at 6 a.m. The guests were long gone.

The train for Leningrad departed that night. A few friends saw us off on the platform, including Lothar and Koni. It would be thirty-five years before we three would meet again.

Only when our train crossed the border from Russia to Finland did our mother tell us the truth about why we were leaving: Markoosha's and Louis's refusal to accept Stalin's murder of millions of good Soviet men and women. "Nothing in my mind had prepared me for this news," George later wrote. "My mother said it with much more sorrow than anger. That made it hard to fight or laugh at. And she stressed all our friends whom the purge hit. Plus the wonderful Soviet military and civilians with whom my father had worked in Spain on behalf of the heroic republic."

It took George years to emerge from his communist conditioning. The reality of freedom and prosperity in the West took time to sink in.

When we arrived in Helsinki, George and I couldn't believe the order and cleanliness that surrounded us, a phenomenal difference from our Russian environment. At Stockmann's department store we were astounded by the quantity, variety, and quality of goods for sale, a display of wealth that outstripped anything we could have imagined (although I later realized that Finland was small and poor compared to other Western countries). Markoosha bought us leather jackets, the dream of most boys. In addition, I got a Finnish hunting knife that served me for many years in Alaska.

George coped with the new experience by simply denying it. He declared the store and the city must have been set up as a propaganda showcase to deceive people about capitalism. He had no such explanation in London, when we attended a demonstration for Spain in Trafalgar Square, with the crowd shouting against the Chamberlain government and marching to 10 Downing Street. Afterward he reported to our mother, incredulously, "No one was arrested."

After we spent a few days in London, my parents allowed me to go on to New York by myself. I was so eager to reach America and be with Paul that I convinced them to let me skip the extended family vacation they had planned in England and France. Louis, Markoosha, and George had a great time, but I never regretted not going with them.

In February 1939 I rode across the stormy Atlantic aboard the *Queen Mary*, the world's largest ship.

For meals, I was assigned to a small table for German speakers with a portly older couple. They were friendly to me, but I felt uncomfortable with them. I could somehow sense that they were Nazis, even though neither sported a swastika or other fascist symbol. After the first meal, instead of going to the dining room, I ate in my cabin or the snack bar for the rest of the voyage. I freely wandered about the ship, swam in a pool, watched movies, and read books.

Entering New York harbor and seeing the Manhattan skyline was a wonderful thrill, a dream realized. I stood along the railing with excitement, watching the skyscrapers go by as the *Queen Mary* slowly moved up the Hudson River to its berth. A massive crowd stood on the pier below the ship. A bit of panic hit: How would I find anyone in that mob?

Yet, marvelously, there was Paul Massing at the bottom of the gangway. We got my bag and walked to his car. "His car." The concept itself impressed tremendously. In Russia, no one owned a car. Getting my own became one of my first goals as an American, although I was only fourteen.

Paul drove me from the pier up the west side of Central Park, past beautiful, solid buildings on one side of the street and trees on the other, to his large but simple apartment in a building just a block off the park on 106th Street, where they now lived. Hede was waiting, food was ready. They had a large library of books in German. I felt immediately at home.

Within a week, I started attending Abraham Lincoln High School, taking German language classes one, two, and three. While other students studied the foreign language, I reversed the lessons to learn English. Movies also helped me with English, particularly westerns, with their simple stories and slow speech. I would walk more than sixty blocks to the theaters at Times Square and Forty-second Street two or three times a week.

When the rest of the family arrived, we moved into a borrowed apartment together. We were living there when Eleanor Roosevelt invited us to dinner in Washington.

I had just turned fifteen. My memory is vivid of walking from the Mayflower Hotel across Lafayette Square to the White House and entering to meet Mrs. Roosevelt and Adm. Richard Byrd, the Antarctic explorer, who was one of my great heroes. Admiral Byrd's dress uniform was resplendent with medals and ribbons. I was in awe.

After a bit of conversation the party walked into a large, ornate room with a round table for twelve set at one side. I was seated between the first lady and Admiral Byrd. A little later, President Roosevelt was brought up to the table in his wheelchair.

I listened to the table conversation as best I could. Unfortunately, my English wasn't good enough yet. To my great annoyance, I couldn't follow all the admiral was saying about his polar adventures. I have no idea what we ate that night, but I do remember following my father's instruction to watch what utensils people were using.

After dinner, the president excused himself, and the rest of the party went down to the basement and watched the movie *Stagecoach*. Featuring John Wayne, it was the kind of western I could follow in English, the action being clear and the language simple.

Washington seemed asleep when we crossed Lafayette Square to our hotel. Before turning in, we walked over to a nearby White Tower and capped the evening with a hamburger.

My process of becoming American had begun, but it had a long way to go.

⇥ 7 ⇤

The Troika at War

I left behind my best friends in Moscow: Lothar and Koni and my classmates from the Nansen school. While I grew through my high school years in the safety of America, their lives were torn apart by World War II. Each member of our troika ended up fighting on a different side.

Following our departure from the Soviet Union early in 1939, the Great Purge abated. Perhaps Stalin's appetite for murder and terror had been temporarily sated. Then, in August, the Soviets and Nazis stunned the world by signing a nonaggression pact and dividing up spheres of influence for conquest in Eastern and Northern Europe. Within a week, Germany invaded Poland and the war began.

The 1939 Soviet–Nazi pact upended reality for the Fischer, Wolf, and Wloch families.

For my parents, the Soviets' opposition to fascism had been the primary and final reason for siding with the Soviet Union. When Hitler and Stalin made common cause, Louis finally had his Kronstadt moment, the historical incident that would no longer allow him to excuse the communists' inhumanity. He ended his silence about the purge. Now he denounced the Soviet Union and began writing what he knew. Markoosha also wrote *My Lives in Russia,* which came out in 1944 and was a bestseller.

The pact affected the Wolf family even more directly. Koni and Mischa's father, Friedrich, had been detained on the way to fight in Spain in 1938 and remained imprisoned in France, in political limbo. Being sequestered there

likely saved him from the purge, when most German intellectuals in Russia perished, but the outbreak of the world war put his life newly at risk.

Friedrich still had a German passport. Declaration of war between Germany
and France made him an alien enemy in France, subject to deportation to
Germany. That would mean certain death as a famous antifascist. But he couldn't
go to neutral America without renouncing communism and leaving his family
in the Soviet Union. Returning to the Soviet Union posed a problem, too. After
the pact with the Nazis, his antifascist writing fell into disfavor there. The movie
based on his play *Professor Mamlock* was withdrawn from Moscow theaters. But
thanks to his wife Else's efforts, Friedrich finally received Soviet citizenship in
August 1940 and eventually got out of France. He arrived in Moscow in the
spring of 1941.

The Nazi–Soviet pact changed Lothar's life most dramatically among the
troika. The Nazis welcomed its citizens in Russia to return to Germany with
a promise of amnesty. Lothar's mother, Erna, had no life in the Soviet Union.
She had finally learned that her husband, Wilhelm, had been executed, and
she remained a political outcast. Besides her unrelenting emotional turmoil, she
declined physically to "a stick, skin and bones," as Else Wolf described her in a
letter to Markoosha. In the middle of 1940, Erna decided to return to Germany
with Lothar and Margot.

Leaving Russia severed Lothar's first love affair, an event that echoed for
decades through several lives. The girl was Zilya, daughter of a famous poet, Ilya
Selvinski. As a favorite writer of Stalin, Selvinski had a huge Moscow apartment
in a building for writers and a dacha at Peredelkino. There, Zilya Selvinskaya
(later Voskresenskaya) participated with our gang of friends like one of the boys.

Zilya was lively and fun, playing volleyball or roaming the woods for mushrooms. She was emotional and dramatic and charmingly flirtatious with all the
boys. And, as we slowly perceived with our advancing adolescence, she was very
beautiful. (In fact, she became a successful actress.)

For her part, Zilya enjoyed the fun as much as the rest of us. She liked being
surrounded by boys and found some of her friends' faulty Russian funny and
exotic. She especially liked the quiet, strong one, Lothar, whose accent was
worst of all.

The summer of 1940 Lothar and his close school friend and Peredelkino con-
federate, Andrei "Anarik" Eisenberger, both fell in love with Zilya. Lothar was
sixteen. He declared his love as he walked with Zilya out of the writers' settlement. Zilya recalled the moment fifty years later in a memoir:

> "I want to tell you something," said Lothar.
> "Yes, please?" I asked, my voice wooden with tension.

We were on the way to the railroad station. End of August. Sun. I had picked raspberries for a long time—the season's last fruit, the sweetest. I filled a glass with effort, because I so wanted to give him a feast.

"No, I probably should not tell you, when I'm going away…"

"Why?" My God, how I wished he would say it, though I well knew what words Lothar would say.

"So, say it?" I ask him gently. We walk on silently for a while.

"I love you."

Silence around us. A locomotive whistles. I try to be calm.

Lothar told no one he was leaving—even his closest friends didn't know until after his train departed for Germany that winter. But the love affair, as intense and yet as innocent as only a romance between sixteen-year-olds can be, continued through that fall while the Wloch family waited for permission to leave.

The couple met for a concert and a play together. Anarik carried messages between them, keeping quiet about his own love for Zilya out of respect for his friend. Lothar feared bringing the GPU down on Zilya's family if he went to her apartment. He visited her there only twice, with other boys for a celebration of the October revolution, and when he left for Berlin.

On that day, December 16, 1940, Lothar took a long, roundabout route to see Zilya, changing streetcars to lose any agent who might follow him. It was the last time they ever met. He made her promise to take care of herself and, snuffing out a cigarette, bade her, "*Auf wiedersehen.*"

A meeting they planned years later, after both were married, was blocked by the construction of the Berlin Wall. Zilya's love for Lothar never faded. When I visited her apartment in Moscow decades later, his photo still occupied a place on her wall like an icon. Lothar answered Zilya's letters after the war, but his affection soon turned in another direction.

Immediately upon arriving on German soil, Erna was detained because she was listed as a communist activist, subject to being arrested on sight. Even after her release in Berlin, the state never allocated an apartment to Erna, forcing her to move between relatives while earning a paltry income as a typist. The Gestapo required her to register and come in for regular questioning.

The world turned upside down again for the three families on June 22, 1941. Despite the nonaggression pact, Germany attacked the Soviet Union.

German columns advanced rapidly across a broad front. The Red Army, although numerically stronger and well equipped with tanks and supplies, collapsed before the German advance. It lacked trained officers. Stalin had killed or imprisoned the cream of his military. Lieutenants commanded battalions on the front. And they were afraid to act for fear of arrest if they made a wrong decision, because Stalin usually reacted to battlefield setbacks by executing officers.

The Fischer, Wolf, and Wloch families now found themselves on three different sides—American, Soviet, and German. The troika and our brothers and friends became enmeshed in the war.

Lothar joined the Luftwaffe, the German air force, although underage at seventeen. He had several reasons. He hoped his service could ease the Gestapo's pressure on his mother. He wanted to avoid being made a laborer for the Nazi state. And he wanted to beat Stalin, who had killed his father.

At first he served at the lowest level, in ground forces, because his history in Russia made him untrustworthy. But eventually he rose in the ranks to fly a short-range reconnaissance aircraft on the eastern front, fulfilling his boyhood dream of being a pilot. A letter home to his mother reported that he had arrived with German forces at Artek, the Crimean summer camp he had attended as a boy when he lived in Russia.

My former schoolmates at the Nansen school joined the military and fought for Russia. Many lost their lives. Boys and girls who were too young for the army were deployed to the defenses around Moscow, digging trenches. After the initial German attack on Moscow was halted at the suburbs and Hitler's forces were pushed back, many of my classmates were evacuated into the hinterland.

Anarik Eisenberger, Lothar's closest friend outside the troika, had promised to look after Zilya and help her wait for Lothar's return. His German family had lived in the Lux Hotel, like Lothar's, and his father had similarly been killed in the purge.

Nonetheless, Anarik considered himself a patriot and eagerly prepared to fight the invading Nazis. He was assigned to a Red Army unit of similar German émigrés. But instead of going to the front, the entire group was arrested as the children of traitors. Anarik spent the war and many years thereafter in a Soviet labor camp and in exile.

Within a few months of Germany's attack, many Germans living in Russia were rounded up for evacuation by rail to the far reaches of Siberia. Crowded boxcars crept across the vast expanse of the country in the chill of autumn, a trip that took weeks with daily rations of a small hunk of bread and warm water.

Trains frequently waited on sidings for trains bound in the opposite direction with soldiers and materials for the front. Some of the people found themselves stranded in indigenous villages as the guests of hostile natives, who didn't want them and could not, in any case, offer them adequate food or shelter. The deep Siberian cold killed off many unfed city dwellers stranded in such desolate places.

A week after the Germans invaded, Koni was separated from his family and sent to a children's camp. Friedrich, Else, and Mischa Wolf, only just reunited after Friedrich's return from France, rode a train four thousand miles east to Alma-Ata, Kazakhstan, a three-week journey with a daily ration of four hundred grams (fourteen ounces) of bread. That provincial capital more than tripled in population with the arrival of refugees and the installation of industries, government, and cultural institutions evacuated from Moscow and other cities. But living conditions, while crowded, were survivable.

Six months later Koni joined his family in Alma-Ata. He and his parents returned to Moscow in February 1942, and Koni joined other teens building defenses. Mischa stayed in Alma-Ata. Friedrich went to the front as a propagandist. In January 1943, Koni joined the Red Army, still seventeen, and was soon at the front as a lieutenant.

The Russian winter had turned the tide of the war in the Soviets' favor. With his fluency in German, Koni operated a van with a loudspeaker along the line of battle, calling on enemy soldiers to surrender. He questioned captured Germans and translated propaganda, both German and Russian.

Koni later became an acclaimed filmmaker and made an autobiographical movie dramatizing his experiences at the end of the war called *I Was Nineteen*. The film captures the chaos created by the collapsing German army and fast-advancing Russians. The young German-speaking Red Army lieutenant gathers up crowds of surrendering Germans, never sure if they will throw down their arms or shoot. He goes to negotiate the surrender of a surrounded castle, is taken away for execution, and is eventually released when the German soldiers ordered to kill him instead escape with him as deserters.

At an earlier point in the film, Koni's character is left behind by a fast-advancing column and with a few soldiers is to take control of a city just abandoned by the Nazis. Standing alone in the street, Koni and his men set out to find the city hall, where his uniform alone will make him absolute ruler, although still a teenager. That really happened, in a town near Berlin.

Meanwhile, Mischa was relatively safe in Alma-Ata. He was exempt from military service as a student of aeronautical engineering. His only fighting came as a German knight in Sergei Eisenstein's film *Ivan the Terrible*—the movie industry had been evacuated there, too.

But the Soviet authorities didn't overlook Mischa's value as a brilliant student and committed communist. Halfway through his engineering studies he received a telegram from the Comintern, the organization dedicated to the spread of communism worldwide, ordering him to Ufa, Bashkiria, to a special school there.

The Comintern school groomed the children of German émigrés to be instruments of the Soviet system in the future conquered Germany. Each student was stripped of his identity and had to pretend not even to recognize old friends from the small community of Germans in Russia. They received advanced academic training in cultural topics and Nazi ideology, as well as communist dogma and extensive military training.

Mischa, like my brother George, his close friend, had accepted the communist belief system in whole, despite the purge. But Mischa also received the brainwashing of the Comintern school, which embedded the Stalinist system of thought control to a further extreme.

Those chosen for power were elevated to a special status above all others, with excellent food while the rest of the country starved, comfortable accommodations, and relative freedom of action. They were drilled with dogma supporting the party above all. And they learned to accept a view of reality defined solely by political superiors, accepting the justice of unjust punishment even when it was directed at themselves.

Sessions of "criticism and self-criticism" were a regular part of life at the Comintern school. Mischa's friend and fellow student, Wolfgang Leonhard, recalled being called into a session with a panel of accusers who tore him down for hours with charges concocted from innocent comments he had made to informers. The last part of the session required the accused to accept the accusations as true, criticize himself, and tear down his own personality with promises to reform the invented faults.

Mischa and his fellow Comintern school alumni worked as radio propagandists in Moscow until Hitler's Germany fell in 1945. He was on the second plane of political Germans sent to Berlin to set up a new government for East Germany, which was in the Russian zone when the country was divided between the Soviet and Western powers. The young operatives were dispatched to rapidly select mayors and administrators for German towns and regions. Leonhard describes in his memoir grabbing a man off the street to be mayor for a town.

George's and my wartime experience followed interesting parallels with our friends' in Russia and Germany, but in the gentler American context.

Like Koni and Lothar, I tried to enlist when I was seventeen, but I was rejected as too young. I recount in the next chapter my long and fruitless efforts to get to the front. While I served with combat engineers in Europe, I never saw combat. All I wanted was to be a foot soldier fighting Hitler.

My brother, however, followed a route more like Mischa's, as a member of the elite, as he had done as a striving Komsomol member in Moscow. Except for his

American context, George was Mischa's twin in intellect and drive to get to the top of the establishment.

George didn't shed his communist conditioning overnight. He spent the war fighting the Nazis, but it took him a long time to give up on the Soviets. When we got to the United States, he abandoned the idea of returning to Moscow and recognized the superiority of the West's economic might, but he did not totally renounce his communist beliefs within his own mind for years.

When the family reunited in New York in 1939, Louis used his connections to get George a scholarship to an exclusive prep school, the Ethical Culture Fieldston School in Riverdale, in the Bronx. Most of its students planned to go to top colleges and become lawyers, doctors, and such. As in Moscow, George excelled, starting the Fieldston Progressive Club and working on the school newspaper. The yearbook predicted he would go to Washington and become president.

He did spend time with the president, Franklin Roosevelt. In 1941, George went to a summer camp, the Summer Student Leadership Institute, which Eleanor Roosevelt invited to Campobello Island, the first family's vacation home off the coast of Nova Scotia and Maine. He remembered Mrs. Roosevelt teaching the privileged young overachievers to sing "Joe Hill," the radical union song. George was the only high schooler among the college student body presidents and other young leaders, but he still tried to organize the camp to approve a joint credo.

At the camp George came to Mrs. Roosevelt's attention, and she told him to let her know when he came to Washington. He did, and she invited him to stay at the White House. They became good friends. He accepted her hospitality for four or five other overnight stays and kept in touch until her death in 1962.

One of George's White House visits merited a mention in Mrs. Roosevelt's autobiography. Arriving for a visit to Washington during the winter break from the University of Wisconsin in 1942, he was invited by her social secretary to a formal dinner, but only if he would wear appropriate clothing. George scrounged an ill-fitting tuxedo, but wore scuffed brown-and-white saddle shoes. It turned out the secret guest of honor was Winston Churchill, making his first wartime visit to the White House.

George later wrote,

> That evening, I was struck by the kindness of FDR and of Harry Hopkins, his close aide. The president was pouring drinks before dinner. Both seemed to go out of their way to put me at ease. Only when I read Mrs. R's memoirs did I guess why they seemed in a rush to my aid. I must have looked like a

fish out of water, like a scruffy teenager among the great of this world. At the time I felt no great strain…That next morning at breakfast I found myself next to Churchill for the meal. All of nineteen at the time, I talked with him for some time. I told him of all the close friends my folks and I had lost in Stalin's purges. He heard me out. Then he shook his round head and growled, "Turrrrrible."

The president personally intervened for George when he decided to join up and fight for the United States. Roosevelt wrote a note to his navy aide to inquire if any branch could use a brilliant young man fluent in German and Russian. Naval intelligence replied that it wanted him, "provided he passes investigation."

The papers from that investigation—an interview by a lieutenant in Philadelphia—confirm that George's conversion from communism was far from complete, despite the high-level attention he received. The reports says, "The subject evinced strong Communistic beliefs and was, in [interviewer's] opinion, as 'Communistic as it was possible to be without being a member of the Communist Party.'" On the navy's written questionnaire, George had listed Moscow as his hometown!

Rejected by the navy, he joined the army through normal channels and attended a ninety-day officer training program. He served as an intelligence officer in the States and England.

George finally shed the last of his communist indoctrination when he got back to the Soviet Union in 1944. He was assigned to an air base at Poltava, Ukraine, where the Allies planned to refuel planes after bombing runs to the Ploesti oil fields in Rumania. The ground crews in Ukraine would extend the bombers' range. As adjutant of the American detachment, George had recruited interpreters and liaison officers for the joint United States–Soviet project. He enjoyed the camaraderie with Russian officers and even took leave in Moscow.

But on the second bombing mission, after nearly one hundred B-17 "Flying Fortress" aircraft flew from Italy to refuel, a catastrophe struck. Nazi fighters had tracked the flight to Poltava, and in a midnight raid, German bombers destroyed 60 percent of the planes on the ground. The Russians had not provided the air and ground protection they promised, and Stalin had refused to allow the Americans to set up their own defenses. The Germans got away without losses. As resulting tensions grew, the Soviets for a time cut off the Poltava base from flights to the West.

George was disgusted, as well, when the Soviets refused to help an uprising by the people of Warsaw against the German occupation, and wouldn't let the

Americans and British help until it was too late. British pilots landing in Poltava told him of the collapse of the uprising, which ended in slaughter of the Poles. When George wrote of the incident forty years later, it still made him weep.

Besides those geopolitical betrayals, the Soviets also undermined individual American officers at Poltava. George saw the Russian-speaking men he had recruited shipped out one after another, each the victim of complaints by Soviet officers, which always seemed to target the most skilled American interpreters. Finally, he and another officer were officially accused by the Russians, purge-style, with false charges of starting a fight and sexually attacking a female Soviet telephone operator. An official investigation cleared George and his colleague, but at that point his conversion to anticommunism was complete.

With the failure of the Poltava experiment, and the first chill of the coming Cold War, the Western allies began withdrawing their forces. In the shrunken force, George became the chief liaison officer and adjutant of the eastern command. When Churchill, Roosevelt, and Stalin came to meet in the Crimea, at Yalta, to divide up the postwar world, George was dispatched to set up the conference. Although his work was only operational, at the airport he saw each of the leaders and was the first and last American officer at the site.

He and his boss, a colonel, had made a crusade of telling their superiors in coded cables and other reports about the Soviets' behavior at Poltava. They believed the Russians shouldn't be trusted; their point was essentially that the Cold War was on. At Yalta, George took the opportunity to grab US Secretary of State Edward Stettinius and tell him this news, but Stettinius shrugged him off.

The war ended in 1945 with Europe devastated. The Western allies and Soviet Red Army had rushed toward each other across Germany, dividing the country into zones of control that eventually became separate nations. Berlin lay on the Soviets' side of Germany, but as the capital its districts were split among the conquering armies, with Soviet, American, British, and French sectors. Half the city eventually became part of West Germany.

In this divided city the young men of the Fischer, Wolf, and Wloch families reunited. George, now a captain, joined a high-level administrative unit in Berlin's American sector. The city lay in ruins, worse even than London, Moscow, or Paris, all of which he had recently visited. Streets were blocked by rubble. Rotting bodies in collapsed buildings kept the scent of death in the air. The people were gaunt and wasted.

Walking in the street, George met Friedrich Wolf, who had been sent by the Soviets to help run the eastern portion of Germany that they controlled.

Friedrich put George in touch with Koni and Mischa. Their roles were nearly counterparts to his own, but on the opposite side of the line, in the east.

Then he found the Wlochs. Lothar, Erna, and Margot were living in a miserable cellar apartment in Red Wedding, the same working-class district where George and I had lived with the Massings as children. Lothar was keeping them warm by burning stumps and branches he dragged in from all over the city.

George found a better place for the Wlochs to live and provided them with military rations to keep them alive. And he reunited them with the Wolfs. He tried to get me transferred to Berlin, to Eisenhower's headquarters, where I could use my German and Russian language skills. I was already in Germany, in the west, and was thrilled at the prospect of reuniting with my buddies, Lothar and Koni. But my combat engineers unit was ordered to the war in the Pacific and my commanding officer categorized me as indispensable to that mission.

So George took my place in the troika, celebrating with Koni and Lothar. A classic photo from that time shows the three of them. Koni, in a Soviet uniform, has deep-set eyes and is slender, healthy. George, in a US uniform, looks strong, well fed, and almost portly. Between them, Lothar, the German survivor, is supported by their shoulders; the civilian seems barely able to stand, thin and hollowed out.

The photo became a symbol, inspiring Koni in his filmmaking career, much later, to represent the trio and the history it represented. We still had a lot of life and friendship to experience together, although our paths now led irreversibly in vastly different directions. At the time, the reunion was simply proof of the power of friendship over politics and change. George remembered it this way:

> We met. Feasted. Laughed and cried. Shared ideas and memories.
>
> We drank a lot, got soused. In that state we'd loll around the streets near Lothar's new place and sing together. Very loudly sang German ditties and Russian favorites…
>
> We argued on the Soviets, of course. And on the whole world, all of life. And our new future, the heavy thick fog of it. How could we master our lives, our Moscow-fed zeal and sorrow?

George's relationship with Mischa did not renew itself in the same way. Once dearest friends, they were adversaries now, important officials on the two sides of the brewing Cold War.

Mischa went as a journalist to the Nuremberg Trials of German war criminals, and George visited and stayed in his lodgings in the Castle of Faber. But their conversations remained polite, constrained by politics and by Mischa's programming, as Mischa himself later recognized. His ideology shielded him from true communication with anyone who was not one of his own kind.

Mischa's training had worked, in the Komsomol and the Comintern school, and then as a communist official. If that had been George's fate on the same path, then the freedom of the United States had likely saved him from losing his moral direction and becoming part of terrible acts. While George went on to be a successful academic in the United States, Mischa became one of the most powerful men in Europe in the hidden world of East Germany's secret service.

Wolfgang Leonhard tells a chilling story of meeting his friend Mischa in Berlin in 1947. Mischa had married a girl he met at the Comintern school. At twenty-five, Mischa had an important official position and high-level contacts in Moscow. Wolfgang visited his luxurious, five-room apartment and the lake villa he owned an hour away, in the country.

After two years of Soviet espousal of democracy and cooperation with the West, Mischa told him that orders would shortly arrive from Moscow to abolish the last bit of East Germany's independence and put its government under direct control the Kremlin. The Cold War had begun. He gave the news by way of friendly advice, so Wolfgang could revise his democracy-leaning beliefs before the new changes were officially announced. (These changes led to Wolfgang's defection, first to Yugoslavia and then to the West.)

Decades later, after the fall of communism, Mischa would wonder in his memoirs about how his development in the party had left him feeling exempt from moral values in his work. But by then, he was being pursued by prosecutors for his part in running the repressive East German regime. Critics questioned if his facile mind was simply accommodating the new political reality in which he found himself, which once again required him to repudiate the old.

Koni had never been a committed believer like Mischa. Koni wanted to stay in Berlin but was afraid he couldn't without becoming a Soviet-controlled political operator, an *apparatchik*, like his brother. Several years later, Koni went to Moscow for film school.

Lothar, ever the responsible one, found work as a stonemason in the Western sector of the city and began studying to be a construction engineer. In the years to come, he would rise at 5 a.m., work at his construction job until 5 p.m., then attend school at night, arriving home at 10 p.m., a schedule he kept six days a week.

Politics didn't come between the members of the troika, of which George was now a part. They met often in the year after the war, despite having fought on different sides and regardless of living on opposite sides of a divided city. One night Lothar, filled with rage at Stalin, shouted his anger at Koni. Koni loved him too much to fight back. George remembered, "He sat with his head bent down...sighed, and said, 'What can and should I do?'"

George had been of a type with Mischa. Now, as a stand-in for me in our troika, he was part of the human connection of close friends that transcends politics. Perhaps he understood me for the first time.

I grew during the war years, too, as I'll tell next.

ᘒ 8 ᘓ

Coming of Age

I was almost fifteen when my father moved out for the last time, in 1939. After a short stint in an apartment with the family, Louis decided to live by himself in a Manhattan hotel. Markoosha got a place in Greenwich Village and during the summer went to the country to escape city heat.

That summer I visited my mother for a week. I spent most of the summer on a farm Paul Massing had rented, helping with outdoor work and enjoying his company. I had fun driving a tractor, haying, and doing other physical work. Best of all, I got a learner's permit and Paul taught me how to drive a car. I bought a 1936 Ford Roadster convertible with a rumble seat for $110. When I turned sixteen the next May, I got a driver's license and could actually use the car. Life in America was great.

Markoosha enrolled me in the top-notch, science- and engineering-oriented Stuyvesant High School. It was a public school that drew students from all over the city. My excellent educational background from Moscow allowed me to keep up despite the language barrier, which was rapidly shrinking.

I kept in touch with Koni, Lothar, and my former classmates at the Nansen school intermittently by mail until the outbreak of the war made communication impossible. As I was well aware, horrifying events were sweeping Europe. In comfortable America I could do little to help other than volunteer in the Fight for Freedom campaign for the United States to enter the war on Britain's side.

My teen years in the United States were lonely without my friends, and I didn't make new friends my own age. There were several reasons. For one, it took time to become fully American. For another, Stuyvesant's geographically spread-out student body made it difficult to develop relationships. Aside from that, I lived in Greenwich Village, where there weren't many families with kids.

My mother, George, and I lived in a series of small apartments in the Village, surviving on Markoosha's meager earnings as a translator and the minuscule support provided by Louis. The division of our family could no longer be ignored. My brother and I resented our father's comfortable hotel life and his three meals a day in restaurants, while our mother, living in the same city, barely scraped by. The difference in lifestyles had existed when we lived in Moscow, but it had not been so obvious to us then.

My father had made his choice. He preferred the posh life of a freewheeling international journalist and author to the role of husband or dad. For years longer, my mother put up with being a part-time wife, available at his call when he needed her as a prop at an event but putting no claim on him as a husband.

George and I saw her anguish and couldn't understand why she let the situation continue. Years later, when Louis made extra royalties on a successful book, he began sending us checks but refused to increase Markoosha's small stipend. We were grown men by then. We forwarded Louis's money to her.

Louis also refused to pay college tuition for George, saying he had worked his own way through school. To the great good fortune of both of us boys, one of Louis's friends recommended the University of Wisconsin, in Madison, which had both a stellar reputation for a progressive environment and low out-of-state tuition. Louis relented and paid some of the cost for both George and me to attend there.

Before I finished high school, Markoosha bought a simple farmhouse— it lacked indoor plumbing—next to a farm owned by Paul and Hede near Quakertown, in Bucks County, Pennsylvania. At seventeen and a high school senior, I lived by myself in a rented room in an apartment in the Village, driving my convertible to Pennsylvania for the weekends. After school each day, for lunch, I bought a hotdog and a slice of apple pie from a stand across the street.

Four days a week I spent the afternoon and evening working in the Slavonic department of the New York Public Library at Fifth Avenue and 42nd Street, where stone lions guard the entrance steps. My main job was delivering Russian-language newspapers, journals, and books to visitors. Some of the patrons, as well as my boss, were my parents' émigré friends, all elderly in my young eyes. One of the older men invariably told people around him that he had held me on his knee and fed me carrots when I was a toddler in Berlin. I would hide from him in the stacks.

The library job allowed me enough time to do my school homework. At the end of my shift, I ate my dinner in an automated cafeteria, alone. In the evening,

I went to a movie or back to my room for more study. It was a lonesome time, until Friday afternoon when I drove to the farm after school.

When I graduated from high school in January 1942, Japan had attacked Pearl Harbor and America was finally in the war. My only focused goal was to fight Hitler. I tried to enlist but the army wouldn't have me because I was only seventeen. For the same reason, my application was rejected to work in the Bethlehem Steel mill in Allentown, less than an hour from our farm. I was dejected.

My mother thought I should be an agronomist. During my summers and after graduation I had enjoyed gardening and doing other work on her farm and Paul Massing's place in Pennsylvania, and for Dr. Joseph Rosen, who had sent my mother to Ukraine years earlier and had a beautiful house up the Hudson River. Growing things became a lifelong interest, but I didn't want to make it my career.

Without a clear direction I followed my brother George to the University of Wisconsin in Madison, almost by default. My memory is vivid of getting off the train on a rainy fall evening in 1942, alone, with a trench coat, a hat, a suitcase, and an address. Nobody was around to meet me, so I walked ten blocks to the Rochdale men's cooperative house. I was shown a bunk in an alcove, got into my dry pajamas, and decided to go find George.

One of the housemates said he was probably at the campus newspaper, the *Cardinal,* a few blocks away. I walked there in my pajamas and trench coat. But, instead of George, I found a beautiful young woman with dark hair, who welcomed me in a friendly, lively way. Her name was Gloria Rubinstein. A couple of years older, she knew George and was part of an active social circle I joined at Madison. She eventually became my wife.

That open social scene influenced my future more than anything I learned in the classroom. At Rochdale and attending frequent student gatherings, I thrived in a free-flowing collection of equals. For the first time in years, I was with people of every background, not just urban intelligentsia like my parents, and I delighted in passing from one group to another. It was my first experience of the Midwestern United States and its fluid culture, accepting new people and treating everyone initially as a friend. Several of my new friendships lasted a lifetime.

In my youth I was quite shy, but here I blossomed. I became confident, actively social, and even an organizer. George left for the military within a month of my arrival in Madison and his circle of friends became my circle. From that base, I came to know more and more people.

My financial circumstances helped stimulate my social connections. My father paid the tuition of $48 per semester, but I had to cover living expenses.

I earned room and board as the food manager for the two dozen students at Rochdale. I organized student kitchen crews and planned menus with the cook. I bought the big #10 cans of beans and other basics that supplied the dining room. In retrospect I realize the diet was Spartan, but at the time I thought the food was wonderful.

Our dining room also served students who lived elsewhere, and we frequently had women guests. I was active in progressive causes on campus, such as working to start a women's co-op. Gloria and I had common friends in several people.

Although we didn't pair up at the time, Gloria and I became well acquainted. She had made a striking impression on me right from our first meeting at the newspaper and, shortly thereafter, when she was playing the grand piano in the grand foyer of the Student Union building. We both attended a party where she was playing the role of a fortune teller. She predicted my meeting a tall, dark-haired girl—describing herself. I was smitten.

Gloria later recounted that she didn't remember our initial meeting, but she did notice me as an interesting, even exotic presence. My English was still accented at that point, although Gloria recalls it being as good as it is today. She also knew of my family's escapes from Hitler and Stalin.

Gloria grew up in the northeast Pennsylvania mining town of Pittston. Her father, a Latvian immigrant, was a doctor. Her mother had been a social worker in Philadelphia when they met. From the day Gloria toured a newspaper office as a Girl Scout, she knew she wanted to be a journalist. When I met her, she was just short of getting her journalism degree from the University of Wisconsin.

Besides her vivid and lively writing, Gloria's personality made her a talented reporter and good at just about everything else she tried. She was outgoing, full of life, game for anything. She had needed an adventurous spirit to get to Wisconsin, a school she chose because she had read about student protests there. If not for her zest for life, mine might have turned out far less interesting.

Despite the fun and the group connections at Wisconsin, one of my clearest memories is of a snowy night on the campus when I cried because I missed Lothar and Koni so badly. As I enjoyed student life, they were in the depths of Europe's war. I wanted to be with them. I knew I would never have closer friends.

I wanted to fight Hitler. I concurrently enlisted in the army and enrolled in the university's Reserve Officer Training Corps. I drilled with other students, creeping along the ground with a gun and stringing reels of telephone wire through the woods with a Signal Corps detachment. In lieu of physical education classes, I took up boxing.

I was called up for active duty after my first semester of college. At the Fort Grant processing center in Rockford, Illinois, I passed my physical exams and received high scores in mechanical and general aptitude tests. I told the interviewing officer of my desire to fight on the front lines in a tank. My second choice was the Signal Corps or anywhere I could make use of my German and Russian languages.

The army wasn't much interested in what recruits wanted in 1943. The officer sent me to Aberdeen Proving Ground in Maryland for four weeks of basic training and a nine-week course in repair of optical instruments, such as range finders, binoculars, and telescopes. Working on periscopes there allowed me to run around in an army tank, and that one experience proved quite enough.

After the army made me an expert on fixing optical devices, somebody decided that my potential was worthy of further development and sent me to Virginia Military Academy for assignment to the new Army Specialist Training Program. For two weeks, we recruits were given nothing to do but try to pick up the few women and direct mockery at the drilling cadets. Finally some army bureaucrat decided my language aptitude called for further study of Russian.

I wanted to fight, not spend my time in senseless training. I made every effort to inform the higher powers that my Russian was perfectly fluent already, but they wouldn't listen. After I had arrived in New York City for advanced Russian classes at City College of New York, it turned out that only basic Russian for beginners was being offered.

Many of the instructors were old family friends and acquaintances from the Slavonic department at the library. They understood as well as I did the absurdity of the army's orders. The Russian teachers and I did everything possible to explain to army officials that if they needed Russian speakers, I was already trained for the job. It was hopeless. In an attempt to salvage the situation somehow, I signed up to learn Italian.

The army was not turning out as I had expected. Barracks life was okay, with its lively discussions and games of poker and dice. But I resented the stupidity and regimentation—what we called chickenshit. As the army wasted my skills and its own resources with pointless training, my enthusiasm waned.

My brother George, by then an officer, was in New York for a while, and some of our friends from Wisconsin had landed there too. For our first get-together, we arranged to meet at the Plaza Hotel for a party of University of Wisconsin students and graduates.

George and I met in the lobby. We hadn't seen each other for a year, so we talked animatedly while riding up in a crowded elevator. After a couple of minutes, we realized other conversation had ceased and that the elevator had fallen silent. The other passengers were staring at us in horror—two men in American military uniforms, speaking fluent German.

The news was full of reports of enemy submarines dropping off spies along the shore of Long Island. The anti-espionage slogan "loose lips sink ships" was posted everywhere. Silently, George and I stepped off on the next floor—and we never spoke German with each other again. Switching to English was one more step toward our full Americanization.

Another major event happened at that party. Gloria was there. She had received her journalism degree and had come to the big city to work as one of the first copy girls at the *New York Post,* the copy boys having been drafted. I invited her to go swimming at Coney Island, and after that outing we began dating regularly.

With this new diversion, I gave in to the reality of where the army had placed me. I was in New York City, young, in love, and without responsibilities. I quit Italian and went back to basic Russian. I tried to help the army a bit by doing some Russian tutoring, but otherwise my time became pretty much my own.

An army private's pay being inadequate for life in the city, and being very healthy, I sold my blood on a frequent basis. By switching blood banks, a friend and I would earn the $25 fee far more often than the six-week interval that was normally required.

Army life also included constant poker games, which I sometimes won. On one occasion, I cleaned up and was able to take Gloria and my mother to a fancy restaurant on Eighth Street in the Village and to a performance by violinist Fritz Kreisler at the New York Opera House. We often attended Broadway shows for free, among them the musical *Oklahoma.* Military personnel didn't have to pay and could stand in the back if a show was sold out.

Gloria lived in a basement apartment in Greenwich Village with two friends from Wisconsin. I spent a lot of my time there rather than the dorm at City College, returning for unavoidable activities, to connect with friends, and to get in on poker games. My absence from the dorm was noted a few times, but it didn't matter much; at worst, the punishment was restriction to quarters for a few days. Gloria was my priority, and I had lots of time thanks to decisions totally beyond my influence.

We were deeply in love by the time the army canceled the entire advanced training program in spring 1944 and sent me off into the infantry at Camp Shelby, in Hattiesburg, Mississippi. At last I would do something practical. While being in a mortar platoon meant having to carry heavy equipment, I felt a new high firing live shells on the artillery range.

Yet even that did not last. Somewhere, a personnel clerk noticed I had taken a drafting class at Stuyvesant High School and that qualification, after all my wasted technical training in the army, was finally enough to get me a real job assignment.

The newly formed 1155th Engineer Combat Group was preparing to go overseas to manage three combat engineer battalions that built bridges and cleared the way for advancing troops. My job would be to prepare route maps, do other basic drafting tasks, and participate in the activities of the intelligence section to which I belonged. After more than a year of temporary assignments, I at last felt part of the military.

A few months after arriving at Camp Shelby, I called Gloria and asked her to marry me. She agreed. She also agreed with her father to send him a copy of the marriage certificate, as he was a bit dubious about our real intentions.

Gloria arrived in Mississippi in the heat of July 1944. We went to a justice of the peace to get married. When the one we had chosen didn't show up for a long time, we impatiently looked in the classifieds and found another. Two young women from the beauty parlor next door were our witnesses.

We stood next to a grand old rolltop desk in a paper-strewn office for the vows to be read. Not knowing any better, we chose a version that included a lengthy oration about God and the Holy Ghost. As a pair of Jewish atheists, we smirked through much of it, and could hardly wait to get outside to burst out laughing.

We spent our honeymoon swimming in Biloxi on Mississippi's Gulf Coast. I had earlier requested a three-day pass for the weekend of our marriage, but the first sergeant denied it. That didn't stop us though, as I earned a pass by qualifying as "expert" on the rifle range the day before Gloria arrived.

I had found us a room in a house at the edge of Hattiesburg. I spent nights in town with Gloria, rising at 4:30 a.m. to get a bus back to the post or riding with another soldier whose wife lived in the house. I was often away on maneuvers for a week or several days, but whenever possible we drove to the coast to swim or to New Orleans for the wild jazz scene there.

Our constant companions were my friend Dino Cechin and his (later to be) wife, Norrie, who was Gloria's roommate after we went overseas. Dino remained my closest friend in the military overseas.

Gloria kept working on her writing career. Although unable to find a job in Hattiesburg, which was glutted with military wives, she freelanced an article about a local woman who had gathered soil from each of the forty-eight states, sewed it into little bags, and sent them to servicemen overseas. On her first try, Gloria sent the piece to *Colliers* magazine, among the nation's biggest media outlets at the time. Entitled "Mrs. Leggett's Dirt," the article sold for $250, a phenomenal sum in our world.

The 1155th was alerted to go to Europe in December, and all men were restricted to quarters, except on weekends. Determined to spend the last days with Gloria, I went into town every night, arranging to have a buddy respond "here" when my name was called during evening roll call. One night the first sergeant realized my absence. When I arrived the next morning, I was given a choice: to be busted from T-5 (corporal) to private, or total restriction to quarters till we left. Without hesitation, I chose the demotion. In a few months, I had my technical rank back.

When it was time for our unit to entrain to New York for shipment overseas, Dino and I realized we had spent all our gas rations joyriding and going to New Orleans and the Gulf Coast. We feared Gloria and Norrie might be stuck in Mississippi. On a tip, Gloria and I went to the town dump to meet a shady character who might have some black market rations. While Gloria waited in fear, I bought the rations, but she felt so guilty, she spent the entire drive to New York watching out for G-men.

The wives made it, and were on the dock to wave goodbye as our troopship left for Le Havre, France, on January 1, 1945. I had been in uniform almost two years.

<hr />

The voyage that had taken just four days from England to America on the luxurious *Queen Mary* now took two weeks on my return to Europe. Traveling at the speed of the slowest vessels in the 150-ship convoy, the tankers, we zigzagged across the ocean to evade German submarines. Our bunks, stacked four high, lay near the kitchen. As the ship tossed through a winter storm, the odors of onions and fat contributed to our misery of seasickness, which fortunately lasted for only the first couple of days.

We occasionally heard the distant sound of depth charges as destroyer escorts fought off German U-boats. Smoke rose from several ships that were hit by torpedoes on the periphery of the convoy. At the very end, the troopship next to ours hit a mine and sank as we entered Le Havre harbor.

From my perspective, the most important activity on that voyage happened inside my mind. I considered my future. I spent the long, empty hours in the ship's library, studying the options for where my life could take me.

The 1155th spent a couple of months in France and several in Germany. Our quarters consisted of everything from a muddy tent camp to a champagne factory and a German castle. Although we were in two battle zones, our unit worked behind the lines.

Occasionally, my language fluency was of use. For a while I supervised German prisoners of war working for us in a bridge equipment storage yard. Later the language was useful for chatting with German civilians, including the many pretty fräuleins, even though the military strictly prohibited fraternizing with them.

While still in France, I went as an interpreter on a reconnaissance through Belgium and Luxembourg into Germany, which gave me a firsthand understanding of the overwhelming destruction of war. We saw minimal damage in French towns and countryside, but some scenes in Germany were beyond imagination.

The whole town of Düren was smashed into rubble. As our jeep followed a bulldozed path through debris, just a few shells of buildings still stood. Aachen, the next larger city to the east, was almost as badly devastated. When we got to the steel town of Essen, fires were still burning, and the boom of artillery sounded in the distance.

In nearby Wuppertal, also badly hit, we stopped by an infantry company headquarters for information but missed the commanding officer. He later turned out to be a Wisconsin friend, Bob Lewis, who remained as such throughout our lives.

I spoke Russian to freed soldiers and slave laborers. A long letter home tells about a dinner with Russian prisoners of war who had just been liberated by American troops. Besides participating in their immense joy, dancing, singing, and copious drinking, I learned about the horrible torture and deprivation the Russians had endured from the Germans. I noted at the time that reconciliation between Russians and Germans seemed impossible, as their hatred had grown into a thirst for revenge (and history records that the advancing Red Army did abuse the German populace terribly).

There were times when I worked around the clock for two or three days. I prepared route maps for movement of troops and materials, mapped passages through minefields, and learned how to blow up bridges and buildings. I found facilities to house liberated slave laborers and did many other jobs.

V-E Day, the end of the war in Europe, found us east of the Rhine River.

My months in the ruins of war-devastated Europe were meaningful in that I finally had useful work to do. But I also had plenty of time, and my letters home and a joint memoir written by members of our unit are full of fun. There was great camaraderie in our outfit, and the memoir records various hilarious incidents, such as the episode when one of the guys drove over the colonel's tent during the night, with the colonel in it, or the time the whole company got lost when the lead truck of our convoy missed a turn on a road in France and we had to camp out in the middle of nowhere.

In France, several sections of the 1155th Engineers were quartered for a month in a champagne factory in Aviz, near Epernay. Most evenings, while we played poker for hours, someone would go down into the cellars and bring up unlabeled bottles of champagne. After a week or so, the plant manager complained to our colonel. To rectify that situation, we established a barter arrangement. A bottle of champagne for a bar of soap, two bottles for a pack of cigarettes. Our trade items were, of course, supplied to us free by the army. We drank champagne by the tumbler. It was years after the war before I could stand the stuff again.

Weeks after the war in Europe ended, we received orders for redeployment to the Pacific, where full-scale fighting was still going on. The summer of 1945 found us camped for another month in the heat and dust of the Arles staging area near Marseilles, waiting for a ship and preparing our gear for the voyage to the other side of the world. We had plenty of time to swim in the Mediterranean, watch movies after dark, and see Marseilles, Lyon, and the French and Italian rivieras, among other places.

It was here that I reunited with my brother, George, fresh from his visits with the troika in Berlin. His rank and headquarters status made it possible for him to find me and get to where I was on the Mediterranean shore. He insisted on sleeping with me and my friends in my enlisted men's tent, over the objections of several of our officers.

We talked far into the night, got up early, and then talked all day. The nineteen hours we spent together forever remade our relationship as brothers.

We hadn't seen each other in almost two years. George and I had never been adversaries, nowhere near that. We had been nonentities to each other, occupants of the same physical and social space but living in different worlds. The line that had divided our bedroom in Moscow segregated his universe of political striving and approval seeking from my self-contained sphere of practical concerns and personal relationships.

The war years had made me more worldly, but the larger change was in George. He had been freed from the conditioning of his youth. Unlike Mischa Wolf, who seemed constrained from connecting on a human level with noncommunists, George had become a more complete person, reveling in the renewal of friendship. And, surely, being older changed both of us too.

We talked in the tent, in a nearby orchard, and while walking along a long, lonely Mediterranean beach under the sharp July sunshine. We talked in a way we never had before—personally—and we left nothing out about our families and friends, our predictions for the future, and our developing career plans. We swam. Long-distance swimming had long been part of our summertime. We swam out to a sailboat far off the French beach, swimming leisurely and talking, on and on, till we realized the boat was slowly sailing away from us.

Afterward George wrote home, describing me:

> He looked very much as always—his black heavy hair, big sunburned nose, puppy smiling eyes, same thick lips, and the very, very white and regular teeth. And his dirtyish fatigue clothes

and general farm appearance—it was like meeting after a very short separation…We talked till almost 4 a.m. and were up again for Vit's reveille at 7 a.m. Vit introduced me to all the fellows in his tent—8 or 9—to whose nice lyrical quick wise-cracking GI repartee I listened for half an hour from behind my sack while "asleep."

From this time on we followed closer paths. After the war, we both went back to the university in Madison, and both of us then went to graduate school in Cambridge, Massachusetts: he to Harvard and I to MIT. Thereafter, we visited each other regularly and often. We stayed close for the rest of our lives.

In his later years, after our parents died, George shared with me the drafts of his many autobiographies. He wrote nineteen of them, some long, some short. The last volume was published by him in photocopies. These were his attempts to work out the pain and confusion created by his political childhood, and to come to terms with his life and our father and mother.

To try to understand his own past, he read the collection of private letters between Markoosha and Louis, which are stored in the Mudd Manuscript Library at Princeton University. He sent me copies and his detailed reactions to them. I read all his manuscripts, too, commenting as thoughtfully as I could, sometimes with far more impact on him than I ever intended.

I expressed my affection for George many times. I have no regrets on that count. But I'm sorry he isn't here to read my own interpretation of the years of our coming of age, which concluded with the end of the war. My version is much simpler than his tortured studies of the times and of the compli-cated molds people tried to place him in, molds that he first welcomed and then fought to escape. I see more the friendships and loves that sustained me, and the bonds with my classmates, my troika of friends, and my brother. These stayed strong, outlasting the grip of Stalin, Hitler, world war, and the Cold War.

Not long after George's visit, our company boarded another troopship for a thirty-nine-day equatorial cruise westward to the Philippines. We were just a week out of the Panama Canal, in the Pacific, when the news came over the ship's speakers that the United States had dropped an atomic bomb on Hiroshima, Japan, and then two days later another one on Nagasaki. It sounded like the war was over. I broke out a package I had received in Panama from Gloria perfect for the occasion: a bottle of scotch, a large salami, and a box of crackers, and we had a joyous celebration below deck.

Reports told of ships in the Pacific turning back to America, and we expected every day that ours too would turn around. We watched the movement of the ship's shadow for evidence of a change in direction. But our ship kept going after Japan announced its surrender. We debarked from the ship in the Philippines near Manila on September 1, 1945. The formal surrender was signed in Tokyo harbor the following day.

Men who had been in the service and overseas longer would get out first, and it was a maddeningly long four months before my turn came to sail for home. Productive work was scarce, though I did learn to survey while helping lay out a military cemetery and worked on architectural drawings as part of a reconstruction project. The memorable aspects of waiting were a lot of ocean swimming right off our tent camp near San Fernando, playing tennis up in the mountains at Baguio, the summer capital, and having plenty of time to read.

I returned to the States after another trans-Pacific voyage through the Panama Canal to New York and was discharged in February 1946. Although I came back with campaign ribbons and two battle stars for the time in Europe, I wondered how much I had contributed to winning the war.

Would I have done more for victory if I had used my languages, Russian and German, more? If I had been in a tank? If I had repaired optical instruments in the field, or lobbed mortar shells into German lines? While I didn't kill any enemy soldiers, I may have saved American lives by mapping German minefields. No way to know.

But I do know how the war changed me. The values that would guide me into the future largely had been set by the war's end. They were, and are still today, liberal and humanistic. They include the belief that people are more important than ideologies, the confidence in freedom that allows each person to fulfill her or his own capacity for good, the responsibility of all to care for those in need, the resistance to discrimination and racism, and the deep distrust of the state's power to kill.

I would carry these values through the next stages of my life, which led to the Territory of Alaska and the founding of a new state.

Beginnings in Alaska

⊰ 9 ⊱

Alaska Bound

The path to Alaska began in the library of the troop ship I rode to Europe in January 1945. The empty hours and days on board gave me a lot of opportunity to think about my future and contemplate what to do with it after the war. My drift through life since arriving in the United States had brought me a wife I dearly loved, good friends, a new pleasure in social leadership, and the beginnings of a good education. But I was no longer satisfied by my early idea of becoming an electrical engineer. I needed a new direction, one with a greater social purpose.

In the ship's library my eye fell upon an intriguing title: *Space, Time & Architecture*, by Sigfried Giedion. It was a monumental book, published a few years earlier, that put architecture and urban planning in a cultural context of history and the arts.

I wonder how differently my life would have developed if another book had fallen in my path. I picked this one up only because Albert Einstein's ideas about space and time had already intrigued me. The word *architecture* suggested the added element of organization, design, and creation. Designing buildings for people to live in would include all the elements I wanted in a career: social relations, making systems that worked, and the application of technical skill.

But as I read the book, I realized the concept of urban planning fit me even better. I'd never heard of a profession called planning. As a planner, one could go beyond filling a city with buildings. The job entailed creating cities that worked for people, a reflection of the hopeful new society I still believed in. Rather than the socialist economic system my parents sought, I imagined the future with aesthetic and well-functioning communities.

Along with thinking about *what* I wanted to do in the future, I also took on the question of *where* to do it.

Most of my twenty years had been spent in big cities such as Berlin, Moscow, and New York, but life there didn't attract me. I had gone west to Wisconsin and found its more human scale and open society. I wondered if going further west would be even better for me. I was still enamored with the dreams of the North and the West originally planted by the stories of Arctic explorers and pioneers I had absorbed as a kid in Russia.

I was blessed from birth with a positive outlook. Unlike my brother, my choices did not comprise reactions for or against my father or my upbringing. Instead, I leaned toward my hopes and enthusiasms. Thus, I was drawn to mountains, wide-open spaces, and a new, growing society in need of planning and building, more so than to what I had seen in the East. I examined books about different regions like a hungry man picking out a delicious meal from a restaurant menu.

As if to produce just such a menu, the New Deal's Federal Writers Project had sponsored a series of books about the states, of which the ship's library had a set. I pulled down various volumes, working west till I got to Oregon and Washington, which grabbed me. Reading about those states, I kept running across references to their ports being jumping-off points for Alaska.

Alaska. I knew about Alaska from Russian history, arctic exploration, and Jack London adventure tales that I had read as a kid in German and Russian. The volume on Alaska, by Merle Colby, a copy of which I still own, entranced me with its copious illustrations, its descriptions of the immense, fresh frontier, and the sense of northern adventure it conveyed.

The Alaska territory stood ready, unconquered, and yet packed with rich natural resources. The largest towns, such as Juneau, Fairbanks, and Ketchikan, had only around five thousand people each. The indigenous people still lived off the land. The book mentioned studies on Alaska, including one by the National Resources Planning Board, which I also still have, but obviously plenty of room remained to chart the territory's future as a planner.

And so, in the middle of the Atlantic on my way to war, I developed the unique ambition to be a city planner in Alaska—without knowing that no such job even existed at the time.

My memory tells this was a definite life plan that I systematically put into effect over the following years. But the work of rereading our old family letters for this book has taught me that the process contained much more uncertainty and many close calls that nearly led me in other directions. During the months in Europe and the Pacific, I often speculated about other pursuits, such as journalism and architecture, and about living in other parts of the United States. The rich experience of researching my own life has opened up my story in many pleasant and unexpected ways.

Yet, my dream must have remained intact through the shifting currents of my youth, because soon after leaving the service I wrote to the University of Alaska about studying to become a planner. I received a friendly handwritten response from Fairbanks, telling me the university had no degree program in architecture, but could offer a course of study in civil or mining engineering and a few other majors. My next check was with the University of Washington, which did offer architecture, but it was full of veterans returning under the G.I. Bill and was not admitting out-of-state students.

I don't know if I shared my Alaska ambition with Gloria. She doesn't remember it. But she was ready to move on from New York when I returned from the war.

Gloria was teaching underprivileged black and Puerto Rican children on the edges of Harlem, having turned down a job at *Time* magazine. She lived in an apartment in the Village with her friend Virginia Vidich, whose Marine lieutenant husband Art had also been in the Pacific, and with Norrie Cechin. Three men's hats hung on their wall, waiting for our return. With great joy, I reclaimed mine and removed my uniform for the last time.

Ultimately, returning to Madison was the easiest course for us, although the University of Wisconsin didn't offer an architecture degree and had only a single city planning course. But I could design my own course of study around a major in sociology, which allowed me enough independence to take courses in economics, civil engineering, political science, real estate, and other subjects that would provide a foundation for planning.

Gloria would be happy there, as it was like going home. We got an apartment in a temporary wartime hospital. Our two six-by-eight-foot rooms, with a three-by-eight bathroom between them, were in the former maternity ward, and looked like it, despite Gloria's attempts to soften the edges. Gloria took some graduate courses, got a job at a food co-op, and did some work at the Bureau of Handicapped Children.

My brother George also came back to the University of Wisconsin, and we took some classes and spent much time together. The Vidichs joined us back at school, too. Dino and Norrie Cechin came to town to finally get married, and Gloria and I and their five-year-old son stood up for them.

Our large circle of Madison friends, old and new, spread well beyond the campus to newspaper people, attorneys, and politicians. The war had given us all maturity and focus. Our group was active and engaged in the world.

Although I didn't realize it at the time, Gloria's gift of enthusiasm and personal connection was helping develop me into the person I became: ever more social, political, and outdoorsy. Our personalities matched perfectly. Life was free and full of playfulness, and we were spontaneous and open to the natural beauty and wide opportunities around us. Without knowing it, we were preparing for Alaska.

During our couple of wonderful years in Madison, we camped all over the state, with other couples and on our own, excitedly describing the adventures in family letters. Probably our grandest outing was canoeing with the Vidichs in the Boundary Waters of Minnesota and Ontario. Each trip became an exploration of nature, our relationships, and our youthful possibilities as the world seemed to be wide open before us.

The place and time were perfect for a budding planner. I soared in the stimulating atmosphere of the exciting new discipline of planning. I studied with frontline thinkers in the field, including political scientist John Gaus and urbanist Coleman Woodbury, both of whom would play a role in my future. In Chicago, I spent time with Saul Alinsky, who had created the practice of community organizing and spread it nationally through his work and landmark book, *Reveille for Radicals*. Also in Chicago, I came to know city planner Martin Meyerson, who later also affected my career path. I began to understand the connections between planning, politics, and real people.

Although the period seems longer in my memory, I spent only two years in Madison, graduating in six semesters, including summer terms. Before my last semester in 1947, a conversation with Coleman Woodbury helped set me on my next stage. He said I should go to graduate planning school at either Harvard or MIT, and sent me to consult with Catherine Bauer, a national housing and planning expert on the faculty of Harvard's Graduate School of Design.

Meeting in Cambridge, Bauer recommended that I augment my strong social science background obtained at Wisconsin with the more technical program at MIT. She called her husband, who was the Dean of Architecture and Planning at MIT. That connection eased my entrance to the small and prestigious program the next year.

Gloria and I left Madison in the spring of 1948 bound for Cambridge in the fall. After a month visiting family, we took off in our old Chevy for a phenomenal three-month camping trip across the United States that opened our eyes to our great country. We saw many revolutionary and civil war battlegrounds, inspected dams in the southeast and southwest, climbed down into caves and up on mountains.

In Great Smoky Mountain National Park a bear chewed holes in our tent while we lay inside. We climbed Half Dome in Yosemite National Park and fished for dinner in the high country. We became part of a community of post-war wanderers and explorers at the Grand Canyon.

We arrived in Boston in early August 1948. Gloria and I rented an apartment near the Red Sox' Fenway Park and Boston's Fen, a small stream in the park across the street from us. MIT was not far, just over the Charles River bridge. Sometimes, when the weather was good, I would assemble my folding kayak and paddle over to my classes rather than walking across the bridge.

George was already in Cambridge, studying at Harvard toward his PhD in history. We attended his wedding. I started corresponding with Lothar again, thanks to the contact George had made in Berlin.

We made friends around us. A doctor in our building helped Gloria get a job as a public information officer for the Framingham Heart Study, which became famous for examining the health of thousands of men and women through their lives and continues to this day.

My class in the two-year planning program at MIT had just fifteen students working closely together in a studio. Most of the students were veterans, many with some professional experience. We developed ties that connected many of us for decades, particularly classmates Dave Loeks, George Nez, and me.

The course of study was intense, the most challenging of my life. I discovered a skill and tendency to throw myself into long, intense hours, sometimes until four in the morning. Learned during my army experience in Europe, the all-nighters served me well later in life, though it sometimes set my life out of balance.

We did fascinating hands-on work. For my required summer practice I did a stint as planning engineer in Peterborough, a lovely little town in the hills of southern New Hampshire. Most people were happy, complaining only about parking in the village center. I developed a parking plan, but realized that a planner need not necessarily advocate for change. I suggested the town protect the good values it already had.

Later I was part of a team working on a redevelopment plan for the Bowery on New York's lower eastside. We lived for a week in that very rundown district, getting a real feeling of what it's like to be poor and live on the street or in horrible housing. I'm not sure our schemes influenced anything, but we certainly learned about life and the severity of the problems faced by serious city planning.

Only after the time in Peterborough did our proximity to Fenway Park mean anything to me. I had caught Red Sox fever hanging out with the kid who worked in the town drugstore. Back in Boston, I realized I could follow the game with my ears. When I heard the roar of a rally, I would walk across the alley behind our building and in through open stadium gates to watch the end of a game. Ted Williams and the Red Sox were my ultimate step in Americanization. It's still the team I root for.

⋯

Job offers for students in our program were numerous as we were finishing at MIT. Besides our presence in one of the nation's best schools, planners were in short supply during the postwar economic boom. Loeks and I had gone to planning conventions in Buffalo and Cleveland, meeting planners from all over. I turned down one job after another for not being challenging enough. Gloria grew nervous and wished I would accept one.

We thought we might end up in a New England town, as much as we preferred the west. Gloria wrote to my mother, "There is of course a certain charm about old towns and houses and a well kept green countryside. But having seen the US we still prefer the bold open beauty of the Arizona desert to the cluttered prettiness of New England."

In Alaska, without my knowledge, fate had taken a hand. My friend Ed Crittenden was there. Originally from New Haven and educated at Pomona, Ed was stationed in Ketchikan in the Coast Guard during the war, where he met his wife Kit, who had then just arrived from Bloomington, Illinois. After his service, Ed received a master's degree in architecture from Yale.

Although already an architect, Ed had wanted to delve more into planning, and so enrolled at MIT in 1948. I got to know him over our drafting tables. The following year, Ed accepted an offer to become technical director of the Alaska Housing Authority, and he and Kit left for Anchorage with their two children.

In 1950, the federal Bureau of Land Management controlled almost all of Alaska, but the end of World War II brought a land rush of young men moving north. Homesteading laws allowed the latter-day pioneers, mostly veterans, to choose large tracts virtually anywhere they pleased. Development was chaotic. Small lots suitable for towns were scarce.

BLM's land planning chief in Alaska, Harold T. Jorgenson, known as Jorgy, had the job of bringing order and foresight to the map. He needed a planner to lay out new towns and deal with problems in existing ones, and he knew they shouldn't just promote a real estate man from within BLM for the job. He turned to Ed Crittenden for advice.

Ed recommended recruiting candidates from university planning and architecture departments around the country, especially MIT. Jorgenson sent a letter to the head of my department. According to my notes from the time, the qualifications included "personal qualities to adapt planning theory to northern frontier growth." When I got wind of the opportunity, I called Gloria at work and told her. Over the phone, I heard her shout out to the room full of her colleagues, "We're going to Alaska!"

I've always remembered that as an example of how open Gloria was to adventure. I'm not sure that we had ever talked about Alaska before. But she confided recently that she also did it because she was tired of my repeated refusal of job offers. I applied.

At the time, I already had an interview scheduled in Greensboro, North Carolina. On the drive south, I stopped off at the Interior Department in Washington, DC, to see if I could talk to someone at BLM about the Alaska job.

My qualifications had already piqued the interest of top BLM officials, as I later learned from their correspondence. I walked into the personnel director's office in Washington with naïve confidence, without an appointment, and was astonished when he took me right away to meet the national director of the BLM, Marion Clawson.

Clawson, an imposing man, took a strong interest in the job and in my application. He questioned me about my unusual background: MIT, Wisconsin, Russia, Germany. It turned out he was a fan of my father's work, too. I got the job in rapid order.

My parents were nervous, and even upset. I wrote to my mother, "It's decided now—we are going to Alaska. Both Glo and I are very happy and excited about it. We feel that this is probably our only chance, since once we are settled and staid we wouldn't be enterprising enough to undertake such an adventure as we are entering now…Be happy with us and tell pap not to be so blue about it."

We staged our move at my mother's farm in Quakertown, packing only what we could fit in the small luggage trailer we would pull behind our two-door Studebaker. With consummate care, we prepared for the unknown in the Far North. On a foray to Philadelphia, we bought a portable player for the new 33-rpm LP records. As if preparing to be cast away on a desert island, we selected the ten most important records to take to Alaska, thinking we would not be able to get more for a long time.

We traveled through Madison to see our many friends, stopped in Minnesota to visit with Nez and Loeks, then went west through Montana and north to Calgary, camping along the way. Pavement gave out forty-seven miles outside of Edmonton, and we began bouncing along for three thousand miles more.

The Alaska Highway and the other roads still required fording rivers at downed bridges and grinding through quagmires caused by melting permafrost. At times, the road narrowed to one rutted lane. But, on the whole, it didn't feel like wilderness, because it was difficult to get away from the dusty roadway, even to camp. The road became a corridor of scrubby black spruce without respite or driveways.

Much of the traffic was going the other direction. North Korea had invaded South Korea a few weeks before, and many Alaskans believed a new world war was starting. They expected the Russians to invade Alaska, just as the Japanese had taken two of the Aleutian Islands in the previous war. In Anchorage, some residents who weren't abandoning the territory were sending their valuables home to the Lower Forty-eight for fear of an evacuation or to keep their possessions out of enemy hands.

A day out of Anchorage we stopped to clean up at Tazlina Glacier Lodge, where we happened to sit with Bob Romig, brother of a former Anchorage mayor and medical pioneer, and his wife Louise. We got their advice on where to live in the city. Their information confirmed what we had heard. Anchorage was vibrant, booming, and full of opportunity; and it was dusty, short of housing, and extremely expensive, with food prices up to triple what we were used to.

After thousands of miles of trees and mountains without seeing two houses together, we were shocked to enter Anchorage the next day on Fourth Avenue, the only paved street in town, and pull up to the Federal Building, where after weeks of wilderness, we found ourselves next to a parking meter. And right across the street, in the window of a store in the Reed Building, there was a large display of record albums for sale. We would be able to increase our music collection after all.

"Even that vestige of pioneering—gravel streets—didn't detract from the stark naked truth that hit us when we drove into town: Anchorage is civilized," Gloria wrote. "But, as Vit says, Anchorage and a few other towns in Alaska are tiny islands in a huge sea of wilderness."

⇥ 10 ⇤
Becoming Alaskan

Before I took the job with the Bureau of Land Management, I negotiated an all-expenses return to Pennsylvania if we stayed in Alaska at least two years. But after only a week, Gloria and I knew we weren't going back. We had already made friends, and we loved the natural surroundings. We felt at home.

Joining the Anchorage community was easy.

Ed and Kit Crittenden invited us to dinner the day after we drove into town, and we had a wonderful evening with them and their other two guests, Elmer and Lile Rasmuson. Alaska-born Elmer had been educated at Harvard and owned the National Bank of Alaska. That evening, we began a warm, life-long relationship.

I was surprised that such a pillar of the establishment as Elmer Rasmuson would accept a last-minute invitation to dinner with newcomers. Ed and Kit later recalled how they saw Gloria and me as valuable new assets to the town.

Within Anchorage's surging and largely transitional population, there was only a small, close-knit core of stable families actually planning to stay and contribute to the community. The young community's professional and business people formed an even tinier cadre.

Our dinner companions were eager to recruit new members socially and for the good of Anchorage. That first night, Elmer Rasmuson, who was chairman of the city planning commission, asked me to be the town's planning director. I had to decline, since I had just arrived for a job with the federal government. Kit enlisted Gloria to act in a play she was directing.

Before the Second World War, Anchorage had been a sleepy railroad town of about four thousand people. War brought the construction of two military bases, rapid development of related infrastructure, and a massive influx of labor and military personnel. After the war, most of the new people departed, but explosive growth resumed a few years later with the escalation of conflict with the Soviet Union. Cold War military spending powered the economy, and the in-migration of new settlers provided a growing population.

In 1950, the city of Anchorage had eleven thousand people, and there were thirty thousand in the entire greater Anchorage area, including the military. By 1960 there were eighty-three thousand.

Many of the newcomers were servicemen or boomtown wealth seekers— young men with no intention of staying. Large areas of town were merely slums of shacks where men went to drink, gamble, and hire prostitutes.

During summer, parts of downtown, Eastchester, and Spenard rocked with all-night activity, like the gold-rush boomtowns of old. But in autumn when the leaves fell and the snow line came down the mountains, the red-light districts emptied and Anchorage quieted for the winter. The population dropped by a third. The boom, based largely on military construction, was very much seasonal.

Gloria and I encountered the consequences of extreme growth when we went looking for a place to live in the summer of 1950. The BLM had put us up in a rooming house on Sixth Avenue, without a kitchen and with bathrooms down the hall. Housing was tight to the vanishing point. The only house for sale stood in Mountain View, a grim and muddy slum-in-the-making, where people lived in tents and shipping crates. Besides being tiny, unappealing, and poorly built, the house carried an asking price of $25,000, for us an astronomical sum at the time.

On the weekend, we roamed around looking for land on which we might build. Driving east out of town on a narrow trail, we came to a lovely hilltop. We climbed up and found a fabulous view of the mountains surrounding Anchorage on all four sides, including Mount McKinley, 115 miles to the north. The hill itself and the rolling country around us were totally undeveloped. We felt like real pioneers as we decided this would be the site of our home—in the wilderness but close to town, with a view.

Back at the office the next day, I asked my boss if we could buy or homestead that wondrous land. The answer was no. The federal government had reserved the land for future institutional purposes. I was disappointed at the time, but that classification certainly made sense from a planning standpoint.

A few years later, when I was working with the Anchorage College Committee as chairman of its land and development committee, I recommended this site for a new private college, resulting in locating Alaska Methodist University there. Ultimately, the area expanded to become the city's U-Med district, with two universities and two hospitals, including Alaska's largest.

We finally found a little cabin, fourteen by twenty-two feet in size, over-looking Chester Creek south of town. It was a converted garage. Living there would be rather primitive: an oil stove for heating and cooking in one corner, a chemical toilet in the other, a big south-facing window, water carried from the neighbors, and showers at their house. But it was all very romantic and suited us perfectly. We immediately bought the lot and cabin for $2,500. Gloria enthused in a letter to the family that it felt like home as soon as she cleaned it up.

In 1950, our home was at the edge of town, outside the city limits, which then ran along Sixteenth Avenue. Today, the great majority of the city lies south of that cabin, and street numbers now go beyond 160th. From our big south-facing window we saw nothing but woods. At night, the only lights blinked from a distant radio tower. Yet, we were less than a mile from the downtown federal building, and I could easily walk to work. In those days, residents walked almost everywhere in Anchorage.

<hr>

Before I came north, Ed Crittenden had written to me: "Being a planner on the Alaska frontier didn't necessarily mean doing work that was new, but doing the traditional work of a planner for the first time." It turned out that little of what I did was traditional planning. I faced as close to a blank slate as anyone ever gets in the urban planning world. But I didn't feel special. Everyone there was creating Alaska. As Gloria said, if you dug an outhouse you felt like you were contributing to building Alaska.

Prior to the war, Alaska's federal landlord was called the General Land Office, part of the Department of the Interior. In 1946, this agency was merged with the Grazing Service to create the Bureau of Land Management. A year later my future boss, Jorgy Jorgenson, arrived to classify and plan the use of federal land in Alaska, which amounted to virtually all of the territory. By 1950, only half a million acres of the 365-million-acre landmass of Alaska was in private ownership.

The land office administered a chaotic hodge-podge of laws for homestead-ing, sale, and lease of the federal domain by simply waiting for land applica-tions to come in. They were recorded with pen and ink in big official books. As a result, great swaths of prime scenic and recreational land disappeared into private hands, but the territory had a shortage of lots suitable for town development.

In many cases, people building homes and businesses simply used whatever land they needed. No one bothered to file a claim. Native communities stood

where people had traditionally lived, or where a school or church attracted settlement. The absence of legal property title didn't stop the growth of towns.
But settlement without property lines created crazy patterns of roads and buildings. Technically, entire communities in Alaska were squatters on federal lands.
And owners faced major obstacles to financing improvements without title to
their land.

Jorgy and his progressive superiors hoped to direct the development of
Alaska rather than simply responding to filings for land. To study the problem, the US Department of the Interior formed a team called the "Inter-agency
Committee on Group Settlement in Alaska," chaired by a University of Illinois
geography professor. A series of seminars in Washington, DC, in February 1950
set the stage for more active policies, including my hiring a few months later.

I had only been at work for a couple of days when one of my coworkers,
Frank Meek, asked if I wanted to go into the Bush with him for the day. He took
me down Fourth Avenue to the Army-Navy Store and outfitted me with an
Alaskan tuxedo: ripcord pants and jacket, a hat, and shoepacks, the waterproof,
insulated boots everyone wore.

The next day, we lifted off in the BLM's four-seat airplane, a Cessna 170, with
Mac McCormick, a top-notch pilot, at the controls. We flew west and within
minutes left Anchorage far behind. I was flying over the wildest country I had
ever seen. I wrote home to my mother:

> The trip took us across endless plains of swamps and muskeg
> and lakes and rivers that meandered so much that in some
> places the loops practically touched each other. Further on
> we hit the Alaska Range, with snow-covered mountains and
> tremendous glaciers all around. We flew through an open-
> ing called Rainy Pass, where the mountains seemed only a
> couple of hundred feet away on either side and nothing but
> rocks below and around. Saw several herds of mountain sheep
> grazing on the thin patches of mountain vegetation. They are
> pretty safe there from hunters—no place to land a plane for
> many miles around.

We flew a few hours northwest to McGrath in Interior Alaska, where we
stopped to refuel and eat lunch. The airfield was built as an emergency-refueling
stop during the war. An old trading post and mining center, McGrath had a
little over a hundred people, close to half of these Athabaskan and Eskimo. I
wandered around, talked to a few individuals, and did some target practice with
my pistol along the wide Kuskokwim River.

A further 145-mile flight over more mountains and unmarked wild terrain took us to Nulato, our destination, on the shore of the mighty Yukon River. At one end of the Nulato airstrip, which lay on a short, narrow ridge high above the town, a wrecked airplane lay where it had crashed. After a deep gulp on my part, we landed and hiked down to the village, which was strung out along the river. I experienced my first visit to an Alaska Native village.

It was July. Everyone in the village was out on the river or "putting up"— filleting and drying salmon outside their little houses. Sled dogs howled and children swarmed around us. While Frank pursued his work, I wandered the village, admiring the sturdy log houses and the boats at the edge of the river. I learned how friendly village people can be. I got lots of smiles and greetings, and received an invitation to tea that I eagerly accepted.

On our return, clouds enveloped the mountains en route to McGrath. For an hour, Mac tried to weave his way among the clouds and through a mountain pass, but couldn't get high enough and so decided to fly back to Nulato. However, the clouds forced the plane ever lower, the terrain below was confusing, and Mac couldn't figure out where we were on his map. We had lost radio contact.

Concerned about fuel, Mac checked a sandbar to see whether we could land to wait out the weather. But the ground proved too soft. So he pulled up and kept flying low, pinned underneath the clouds. He finally found a stream that flowed in the right direction and headed downstream until we reached the Yukon, far above Nulato. There Mac finally could pick up a radio beacon and was guided to the air force station in Galena, a Native village on the Yukon, thirty-five miles upriver from Nulato.

I admit that it was a great relief to land and get out of the plane. But it was only over time that I realized how near we had been to disaster. Fortunately, that was my closest call in many more years of flying all over Alaska.

Our weather-forced visit to Galena lasted three days. Besides wandering around the village and playing poker with the airmen, I used the opportunity to learn from Frank about the federal land business and the BLM bureaucracy. Even more usefully, he taught me how to pace out distances, along the two-mile airport runway and cross-country through brush and woods, and how to find old survey monuments in the wilderness, some of which could be left over from the gold rush of forty years before. I also learned patience, a necessity for travel in Alaska's Bush.

These were skills that were not taught at MIT. I was ecstatic. I kept thinking of how different my life had become compared to where I might have been if Alaska hadn't opened up for me, in Greensboro, Cleveland, or Philadelphia. What a fabulous beginning of my Alaska adventure, far better than I had ever imagined!

I spent much of my eighteen-month tenure with BLM traveling the length and width of Alaska in small planes, riverboats, railroad trains, and pickup trucks. The work was interesting, useful, and exciting. I saw more of Alaska and met more Alaskans than most ever could. The experience also served me well later when I got into politics and sought to make laws applicable to diverse land, peoples, and living conditions in this vast territory.

Among my most challenging but often interesting responsibilities was resolving the title to property underlying towns that already existed. An example is Dillingham, a regional center at the edge of Bristol Bay. BLM surveyors platted lot lines along the community's crooked roads and around buildings where custom dictated lines should exist. My assignment was to transfer these newly platted lots to the people who lived on them, essentially giving the locals legal property rights to the ground they already felt they owned.

Ed Crittenden had given me the name of a friend in Dillingham who could help me get started. As I approach the log cabin door, I heard voices inside. When I knocked, silence. I knocked again, and again. Finally, through the door, someone responded. I identified myself as a friend of Ed's looking for Jack Bennis. The door opened cautiously, and a hand pulled me inside.

There were several men in the hot and steamy room with a large pot boiling on the wood stove. It turned out they'd shot several geese out of season and were afraid I might be a US Fish and Wildlife enforcer. Instead, Jack and his wife Esther became good friends of ours, and introduced me around the community, where I made other lasting friendships.

I conducted large community meetings to explain the process of applying for title to land. After lots of questions, most people understood what they needed to do. But at the Dillingham meeting, a slender and somewhat reticent Russian Orthodox priest, speaking with a thick accent, just couldn't seem to get it.

After the meeting broke up, I pulled aside the priest and asked him in Russian if he would like me to explain further. He threw his arms around me and kissed me on both cheeks. He was Father Merejko Amvrossy, who would in 1955 be consecrated as Bishop of Sitka and Alaska. In short order, I clarified everything and the Russian Orthodox Church received the land to which it was entitled. During later years, we frequently visited at the Bishop's House in Sitka.

By the time my work was done in Dillingham, residents and other occupants had legal title to their land, for little or no money. Under rules at the time, Alaska Natives could normally receive land only if the Bureau of Indian Affairs held it in trust, but I worked with a counterpart at the BIA to waive the requirement. All the titles we conveyed were free and clear.

In Seward, a port city south of Anchorage on the Kenai Peninsula, the legal status of the land I was selling required me to put lots up for outcry auction to the highest bidder, rather than giving preference to existing occupants. Some people had built substantial houses, worth perhaps $80,000, on federal land. However, in the auction, the owner of such a house would have to bid along with everyone else.

I managed the situation by auctioning those valuable properties first, explaining the situation to the bidders in hopes all would show restraint with their neighbors. In each case, existing homeowners were able to get their lots just for the appraised price of the land without anyone bidding against them.

Traveling from Anchorage to Seward is one of the most scenic trips I've ever experienced. The route follows the mountain-ringed shore of Turnagain Arm before rising over glacial mountains and back down to Seward, on Resurrection Bay. No road led to Seward at the time, only the railroad, with infrequent passenger service. Most of my work trips were in the caboose of freight trains on the federally owned Alaska Railroad, available free to the BLM.

Adding to the childish joy of traveling in a caboose, the ride was thrilling, through rugged mountains and over high bridges, especially where the train looped the Loop. Here the track made a complete circle above itself, about fifty miles north of Seward, to climb terrain that otherwise would be too steep.

The first time I rode the Loop, the trestles swayed scarily as the long freight train struggled higher and higher. At one point, the three steam locomotives were directly above our caboose and I thought the whole massive wooden structure would collapse on us any minute, with the locomotives driving us down into the abyss below. The brakeman in the caboose calmly assured me that wouldn't happen.

I was among the last to have that ride. A new railroad track was built using ground opened up by the retreating Bartlett Glacier. The Loop was abandoned by the end of 1951.

Part of my job was to design new towns. The proposed townsite of Cantwell would be just south of McKinley (now Denali) National Park, at the intersection of the Denali Highway and a future road between Anchorage and Fairbanks (now the Parks Highway), and several miles east of the existing Athabascan village of Cantwell.

Until my arrival at the BLM, federal engineers had surveyed townsites with little regard to the topography or expected uses of the land. They would produce a rectangular grid, even if the straight roads would go through swamps or over impossibly steep hills. I laid out Cantwell's roads and blocks using curves and leaving highway buffer zones to make it more livable than the typical federal checkerboard. The chief of surveyors objected that my layout would cost twice as much as normal, but I had the authority to make him do it the proper way.

In Southeast Alaska, I spent a week evaluating the idea of a new town at Wards Cove. The superintendent of Tongass National Forest had asked if forest lands should be set aside for a community to support a large pulp mill that was planned. Despite the enthusiasm of a nearby grocery owner who wanted to name the new town for himself, I concluded that it made more sense for businesses and workers' homes to be located in nearby Ketchikan. The national forest didn't release the land and the idea of the new town died.

On that trip, I spent days climbing around in the rainforest near Wards Cove, with its enormous spruce trees. I was entranced. In that virgin forest some of the trees were six feet across at the base. To this day, most of that land remains a protected forest recreation area.

The job in 1951 also took me on an all-day drive on one of Alaska's new highways to sell lots in a newly surveyed townsite at a junction called Tok. Gloria went along. I stood on the back of my BLM pickup truck, auctioning lots to locals and speculators. About fifty people stood below me on a dusty clearing in the woods near the gravel road. The scene was out of the Wild West.

All sales were on a cash basis and I ended up with thousands of dollars. Everyone knew I had the money. But the US marshal had advised me against carrying my gun, as any robber would probably shoot a lot faster than I ever could and, in any case, whatever I carried was insured.

Driving back from Tok, we saw the turn-off for a narrow gravel road the Corps of Engineers had built to the army's recreation area at Lake Louise. An hour of very rough trail brought us to the shore of Lake Louise. We always carried the folding kayak in those days, ready for spontaneous paddling and camping whenever the inspiration hit—which was often. Leaving the government's money in the truck, we launched out onto that vast, spectacular lake, barely able to believe the beauty of the wilderness opened for our private exploration.

We crossed some twelve miles of lake from the south to the north end, paddled through a channel into Lake Susitna, caught a large lake trout, and then started back into Lake Louise. But while we were fishing, a wild wind had come up, driving waves over the sandy shallows on the north end of the lake. We worked our way along the north shore until we could pull the kayak up into brush above the crashing waves. We were totally soaked by the time we crawled into our pup tent, which shook in the wind and rain all night.

In the morning the air was calm, the sun was out, and the lake was placid. We found ourselves just above an extraordinary sandy beach, more than twenty feet wide and a mile long.

When I got back to BLM (with the money safe), I learned that the land along the beach we had discovered was unclaimed. I arranged to have it withdrawn from private entry, so it would remain public forever. Our love for Lake Louise continued. Years later, after camping all over Alaska, we got our own five acres elsewhere on the lake and built a cabin. The sandy beach is still there for us and others to enjoy.

Gloria was as eager to camp and explore as I was. During our first autumn in Alaska, I was on the Kenai Peninsula laying out property for future settlement. As the road to Anchorage was not yet completed, she put our Studebaker on an Alaska Railroad flatcar to the Moose Pass stop and drove onward to join me. We spent Labor Day weekend in an abandoned cabin at the confluence of the Moose and Kenai rivers, catching enough silver salmon to last us through our first winter.

We also had moose meat that first winter. Working south of Anchorage in Girdwood with a colleague, George Gustafson, we learned a big moose had been seen on the flats beyond the railroad tracks. After we finished our work, we bushwhacked after the moose and George shot it. A local fellow hauled the carcass back to the tracks with a bulldozer, and a group of men helped us heft it whole onto a freight train for the ride back to Anchorage, the Seward Highway not yet being open.

———

Besides joining me for outdoor forays, Gloria got involved with the League of Women Voters, took art lessons, and started writing a novel. It was easy to be busy as a member of that community. She also went to the *Anchorage Times*, the largest newspaper in the Territory, to see about getting a job.

The city editor, Bernie Kosinski, was immediately interested in hiring her as a reporter. The *Times* in those days had about half a dozen writers. It was an exciting place. I remember coming into the newsroom one day and seeing the publisher, Bob Atwood, putting out a special edition for a fire that was burning in the railroad yard (Kosinski was on leave). Bob's shoulders held two phones to his ears, one to hear the reporter on the scene and the other to dictate the headlines and layout to the composing room, while his hands banged out the breaking story on a typewriter.

When Gloria came in looking for a job, Kosinski said she would have to go upstairs to talk to Atwood. He told her, "We don't need a social editor." Gloria countered that she was interested in working in straight news, and had the background for it. Soon the paper was pursuing her, and Gloria ultimately took a job and stayed five years.

Bob Atwood and his wife Evangeline became good friends of ours, despite their very different political outlook and lifestyle. I recall once taking a visitor from Juneau to have dinner at Bob's home. I told the guest we would have to drive out to the edge of town, where the Atwoods lived in a log home. I knew he would expect a cabin. With pleasure, I saw the visitor's amazement when we arrived at the Atwood's palatial log mansion and his surprise when the door was opened by a servant wearing a red-coated uniform.

Gloria's job covering city hall and the courts put her in the middle of the action in Anchorage. She knew everyone and everything. Sometimes, she even covered my land sales—including a ridiculous sale creating the town of Portage, a railroad junction about forty miles south of Anchorage, which was placed, at the Alaska Railroad's insistence, in what was a salt marsh. Bidders at the auction, held in an old passenger railcar, joked that they had surveyed the lots wearing hip boots.

Like Gloria, I developed involvements outside of work. A month after arriving in Alaska in 1950, I wandered into the first meeting of the League of Alaskan Cities, in the Fourth Avenue Theater in downtown Anchorage.

In those days when Alaska was a territory, civic organizations such as the league (which became the Alaska Municipal League) played an outsized role, taking the place of government in addressing problems. I later became the executive secretary of the league, which put me in the center of Alaska politics, representing various community interests to the territorial and federal governments.

At the league's second meeting, in Kodiak, I met Bob Bartlett, then Alaska's sole nonvoting delegate to Congress, a position he had held since 1945. I saw him standing alone at the cocktail reception and quizzed him on his view of Senator Joseph McCarthy's attack on the "Red menace." Bob expressed disgust at McCarthy, and I liked him immediately.

Bob's personality secured our friendship. He stayed with me for some twenty minutes at that party, asking sincere questions about my work, family, and Gloria. His warmth and personal interest were real. Moreover, he taught me how to avoid being interrupted by waiters or getting tipsy at a reception. He never took a sip of his drink, always holding a full glass of water.

In those days, Bartlett didn't have many friends in Anchorage. When I would learn he was in town with nothing to do over a weekend, I invited him to our humble house for brunch, at times with some of our friends. Those visits became a tradition through the 1950s, and I continued to spend time with him until his death in 1968.

The Crittendens, Fischers, Charlie and Molly Tryck, and several other couples formed a circle of friends, with frequent parties and impromptu gatherings. I had looked forward to a long winter of undisturbed reading, but our time seemed totally full with work, socializing, plays, concerts, and other events. Together with watching sled dog races, skiing, and snowshoeing, this busy world kept Gloria and me happy and involved.

As the winter sun began setting around three in the afternoon for the first time in our experience, I explained in a letter to the family that the darkness didn't bother us:

> Going out at night is like going out in the dusk, the snow making everything appear light. Last weekend we sledded down our hill with the Morley kids, and that night had a picnic outdoors! The Morleys (our only neighbors) had shoveled out their outdoor fire spot, built a fire, and luckily we had some hot dogs for supper that night and were able to roast them over the fire. Followed by roasted marshmallows, with snowballs flying around meanwhile! Actually, it wasn't at all cold, partly because we were all warmly dressed, as everyone is here.

Our little dwelling, surrounded by spruce trees and the broad swath of undeveloped land to the south, sat in the deep snow like a wilderness log cabin—no road, no people, no buildings in sight or sound. Except that it was located at the edge of Alaska's largest city, it *was* such a cabin. Our friend L. T. "Peanuts" Main, an office mate at BLM, said that as long as we lived in Alaska, we would never have a more pleasurable winter. Indeed, it was an Alaska winter beyond our fondest fantasies.

But, like everyone else, we wanted a home with plumbing and our own shower. Ed Crittenden, who was building on the adjacent lot uphill from us, designed a house for us, and I arranged for a loan and a contractor. But on the first morning of work that spring, the contractor's equipment got stuck. The shaking of the ground by the backhoe had liquefied the claylike soil to a depth of up to four feet.

After a rapid series of consultations with my engineer and architect friends, it became clear we could not build with a conventional foundation. The FHA-approved house plans were out, and so was the financing.

Until the ground could be stabilized, our house would have to sit on logs that would lie atop the ground. The water and sewer lines would be dug by hand. I stayed up all that night designing a completely new, smaller house, the only given being the large windows that we had ordered and that were on the way from Seattle.

We built without a loan, buying supplies from our paychecks, and doing most of the work with our own hands. Each stage of the project meant learning a new construction skill. Gloria and I worked side by side. She was as strong as I, and I was strong in those days. We lifted heavy birch paneling to the ceiling and banged together the warped, home-dried, tongue-and-groove boards.

I bought a book on electricity and wired the house myself. The city inspector said it was one of the best jobs he'd seen—naturally, since I did it literally by the book. In the first room we enclosed, our bedroom, we created cabinets and a closet by stacking wooden apple crates, and set a Coleman camp stove on a makeshift kitchen counter for cooking. The bathroom came next, and then a real kitchen. For four years, we finished one room at a time.

Everyone in Anchorage seemed to be doing the same thing. It was all part of building Alaska, part of the adventure.

By the time we had been in Alaska for a year and a half, I was ready to change jobs. I had done most of the town planning projects that were needed. Also, the federal budget process frustrated me at BLM, and the constant travel gave me insufficient time to work on house construction. So I seriously considered accepting the long-offered job of becoming the first planning director for the city of Anchorage.

My friend Charlie Tryck, born in Wasilla, Alaska, and a graduate of the University of Alaska, was as city engineer responsible for planning and zoning. City manager Bob Sharp was also a friend. Elmer Rasmuson was chairman of the Planning Commission, as well as owner of the largest bank. I couldn't ask for better backing to become a real city planner.

In those days of building, bankers were the most important city fathers, and Elmer's support for planning helped make it a priority for the city. I recall well the talk he once made to the city council about the economic benefits of planning, arguments more persuasive on the subject than any I ever heard at a planning conference or in a university lecture hall.

The support of such progressive ideas belies the typical image of a boomtown like Anchorage. Even active promoters of growth and development like Bob Atwood were on board. Outside the city limits, the quick-profit values of boomers produced careless sprawl. But among the families that expected to make a life in Anchorage, there was a strong consensus to do things right, and those people controlled the city government. Community planning suited their shared vision, along with other goals, including Alaska statehood.

I decided to quit BLM at the end of 1951 and take the city job after New Year's. In the fall, Gloria went on leave from the *Times* to visit her ailing mother on Long Island.

Our decision to live in Alaska permanently still hadn't sunk in with Gloria's extended family, and she came under intense pressure to move back to the East Coast and share responsibility with her sister for their mother's care. Instead, we offered to bring the mother to our home in Alaska (she never came).

While I was alone, I worked long hours to get the new house enclosed and insulated for winter, and to make it decent for Gloria to return to. I had spent so much money on the project that I had to take out a bank loan against my accumulated vacation pay to buy her return ticket.

Gloria never considered giving up our life in Alaska. During that separation she wrote to me:

> Oh baby I love you so very much and I wish you were here. No I don't, I'm glad you didn't come. Believe me, I'm glad I came to the States because I can't wait to get back to Alaska. Now I know exactly what people mean when they go Outside and say they're glad to get back and that there's nothing here worth sticking around for. When I was driving to New Jersey yesterday, there was just house after house, car after car. How I longed for the sight of the Palmer Highway or the Potter Road or the view from our window!

⊰ 11 ⊱

Little Men for Statehood

Coming to Alaska was perfect in every way except one: I became a second-class citizen. When Gloria and I arrived from Pennsylvania, I was astonished to learn that I had lost the ability to vote for president or for senators or representatives. I had voted in the 1948 presidential election. Now I could no longer do that because I lived in a territory.

As the 1952 presidential election neared, I wrote to my family that my interest in it steadily waned, "as the day approaches when everyone but Alaskans can cast their vote—revolting thought!"

Like many other veterans of World War II, steeped in patriotism and empowered by victory over powers that suppressed democracy, it struck me as outrageously un-American to now be denied my political rights. These would only be returned when Alaska became a state. I followed the ongoing efforts for Alaska statehood with interest.

Statehood for Alaska had been discussed seriously since the gold rush at the beginning of the twentieth century. In the 1940s and 1950s, modern legislation to establish a state was proposed by the territory's nonvoting congressional delegate Tony Dimond and his successor Bob Bartlett, and by other members of Congress.

Alaska voted for statehood in a 1946 territorial referendum. An official Alaska Statehood Committee was created in 1949 by the territorial legislature to lobby Congress for statehood. Congress did repeatedly address the statehood issue, but no bill was enacted. The center of action on the issue was in Washington, DC, with Alaskans in the role of spectators from afar.

My personal involvement was inspired by a comment made in April 1953 by Senator Hugh Butler, a conservative Republican from Nebraska opposed to statehood. He was chair of the Interior and Insular Affairs Committee, which heard statehood bills in the Senate. After another Washington lobbying effort and defeat of a statehood bill, Butler announced he would go to Alaska for hearings to seek "the reaction of the little people—not just a few aspiring politicians who want to be senators and representatives."

We were at a party of our circle of friends when the subject of Butler's remark came up. Roger Cremo, an attorney who was rather short, quipped that he was a little man and would gladly tell Senator Butler what he thought about statehood. He and Cliff Groh, also an attorney, had already thought of creating a Little Man Club.

Ideas sped around the room about organizing many "little men" to give Butler the message that the people wanted statehood. We knew how to organize the community—we did it all the time, for all sorts of purposes—and this time it could be for a much bigger cause.

Our theme would be "I'm a Little Man for Statehood."

We held a strategy meeting a few days later in Roger's office in the Reed Building on Fourth Avenue, with Cliff, the attorney; businessman Barrie White; Gloria, a journalist; Molly Tryck, a full-time mother; and others. All were good friends. We were a pragmatic bunch. Being Alaskans meant, if you had a common purpose, you just did things, you took action. No one was around to stand in your way, so you learned to take the initiative.

The idea for the "Little Men" was to overwhelm Butler and other members of the Senate Interior Committee with the people's support for statehood. We would fill his hearings with well-reasoned and strongly felt testimony. We would make sure that everywhere he went in the Territory of Alaska, he would be swamped with pro-statehood messages. And to accomplish that, participation in the effort had to go far beyond our group.

We each threw in a few bucks to cover initial expenses. Our loose-knit, volunteer organization resembled a political campaign, although we were nonpartisan. Mitch Abood gathered petitions. John "Mickey" McManamin produced banners, with the help of many. Barrie White oversaw and handled distribution of materials. Kit Crittenden managed the setup and staffing of an informational booth. Molly Tryck was our secretary. Gloria oversaw publicity. I worked on organizing and contacts with other communities. Roger Cremo spearheaded the effort and handled finances. Bob Bartlett fed us intelligence on the senate committee that was coming and provided congressional data in support of statehood.

We recruited chairmen in each of Anchorage's neighborhoods. Molly and I called and sent letters to the other towns the senate committee would visit: Ketchikan and Juneau in Southeast Alaska and Fairbanks in the Interior. We supplied them with bumper stickers, banners, buttons, and other materials, and they organized their own Little Man groups.

We even developed organizations in towns such as Kodiak and Nome that the committee would never visit. Residents there held up banners and were photographed for senators to see. Other communities sent in scrolls with signatures and statehood comments. Extensive newspaper coverage was arranged.

It was fun. We loved gimmicks—women arranging bouquets of forget-me-nots, the official territorial flower, and stores putting on weekend sales in honor of the event, with advertising to match. The number 49—for the forty-ninth state of the Union—was painted in gold all over town. Bookmarks and name-tags said I'M A LITTLE MAN FOR STATEHOOD. And banners that said THIS IS THE YEAR! and STATEHOOD NOW! We were often on our hands and knees on the attic floor above Cremo's office painting placards.

Gloria's position at the *Times* made publicity easy to organize. She faced no obstacle at work. Atwood had supported statehood for years and was chairman of the territory's official Alaska Statehood Committee. He used his *Anchorage Times* to advocate for the cause through editorials and, unabashedly, through his news stories. For years, Atwood also put out a Sunday tabloid, *The Forty-Ninth Star*, devoted strictly to promoting statehood.

Atwood and other leaders had made a solid case for statehood. Powerful interests from outside Alaska controlled and abused our salmon fisheries through their influence on Congress and federal agencies. Mining syndicates likewise ran roughshod over local interests, and shipping companies used political influence to gouge Alaskans for delivering freight.

As a territory, Alaska lacked the power to defend itself. Our sole nonvoting congressional delegate, Bartlett, had little influence on federal operations in Alaska. Yet the federal government controlled 99.4 percent of Alaska's land, all its resources, the transportation and communications systems, the courts, and other services and facilities; and it did so poorly.

Agencies in Washington ran everything. The authority of the governor in Juneau was minuscule, and besides he was appointed by the president and served under the Interior Department. We had some capable local bureaucrats, including some of my colleagues at the BLM, but they answered to Washington. Alaska's problems often disappeared in the labyrinth of the bureaucracy thousands of miles away.

Our own territorial government didn't help. Its budget was tiny and its powers flaccid. The weak authority it did possess was squandered through complex lines of control. Since we could not elect our own governor, the territorial legislature, which we *did* elect, took pains to split administrative oversight among many minor elected officials. This divided Juneau's modest power into tiny fractions held by a locally elected attorney general, auditor, commissioner of labor, highway engineer, and mining engineer.

The legislature itself met only once every other year. Its limited powers were often used to counter the appointed governor, turning down some of his nominees for appointed boards and commissions, and sometimes all of them. We voted for territorial officials, but no one was really in charge.

Despite these problems, and the efforts of Atwood, Bartlett, and Governor Ernest Gruening, no broad popular movement for statehood had developed. Our group contributed this historic new ingredient.

Senator Butler had been partly right in his offhand comment about hearing only from "aspiring politicians." Members of the Alaska Statehood Committee were major businessmen, territorial senators, and other community leaders. We knew ordinary people also wanted Alaska to be a state, but our young, energetic generation had mostly been content to stay on the sidelines of the debate in faraway Washington, DC.

The "Little Man" campaign had nothing to gain from statehood other than good government and basic political rights as Americans. It was this sort of idealism that galvanized the citizens' movement from the time we mobilized to respond to the Senate Interior Committee's visit, right through our constitutional convention and action by Congress five years later.

Perhaps our idealistic motives helped keep us together. It was a time of consensus and camaraderie. Liberals such as Gloria and I, Gruening, and Bartlett had no trouble working side by side with conservatives such as Barrie White, Cliff Groh, Bob Atwood, and Wally Hickel. We all shared the same self-government goal.

When the August evening finally came for Senator Butler's party to arrive in Anchorage by train from Fairbanks, the weather was miserable, cold and rainy, and the sky was already dark. The dreary setting at the railroad station, waiting for the senator's train from Fairbanks, seemed unlikely to turn out a crowd, and we worried that our plans might flop, with only a handful of supporters showing up.

Instead, the city's turnout was enormous, with hundreds of people waving signs and holding banners, and shouting that they were little men and wanted statehood now. Cliff Groh made a speech on the train platform. The senators were tired but gracious, thanking us and shaking hands.

Good crowds turned out for the congressional committee's two days of Anchorage hearings in Carpenters Hall on Fourth Avenue. Almost sixty people testified, many of them part of the Little Man movement, including me. Just two spoke in opposition, arguing that Alaska did not have the financial base to support a state; one of them was bush pilot and future governor Jay Hammond.

Margaret Rutledge made the greatest impression on the senators. As Republican National Committeewoman, she described the excitement she felt in anticipation of a trip to see the inauguration of President Eisenhower earlier that year, the first Republican president in two decades. And then, on arriving in Seattle, she had been subjected, as were all Alaskans, to the indignity of being required to go through US immigration, as if coming from a foreign country.

"Some degrading influence had robbed me of the thing I value most—my birthright as an American, my freedom in my own country," she said. And with that she broke down in tears, obviously moving the senators.

During its travels to Ketchikan, Juneau, Fairbanks, and Anchorage, the senate committee heard testimony from more than some two hundred speakers, of whom only twenty opposed statehood. Wherever they went in Alaska, members heard and saw that Alaskans were eager to become a state. We learned, to our surprise, that the anti-statehood Senator Butler wore a Little Man button at a banquet in Fairbanks and smiled for the first time.

We had achieved our goal of giving voice to the people's stand on statehood. Now the group considered what to do next. The movement we had instigated was worth continuing. But, while the Little Man idea launched a spontaneous mobilization of support, we would need a more organized effort to sustain a citizens' movement over the years till Congress actually approved statehood.

So the "Little Men for Statehood" became "Operation Statehood," incorporated as a nonprofit, with a charter and by-laws. Its purpose would be to provide private citizens an opportunity to band together in a volunteer, nonpartisan, nonpolitical organization "to devote such time and energy as they are able to achieve statehood." Initially our president was Cliff Groh, and then Barrie White. I was vice president. Our board pledged to meet weekly until statehood was achieved.

The fun outlook of our group persisted. Our Gimmicks Committee sent silk forget-me-nots to congressmen with notes to "forget-us-not" when a vote was coming up. We sent a telegram to each of the forty-eight states (in care of the governor) on the anniversary of its own "birthday" of admittance to the Union. And we raised money by selling Christmas cards that showed Santa Claus carrying a gift labeled "Statehood." Women from our group even went to the airport to buttonhole departing passengers with pro-statehood information.

We encouraged Alaskans to write to their stateside newspapers outside Alaska. We held a banquet, with five hundred in attendance on a February night. On the spot, everyone signed form letters to their relatives, friends, and business associates down south, asking them to write to their own senators and representatives. My family participated. The letter-writing campaign went on for several years.

Most of our efforts concentrated on mobilizing ordinary people in America to express their feelings in favor of statehood. A Gallup Poll indicated that over 80 percent of Americans endorsed statehood for Alaska and Hawaii, and most newspapers around the country supported us, too. Our idealistic notion was that Congress couldn't resist such a majority if we kept the pot boiling.

But politics doesn't necessarily work that way.

Statehood bills repeatedly came close to passage in Congress, but again and again didn't make it through both houses. The stated arguments of the opponents included the territory's great size and small population, which made government too expensive for the local economy to bear. Some business interests worked against us because they were profiting from low territorial taxes and lax federal regulation of natural resource exploitation.

But national politics damaged our prospects more. The Eisenhower administration and the Republicans in Congress supported bringing Hawaii into the Union, as it was then a Republican-leaning territory, but they opposed admission of Alaska, which usually voted Democratic. In the narrowly divided US Senate from 1952 to 1956, two more senators from either new state could sway control.

Also, new senators from either territory could be expected to support civil rights legislation. That fear set southern Democrats against both Alaska and Hawaii. They still had sufficient numbers to kill any civil rights bill by filibuster, blocking it with endless debate. Senators from Alaska or Hawaii could contribute to the two-thirds needed to end a filibuster in the Senate.

But, in 1954, opponents seemed to be giving way. Senator Butler dropped his ardent opposition to statehood and suddenly became a strong supporter. Privately, his feelings hadn't changed, but Butler believed popular support for statehood had become too strong, and he didn't want Democrats to get all the credit when a bill inevitably passed. He also saw that Alaskans could vote for Republicans, as they had in the 1952 territorial legislative elections.

We didn't know Butler's motivations at the time. We only knew that he now supported us, and we gave him a standing ovation the next time he appeared before Operation Statehood. Documentary research by historian Terrence Cole, of the University of Alaska, has uncovered the private communications of Butler and others involved in the fight. As I tell the story now, I keep in mind both our perceptions about the politics at the time and the historic record that now shows how inaccurate our read of the situation really was.

A bill for both Alaska and Hawaii statehood made progress in Congress that spring of 1954, but got stuck in the House, where both Speaker Joseph Martin, a Republican, and Democratic Minority Leader Sam Rayburn opposed it, making it unlikely ever to come up for a vote. Our group hoped that we could convince congressional leaders and President Eisenhower to move the bill. A Hawaiian delegation planned to make a lobbying blitz to try to force the bill forward. With little time to organize, we decided to join them.

We jumped into high gear after a phone call from Bob Bartlett on April 30, with just a week to organize a flight of fifty Alaskans to Washington on a chartered Alaska Airlines DC-4. Barrie White and I worked with the rest of Operation Statehood and the two political parties. Each person traveling would have to pay $295 for the flight (more than $2,500 in today's dollars), plus expenses in DC.

Persuading Alaskans to go at that cost seemed a tall order. It was certainly a tough decision for me. Gloria and I had fretted about plans to go Outside and had long delayed a trip. We couldn't consider the expense for ourselves unless the trip was at least a month. But under the circumstances, we agreed I had to go.

To raise money, Operation Statehood printed ten thousand tickets to raffle off a seat on the plane. We launched a campaign to call around the state to recruit passengers. As the date approached, Vic Rivers signed a voucher on behalf of the Alaska Statehood Committee to advance the money for the charter until we could raise the full amount we needed.

We fired off requests through every available channel to meet with President Eisenhower. Barrie worked a family contact to White House Chief of Staff Sherman Adams. Wally Hickel, who served on the Republican National Committee, made the request through his party. Bob Bartlett tried to set it up from his Washington office.

We also planned our gimmicks: more forget-me-nots, as well as flags, stickers, matches, stamps, and maps of Alaska's resources, plus hundreds of pounds of king crab and bags of Matanuska Valley potatoes.

The mood was ebullient as we flew east on our specially decorated plane. We would finally meet the people who would decide Alaska's fate and overwhelm them with the arguments that seemed irresistibly persuasive—at least to us. Bartlett cabled on the eve of our departure that President Eisenhower had agreed to meet a group from our delegation, and he suggested we decide during the plane ride who would go to the White House.

We arrived with absolute confidence in the rightness of our cause. We did make an impression at the airport. My old Wisconsin friends Bob and Martha Lewis, who were living in Washington and came to meet me, described the general amazement at the sight of the first Alaska Airlines plane to land there. We looked like a circus, posing next to the plane for press photographs, with almost every member of our group waving a sign or a flag or wearing a fur parka.

We had a joint dinner with the Hawaiian delegation in the Capitol. Miles Brandon, a Native youth and legislative page, sang the Alaska Flag song in his well-trained voice, bringing tears to the eyes of Alaskans present.

But our reception in congressional offices came as a cold shock. Eisenhower had taken the position that Alaska statehood would impede defense against the Soviet Union. Congressmen would not go against a national security concern expressed by our war-hero president.

Just as some Alaskans had abandoned the territory at the outbreak of the Korean War, many Americans still feared an invasion by the Soviet army. The military build-up that had powered Alaska's growth was intended to counter that threat, but doubts persisted about whether our vast territory could be held against a massive surge of Soviet troops or a nuclear attack.

We didn't challenge the likelihood of an invasion, but we argued that statehood wouldn't impair the ability to defend Alaska. Air Force Chief of Staff General Nathan Twining had said in 1953 that statehood would make Alaska easier to defend, not more difficult. Eisenhower administration officials could not offer a coherent explanation for their contrary position.

Statehood advocates concluded that the administration had advanced the defense argument as a pretext for political opposition. Confronted with the justice of our cause, they would surely relent.

We did not know at the time that the defense objection in fact came directly from the president, a pet theory he had developed based on geography and his outdated knowledge about Alaska. Historian Cole reports that Eisenhower still believed only Southeast Alaska had a significant population, which would leave most of the territory available for military use.

Eisenhower had supported Alaska statehood before running for president, stating while president of Columbia University that statehood for Alaska and Hawaii would prove to the world that America practices what it preaches about democracy. Once in office, however, Eisenhower instead saw the territory as a defensive line against the Soviets. Perhaps he believed that keeping its land mass undeveloped would allow easier use of nuclear weapons in case of a Soviet invasion.

Eisenhower also came up with the administration's solution to the problem. He drew a line across the map of Alaska and said he would agree to the southern, more populated portion entering the Union, with the northern and western part remaining permanently as an enormous military reservation.

This proposal was put forth through the mouth of Alaska's already unpopular appointed governor, Frank Heintzleman, as his own idea. We were outraged, as were the Iñupiat residents of Barrow who objected to being left out of the future state. Defeating the partition of Alaska became a major goal of the Operation Statehood visit to Washington.

At that point, it was secret that national security was the rationale for partition. But regardless of the reason for it, members of the House Interior Committee with whom we met insisted that we had to accept Alaska as a state divided or have no state at all. (I still have notes from the meeting.) Col. Marvin "Muktuk" Marston asked what would happen to the Eskimos with their homeland stranded in the military reserve. Committee Chairman A.L. Miller, a Nebraska Republican, said, "I guess there will always be Eskimos."

Miller went on to tell us, as "friendly, frank advice," that we should change our attitude: "You didn't come here to tell anyone what to do. You're coming hat in hand."

We didn't follow that advice. In the meeting with the president, our delegation chose as one of its two speakers Johnny Butrovich of Fairbanks, known for his straight talk. Johnny lectured Eisenhower for five minutes, face-to-face, in front of the president's desk, respectfully but forcefully, making our arguments, while pointing out that it was in the president's power to push the bill out of committee in the House and on to passage. Eisenhower visibly reddened and those present thought he would explode. He clearly wasn't accustomed to being spoken to that way.

The mood on the flight back to Alaska was dark, a complete contrast to how we had felt on the way east.

Barrie White, writing to thank Bob Bartlett for his help, admitted he had been "scared to death" while leading the group, and felt "the gradual awakening of how mean and petty and frustrating politics can be." Bob wrote back to Barrie:

> I am persuaded that the accumulative effect was helpful. More than that, possibly, were the revelations made during that fateful week. Suspicions became translated into realities. That of which we had only guessed was demonstrated to be the fact. Every member of the delegation, I should think, went home with a much clearer understanding that great legislative issues such as this are not always resolved on the basis of merit. Sometimes, one would think, not at all!

That summer after the spring Washington flight, Secretary of the Interior Douglas McKay came to Alaska for a tour and met with the Operation Statehood board at the Anchorage Westward Hotel (now the Hilton). According to my notes, we all rose when he entered the room, and Barrie introduced us as a volunteer group brought together by a single purpose. He respectfully submitted our list of written questions, which had been requested and provided to the secretary in advance.

To our amazement, McKay refused to answer the questions and launched into a diatribe, saying senators and representatives had complained of our assertiveness during the trip to Washington, and advising us not to be so "belligerent."

"Your people's attitude has got to change," he said. "I don't tell them what to do. I go up with hat in hand."

We were stunned. For a cabinet member to come to our hometown and give us a tongue-lashing was unreal. But we didn't back down. Board members challenged the need for partition and restated our fundamental rationale for statehood. McKay said he supported statehood, but couldn't do anything for us because the president sets the policy. "I'm just a hired hand working for the president," he said. When asked what we could do, he advised, "Get back down to earth, and act like ladies and gentlemen."

At the end of the meeting, McKay admitted he "got a little too mad," but it was too late to take back his comments, which flashed through the news in Alaska and around the country. The national press reacted strongly to the secretary of the interior speaking to us, Americans asking for our rights, as if we were unruly children. Oregon Senator Wayne Morse took to the senate floor to call McKay "a mental peanut" and "stage character tyrant."

McKay's tirade was a public relations fiasco. But, for the statehood movement, the moment was a turning point. In the face of his insults and condescension, the resolve of Alaskans hardened, and compromises such as partition became even less acceptable.

The prospect of passing statehood legislation receded years into the future. We needed to settle in for the long haul. Gimmicks and one-shot plane trips would not be enough.

My young friends and I had entered into the statehood movement motivated by idealism and in a spirit of fun and excitement. The work had taken us to the corridors of power in Washington, where we had been cleansed of our naiveté about how the decision would be made. We had become leaders, with a sense now of the difficulty and seriousness of the job we had taken on.

Alaskans needed to prove our readiness to be a state, politically as well as economically. With legislation dead in Congress we now had the time to build that case. We decided to draft a constitution.

⇥ 12 ⇤

Constitutional Delegate

I had lived in Alaska five years when, in 1955, I put my name forward for election to the Alaska Constitutional Convention. Only sixteen years had passed since I had arrived in America from the Soviet Union, speaking not a word of English. I was thirty-one years old and five years out of school—hardly the stereotypical profile of a founding father. Gloria was skeptical of my candidacy from the start.

But sprouting careers grew fast in Alaska's virgin political ground. I did become a delegate. Two other delegate candidates had lived in Alaska no longer than I. Eight had arrived since the end of the war. Everyone seemed to be new in those days. The rapid growth of Alaska's population, after a long period of economic stagnation, meant that a large percentage of the territory's leadership came from the World War II generation, then just reaching its prime. When I became planning director for the city of Anchorage, everyone I worked with, including the mayor, was under thirty-five.

Nor was I the youngest delegate elected, with two others my junior. More than half the delegates were under fifty. It was hardly possible to have been born in the territory and be much older unless you were an Alaska Native, because prior to the 1898 Klondike Gold Rush there was scarcely any non-Native population. Sixty-year-old Frank Peratrovich, from Klawock in Southeast Alaska, was the only Native delegate.

The delegate with the next-longest Alaska longevity was E. B. Collins of Fairbanks, who had arrived in 1904. He was elected in 1912 to the first

Territorial House of Representatives and served as its Speaker from 1913 to 1915. Collins, at eighty-two, seemed to me to be fossilized with age. I couldn't imagine him helping write a constitution. (As I write these words, I am six years older than he was then.)

I was probably the most recent arrival of the five convention delegates born outside the States, though I was the only one of them born a US citizen. In my time in Alaska, I had suffered no prejudice either as an ethnic Jew or as a child of Nazi Germany and Soviet Russia, the United States' greatest twentieth-century enemies. Even today, friends often don't know where I came from.

Some of my friends from those years cannot remember if I spoke with an accent when I got to Alaska, although others confirm that I had some. Charlie Tryck, who grew up in Wasilla, was surrounded as a child by the accents of the area's immigrant settlers. He says he would have thought nothing of it if I spoke like a German or Russian. Alaskans tended to consider arrival in the North as a sort of new birth and rarely inquired about one's place of origin or previous life. Participation in the community alone created nearly complete social equality.

In the Anchorage of the 1950s, Gloria and I, with our energetic, outgoing personalities, found ourselves in an ideal society, where leadership came as a natural reward for ideas and involvement. It was the world we had envisioned when we looked to the west to make our home. It was a largely classless social structure, resembling the dream of my parents and their socialist friends—but in a free rather than coerced form.

Unconsciously, I enacted the values taught by my upbringing in Russia's Soviet society through my work as a statehood advocate and constitutional drafter. Regardless of the dreadful political realities in Russia, our education as children there emphasized a vision of a perfected human civilization, a goal we accepted and took seriously, even though Soviet reality did not live up to those dreams. My idealism was no less in our work for a new government for Alaska. Those dynamic times made the ideal seem possible.

Besides living in the hothouse of Alaska's growth, good fortune also helped me on my five-year path from fresh university graduate to constitutional delegate. My master's degree from MIT gave me the aura of an expert. Everyone had heard of MIT's brilliant engineers. I didn't always trouble to explain that, as a city planning graduate, I was of a different species, one that most had never heard of.

I was also lucky with my job at the BLM. It gave me an extraordinary introduction to Alaska and its communities. Having traveled to towns across the territory, I got to meet Alaskans of all types. When I campaigned to be a constitutional delegate, many people already knew who I was.

On the other hand, my famous parents did not add much to my fame in Alaska, despite a few odd encounters over the years. For example, in the early 1950s, I went sheep hunting with Don Coolidge, one of Ed Crittenden's architecture partners, in the mountains of the Kenai Peninsula south of Turnagain Arm. Stopping in the tiny, forgotten gold-rush community of Hope, we visited a ramshackle little cafe for coffee. Out-of-town guests were so rare, the proprietor asked us to sign a register. On seeing my name, she asked if I was related to Louis Fischer. She had heard him speak at a town hall meeting in Chicago years before. It truly was a "small world" moment.

Markoosha contributed to our lives personally. She came to Alaska many times over the decades, sometimes for several months at a stretch. She delighted our friends, becoming a source of wisdom and solace for an amazing number of people in Anchorage. Friends like Kit Crittenden kept up correspondence with her, and she became a confidante to our friends' children when they reached adulthood as well. She is still remembered for her cheer, her smile, and her ability to gather a young adult into her circle of warmth. Her young visitors would sit at her feet, literally, and emerge with a glow and new love of the world.

Markoosha spent much of the late 1940s and the 1950s working with refugees in Europe. She never lost touch with the Wloch family in Berlin, and in the early 1950s developed a plan with Lothar to emigrate to the United States and stay at her farm in Pennsylvania. I worried that Lothar wouldn't want to be dependent and suggested he instead come to Alaska, where summer construction jobs were abundant and well paid, and where language difficulties didn't matter much. It never happened. I didn't see Lothar until years later.

In the postwar years, Louis broke with the *Nation,* where editor Freda Kirchwey remained an apologist for Stalin, and focused more of his attention on India. He seemed to mellow through his trips there, particularly with the days of long, thoughtful discussions with Mahatma Gandhi that he described in *A Week with Gandhi.* In 1947, he also wrote a short book that compared Gandhi and Stalin, and, in 1950, he published *The Life of Mahatma Gandhi* which remains one of the most respected biographies and was the basis for the Academy Award–winning 1982 film by British director Richard Attenborough.[3]

---

3. In the course of researching the book I came across a 1964 agreement promising royalties for the film. None were ever paid.

When I began writing this book, my emotional image of Louis was of the cold, sometimes brutally uncaring man in the story of my childhood and in his relations with my mother. He was a bad father and a bad husband. But in the research of my own life—reading hundreds of old letters—I uncovered more of a picture in three dimensions. I realized that Louis became much more interested in his sons and our families in our adulthood. He wrote often and planned times when we could be together to keep our relationship alive.

The change seems to have come soon after his work in India. I noted in a family letter at the time that "Pap" had changed. He had become warmer and more caring. I think he realized and regretted that he had been a cold and forbidding father. George still struggled with his complex feelings about Louis. They worked in generally the same field—the academic study of the history of international relations—and their discussion had many levels. I still resented Louis's rotten treatment of my mother, which never relented. Yet, he was my father, and a fascinating man, wonderful writer, and deep believer in democracy and freedom. So we got along and enjoyed each other's company, although always with some distance between us.

How did I forget this change when I got older? At some point, after his death, I developed a stereotypically negative image of my father and his coldness. When I began rereading the early pages of this book, I began to realize that I was being unfair. Delving into our family letters in the Princeton University archives brought back a very different person from the one I had portrayed. Later events and perceptions, falling in the forty years since Louis's death, had unconsciously reshaped the impressions of earlier events—and so my later life edited the middle part of my life.

Louis doubted the choice Gloria and I made to move to Alaska, which he believed would put us beyond the reach of "culture." I'm not sure he changed his opinion much on his first visit. He stopped off in Anchorage, in December 1952, toward the end of a round-the-world trip to collect material for future books. While in Tokyo for two weeks, he took daily cold showers to prepare himself for Alaska. My father was quite surprised when he found our temperatures well above freezing, and was particularly pleased that we had completed our indoor plumbing.

During his Anchorage stay, Louis met many of our friends and coworkers. He also had good conversations with federal judge Tony Dimond, politician and attorney Wendell Kay, and others who helped him realize that we had not really dropped off the planet. But while he came to appreciate why we loved our new life, he didn't care for Alaska. It was too alien to his lifestyle. Nor were all our close friends impressed with Louis. To many, he came off as a snob, even if a most interesting one.

But Louis's reputation, experience, and charm worked well on Bob and Evangeline Atwood. Evangeline wrote Gloria a star-struck letter describing her meeting with my father in San Francisco after he left Alaska, in which she said she had asked Bob to order all of Louis's many books. From then on, our letters teased Louis about "his friend Evangeline."

Louis also knew Alaska's governor, Ernest Gruening. As the managing editor of the *Nation* in the early 1920s, he had given Louis his first chance to write for the magazine. Gruening came from a privileged family and knew Franklin Roosevelt as a friend. In 1934, he became the Roosevelt administration's head of territories and possessions, spending much of his time on issues in Puerto Rico and Alaska.

In 1939, Roosevelt made Gruening governor of Alaska. I stopped in to see him in Juneau in the Governor's Office in 1951, when I was passing through on BLM work—the same trip when I decided a new town was not needed near Ketchikan. He was most pleasant when we met then, but our acquaintance became established only later, with the work on statehood and the constitution.

As an intellectual and a well-connected political insider, and a hard worker, Gruening was a major asset to the territory and the statehood movement, and was arguably our greatest governor. He brought his progressivism and anti-colonialism with him to Alaska, planting the intellectual seeds for statehood. Gruening's indignant writings and speeches about the abuse of Alaska as a colony leapt from the page. He invested prodigious knowledge and intelligence in his words. Early on, he built Alaska toward statehood by enlarging the legislature, raising taxes to pay for a more active government, and appointing Republican Bob Atwood chairman of the new Statehood Committee, a decision that angered Gruening's own party.

Personally, he could be charming and friendly, but he also frequently came across as haughty and difficult, as if wrapping himself in his power and importance. Besides, his policies often threatened the status quo, including his work for racial equality and his challenge to the corporate abuse of Alaska's natural resources. And he could play political hardball (including against me, as I'll describe later).

Gruening made many enemies. He had arrived as a carpetbagger, following previous governors who had enjoyed the advantage of being Alaskans before they were appointed. His patrician upbringing made it difficult for him to relate with the down-home style of Alaskans. His assistant, Katie Hurley, also says she heard some prejudiced remarks directed against him as a Jew.

Katie became Gruening's assistant not long after he took office and stayed for thirteen years, advancing from a job she landed with her shorthand skills to being the equivalent of the governor's office manager. She was Gruening's confidant and a good judge of people as well. Gruening had few close allies, and her social aptitude helped him navigate the workings of the territorial capital of Juneau. After his gubernatorial appointment ended, she became Secretary of the Territorial Senate.

Gruening left office after Eisenhower won the presidency in 1952, when I was Anchorage's planner. In my job, the failures of territorial government mainly concerned me as I saw them in Anchorage. Our city boundaries were small compared to the great expanse of the Anchorage bowl, between the Chugach Mountains and Cook Inlet, where most future development would occur. That broader area had no local government at all.

Anchorage was a real city. As in council-manager cities around the United States, operations were efficiently run by a city manager, appointed by a nonpartisan mayor and council. Unlike my time with the BLM, where I largely worked alone, I was now part of a team and involved in much current decision making. The daily rush of development required constant attention. It was exhilarating.

Military spending continued to power the city's boom. Construction of the Anchorage International Airport at about this time added a large aviation industry. Lying on the route between Asia and the United States and Europe, Anchorage became the refueling base for flights between continents and adopted the motto "Air Crossroads of the World."

Employment increasingly became year-round, more and more families located in Anchorage, and population doubled and redoubled in a matter of years. The city's infrastructure was under constant pressure to expand, with decisions to be made on extending and improving streets, water lines, sewers, and other services into new areas. I became deeply involved in these choices.

One of our successes was stopping repeated proposals to divert centrally located land running along the edge of the original Anchorage townsite, now the city's downtown core. This open land had initially served as a firebreak and an early landing field. We turned down a parking lot, a school, housing, and a curling rink. Today the land is known as the Delaney Park Strip, Anchorage's extensive central park, which extends one block wide and fifteen blocks long from the ocean toward the mountains. It is a centerpiece of downtown Anchorage.

Much of the new residential growth was occurring outside Anchorage city limits, in areas that lacked local government. It was clear that an areawide approach was needed to deal with the region's growth problems and to provide a basis for its future. Several public utility districts cropped up on the city's periphery, but they were limited in function and size and would not cooperate with the city.

All existing states had an intermediate municipal level between cities and the state, in most cases counties, but Alaska did not. Thanks to lobbying by fishing and mining interests that wanted to be free from taxation on properties outside cities, Congress specifically prohibited the Alaska legislature from creating counties. That would have to wait for statehood. More than any other single cause, today's sad pattern of sprawl can be blamed on this too-late organization of areawide local government.

As Anchorage's planner, I pursued annexation of lands adjacent to the city, efforts that usually ended up in federal court (the only court Alaska had at the time). Utility districts fought the loss of taxable areas. Questioning by the opposing attorney could be tough. City Attorney John Rader advised me that when on the stand I should always keep my cool and remember that I knew more about the issues I was speaking on than anyone else in the courtroom. I've always remembered that counsel, whether appearing in court or before congressional committees. We won all these cases, and the people in each area voted to join the city, more than tripling its size.

Our accomplishments from those days remain evident across Anchorage. The areawide recreation plan, prepared with extensive citizen participation, proposed a system of parks for the entire Anchorage region, much of it implemented over the past fifty years.

The plan called for an inland recreation area on the east side of town at Goose Lake with a connecting greenbelt along Chester Creek, which flows from the mountains into Cook Inlet. My friend Ed Fortier suggested building a pond at the estuary of the creek, now known as Westchester Lagoon, and we put that on the map too.

Some of the land needed for the Chester Creek greenbelt was in public ownership and more was later set aside by two urban renewal projects in which I was involved. The city acquired other key areas through bond issues and appropriations. With continuing citizen and municipal support, what started as a highly speculative idea in the 1950s has evolved into today's system of regional parks, greenbelts, and city-spanning trails that are distinguishing features of Anchorage.

Planning worked because of the town's booster spirit and the oft-stated desire to avoid the mistakes that had been made Outside. But this support had limits. At hearings on our proposals I heard, time and again, statements like "I came to Alaska to get away from government controls" and "I have a God-given right to do whatever I want with my property." I had come to Alaska for the freedom of the frontier, too. I understood the essential Alaska conflict between individual freedom and community connection. In my case, they are both part of me.

Work seemed to occupy every waking hour, with evenings usually taken up by meetings for the city, for Operation Statehood, for the League of Alaskan Cities, or for my other community involvements. On weekends and rare free weekday evenings I worked on the house. Gloria felt my absence and hoped for a change that would allow us more time together. Work at the *Anchorage Times* brought frustrations, too, and she pondered quitting to solve both problems.

My part-time role as executive secretary of the League of Alaskan Cities first took me to the capitol in Juneau for several weeks during the 1953 legislative session. I lobbied for the League through the entire 1955 session. (The legislature met only in alternate years.) On my shoestring budget, paid by the city of Anchorage, I couldn't pick up a lunch tab for a legislator. Instead, a legislator such as Senator Bill Egan would sometimes buy me lunch.

That two-month 1955 session proved to be the most important in the history of the statehood movement. It issued the call for a constitutional convention.

Hawaii had written its constitution in 1950, but Alaskans had decided to wait. Those who supported the idea in the following years were defeated by the belief that statehood was coming quickly without a constitution, and that engaging in writing one might provide an excuse for opponents to delay congressional action.

After the disappointment of our charter flight to Washington in 1954 and the failure of the statehood bill in Congress, the prospect of Alaska joining the Union seemed to be years away. We had time to draft a constitution and prove ourselves politically mature enough to be a state. It was the only positive thing we *could* do.

Operation Statehood formed a study committee to advocate for a constitutional convention, and a group in Fairbanks got together on its own for the same purpose. Other than the *Model State Constitution*, published by the nonprofit National Municipal League, our committee found little existing information on how to draft a new state constitution.

The last states to be admitted, Arizona and New Mexico, had entered the union in 1912. Many state constitutions were outmoded, clogged with detail, and poorly suited to the contemporary roles of the state and federal governments. They provided examples of what not to do rather than models to follow.

A political debacle for Alaska's Republicans helped set the stage for legislative action. The 1953 session was a disorganized mess. It concentrated, in part, on searching out communists in the style of Senator Joseph McCarthy (one communist was found, a longshoreman working on the docks in Skagway). The House of Representatives never formally adjourned at the end of the session: The Speaker and various members were too drunk to act and the body simply disintegrated. That summer, Interior Secretary McKay compounded the Republicans' problems with his infamous comments about Alaskans coming "hat in hand" for statehood and behaving "like ladies and gentlemen."

Democrats swept the fall 1954 legislative election, taking all but four seats in the Territorial Senate and all but three in the House. After the landslide, Democratic legislators met to organize and discuss priorities for the 1955 session. A bill to create a constitutional convention became their top priority. Attorney Tom Stewart of Juneau, a new member of the House, took on the research to prepare a bill.

Tom had grown up in Juneau, the son of a well-known mining geologist. He studied Russian and foreign relations (he later had Alexander Solzhenitsyn to his home in Juneau), and obtained a law degree at Yale. During the war, Stewart trained army ski troops and led them into battle in the Italian Alps, an experience he could recount as a gripping and hilarious yarn. Besides his intelligence and talent, he was well liked.

Stewart took on responsibility for the constitution with a level of energy and attention to detail that would ultimately put him in the hospital with exhaustion. To tackle the dearth of information about constitution making, Tom quit his job as a territorial assistant attorney general in November 1954 and, at his own expense, traveled the country to talk to experts at university political science departments, and public-policy and legal organizations. He studied the theoretical and practical aspects of writing a constitution, and learned about the expertise and required resources to do the job successfully.

Tom's most important stop was in New Jersey, which had written a new constitution in 1947. He met with their convention's vice-president and other leading delegates. They emphasized the need to insulate the process from day-to-day politics, with its lobbyists, horse-trading, and partisan battling. They attributed their success, in large part, to holding their convention at the state university, Rutgers, rather than at the capital in Trenton.

The process to complete the constitution would require many steps. The legislature would have to pass detailed legislation calling for the convention and make an appropriation to pay for it. Delegates had to be elected. Research and background studies would be needed. The convention itself would take months. And then the people would have to vote on approval of the constitution at the primary election in April 1956.

To finish the process in a timely manner, each step would need to be completed smoothly in sequence. And the convention itself would have to be held in the coldest part of the winter, so it would not interfere with the warmer fishing, mining, and construction season.

When the Alaska territorial legislature convened in January 1955, Tom Stewart led a joint committee of the House and Senate on the constitution. Bill Egan, the Senate's committee chair, deferred to Tom's expertise in drafting the convention bill. Juneau merchants angrily opposed holding the convention at the university near Fairbanks, in Alaska's Interior. They feared the site would threaten Juneau's role as the future state's capital. Tom successfully insisted on that provision, against the wishes of his own constituents.

This decision was among those that proved critical to success of the convention. Another was to elect delegates on a nonpartisan basis, an idea that was readily accepted. However, creating districts for electing delegates required much creative thinking and discussion.

Federal law mandated that territorial legislators be elected at-large from only four districts, which matched Alaska's four judicial divisions. The divisions bunched together cities, towns, and villages, allowing a few larger cities to dominate elections. For example, the Third Division covered a vast region from the Copper River country and the Canadian border to Bristol Bay and the Aleutian Islands, a distance of more than one thousand miles, including the Kenai Peninsula and Matanuska Valley. Yet, all ten House representatives in the 1955 session came from Anchorage, which had only half the division's population.

Statehood advocates believed the convention would need to be far more representative to gain acceptance by the public. After extensive debate, the legislature devised a three-tier system for electing fifty-five constitutional convention delegates, the number who convened in Philadelphia to write the US Constitution in 1787.

A single election district covering all of Alaska was designed to attract leading statesmen and help overcome regionalism. A second level of seats, allocated according to population by the four existing judicial divisions, would cover the largest population centers. At the third level, single-member districts, each representing one or two land recording districts, would assure that communities throughout Alaska would have their own local delegate, and would bring new recruits into the public discourse.

This allocation system worked out well. The range of votes per candidate to the convention ranged from just under fifty to more than seven thousand. But once seated, all delegates were equal.

My lobbying assignment to Juneau that winter, for Anchorage and the League of Alaskan Cities, put me on the scene of the constitution writing decisions, for which I represented Operation Statehood. I got involved in convention details,

Louis Fischer, the author's father, in a famous 1922 group photograph with Vladimir Lenin. Fischer (2) is to the right of Lenin (1). As a foreign correspondent, Louis maintained contact with many world leaders through his career. —RUSSIAN STATE ARCHIVE OF SOCIAL-POLITICAL HISTORY, RGASPI 393, DOCUMENTARY PHOTOGRAPHS V. I. LENIN IN HIS LIFETIME, INVENTORY 1, FILE 369 OR 370.

Louis and Markoosha Fischer, the author's parents, early 1920s.
— LOUIS FISCHER PAPERS. MANUSCRIPT DIVISION. DEPARTMENT OF RARE BOOKS AND SPECIAL COLLECTION. PRINCETON UNIVERSITY LIBRARY

Markoosha Fischer, the author's mother, translated for the Russian delegation at the 1922 Genoa Conference, when the Soviet Union gained a place on the world stage. She is the second woman from the right.

Markoosha and sons George, left, and Vic Fischer, the author.

Vic with German leftist Paul Massing, Berlin, 1932. Brothers George and Vic lived with the Massings when scarcity in Soviet Russia forced their removal to Berlin in 1931. Massing, a lifelong mentor and father figure, was imprisoned by the Nazis for his resistance to fascism.

Louis Fischer with George and Vic. The boys returned to Moscow after Hitler came to power in 1933. Traveling as a journalist, Louis spent little time with them. Markoosha faced alone the challenges of raising sons in Stalin's Russia.

Vic Fischer, Koni Wolf, and Lothar Wloch, the "troika" whose friendship would remain unbreakable across a lifetime, at the Peredelkino writers' colony outside Moscow, 1937.

Koni Wolf, George Fischer, Markoosha Fischer, Koni's mother Else Wolf, the author, and Lothar Wloch, Peredelkino, 1938.

The Russian passport issued to Markoosha Fischer and sons with the intervention of Eleanor Roosevelt, allowing the family's escape from Stalin's secret police and the Great Purge in 1939.

Vic seen off by his father, Louis, on his solo voyage to America aboard the *Queen Mary* in 1939.

Brothers George and Vic in U.S. Army uniform, New York, 1943. Vic was stationed in New York to study Russian, even though he was fluent already. —LOUIS FISCHER PAPERS. MANUSCRIPT DIVISION. DEPARTMENT OF RARE BOOKS AND SPECIAL COLLECTION. PRINCETON UNIVERSITY LIBRARY

George and Vic met near Marseille, France, in 1945, as Vic's unit redeployed to the Pacific. The visit remade the men's relationship.

Gloria and Vic Fischer as newlyweds in Biloxi, while he was stationed in Mississippi, 1944.

The author, right, with his new wife, Gloria, and friends Norrie and Dino Chechin, left, at a nightclub in New Orleans, 1944.

This fabric-framed photo of Vic's wife, Gloria, traveled with him through World War II, hanging by yarn from tent walls in camps from Germany to the Philippines.

George Fischer, left, met Lothar Wloch and Koni Wolf in Berlin, 1945. George is an American officer and Koni a Soviet officer. Lothar is in civilian clothes after defeat of the German military he served.

Lothar Wloch, 1940. He joined the Luftwaffe to ease Gestapo pressure on his communist mother, having left Russia after his father's execution. —COURTESY EVA WLOCH

A one-room cabin at 1601 F St. in Anchorage, then at the edge of town, became Vic and Gloria's first home in Alaska, 1950.

Vic auctions lots for the federal Bureau of Land Management in Tok, 1951. The job also involved planning new towns.

Constitutional Convention plenary sessions met in a newly constructed building on the University of Alaska campus near Fairbanks. President Bill Egan is on dais at the right, the author is at the far left.
— STEVE MCCUTCHEON, MCCUTCHEON COLLECTION; ANCHORAGE MUSEUM, B1990.14.5.CONCONV.12.15

Vic addresses a plenary session of the Alaska Constitutional Convention. From left, delegates George Cooper and Barrie White. —STEVE MCCUTCHEON, MCCUTCHEON COLLECTION; ANCHORAGE MUSEUM, B1990.14.5.CONCONV.20.5

The convention's Local Government Committee at work on the constitution. The board in the background shows the status of committee work on each article. —STEVE MCCUTCHEON, MCCUTCHEON COLLECTION; ANCHORAGE MUSEUM, B1990.14.5.CONCONV.2.25

Vic Fischer signs the Alaska Constitution on February 6, 1956. Behind him, from left, Convention First Vice President Frank Peratrovich, President Bill Egan, and Second Vice President Ralph Rivers. —STEVE MCCUTCHEON, MCCUTCHEON COLLECTION; ANCHORAGE MUSEUM, B1990.14.5.CONCONV.14.9

Early years in Alaska were busy with outdoor activities; here, duck hunting, 1954.
—ED FORTIER

Fischer children Yonni, Greg, and baby Joe. The Fischers adopted all three children in a span of three years.

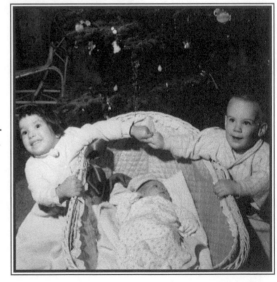

Senator Bob Bartlett, left, attended the author's swearing in as assistant administrator of the Housing and Home Finance Agency, Washington, 1962. Next are Gloria Fischer, Vic, HHFA Administrator Robert Weaver, and Assistant Administrator Morton Schussheim.

Work as University of Alaska professor and ISER director took Vic across Alaska. In St. Paul, Pribilof Islands, he swam in 38-degree Bering Sea waters to retrieve a glass fishing float, 1967.
— PHOTO BY ANN BALTZO, ALASKA MAGAZINE

Vic and others watch Iñupiat hunters butcher one of three bowhead whales taken near Point Hope on a single day in spring 1969. —HOWARD ROCK

A science conference on the coming of big oil to Alaska, hosted in Fairbanks by ISER in 1969, exploded in acrimony when US Senator Ted Stevens, center, blasted environmentalists in a luncheon speech. Chair Vic Fischer is left and University Vice President Don Theophilus right. The banner was designed by Ron Senungetuk.

The author with Bill Egan and Bob Atwood at the release of his book on the Alaska Constitutional Convention, 1975. —ANCHORAGE DAILY NEWS

Signing copies of *Alaska's Constitutional Convention* at a book launch, Anchorage, 1975. —ANCHORAGE DAILY NEWS

made many lifelong friends, and learned about politics and the legislative process. Most of us were young and had fun in the evening, too.

I decided to run for delegate to the constitutional convention that summer of 1955. It would be a natural extension of my commitment to statehood and my planning work.

There would be no primary due to limited time and to keep party politics out of the constitution. All candidates would be listed together in their particular districts. In my race, voters would choose twelve delegates from a field of about fifty Third Division candidates. It was a horserace, as each candidate ran against the whole field to make it over the line as one of the twelve elected. Some didn't campaign. Those who did simply emphasized their qualifications and assured voters that they supported statehood and had no axe to grind.

I resigned as city planning director a month before the election so I would be free to devote myself to the campaign and to start a planning consulting practice. I expected voter support in Anchorage, where my name was well known as a planner, community activist, and statehood advocate. My years as League executive secretary and townsite work with the BLM gave me a positive reputation in the rest of the region. My training in planning and government added to my qualifications.

I thought I had enough going for me that I could get by with a few contacts in other towns for local support. I made a campaign swing down the new highway to Seward with George McLaughlin, a fellow candidate, neighbor, and friend. George and I stopped in at every bar along the way, and there must have been at least a dozen—it was a bit hard to remember afterward.

Gloria thought we needed a stronger campaign to overcome the deficits of my young age and short experience for such an important job. She was excited about running an aggressive door-to-door campaign like the one that had made young John F. Kennedy a Massachusetts senator the year before. She urged me to campaign door to door outside of Anchorage, a prospect that made me distinctly uncomfortable.

Steeling myself, I finally drove an hour up the Glenn Highway to the Matanuska Valley, pulling off on Bodenburg Butte Road near Palmer. I drove into the first driveway, lost my nerve, and pulled out again. At the next house I stopped and knocked. A woman answered the door. She had no idea an election was coming, but she listened to me very politely, even asking a few questions. I told her about the upcoming ballot, explained the constitutional process, and said a few words about my qualifications. With that, I got back in the car and returned to Anchorage.

This process obviously would not win me the election, but it gave me a topic for a letter we then sent to every voter outside of Anchorage. I told of going out to contact voters, without mentioning the number of people I had met, and said, "I only wish there were enough time to tour the entire Third Division. Since that isn't possible, I'm sending you this letter." I continued:

> Everyone we talked with agreed that the Constitutional Convention Election is probably the most important election we'll ever participate in. As one woman put it: "It's the election we'll be telling our grandchildren about." The delegates we elect must write a constitution that will serve many future generations of Alaskans.

We printed six thousand copies on a mimeograph machine, and Gloria recruited a gang of neighborhood children to fold the letters and to stuff, hand-address, and stamp the envelopes. I spent all available time over several days signing every letter by hand, and it was great to get the last batch in the mail. It was only later that I learned Gloria had signed about a thousand for me, but I doubt anyone noticed the difference.

I also benefited from the endorsement of the Central Labor Council, which sent out its own letter to union members. The entire campaign cost less than three hundred dollars, which we paid out of pocket.

The turnout was not large. It was an unusual election, coming in September, when Alaskans were still hunting and fishing for their winter food supply. To many, after years of futile lobbying for statehood, the whole constitution writing exercise seemed speculative and even hypothetical.

When the results came in, I had done well, finishing sixth out of the twelve winners in the Third Division. That was above even Bill Egan, who been previously elected from this region to a number of terms in the Alaska legislature. But this was certainly not because of superior merit—Egan ran from Valdez, with a far smaller population than my base in Anchorage.

Within two months I would be serving under his leadership to draft Alaska's constitution.

⇥ 13 ⇤

Convening the Convention

Bill Egan's gentle leadership of the convention left an imprint on the body and the Alaska Constitution itself. As president, he helped create an atmosphere of friendship, equality, and idealism that pervaded the deliberations.

That observation doesn't come only through my fond retrospective view of this work, the most rewarding of my life. Private letters and articles from the time noted the remarkable level of comity and thoughtfulness. We were a truly unique political body—listening, learning, exchanging the lessons of our experience, and hammering out words that delegates with different beliefs could sign with pride.

But Egan nearly didn't run for a seat at the convention at all.

Some months before the delegate election, Bill had decided to quit politics. Returning to Valdez after the 1955 legislative session, he needed to devote more time to his business, Valdez Supply, and to his wife Neva and son Dennis, then nine. When the constitutional convention election came around, he did not file for the seat set aside for his town, Valdez. But Burke Riley pressed Egan to run, and I'm sure Egan felt pangs as the deadline approached, knowing the convention he had helped set up would happen without him.

I had made friends with Burke during that year's session in Juneau. He was a lawyer from Haines, serving in the House. Close to Bob Bartlett, whose daughter he later married, Burke often served as the congressional delegate's advisor and eyes and ears in Alaska. He was bright and quick on his feet, always in the know, but secretive. He enjoyed the role of political chess player, behind the scenes. Katie Hurley tells a story of Burke sending notes to her in shorthand, which he would end with the phrase "Burn this." She joked about the practice until he sent her a note that said nothing but "Burn this note."

Everyone knew Bill Egan would be an exceptional delegate. After several sessions in the House, including one as Speaker, and one term in the Senate, he had shown an exceptional ability to bring people together. In photographs, Bill often looks ill at ease, and he was, in fact, shy and unwilling to push himself forward. He spoke with a soft voice and as an orator was uninspiring. But personally, he created a connection that reflected real caring.

Bill's uncanny ability to remember the name of everyone he met—and the names of spouses, children, and other facts—didn't come about only because of a prodigious memory, but also because he listened to each and every person he met and thought about what they had to say. In a deliberative body, that empathy became invaluable. As a presiding officer, Bill understood what each member wanted and how to mesh that with the needs of others.

Egan finally decided to file for candidacy the day before the deadline. Having already persuaded Tom Harris to run for Valdez's own seat, he filed to run along with all the others seeking to represent the entire Third Division. That Sunday, he quickly collected the fifty petition signatures from his Valdez neighbors required to be a candidate. But he began to wonder if a postmark would be adequate to make the deadline, so on Monday he boarded a plane to Anchorage and filed with the clerk of the court there. I doubt he did anything else to campaign. Tom Harris, by the way, won the Valdez seat with forty-nine votes.

Weeks before the convention opened, Vic Rivers began gathering delegate votes to be president of the convention. Vic, a civil engineer, was a forceful and effective politician. A Democrat, he had first served in the legislature in 1936, and he knew delegates from all over the state. But, when he approached me, I politely declined to support him for the presidency. I didn't think his partisanship and dominating attitude were right for the convention.

Burke Riley meanwhile began rounding up votes for Bill Egan to be president, partly in response to Rivers's move. But Bill did not agree to take the job.

Gloria and I drove to Fairbanks, arriving at noon on Sunday, November 6, before the Tuesday opening of the convention. The temperature was nine degrees below zero. We moved into an apartment on the second floor of the downtown Northward Building, where a window opened on the top of the awning over the sidewalk, making a handy freezer shelf for anything we wanted to keep cold. (Gloria's detailed letters to our family Outside provide a wealth of such details.)

The next day I got together with Barrie White, also a delegate, and we set about talking to other delegates on behalf of Burke's plan to make Bill Egan our president. Delegates had gathered in our building and in the Polaris Hotel. Talking with Tom Stewart and others, we realized the momentum behind Egan was real. We thought we had the votes. But we couldn't find Bill.

Egan arrived the morning the convention started, tagging a ride from Valdez in a freight truck. Burke was eating breakfast with George McLaughlin in the Model Cafe when he saw Bill jump down from the passenger side of the rig on Second Avenue. Hurriedly paying the check, Burke and George rushed into the street and intercepted him and immediately started pushing the job of convention president on him.

Bill wasn't ready to accept. He had been sincere in his desire to quit politics, and he didn't want responsibility for the convention on his shoulders. Burke took him to see Bob Bartlett at his office just down the street in the federal building at Second and Cushman, and Bob finally convinced Egan to go for the position.

The convention began amid of flurry of preparations and arrivals. The new student union building where we were to meet—now called Constitution Hall—hadn't been completed. In the morning workers were still installing ovens in the kitchen where university cooks would prepare our first lunch.

But the opening ceremonies brought the importance of the event back to the front of our minds with great solemnity and symbolism. A stage had been built in the gymnasium, decorated with blue and gold and big bouquets of yellow chrysanthemums. A school band played while we delegates marched in, each with a yellow rose in our lapel, and then we sat to hear a series of serious speeches.

The orations given that day by Bob Bartlett and the next day by Ernest Gruening were among the most important and best remembered of their careers. Everyone understood the significance of the moment. In two days we heard the greatest speeches of two of the greatest leaders in Alaska's history. Bartlett delivered a thoughtful and prescient analysis of the hazards of creating a state like ours, whose major wealth lies in publicly owned resources, and offered warnings and advice to guide our work. Gruening slashed the injustice of territorial status—colonialism, as he called it—with the precision of a surgeon and the ferocity of a swordsman.

All went well until Governor Frank Heintzleman rather ineptly presided over the election of temporary officers. Confusion about procedure reigned. Nominations for president came forth. To our surprise, Vic Rivers, the principal adversary against Bill Egan, nominated elder Mildred Hermann, a lawyer and experienced bureaucrat known for joking at the expense of her own huge size. No one had mentioned her as a contender for convention president. One of our allies, John Rosswog of Cordova, nominated Egan. The vote came down and, to our astonishment and dismay, Hermann won.

We were stricken. We thought we had been betrayed. It turned out we were showing our inexperience. The temporary president would merely run the election of the permanent officers the next day. Being in that role would have hurt Egan. But even Bill voted for himself, along with most of our other political novices and rural delegates who had committed to support him.

As the convention began, it was clear we had a lot to learn. The next day, Egan won the real vote for convention president. He soon proved his talent for the job.

Egan drew out the thoughts of inexperienced delegates who might be intimidated by formal procedures. He defused angry debate and short-circuited parliamentary confusion by calling frequent "at-ease periods" for delegates to cool down and work out their differences. While maintaining the dignity of the proceedings, he used humor and a homey manner to remind us we were all Alaskans working on a common goal.

Most of us were ordinary Alaskans. Egan himself, often described as a businessman or grocer, owned a store so small that when he went away to Juneau to serve in the legislature his wife Neva had to run the cash register and carry heavy boxes of supplies herself. Jim Doogan of Fairbanks delivered coal for a living. He came home with clothing, face, and hands jet black. I remember waiting in his big kitchen as he washed up, half a dozen boys and girls noisily romping through.

Yule Kilcher, a Swiss immigrant who raised a large family on Kachemak Bay, wore his homesteading clothes on the floor of the convention, including heavy-treaded boots still caked with dried mud from his corral. He kept a hunk of smoked moose in his pocket, cutting off chunks with a hunting knife to offer snacks to the other delegates, which we devoured appreciatively.

The delegates didn't divide along political party lines, but we did split into loose groups. The younger and less-experienced delegates allied with those from rural communities. Our votes put Egan in the president's seat. The convention he ran equalized the delegates rather than giving sway to those who knew more about operating in the political arena.

On substantive issues, a divide developed between liberals and conservatives, with the larger group carrying the day for progressive policies, such as the convention's decision to lower the voting age from twenty-one to nineteen, one of the convention's most vigorously debated issues. (I proposed lowering it to eighteen, as it became years later.)

Compromise usually was available in this collegial group, with Egan's encouragement. My first attempt at it came during the initial voting on convention rules. John Hellenthal and I objected to a rule that would close all committee meetings to the public except by special request for admission. Several former legislators supported the proposed rule, pointing out that the public wasn't included in their committee meetings in Juneau and that privacy made work go faster.

We didn't get much support on the floor and appeared headed for defeat when Egan called a lunch recess. During the break, I worked out an alternative, allowing the committees themselves to determine whether to hold open meetings. This idea received unanimous consent after we reconvened.

The next day newspapers across the Territory objected to closed meetings at the convention. The *Fairbanks Daily News-Miner* editorialized, "They have opened a great exercise in Democracy with a very un-Democratic act." But the compromise worked as I had hoped. As the convention progressed, all committee meetings were announced in advance and were open to the public.

Success on that issue boosted my own confidence. I found a new skill for crafting words that could resolve a dispute and for speaking to issues on the floor. I became one of the more active delegates in voicing my opinion and seeking agreement.

A few individual conflicts arose during the organizational phase of the convention. An ugly debate, later expunged from the record, erupted when the vote came to elect the convention secretary.

Tom Stewart had not run for delegate because he wanted to carry on the work of guiding the convention as Secretary. But when the president called for nominations, a delegate put forward Katie Hurley's name in competition with him, against her wishes. Derogatory remarks were made against Katie, while Tom was opposed by others on the grounds his service would be illegal, since he had been in the legislature that created the job. (Several legislators were serving as delegates under special legislation Bob Bartlett got through Congress.)

Egan adjourned the convention, and the next day the issue was resolved by Katie withdrawing—she became chief clerk rather than secretary—and by the Rules Committee, led by chairman Burke Riley, ruling that Tom could serve.

Petty or personal disagreements were rare. Generally, the level of debate remained at a high level. We began the convention aware that, for the sake of the statehood movement, we must prove ourselves to the Congress and to the rest of the country with our maturity and the quality of our work. Once we began, the realization sank in that we were writing a document for the ages, one that would shape our state and the lives of our people long after we had passed on. This was no place for deal making or cheap politics. We delegates totally committed ourselves to doing our best.

As the convention got down to work, we adopted a studious attitude. The setting helped. After the opening sessions, spectators were few, with several wives and reporters present at plenary sessions, and committee rooms rarely visited by outsiders. Our meetings in classrooms often felt more like seminars than political arenas. Students continued to use the same buildings, passing us in the halls and eating with us in the cafeteria. Since we were five miles from downtown Fairbanks, we couldn't easily wander off to a bar or restaurant, so we stuck to our work.

Most delegates stayed in hotels and apartment buildings downtown, riding back and forth to the convention site in school buses, from which they often could not see out because the windows were solidly frosted over in the bitter cold of the Interior winter. Gloria and I had brought our car, but it froze up soon after we arrived and keeping it running through the winter was a challenge. The months of the convention were among the coldest and snowiest on record in subarctic Fairbanks.

The cold and dark kept us at our work. One didn't want to go outdoors. Delegates might stop in a hotel bar after getting off the bus, but the convention didn't have the wild nightlife of Juneau during a territorial legislative session. Katie Hurley often held a potluck on Sundays in her little apartment, gathering delegates who had come without their spouses. She says they always ended up singing, led by Bill Egan, whose infallible memory gave him total recall of the words of all the old songs.

The work Tom Stewart had invested through the summer supported our seriousness. Despite the territorial treasury's poverty, the legislature had allocated $75,000 to the Alaska Statehood Committee for preparatory material to provide the factual and intellectual grounding for the convention (about $650,000 in today's dollars).

Chairman Bob Atwood hired the nonprofit Public Administration Service, based in Chicago, which sent a team of consultants to work with Tom. They traveled around the Territory and wrote preparatory research papers, explanatory newspaper columns, and some suggested constitutional provisions. The service provided each delegate with three paperbound volumes of this work. In consultation with committee chairmen, Tom recruited top specialists from universities and other institutions around the country to advise convention committees.

The research helped set the stage for thorough debate, bringing to bear current political theory and examples of failures and successes from other constitutions and government structures around the country and internationally. Convention delegates committed themselves to public policy analysis in a wholehearted way with no parallel in Alaska's civic life. The convention represented a moment of high seriousness and resolve when reasoning and deliberation triumphed over politics.

The irrelevancy of our constitutional enterprise to the day-to-day functions of territorial government made it easier for delegates to think abstractly for the benefit of the distant future. We received little outside pressure, because, short of statehood, our decisions would not have any practical impact. To some, the convention seemed an academic exercise fit for a college campus. As a result, the usual Juneau lobbyists were absent from Fairbanks.

A more fundamental factor also set our work apart from the concerns of the present. Change came so rapidly in Alaska during those years that the future for which we were organizing the state could not be imagined. Political and economic history had barely begun. And, we knew little more about the complexion of the coming state and its problems except that they were unpredictable. With only the foggiest idea of what decisions Alaska's future leaders would face, we never thought we were guiding their hands other than with respect to basic principles, such as equality, fairness, accountability, and local self-determination.

This perspective gave Alaska's constitutional convention a critical advantage. Politicians rewriting or amending state constitutions often used the documents as a stronger kind of statute, one that allowed them to address legislative priorities in a more permanent fashion, imposing their views on the future. We, instead, saw Alaska's constitution as a foundation that could support whatever government the changing times and needs of the people would require, leaving as much flexibility as possible to addresses problems and opportunities we couldn't yet conceive. Delegates agreed the constitution should limit the power of each new generation to find its own solutions as little as possible, laying down just enough rules to protect individual rights and empower the state.

We were acutely aware that this opportunity to do the job right would never come again. As the convention worked on creating the future state of Alaska, delegates wrote on a blank slate. We started with a shared base of knowledge from having lived through the misgovernment of territorial Alaska. The frustrations of the failed territorial system traced their causes to divided authority, institutional rigidity, lack of accountability, and a disempowered electorate. These problems pointed toward a state government structure that would be their opposite.

The research provided by Tom Stewart's colleagues allowed us to draw on contemporary political theory. An example was the design of the judicial system. Delegates overwhelmingly agreed that judges should not be elected, as in many states, because that process can lead to money and politics corrupting the courts.

Instead, the convention provided for a merit system of selecting judges, including a nonpartisan vote on their subsequent retention. The framework had been laid out by the American Bar Association and applied in the eight-year-old New Jersey constitution. That, together with integrated administration of the courts, has given Alaska a model judicial system that has been one of the nation's most professional and efficient.

Each of these approaches evolved through a structured convention process. Under convention rules, a committee was established for each article of the constitution. Each committee essentially wrote its own article for presentation to the convention as a whole, which amended and approved the draft, and then referred it to the Committee on Style and Drafting. That committee edited each article to make sure it fit in with the rest, with uniform language, clear and declaratory statements, and simple grammar.

A temporary Committee on Committees assigned delegates to committees. Each of us put in our top three choices, and most got their first and third choices. Mine were Local Government, my area of special concern, and Style and Drafting, which would allow me to work on all aspects of the constitution. Bill Egan chose the committee chairs, who then served as an ad hoc steering committee for the convention.

I recall how earnestly Egan apologized to me for not making me chairman of the Local Government Committee. Although he said I was the most qualified, he wanted to appoint a small-town delegate rather than one from Anchorage, which made sense to me. He was also concerned about offending Barrie White, who was my friend and Operation Statehood colleague and not in consideration for a chairmanship.

I didn't care. The wonderful deliberative atmosphere of the committee, chaired by John Rosswog of Cordova, gave me all the influence I needed. As committee secretary, I kept the minutes, which have become the official record of committee discussions and intent.

The article on local government was one of two that would have to be built almost from scratch. The other was the resources article, an essential for Alaska that did not exist in any other state constitution. Neither could readily import its form from another state.

According to terms of pending statehood bills, Alaska would receive 104 million acres of land, an area equivalent to all of California, to be transferred from federal to state ownership. Along with other rights, the state would own all mineral resources on and under its land, and it would obtain control over commercial and sport fisheries and wildlife resources. No wonder drafting provisions covering natural resources was one of the major challenges of the convention.

No state had a resources endowment approaching Alaska's scale, and none provided a comprehensive model for its management. The Resources Committee had to draft its article from scratch. The foundation of the article is that the resources belong to all of the people, and that they are to be developed and preserved for the maximum benefit of the people. But the meaning of that benefit—whether financial, recreational, or spiritual—is left for each new generation to define.

The article provides for renewable resources to be managed on the sustained yield principle, and lays the basis for dealing with public lands, minerals, waters, and other responsibilities. Public notice and other safeguards of the public interest are assured in disposal of lands and resources.

The resources article emerged as an amalgam of modern ideas in resource management with the experiences of Alaskans, both positive and negative. No basis existed to project the resource future, so the emphasis was on maximizing the public interest and preventing exploitation by special interests. Wisely, the resources article lays out fundamental structures, policies, and management principles, leaving implementation to future legislatures.

This flexible framework proved strong enough to handle the 1968 discovery of North America's largest oil and gas deposit, located on state-selected land at Prudhoe Bay, along the arctic coast of Alaska. The state successfully adapted to dealing with the world's largest multinational corporations, regulating oil field production, and managing more than $150 billion in state revenues. The delegates at the 1955–1956 convention never anticipated development at this scale, yet the constitutional framework has worked.

The Local Government Committee faced a different kind of challenge. Alaskans had but limited self-determination at the local level in the few dozen cities and special districts. The vast bulk of the territory had no local government whatsoever. Federal law prohibited establishment of counties, restricted city borrowing through bond sales, and did not authorize home rule. We began with as close to a clean slate as could be possible in the 1950s. But it took much effort to figure out what we should do.

Our committee represented the expanse of Alaska. Four members were from small communities: bush pilot John Cross from Kotzebue on the northwest arctic coast; Eldor Lee, a commercial fisherman from Petersburg, about 1,500 miles to the southeast; Maynard Londborg, a clergyman from Unalakleet on the Bering Sea; and Rosswog, the chairman, a merchant and city councilman from Cordova on Prince William Sound. The other three members, Doogan, Vic Rivers, and I, were from Fairbanks and Anchorage.

We spent the first weeks of the convention studying the local governance systems of the states, Canada, Australia, Finland, Switzerland, and other countries. The learning process brought together our disparate group of men as a team sharing a common understanding, as well as revealing to us what had worked or failed in other jurisdictions. We came to agree that their problems provided useful lessons, but no system we could find was a worthy model for Alaska. We would have to start from basic principles and build something new.

Stating basic ideals and values as a starting point for the constitution was inspiring and invigorating. We agreed that self-government at the local level was the basis of democracy and that the fundamental purpose of our article would be to provide for maximum local self-government. At the same time, we shared the goal of preventing the proliferation of overlapping tax-levying jurisdictions, with a single areawide unit covering an entire region, whether urban or rural.

We decided we did not want anything like conventional counties, as they were too rigid, suited neither to urban regions nor vast rural expanses. Instead, we would invent a highly flexible local government system able to adapt to different areas of the state and to changing economies and populations. And we wanted the state government to play an active role in making the local government system work.

Rarely does anyone have such an opportunity to see his or her values expressed at such a fundamental level.

Over the course of our meetings, as the weeks advanced, we slowly worked through the possibilities and problems. Could we have just one level of local government, a regional entity that would abolish towns and cities? Alaska already had about thirty cities. Politically we couldn't do away with them, and, besides, they had a purpose. Could we get rid of independent school districts and utility districts and make them a part of a broader, general, local government? That did seem possible.

As a group of seven individuals, we had arrived with some ideas based on our experiences. Together, we developed basic concepts and then definite plans. Finally, with the help of a national expert on local government who became a virtual committee member, consultant Professor Weldon Cooper of the University of Virginia, we wrote a first coherent article, which then went through a dozen committee drafts. Economist George Rogers of Juneau, the only Alaskan consultant at the convention, helped us test how our ideas would work in our various areas, including the most urbanized and most isolated regions of Alaska.

The kind of self-government we devised was a radical departure from prevailing practice. Many states had varying degrees of local home rule, allowing cities to adopt charters delineating their organizational arrangements and the powers they would exercise. Under existing statutes and court decisions, however, local governments could only do what the state authorized them to do and what had not been preempted by state action. In the spirit of statehood and removing the shackles of federal control, we wanted to provide more control at the local level.

We created a home rule system in which a local government could exercise any legislative powers not prohibited by state law or its own charter. A home rule charter is to the local government as a constitution is to a state, wherein the city or region designs its organizational structure and the functions it performs to suit local conditions, needs, and desires. Cities and regions without home rule charters function under the general laws of the state applicable to municipalities.

Our committee's largest innovation was to restrict taxation and governmental powers to only cities and the larger regional unit, which we eventually named a borough. The borough we conceived as a new kind of county adaptable to Alaska's variety of conditions. All of the state would be divided into regional boroughs based on population, geography, economy, and other factors. Boroughs could be organized, with their own governments, or could remain unorganized and overseen by the legislature until ready to take over local government functions. This system would be unique in the world.

We had invented something new in these regional units of government and we agreed early in the process that it would be confusing to call them "counties." But what should we call them?

I preferred a brand new name to match a new kind of local government: *munipuk*, combining *muni*, as in "municipal," and *puk*, the Yup'ik word for "area." As discussions proceeded, more and more names were suggested. By the time of our twenty-ninth committee meeting, with the convention half over, we had about forty ideas on the table and still hadn't chosen. According to committee minutes:

> The following names were considered by the committee: county, town, township, shire, parish, borough, precinct, burg, burgar, tundraburg, nunat, munipuk, authority, municipal district, rural municipality, division, circle, unit, areas, syzygy, couperie, ganglion, aurora, environ, locus, venue, aerie, polaris, commonwealth, poloria, mural district, rurban district, tundarea, constellation, munit, compos, compass, local unit, ruripality, political unit, district, unitality, denali, province, department, canton.

Ultimately, *borough* won the day, somewhat by default. The word had a local government sound to it, but didn't have a specific meaning in American law and the minds of most delegates. It seemed a somewhat alien term at the time, but has since become totally accepted.

My pride in the local government article endures. This unique form of government has proved as adaptable as we hoped it would. The early idea of just a single local government layer under the state has actually been realized by creating unified city-borough governments in Anchorage, Juneau, and four other areas. In other parts of Alaska, such as the Kenai Peninsula and the Matanuska and Susitna valleys, at most two levels of governance exist—the borough performs the role of a regional government and cities exist within it to provide local services. Independent districts no longer exist in Alaska.

The goal of "maximum local self-government" has been successfully realized in diverse regions. The entire Anchorage metropolitan area has a single government under its own home rule charter. A very different home rule charter provides the governing basis for the North Slope Borough, a local government the size of Minnesota along Alaska's arctic coast. That borough's charter takes into account the whaling and subsistence culture of its Iñupiat Eskimo population and, at the same time, allows for environmental oversight and taxation of the largest oilfields in North America.

Writing a strong home rule provision was one of my goals when I decided to run for convention delegate. My work at the city level and representing municipal interest before the legislature had convinced me that local home rule was a necessity in Alaska. Bob Bartlett told me home rule would be hard to get through the US Congress, a requirement under territorial status. Preparing for the convention, I worked with the National Municipal League and others to design a home rule provision for the Alaska Constitution. It has become the foundation for effective self-government for most of the people of Alaska.

And yet, important elements of the local government article still have not been implemented by the legislature. The constitution requires that the state government would divide the entire state into boroughs, organized and unorganized. Over time, the local population of each area would make its own decision whether its borough would organize. We visualized all unorganized boroughs with some self-government, through regional planning and guiding state services in the regions.

Instead, the legislature lumped all parts of Alaska not included in an organized borough into a single "unorganized borough," contrary to the regional concept of the constitution. As created by the legislature, a single unorganized borough now covers more than half of the state, an immense area totally unsuited for local government. It is larger than the entire state of Texas. It extends from one end of Alaska to the other, equivalent to the distance across the United States.

Additional detail in the constitution would have helped to implement our ideas. The local government article *does* give more specifics than the other articles, but the convention as a whole resisted including even those details. While the basic principles we laid out passed with little discussion, some specifics sparked extensive debate on the convention floor. The delegates had learned well that constitutions should be general.

For example, our committee also had to fight for our proposed state commission to determine local boundaries and an agency to assist local government organization. We narrowly won the day, mainly because our work had been so careful and these provisions seemed the minimum necessary to create a flexible governmental system that did not exist anywhere else.

But that floor fight was like a preliminary to the major debates ahead, as the convention struggled to resolve some of Alaska's most fundamental conflicts before a fast-approaching adjournment deadline.

⊰ 14 ⊱

Constitutional Battles

As the convention progressed, action shifted to the convention floor. Each article came before the delegates for action twice: once as written by a committee for discussion and amendment, and a second time after stylistic editing for insertion in the constitution. Both stages could extend over many days and bring forth deep emotions.

The Committee on the Preamble and Bill of Rights brought forward its draft in mid-December. Most sections simply restated the federal constitution's Bill of Rights. At the initial readings, the convention debated a variety of changes, but few substantive amendments succeeded. One that was approved protects the right to fair and just treatment in legislative investigation, a response to abuses of power by Senator Joseph McCarthy and others during the Red-baiting period of the early 1950s.

The preamble itself bothered a number of us. As proposed, it read:

> We, the people of the State of Alaska, grateful to Almighty God for our civil and religious liberty, seeking His continued blessing upon our endeavors to secure and transmit these liberties unimpaired to posterity, do ordain and establish this Constitution.

Some of our friends in Anchorage were furious with this "churchy" wording, but on the floor we were initially cautious in challenging the language.

Delegates Barrie White of Anchorage and Yule Kilcher, the homesteader from Homer, questioned the references to God in terms of how they might strike non-Christians, and asked whether they conflicted with the clause prohibiting establishment of religion. That day's debate ended when Frank Barr, a conservative delegate from Fairbanks, declared, "Our [federal] government is based on a religious belief and since we are writing a constitution which is to be based upon our national constitution, that is the kind it [Alaska's] should be."

The next day we took the issue on with more vigor. Vic Rivers wrote a new preamble that left out God entirely and gathered signatures of delegates to support it. However, some of us feared that with God eliminated, the convention might go back to the original version. I wrote another preamble, as did George Sundborg of Juneau and several others. Gloria suggested we put them all in a hat and choose one. I said, "Yes, but we might get the worst one," to which Eldor Lee, the fisherman delegate from Petersburg, replied, "We've already got that."

As the session progressed, we still didn't have a single version. George Sundborg took Vic Rivers's draft, his own, and mine to the gallery where Gloria was watching the proceedings, and asked her to put them all together, polish the language, and mention God once, at the appropriate spot. He passed her version around for signatures, sent it to the mimeograph, and gave it to Vic Rivers to present as his own. It now read:

> We the people of Alaska, conscious of our heritage of political,
> civil, and religious liberty, faithful to God and to those who
> founded the nation and pioneered this great land, reaffirm our
> belief in government by the consent of the governed within
> the Union of States, do ordain and establish this Constitution
> for the State of Alaska.

When the new proposed preamble came to the floor, Barrie objected to its one reference to God, saying that, although he was a churchgoer and had been educated in a church school, he thought it conflicted with the establishment of religion clause, and noted that the federal constitution contained no such reference to God. Fairbanks delegate James Doogan disagreed, speaking quietly but powerfully. You could hear a pin drop. He said mentioning God in the preamble was like saying grace before a meal or taking an oath of office using the Lord's name.

Doogan went on to point out that the convention should respect the author of the original draft preamble, Rolland Armstrong, a Presbyterian minister from Sitka, who had been delayed on a three-day excused absence. Eerily, Armstrong returned to the session at that exact moment. As Gloria wrote in a letter, "It was almost enough to make a believer out of me." Egan called a two-minute recess, the speeches ended, and the delegates voted, keeping God in the constitution by a voice vote. The new preamble Gloria had edited passed overwhelmingly.

Some people wondered if Barrie White had damaged himself politically, as the newspapers reported his stand around the state. Evangeline Atwood sent him a magazine clipping titled "Belief in God," with a note that said, "Brains are not enough. Show this to Vic Fischer, too." It didn't matter. Barrie never ran for office after the convention. And it certainly never bothered me.

One omission in the preamble bothers me today far more than the mention of God. We gave credit to the pioneers, but not to Alaska Natives and their cultures, which came long before. That flaw simply didn't come up when the preamble was considered. By the time it was pointed out, it was too late and in the wrong context to fix it.

Anchorage delegate M. R. "Muktuk" Marston, the strongest advocate for Alaska Natives among the delegates, pointed out this shortcoming during his discussion of Native land rights much later in the convention:

> In our preamble we speak of the pioneers of Alaska. Well, they are great. You see a man with boots on, a packsack, a pick and shovel, and a pan. We speak much in our convention about founding fathers—great men they were, but greater men and many more of them lived long ago before the founding fathers and before the prospectors hit Alaska, and there are thirty thousand of these people living here now in Alaska, and we have passed them by...too long.

Marston was already an Alaska legend, although he had been in the territory only since 1941. He received his nickname in a village *muktuk*-eating contest (muktuk is the skin and blubber layer of a whale, a delicacy prized by the Iñupiat and a few of us non-Natives.) As an officer in the army air corps during World War II, Marston organized hunters in 157 Alaska Native villages into fighting units called the Alaska Territorial Guard.

His speech for recognizing the Native land rights was among the most dramatic moments at the convention, as he begged us to address the inequities of government and white settlers taking over land that individual Alaska Natives had used for fish camps, trap lines, and homes under their prior, indigenous system of ownership. He read a letter from a man in Unalakleet whose fish camp had been taken over by a construction crew. Other delegates related similar stories, including Jack Coghill, who told of a Native family in his region whose age-old trap lines had been appropriated by a white newcomer.

Marston wanted to bestow property rights on Alaska Natives for their home sites and fish camps when Alaska became a state. He had presented his proposal to the resources committee, but it was rejected. When the resources article was before the convention, he submitted his idea as an amendment to the committee's proposal.

Unfortunately, his legislative skill did not equal his oratory or his moral authority. Quite a bit of time was taken up to deal with problematic legal language in his amendment so it would carry out his intent. Then ensued the longest debate of the convention, with amendments to his amendment, and amendments to the amendments.

A major point of contention was that the constitution was dedicated to the proposition that all persons are equal and entitled to equal rights and opportunities—so how could the state grant land to some and not to others? Proposals were fielded to give all Alaskans small tracts or even homesteads at the time of statehood.

After many hours of debate, the proposal suffered a long, messy death of amendments and parliamentary maneuvering. In the end, delegates never had the opportunity to vote up or down on a more practical version of Marston's idea. Resolution of Alaska Native land claims would be left to the Congress. Indeed, Congress had the responsibility and power to directly address the obligation, and the state constitution acknowledged that.

The Alaska Constitution's scant acknowledgment of Alaska Natives reflects the political thinking as well as the realities of the 1950s.

We were keenly aware of the civil rights movement. Severe discrimination had been endemic since the gold rush, with Natives barred from living in white towns, denied employment, and faced with signs on businesses that said NO NATIVES OR DOGS ALLOWED. But Governor Gruening and Native leaders moved Alaska ahead of the rest of the country in the 1940s. In 1945, the territorial legislature outlawed racial segregation.

In 1955, we conceived of civil rights as simple equality before the law. In the debate on Marston's amendment and the constitution's resources article as a whole, the concept of equality and equal access weighed against the legitimate claims of indigenous people to their traditional uses of land and resources, which to my mind were not equal to others' but superior.

That conflict between equality and justice was not yet clear. We saw little competition for fish and game in rural areas. We didn't think about what should be done when times of scarcity would force a choice between equal access and traditional subsistence uses.

Ultimately, the equality provisions of Alaska's constitution, and the failure of the legislature decades later to approve a necessary constitutional amendment, led to the loss of state management of fish and game on federal lands, comprising 60 percent of Alaska. The federal government stepped in to protect rural subsistence rights to fish and game in the 1990s. In that outcome, one of the key goals of statehood was lost.

The constitutional convention paid no attention to tribal governance. The word *tribe* never came up. Early discussions of the local government article touched briefly on village councils that provided traditional governance, mostly informally. Under territorial law, they could incorporate as fourth-class cities.[4]

The convention reflected the times. It had little specific concern for Native Alaska. At the same time, Natives had minimal interest in the convention, as it had little immediate relevance to them. Other than in Southeast Alaska communities, most Alaska Natives lived in remote, isolated villages, subsisting on wild fish and game, and interacting little with government other than the federal Bureau of Indian Affairs, which ran schools and offered minimal services.

Although 20 percent of the population was Native, only six candidates were Native out of the more than 160 who ran for delegate to the constitutional convention. Only one was elected.

The status of the convention's single Alaska Native delegate provides an example of the body's simultaneous lack of prejudice against Natives and the lack of awareness of their concerns. Delegate Frank Peratrovich, a Tlingit from Klawock, enjoyed wide respect. A former Territorial Senate President and Grand President of the Alaska Native Brotherhood, he carried himself with great dignity. Although weather kept him from attending the opening of the convention, fellow delegates elected him in his absence as first vice president, as an honor both for him personally and for Native people in general.

But Peratrovich was not as outspoken for Native rights as was Muktuk Marston, who was not Native. Frank rarely took the floor at the convention. The Alaska Native Brotherhood, formed in 1912 and based in Southeast Alaska, had emphasized English language instruction and participation in economic development that pointed more toward assimilation rather than militancy. Since the

---

4. Under the Alaska Native Claims Settlement Act (ANCSA) of 1971, all Native communities have for-profit village corporations with elected boards of directors. More than 200 Native communities now also have federally recognized tribal governments, with elected councils, and receive federal support. And more than a hundred villages are also incorporated as cities under the state government, with elected city councils, receiving state municipal revenue sharing. The triple layering of government in tiny communities often creates conflict. Villages are fortunate when even two out of three of these governing bodies cooperate.

1930s, the Southeast Tlingit and Haida Tribes had pursued their land claims through lawsuits and the US Court of Claims, not through politics.

When voting qualification provisions were before the convention, they included a Peratrovich proposal that would pave the way for more Native involvement in politics. Territorial law then allowed voting only by persons who could read and write the English language. Frank's action would give the vote to anyone who could speak English, regardless of literacy. He strongly argued that it was unfair to deny the vote to citizens who could not read when the government had, in many cases, provided no opportunity for them to learn.

Muktuk Marston supported that position as well. He said, "I think these people who lived here and inherited this country might turn around and ask us…how we vote, instead of our telling them how they can or can't vote. It is their country, and I think every man should vote and we should not stop him."

The majority of delegates agreed that it would be unconscionable for Alaska to have an English language requirement that could be used, as in the southern states, to deny citizens the right to vote. To the credit of the convention, Peratrovich's proposal passed overwhelmingly.

Convention days kept getting longer as the weeks went by, starting early in the morning and continuing, with breaks for meals, far into the night. The call for the convention allowed only seventy-five days to finish the constitution, plus a fifteen-day recess around Christmas for hearings and gathering information back home. A blackboard showed the status of each article and the number of days till adjournment. Sitting nearby, Juneau delegate Mildred Hermann daily urged delegates to keep moving along, pointing to the schedule with an autographed rolling pin, presented to her as the "nagging wife" of the convention.

The time went rapidly, especially for those of us on the Style and Drafting Committee. Our challenge was to edit each article without affecting its meaning, so the entire document would read with a single, unified voice. The task required a deep exploration of the intent of the material, as a single word choice could carry great legal significance. We dissected the constitution like anatomists seeking to understand the function and relationship of every part of a body. Through this process, our committee sometimes discovered conflicting provisions that had to be resolved by the convention. We would present the smoothly rewritten version for referral back to the original committee that drafted it, and then to the convention as a whole for approval. Finally, we edited the entire constitution together as a single document.

Our committee included many of the convention's sharpest minds and literary talents, and was chaired by delegate George Sundborg of Juneau, an author and journalist. Others were four attorneys, a businessman, clergyman, teacher, and I, a city planner. We had the assistance of an extraordinarily able and hard-working consultant, Kimbrough Owen, a constitutional expert from Louisiana. To get through the work, we divided our nine members into three-member working groups. We took turns presenting article redrafts to the convention. Still there wasn't enough time.

As the convention neared its end, with much of the floor work still unfinished, plenary sessions extended far into the night, then into Saturdays, and finally seven days a week. Our committee members did not want to miss those important deliberations, so we had to steal away at every available break to work on the language. We worked through our meals and into the small hours of the morning. The work became continuous. Toward the end, the Style and Drafting Committee would meet separately in the gallery, behind a wall of windows, listening to floor action through a sound system, while we worked over drafts.

On January 25, the sixty-fourth day, the convention met all day and into the evening. I presented the final style and drafting version of the legislative article, which involved a series of technical questions over matters such as how to count residency dates for eligibility for election. Frustration rose on the part of delegates. Some of the words that members did not like were unchanged from the language they had previously approved. We were rehashing weeks of debate.

Under convention rules, substantive changes at this point required a two-thirds vote, while a simple majority could approve stylistic changes. The complex parliamentary situation added to the time and difficulty of the session. Delegates began skirmishing over whose turn it was to speak. New amendments began to draw audible groans from the body. After dinner, work continued till we finished with a series of substantive amendments of the legislative article. At the slow pace we progressed, it appeared impossible the convention could finish on time.

That same evening, we turned to the Preamble and Bill of Rights, which paralleled the part of the US Constitution with which Americans have the deepest knowledge and strongest emotional attachment. The committee that drafted the article had followed the federal model closely, even including obsolete material such as the prohibition on quartering of soldiers in private homes.

English teacher Katherine Nordale led the convention through the style and drafting revisions, explaining, "As you read the thing out loud, it seems to me every once in a while a sentence sort of comes out of the Bill of Rights as it originally was written that doesn't seem to quite fit the tone of the rest of the article, and we were attempting to smooth the language as much as possible." But it soon became clear that many delegates were uncomfortable with revisions to these cherished words and wanted to go back to the original text.

Barrie White didn't like the committee's redraft of the preamble that Gloria had edited and that we had weeks before fought for on the floor. The newly revised version said:

> We the people of Alaska, grateful to God and to those who founded our nation and pioneered this great land, in order to secure and transmit to succeeding generations our heritage of political, civil, and religious liberty within the Union of States, do ordain and establish this constitution for the State of Alaska.

The changes fulfilled the Style and Drafting Committee's mandate: the language was simpler and tracked better. But Barrie disagreed with the deletion from the preamble of the phrase attesting to "our belief in government by the consent of the governed," which had been moved elsewhere into the bill of rights. Some suspected Barrie was somehow trying to downgrade the mention of God. As the evening grew later and testier, he made a motion to cast aside the committee's work on the preamble and revert to the previous version.

That motion failed, but it opened the floodgates. Delegates called for wholesale reversal of the committee's work on one section of the bill of rights after another. Following some banter and complaints about the time we were taking in reworking everything, John McNees of Nome tossed a verbal grenade into the session. He said much more time would be needed and that it was all the fault of the style and drafting committee. He declared he had given up on the committee days earlier and from now on intended to keep advocating to discard its work.

A member of the committee, Ed Davis, rose to respond to McNees with a point of personal privilege, a type of statement that is not recorded in convention proceedings. Davis was a serious, quiet, and highly regarded lawyer and civic leader from Anchorage. He commanded great respect on the floor of the convention. Exploding with anger, he explained the process of stylistic revision, and then said that if the convention had lost confidence in the Style and Drafting Committee, we should be discharged.

Others spoke up to defend the committee. Out of respect to Davis, John Hellenthal of Anchorage tried to withdraw an amendment he had offered. But others objected to the withdrawal and kept up the march to delete style and drafting's work—without success, but with some close votes. Emotions got ever hotter, late into the night, as the hour passed when the bus was available to take delegates home to Fairbanks, until Bill Egan tried to cut the tension, saying:

The Chair would like to announce that the temperature is now about 40 degrees below, and, if the delegates have their cars out there, they probably should start them in order that they will start. There has been a sudden drop in the temperature—outside. (Laughter) The Convention will come to order.

As the hour reached midnight and motions to discard the committee's work continued, Ed Davis made a formal motion to abolish the Style and Drafting Committee, seconded by another member of the committee.

Seaborn Buckalew, an Anchorage attorney, responded, "We have been working hard and our nerves are a little shattered and we're getting tired, and things sort of disagree with us a little, but I think that is the cause of this whole furor...I don't think that there is anybody that has lost any confidence in Ed Davis or anybody that are members of his committee."

Egan ruled Davis's motion out of order. Instead of disbanding the committee, Davis offered to take the entire article back for more work. The convention adjourned for the night, with delegates sharing cars and cabs to get back to Fairbanks. The next day we resumed voting on the preamble and bill of rights. After all the conflict, the words ended up in the final constitution almost exactly as the style and drafting committee had proposed.

Work went on around the clock at the end, but we finished the whole constitution on time.

During the dramatic closing ceremonies, our emotions poured out. The sleepless nights and the stress of last-minute work heightened everyone's feelings. One delegate, R. E. Robertson of Juneau, walked out and refused to sign the constitution. But most of us felt enormous pride in our accomplishment and warmth for one another.

The experience we had passed through bonded us like brothers and sisters. With the document finished and signed, we were overwhelmed by the magnitude of what we had done and by the reach of our collective imprint on the future.

The final, seventy-sixth day of the convention included many resolutions of thanks—to the university, to the talented *Fairbanks Daily News-Miner* reporter Florence Douthit who covered the convention, to the wives, even to the cleaning staff—and heartfelt and humorous remarks, plus details about turning in receipts.

We paid the final and greatest tribute to Bill Egan, whom all now recognized as "the father of the constitution." We had subscribed to have a portrait painted of him, and gave it as a surprise, with a resolution, on the final day. James Hurley of Palmer, Katie's future husband, made the presentation, saying, "I think this occasion is somewhat similar to a group that has been through a major battle. We have earned a respect for our leader that can only come from having gone through all of the trials and tribulations of presenting to the future State of Alaska the document that they will live by for many years."

All this was too much for Bill, who said, through tears, "All I can say is that I certainly appreciate it. I will never forget a single one of you. You have done a wonderful job." Everyone was crying. First Vice President Peratrovich called a recess for us to shake hands and collect ourselves.

The final speaker of the convention was Earnest Collins, whom I had once perceived as such an ancient fossil. He had participated in the first territorial legislature, which had set up its government much as we were doing now for the state. He was one of three from that body still living—just as today, as I write this more than fifty years later, there are only three of us left alive from among all my friends and colleagues at the constitutional convention.

"Bear with me just a moment," Collins said. "I realize that this has been a great emotional scene. It brings back to my mind the organization of the First Territorial Legislature." He continued:

> Little did I think that forty-three years from that date that there would be only three surviving members of that legislature. In all those years that friendship has become stronger and closer between the three of us, and I can see here today that the association and the friendship...within this convention is going to bind the personalities of each and every one of you, that will endure for time to come when we enjoy the statehood of Alaska...Little did I think at that time, forty-three years hence that I would be a member of a convention that was drawn here by the people of the Territory of Alaska to draft a constitution for the first statehood, and I say to you, it has been a wonderful experience, and as years go by the younger members will remember the meeting of the individuals of this convention, and it will be cemented in friendship that will endure to help carry on the workings of the future State of Alaska.

With that, the Alaska Constitutional Convention adjourned, February 6, 1956.

⇥ 15 ⇤

Fatherhood and Statehood

Gloria and I wanted to start a family after I got out of the army in 1946 but soon learned we were very unlikely to conceive a child. We began thinking about adoption while I was still working on my planning degree at MIT. After we moved to Alaska in 1950, we seriously sought a child, but it was difficult and we went through many twists and turns.

We tried to pursue adoption through a social service agency, but Alaska adoption officials kept telling us there were no children suitable for us. After several years of trying, I finally had a confrontation with an adoption bureaucrat. He said a child's background must match the adoptive parents'. We had always insisted that we were nonreligious and didn't care about the race, ethnicity, social class, or intelligence of our child's progenitors. But the agency decided that, as college-educated Jews, only the child of Jewish intellectuals would suit us.

We knew no such child would be available in Alaska, so we gave up on the social welfare establishment. Instead, I passed word to lawyers and doctors in Anchorage that we were searching for a child to adopt. We did not have to wait long.

In early 1956, Anchorage attorney George McLaughlin, one of our neighbors and a fellow constitutional convention delegate, told me he had arranged the adoption of a Greek child for another couple, and he would help us, too. In Greece, the Ahepa Refugee Relief Committee was seeking homes for kids orphaned by a civil war and for other needy children.

We studied a book of children's photographs from Ahepa. We chose a seven-year-old boy and mentally bonded with him, only to feel heartbroken when he instead went to another family. That summer, we picked another face from an Ahepa book—a little, round-faced girl of seven months with jet-black eyes. And then we waited, banishing hope.

Since quitting my job with the city of Anchorage in 1955, I had worked as a planning consultant, forming a partnership with Ed Crittenden called Alaska Planning Associates. It was all very convenient. His architecture office was just uphill from his house, which was just uphill from mine.

Most of my work came from the Alaska Housing Authority, which was the urban renewal agency for the entire territory. I planned large, complex projects to remove obsolete and substandard buildings and replace them with modern facilities, housing and businesses, working with local governments in Fairbanks, Anchorage, Sitka, and other towns. We also worked on city planning projects and major subdivision designs.

In January 1957, Gloria and I had just arrived in Ketchikan to discuss an urban renewal project with the city, when we received a message from George McLaughlin that the beautiful black-eyed girl we had chosen, now 14 months old, would be ours. We tried to contain our excitement but failed, and immediately began trying on names. We settled on Susie, with hopes she would come from Greece to be in our arms within a few weeks.

George said we should fly back to Anchorage immediately to complete the adoption. Time was short. Bringing Susie into the country depended on the Refugee Relief Act of 1953, which could be used only until the end of January, just two weeks away.

The next morning, a Thursday, George called us at the Ingersoll Hotel to say another lawyer friend from the convention, Tom Stewart, could probably get the papers through faster in Juneau. Sure enough, Tom got a hearing before a judge there on Saturday, and the papers were on their way to Greece and Washington, DC, on Monday.

At the time, we were moving into an apartment in Juneau for the legislative session, in which I would serve as a member of the Territorial House of Representatives.

My decision to run for the House had come a year earlier, during the campaign for ratification of the constitution in the spring of 1956. Ratification would be on the same ballot as the party primaries in April. Being a primary candidate would give me an added platform to speak in behalf of the constitution during campaign meetings with chambers of commerce, labor groups, service clubs, and the general public. Seventeen convention delegates followed the same strategy, and all but three made it into the legislature.

We also campaigned energetically for ratification through Operation Statehood. Our approach emphasized the excitement of the convention and the praise the document had received nationally, which reflected well on Alaska and stood as a point of pride. We didn't engage with details. We held the constitution up as a great civic accomplishment that represented statehood itself, underlining the boost a strong "yes" vote would give to the movement.

At first we feared the campaign would fail to bring out many voters, as had the election for convention delegates, because of the lack of controversy. But a primary challenger to Delegate to Congress Bob Bartlett helped with that. Peter Wood of Juneau tried to bring attention to himself by attacking the constitution, the convention, and the delegates with broad, wild charges. Given his lack of credibility and the viciousness with which he attacked me and some of the others, he was just the opponent we needed.

The constitution passed by a ratio of 2 to 1. The convention's ordinances also won big victories, calling for the abolishing of fish traps and adoption of the so-called Tennessee Plan, the idea of electing senators and a representative, even without statehood, to show our resolve and to lobby Congress.[5]

The ratification vote again brought a flood of journalistic and academic praise, such as a *Washington News* editorial stating, "Those who have had their doubts that the Territory of Alaska has achieved political maturity and is ready to take its place as a State of the Union need only look at the returns from Tuesday's election."

That the Alaska Constitution is exceptional is not just the opinion of a proud old man. Experts at the time and since have noted our constitution's brevity and clarity and the way in which it avoided difficulties created by the charters of other states.

Most important in Alaska's history, the architecture of our constitution makes the governor and legislature of each generation strong enough to address problems facing the state in their times, with the accountability to answer to voters for their results. By simplifying government and concentrating authority, the constitution takes excuses away from elected leaders. With the power to succeed comes the inability to evade blame for failures.

The constitution also concentrates authority by giving as much power as possible to the present rather than the past. We had no idea where Alaska was

---

5. The Tennessee Plan delegates sent by Alaska—Egan, Gruening, and Ralph Rivers—were not a major factor in bringing about statehood. They got in Bob Bartlett's way more than accomplishing anything.

going and didn't try to predetermine solutions to unforeseen problems. And we endeavored not to limit future Alaskans in addressing their own times as well. The prohibition on dedication of funds is an example of this philosophy—the lawmakers of each period would be free to spend their money as they saw fit, but could not decide the priorities of legislatures to come.

With these qualities, the Alaska Constitution reflects the values of those who wrote it. The central idea relied on good citizens. Our structure, with strong leaders directly accountable to voters, could succeed only with the diligence of citizens actively addressing their roles. With our faith in democracy, we trusted Alaskans to uphold that responsibility. They have done so to varying degrees, yet I remain optimistic and would not choose another system.

The constitution itself and the strong ratification vote created new momentum for statehood, just as we had hoped. But some other events at the time also were critically important.

Our powerful opponent, Interior Secretary Douglas McKay, resigned in May 1956. He was replaced by Fred Seaton, a Nebraska newspaper publisher who was a friend both of Bob Atwood and of *Fairbanks Daily News-Miner* publisher C. W. Snedden. The new secretary strongly supported statehood. On Snedden's recommendation, Seaton hired as Interior's top lawyer a former US attorney from Fairbanks—Ted Stevens, who became a key political and technical operator for statehood legislation in Washington.

———

Seaton also helped birth Alaska's oil industry, which became the key to the economic case for statehood, as oil revenue was the only credible source to fund the future state's expanded government. The oil company Richfield had filed oil leases on the Kenai Peninsula within the Kenai National Moose Range. The wilderness lands were closed to drilling or additional leasing, but Seaton opened up an area on the Swanson River leased by Richfield and a group of Anchorage businessmen. In 1957, Richfield made Alaska's biggest oil find to date on those lands.

The Anchorage businessmen called themselves the Spit and Argue Club. They included some of the city fathers surrounding Elmer Rasmuson and doing business with his National Bank of Alaska. (The competing group of businessmen in town was led by the Cuddy family, owners of First National Bank of Anchorage.) Bob Atwood, Elmer's brother-in-law, had bought the *Anchorage Times* with a loan from the bank. Their club had a special lunch table in the Elks Club dining room, located on Third Avenue at G Street.

John "Mickey" McManamin, owner of the Army-Navy Store on Fourth Avenue, was a Spit and Argue Club member. A clerk in Mickey's store, Locke

Jacobs, would camp out in the Bureau of Land Management land office, watching oil leasing activity. As the story goes, he saw an opportunity to lease lands around Richfield's area, alerted the club members, and they grabbed up the adjoining leases. It proved a very successful business move.

Federal oil leasing in those days had a noncompetitive phase that let people of ordinary means get into the oil business. In areas where no oil had been located as yet, the first person to file for a lease and pay a relatively small fee could receive a lease with the obligation to pay royalties if oil were found.

But the law limited the number of leases any one person or company could obtain, so the oil companies were tempted to put up fraudulent "straw men" to file as stand-ins, later buying the leases from them, as if in an unrelated transaction. For a century, the scheme was a common and well-known style of theft of public wealth in the west.

I didn't attend the Spit and Argue Club lunches, but I knew the members well, including Mickey McManamin, who was a member of the Planning Commission. One day, while Secretary McKay was still in office and the Kenai Moose Range still closed to oil exploration, Mickey took me aside and said, "Vic, a group of us are going to file on some oil leases. And we've discussed and agreed we would invite you in."

Mickey laid out the opportunity for leases next to Richfield's tracts. Locke Jacobs was putting it together, and Elmer, Bob, and several others I knew were involved. I told him I wasn't sure I would want to participate, but in any case I did not have money to pay for oil leases. But Mickey said Elmer was ready to lend me as much as I might want to put in, and that the profits would be quick and certain.

The offer made me uncomfortable, and I said I would talk it over with Gloria. That night we agreed that this deal was pure speculation and had an evil odor to it. Buying in would violate our basic values and we wouldn't do that, regardless of the potential reward. The next day I told Mickey that I would not participate.

I have never regretted my decision. I might have gotten very rich, as did those who participated, but I never cared that much about money. Besides, I might have gotten fat and died years ago.

I didn't know at the time, and learned only when it was documented decades later by David Postman of the *Anchorage Daily News* that the deal pulled off by the Spit and Argue Club was probably fraudulent.

The leases were issued during a leasing moratorium in the Moose Range. Richfield made huge deposits in National Bank of Alaska at the same time Elmer was offering loans to his friends to buy the leases. And he bought many himself. The agreements the group made, transferring the leases to Richfield, had a special provision—the company would repay their lease fees if the deal didn't work out.

In view of all that, it is more than likely that Richfield actually advised Locke Jacobs and the Spit and Argue Club of the opportunity to lease the adjoining lands.

———

My ambitions were more modest, including in politics.

After the April 1956 election ratified the constitution and gave me the Democratic nomination for the Territorial House, much of my purpose for running was achieved. Other than funding the Tennessee Plan representatives to Congress, the ability of the Alaska legislature to carry forward the constitutional convention's work would be modest.

As during the convention delegate election, I was running from southcentral Alaska, one of the four huge judicial divisions. During the general election campaign, the Democratic Party chartered a DC-4 to carry candidates campaigning on the ticket, led by Bob Bartlett. We flew to Kenai, Homer, Kodiak, King Salmon, and Dillingham, the larger towns in the district. When the plane landed, we would fan out rather than moving as a crowd of candidates. I knew people in each of the towns and enjoyed catching up with them.

One of my few difficulties as a candidate arose from my name. Helen Fischer appeared next to me on the alphabetical ballot. She had served with me at the convention and was secretary of Operation Statehood. Although we were unrelated, people who didn't know us assumed we were married.

Once I dealt with the problem in a public way. At a big campaign party in Dillingham—with a lot of drinking—an old acquaintance approached and said he couldn't vote for me, with my wife also serving and both drawing legislative pay and per diem. I knew Helen was right behind me, so I declared in a loud voice, "Oh, Helen Fischer is not my wife. Why, she's old enough to be my mother." Helen spun around and began beating on my shoulders with her fists. The incident made a great story, which quickly spread and settled the question, at least in that community.

In the absence of strong issues, my campaign speech emphasized values. It matches up remarkably well with a speech I might make today. After denouncing wire tapping, which had been a hot topic of debate at the convention, I went on to say,

> In addition to upholding the civil rights of the individual, I
> believe that we also have the duty to promote his other basic
> rights: his right to make a decent wage, to receive an edu-
> cation, to attain a minimum standard of living, and others.
> Equality of economic opportunity is a basic right. Where this

right is abridged, be it by the use of fish traps or through racial discrimination, it is the duty of the legislature to take all possible steps to correct the abuse.

My actual experience as a legislator fell far short of such idealism. The session lasted only sixty days, and federal law controlled much of what we would like to legislate. Unlike the convention, which had been public spirited and deliberative, the legislature worked under the manipulation of party bosses and lobbyists for various interests, especially, in the case of Democrats, labor, gambling, and liquor.

One Monday in February, a furor erupted when Juneau's *Daily Alaska Empire* published a column by Bob Kederick reporting a rumor, in the vaguest of terms, that a certain legislator received a certain sum in connection with a liquor bill.

Speaker of the House Dick Greuel, a Democrat from Fairbanks, expressed outrage at such slander and announced to the House he would appoint a committee to investigate where Kederick had obtained the information. I rose and suggested that rather than the source of the information, the veracity of the allegation needed to be investigated. So Greuel appointed me to the three-member committee chaired by Bob Ziegler of Ketchikan.

The investigative committee invited Kederick to a closed hearing. He came accompanied by an attorney and refused to disclose the source of his information about the alleged crime. With that, chairman Ziegler adjourned the hearing, reporting to the House that Kederick would not provide the requested information and that the committee's work was done.

To my disgust, the committee's only interest was to criticize Kederick and label him "irresponsible," not to uncover possible corruption. I submitted a minority report, requesting that a law enforcement agency be asked to find the facts behind the reported rumor, or that the committee continue investigating it. And that was that.

I ran into a similar attitude while pursuing my primary legislative initiative, a bill to establish an Alaska Department of Highways. At that time, a hodgepodge of agencies managed Alaska's roads, with a politically elected highway engineer overseeing only a small mining access program.

Our roads were largely unpaved and poorly maintained, and I knew from my work with the League of Alaskan Cities that a professional highway department would qualify Alaska for more federal money. I also saw this modernization measure as a step toward statehood.

I served on the House Resource Committee, and committee chair Irene Ryan agreed to have the highway proposal introduced as a committee bill if I would have it drafted. With help from Delegate Bob Bartlett and the Bureau of Public Roads, I came up with a measure that met federal-aid criteria and was up to the latest national standards. When the draft was ready, Irene said that in recognition of my efforts it should be introduced with just my name as sponsor rather than the committee's.

The highway bill came before the House and I made a brief statement about its purpose. No one else spoke up, so without debate, the members proceeded to vote. To my amazement, the bill was defeated by a single vote.

My own party had shot down my bill. Even Irene Ryan had voted against it. I was dumbfounded. Seeing the shock on my face, Clint Gray of Nome gave "notice of reconsideration," which meant the measure could be voted on again the next day.

It was clear the defeat of my bill had been wired. But why?

In the corridor outside the chambers right after the vote, Democratic Party boss and liquor lobbyist Alex Miller explained. The elected highway engineer was a member of the Alcoholic Beverage Control Board, along with the governor and three other elected territorial officials. My bill would eliminate the position of the highway engineer and provide for a qualified professional rather than a politician to manage the new highway department. Miller didn't like that. Changing membership could loosen his control of the alcohol board. He could count on the existing board membership to do the bidding of the liquor interests. To keep it that way, he lined up House Democrats to kill my bill.

I was angry, but I also saw who had the power, the votes. I revised the bill to allow the current highway engineer to head the newly created department for the remaining two years of his term. The next day, the bill passed the House unanimously, with the liquor lobby's clout safeguarded.

I never got a clear answer why Irene Ryan and the rest of the party leadership had secretly set me up for defeat rather than asking me to change the bill in advance. I'm convinced they wanted to punish me for earlier seeking to investigate what special interest (liquor!) was bribing which legislator.

The high point of my otherwise dispiriting time in the legislature came on a much more important issue: abolition of the death penalty. It became my privilege to cosponsor that bill, as I sat next to Warren Taylor, who drafted it and carried it to passage.

I knew and treasured Warren as a friend from the constitutional convention and before. He was an attorney from Fairbanks with thirty years' experience, a gentleman with courtly manners and an old-school gift for formal oratory. As he was known for solving his clients' legal problems through legislation, I sometimes resisted when he leaned over to ask my support on bills. But when I needed his help on a local government bill, he fought my battle with skill and panache, and we became firm allies.

I needed no convincing to cosponsor Warren's death-penalty bill. I had met Roger Baldwin, founder of the American Civil Liberties Union, before coming to Alaska and briefly served on the ACLU national committee. But Warren Taylor had a much deeper knowledge. He had been involved in death-penalty cases and had seen a man hung, which he described as one of the worst experiences of his life.

The moment for the bill may have been right because of the optimism and idealism of the new constitution and coming statehood. Although murder was common in Alaska, it tended to occur in drunken fights that threatened only the young, transient element of society. In the stable middle class people felt safe. We didn't lock our doors or cars. We had no fresh memory of heinous crimes and no one had been executed for seven years.

When the time came, Warren rose and gave the greatest speech I ever heard in the legislature, an oration worthy of Clarence Darrow. He went through the history of the death penalty in Alaska, the eight men hung, only two of whom were white Americans, although most murders were committed by whites. He related the shoddy evidence and procedures that sent the men to death, in cases that no jury would convict today.

And he re-created the scene of the defendant standing before the judge, the judge intoning: "The jury has found you guilty...and I sentence you to hang by your neck until you are dead...dead...dead." With each case he described, Warren repeated these words, drawing out the final syllables to hang in the air. The House was utterly silent, without a breath.

Sadly, there is no record of that monumental speech besides the memories carried by a few of us. The House did not record floor sessions in those days, the clerk's notes were general, and Warren, incredibly, was speaking without a written text or even notes.

The House debate lasted a day and a half, before a packed gallery. The bill passed by a vote of fourteen to five. Warren and I met with individual senators to make our case and won by a large margin there as well. Alaska has never executed a prisoner since.

Gloria and I had expected that she would have to leave Juneau during the legislative session to meet our new daughter and bring her to Alaska. But as the session neared its end, we heard from George McLaughlin that the State Department had refused the child entry into the country.

Tom Stewart happened to be in Washington and made inquiries for us, including meeting a top State Department official he knew from college. We learned that although our papers had made it in time, the Greek court had taken weeks more to complete the adoption and get the necessary documents back to Washington, by which time the legal window had closed.

Our frustration verged on desperation. We needed the law that had expired. Under the normal immigration quota, our daughter would be ready for marriage by the time we could finally get her out of a Greek orphanage to Alaska.

We pulled every string we could find, including contacting my father's many friends in Congress and the administration. In June, Bob Bartlett introduced a private bill to get Susie into the country, H.R. 8176, "A bill for the relief of Yannoula (Gianoula) M. Lapa," using her proper Greek name. But the bill sat dormant while Congress worked on legislation to address the situation for all the thousands of families in our situation.

In the meantime, another child fell in our lap, through an Anchorage lawyer who had been a classmate at the University of Wisconsin. He told us about a young married couple temporarily in Anchorage, his cousin and her husband. She was pregnant, but they were not ready to raise a child because they still had years of college ahead of them.

The couple had considered potential parents for their child and specifically chose us to raise the baby. That had taken place the previous November, but we had learned not to hope. Then, one April day, Greg arrived from the hospital at our door, a big, healthy, happy infant. He brought pure delight into our life.

My father arrived on a previously planned visit when Greg was only a few weeks old. We were too busy and tired to clean the house or set up any special get-togethers, so Louis got to experience real family life for once. I wrote my mother, "It's done much good, he even wrings out dirty diapers in the toilet! For the first time has fed a baby from a bottle."

My consulting work slowed down considerably, so we spent much of the summer of 1957 camping. Gloria washed diapers and baby bottles by the campfire. Greg was fine as long as we kept a mosquito net around him. But we were depleting our savings. In October, I started a job as assistant executive director with the Alaska Housing Authority, the largely federally funded agency that had been our main consulting client. My principal responsibility was for urban renewal and planning for cities in Alaska.

Immigration legislation allowing our daughter to come to us finally passed and was signed by the president that fall. But she still didn't arrive until January

1958, a year after we had adopted her, and almost two years since we began the process of trying to adopt a Greek child.

The original picture of a seven-month-old baby from which we'd chosen her and named her our black-eyed Susie was completely out of date. Now she was two years and two months. We instead chose to call her Yonni, based on her Greek name.

She was a toddler, chattering in Greek as if not realizing we couldn't understand her, and oscillating in her emotions from subdued to happy to furious. The shock of adjustment was traumatic for her and for us. Yonni's screaming, biting tantrums were almost constant. She attacked Greg, although he already outweighed her at only nine months. She slapped Bob Bartlett across the face.

Fortunately, this lasted only a few months. By spring, she began to feel more comfortable in her new home, proving to be an active and creative child.

We completed our family later in November 1958, when a doctor friend asked if we were still interested in adopting. He had a patient, an Alaska Native woman, who was giving birth in Anchorage and needed to give up the child. We thought about it only briefly before deciding to adopt one more, and Joe came to us shortly as a newborn. Greg was now seventeen months and Yonni three years old.

It was a busy but joyous time. I was traveling extensively and doing interesting work, but life at home was the focus. Next door, Ed and Kit Crittenden and their six children were constantly part of our lives, as were Charlie and Molly Tryck and their kids, Cliff and Lucy Groh, Roger and Ghislaine Cremo, Barrie and Daphne White, and Drs. John and Betsy Tower (and John was everyone's pediatrician, too).

We were the "station wagon set." All these friends and others joined in big, noisy picnics and holiday parties, as well as adult parties and dinners.

Yonni, Greg, and Joe were my playmates. Whenever I arrived home, I was soon down on the floor with them. Although temper tantrums and colic certainly occurred, it's the happiness that enveloped us and fun with the kids that I remember most of all. We added two bedrooms as the family expanded. The new rooms were four feet down from the main part of the house. Alongside the wide descending steps, I built a slide made of Masonite, which the children used in an unending circle of frenetic up-and-down activity.

We lived at the edge of town, with the whole undeveloped Chester Creek valley below. The groups of kids wandered freely through the woods and down to the creek, where they fished as they grew a bit older. Most summer weekends were spent at our Lake Louise cabin or camping elsewhere in Alaska. Life was good.

That same happy year, our dream of Alaska statehood was finally realized. Rather than a single dramatic event moving the issue, a series of pieces fell into place, helped by the force of overwhelming popularity built over years of effort.

In 1957, Bob Bartlett had persuaded Speaker of the House Sam Rayburn and Senate Majority Leader Lyndon Johnson to support statehood. (Bob later told me that Johnson extracted a promise to support him for president.)

At the same time, according to recent research by historian Terrence Cole, Ted Stevens played a critical role in addressing Eisenhower's desire to partition Alaska with a vast military reservation removing the northern and western part. Stevens came up with a provision in the statehood bill to allow the president to withdraw military land if needed for defense later rather than excluding it from the start—a provision that, in fact, would never be needed and mainly served to mollify Eisenhower's concern about national security.

When the president included Alaska statehood in his 1958 State of the Union address, the dam clearly was breaking. Opposition remained only from the South, because of the civil rights issue. The Virginian who chaired the House Rules Committee wouldn't allow the Alaska statehood bill to the floor, but Rayburn finally decided to break it loose, using an esoteric rule that gave statehood legislation special privilege. Debate began on amendments on the House floor on May 21, 1958.

I happened to be in Washington on business involving my Alaska Housing Authority job. As the debate continued on May 26, I dropped by Bartlett's office to visit with my friends, his long-time aides, Mary Lee Council and Marjorie Smith. By luck, while we were talking word came that the vote on the bill had begun.

We walked together down the long marble corridors from the House office building to the House Chamber in the Capitol and up into the gallery. I felt like a bundle of nerves with the tension of the moment, and I could tell Mary Lee and Marjorie were totally on edge, hoping for the moment to come that we had anticipated for so many years. We had made it this far before and failed.

On the floor, as the vote progressed, we watched Bob, who knew how to count each vote as it came in. At a certain moment, he turned to us in the gallery and raised his arms in a signal of victory. With an incredible release of tension and a huge burst of happiness, the three of us exploded in tears and hugs of celebration, letting ourselves go as far as was appropriate in the congressional gallery. Then we waited quite some time as the rest of the members straggled in to complete the vote.

Back in Bob's office the celebration recommenced with hugs, handshakes, and phone calls. And then came the worry about what would happen in the Senate. We had the votes, but if the bill were amended it could become bogged down in a conference committee and die by endless procedural moves. Bartlett and others met with senate leaders and won their agreement to abandon their own bill and pass the House bill without amendment, removing the need for a conference committee.

I was working in Juneau as the senate debate progressed in late June. Plans had been simmering for a huge celebration in Anchorage and I was antsy about missing it, so I made plane reservations for Monday, June 30, and each of the following two days. On Monday, I dropped in to see Bill Tobin, the Associated Press bureau chief in Juneau, to find out what was happening in DC. He told me the statehood bill was about to pass, so I boarded the first flight to Anchorage and got home even before Gloria received the message that I was coming.

Gloria's letter to Markoosha describes what happened next better than I can:

> He had no sooner gotten in the door than we heard the sirens go off. We rushed to the radio and turned it up. The Star Spangled Banner was playing, so we knew the bill had passed. I'm sure the kids thought we were completely nuts. We shouted and laughed and cried and danced around with each other and the kids. We grabbed up some clothes and rushed downtown to be on hand for the ceremony pinning the 49th star on the giant Elks flag to be draped over the Federal Building. There were lots of people headed towards Fourth Avenue just like ourselves, and everyone was smiling and blowing horns. Greg and Yonni were right in the spirit of the thing and when the flag was lowered from the roof of the Federal Building over the side, they clapped and shouted hooray for the flag just like everyone else. After milling around downtown for a while, we went down to the *Times* office to watch the extra roll off… It was a thrill to see the papers plop down with the big headline.

The enormous headline that day read, simply, "WE'RE IN."

Gloria and I ate dinner that night with many friends at the Chart Room restaurant atop the Anchorage Westward Hotel and then met at the huge bonfire on the Park Strip. We watched the scene from the roof of Ed Crittenden's new architecture office on Ninth Avenue with many of the people we'd worked with on statehood for so many years, including Roger Cremo.

Cowboys on their horses pranced around the fire, including my friend Peanuts Main. People milled and danced by the firelight. Some twenty thousand were there. And the parties went on into the night. Ours was at the Crittenden's next door, ending only with breakfast at the home of other friends, Corinne and Harry Blair.

The political talk began before the bonfire embers had cooled. With elections that fall, we would choose our first governor, a state legislature, two US senators, and a congressman. The same friends I had worked with for a decade moved quickly to the top. We were to elect Bill Egan as governor, Bob Bartlett and Ernest Gruening as US senators, and Ralph Rivers to the US House of Representatives.

There was wide expectation that I would run for the state legislature. Feeling confident that I could be elected, I wrestled with the idea myself, despite not having enjoyed my service in the territorial legislature.

I wrote to my father explaining my decision to turn down a chance to run:

> My job is such that I would have had to resign. This I couldn't do as the kids like to eat and there are no other professional opportunities here. So I will sit it out now; there are many years ahead.

I was thirty-four years old.

Making Connections

⇥ 16 ⇤

Seeking Challenges

A letdown followed statehood. Politics returned to the more mundane battle over day-to-day trivialities. Personally, I became restless and dissatisfied with routine work.

When I set about writing this book, I had to dredge up these feelings. I had forgotten about the letdown until I reread my old letters. In October 1959, I wrote to Bob Bartlett, "The tremendous effort that went into statehood has been dormant since its achievement. I believe that in part this is due to lack of anything else even approaching the significance or imaginativeness of that goal." Later I let him know, "Am getting fed up with a multitude of piddling little local projects, keep having a hard time holding enthusiasm."

Bob and I corresponded constantly, a habit we continued until his death in 1968. He exchanged letters with many Alaska friends, keeping up with political gossip and private opinions out of a sincere interest that contributed to his great skill as a senator.

Bob cared about the people around him. His colleagues liked and admired him. In the nation's capital, he would strike up conversation with tourists or elevator operators with consummate natural politeness and curiosity, always stepping aside to let others go ahead. His knowledge and humble personality made him hugely effective in Congress. As the sole nonvoting delegate from our territory, he was said to have passed more legislation than any congressman with a vote.

Among the other friends from the statehood movement with whom I kept constantly in touch was Burke Riley, Bob's son-in-law. In the 1957 territorial legislature, I had helped Burke in an unsuccessful bid to become House Speaker and I sat next to him in the back row during the session (with Warren Taylor on my other side). Burke became Bill Egan's top aide in the governor's office, which often put us in touch on issues about how the new state was being organized.

Reading through my papers has reminded me how closely my friendships and experience tied me in with the people setting up the state government. Colleagues from the constitutional convention, the statehood movement, and the territorial legislature held positions in the new Alaska legislature, administration, and governor's office. Other, younger people, including Joe Josephson and Hugh Gellert, came on the scene and treated me as a mentor and elder statesman (although I wasn't yet forty). My advice was frequently requested and I enjoyed giving it, in long, detailed letters, combining my view on the need for planning with details on the political situation.

The state had a rocky start under Egan's governorship. First, he became seriously ill and was rushed away for a hospital stay that lasted the first months of his administration. When he returned to the capital, he didn't initially take on the job with the broad view needed for the chief executive of a state, getting caught up in minutia. He groused to state officials about using the phone too much rather than saving money by writing letters. Meanwhile, the new state faced daunting problems.

Our euphoria over gaining statehood had blinded us somewhat to the challenges we would face. Besides taking over many functions from the federal government—from roads to schools to fish and game—the state would have to provide a far better level of service to meet citizens' basic expectations.

The court system is an example. We had used the federal courts only, which provided merely four judges in the entire territory. As a state we would need an entire court system, with district, superior, and supreme court judges. The three-member Alaska Supreme Court alone was almost as large as our former federal court system.

The 1959 legislature created a five-member Alaska State Planning Commission to prepare a capital improvement program for the new state's first six years. Charlie Tryck was chairman, and it included several other friends. George Rogers and I each turned down the job of undertaking the project for the commission, but we agreed to do it jointly. (I also continued as assistant director of the newly renamed Alaska State Housing Authority.)

Putting us together proved fortuitous. Given the short time allowed, it's doubtful anyone but we, two old friends, an economist and a planner, could have managed the job. I worked with the governor and other officials to project school, transportation, and other infrastructure needs. It was a difficult task, for at the time few agencies looked beyond a two-year time horizon.

As Alaska's preeminent economist, George had fiscal analysis skills that were key. He showed how the Alaska economy had slowed with a reduction in military Cold War spending. Nothing appeared on the horizon to replace those jobs or tax revenues. Meanwhile, the statehood transitional funds provided by Congress were dwindling.

Our report, issued on the eve of the second legislative session, in January 1960, said:

> While the future holds tremendous promise, Alaska is entering a very difficult stage. Truly, a financial crisis looms large...Beyond 1961, the State will not have sufficient funds to provide capital facilities, it may not have sufficient funds to meet regular operating costs.

Newspapers across the state ran our prediction of financial crisis in apocalypse-sized headlines. Governor Egan said we were far too pessimistic. Legislators blasted our conclusions as unrealistically negative. Editorials argued for a much rosier future.

Reality sank in a year later, by the time the 1961 legislature convened. Bill Egan recommended a series of tax increases to meet revenue shortages in the coming fiscal year. When lawmakers complained that they had not been warned about the state's fiscal situation, the governor cited our report as having forewarned them. The legislature took the necessary steps, and some oil-lease sales brought in enough money to keep the state solvent.

But I was disappointed by the slow action for economic development. Major economic growth and increased state funds could only come from opening up natural resources. The problems were complex. No one could doubt the richness of Alaska's petroleum and mineral resources, but converting them to revenue would require access, exploration, and the ability to get products to market in economic competition with other sources around the world.

Success would require a series of steps, beginning with the state selecting the right lands among the 104 million acres promised by the federal government under the Statehood Act, and also including building the right roads, training workers in appropriate skills, and attracting private capital through an aggressive sales effort.

I pushed to have the planning commission turned into a state department that would be responsible for planning and economic development. Our state was like a third-world country in its resource development, but we were trying to provide our people with first-world services. Without taking on the challenge of modernizing our economy, we could squander the promise of statehood. With this in mind, in September 1960, I sent Bill a nine-page letter on the subject, with a blast of ideas and encouragement he could only have taken as criticism.

> In general, Bill, there seems to be a real need to give Alaskans some ideals, goals, purposes or whatever one might call it. There seems to be little direction in where people are going, in what we are striving for. Statehood was a tremendous unifier for Alaska—it welded everyone together for a common goal, and very enthusiastically so. It was something that people believed in and selflessly worked for. But since we have become a state, there has been nothing that has become a common driving force. Everyone is going his own way, sectional differences are becoming greater, there is a marked lack of enthusiasm. We need something new, something vital, something related to the future and not the past. You actually are the only person who can supply this.

In this frame of mind, I traveled on business to the East Coast in the fall of 1961 and got excited about the work in planning and development being done around the nation and the world, far beyond the scope anything Alaskans had in mind. The new energy and optimism created by the Kennedy administration was exciting. I visited Harvard, where my brother, George, was organizing the papers of Leon Trotsky, and made a friendly call on a former professor, John Gaus, who had a wonderful office high in an attic in one of Harvard's historic halls.

Our talk lasted much longer than I expected, ranging over many issues, including my feeling that I needed something new. He was interested in my theory about Alaska as a third-world country, and recognized my need to learn more about the growing field of international economic development.

On the spot, Gaus marched me to the office of the Littauer School of Public Administration (now called the Kennedy School of Government), which had a program to give credit toward a master of public administration to students with extensive experience in government. I was told I would be virtually certain of a fellowship there, should I apply.

I did apply, and the Littauer fellowship offer came. And with it, indecision over whether I should accept it.

There were several considerations. At the time, I was weighing getting a grant to study Siberia and its possible relation to Alaska. I had received an offer to go to Chile to help with earthquake reconstruction, though they would not allow me to take the family. At Harvard, we would have to scrape to get by on the $5,000 fellowship, a fraction of the income I earned at the housing authority. And I loved Alaska and feared that if we left, we might not get back for a long time. Gloria was dead set against accepting the fellowship.

We had reached a stalemate when a letter came from Bob Bartlett. He said getting the fellowship was a once-in-a-lifetime opportunity that no one should pass up, and he claimed he would do it himself if he'd been qualified. With that, Gloria changed her mind, I quit my state job, and we took off.

We rented our house to friends Jack and Martha Roderick, loaded our belongings in the same luggage trailer that had brought us north eleven years earlier, and headed off down the Alaska Highway and across the country in our station wagon, crowded with Yonni, Greg, and Joe, and our tailless, adopted stray dog, Stubby, as well as my mother, who had been visiting us in Anchorage. The trip had the feeling of an adventure. To the children, Boston was an exciting new place very different from their home, while Gloria and I found many old friends there, as well as my brother and his wife, Nell.

Harvard's family housing was full and we couldn't afford to stay long in a motel. As soon as we arrived, I called Nell's mother in Cambridge to ask her advice on finding a home. She suggested we stay until the onset of cold weather at a cottage her family owned in Manchester-by-the-Sea, an hour north of the city.

When we arrived at the Manchester address, we couldn't believe our eyes. The long driveway wove through beautiful seaside woods to a great seven-bedroom, seven-bathroom house with a big deck overlooking the Atlantic, one of six houses on a forty-acre seaside estate. We stayed at the "cottage" for more than a month, and returned many times to "Manch" as a borrowed vacation home, keeping a warm friendship with Nell's family, even after George and Nell divorced. Fifty years later, I still visit the Manch estate with my brother's family, staying in one of the larger houses.

I devoured the work at Littauer and the cultural life at Harvard. Hardly anyone had studied the particular subject I was concentrating on—how to bring about state economic development through the legislative process of budgeting. The family was happy as well. We rented a house in Arlington on a lake, where the children could skate all winter; I skated for the first time since I was fourteen years old in Moscow.

When the school year ended, we were determined to return to Alaska, despite several intriguing work opportunities. MIT wanted me to serve as an urban development advisor to Turkey's government. Harvard pursued me to go to Jakarta to represent the university under a cooperative planner training program with the Indonesia Institute of Technology. A federal housing job was available in Portland, Oregon. A former MIT classmate asked me to join him in a lucrative consulting practice in San Francisco.

My skills once again were rare and in high demand. Alaska was the one place without job prospects. Burke Riley and I corresponded about the governor's lack of interest in my services, which I couldn't comprehend.

Gloria and the children desperately wanted to get back to Anchorage, and I strongly believed that planning and working for development in a place you cared about and where you expected to stay would make a more fulfilling career than being a visiting expert somewhere else in the world. I figured that, if nothing else, I could always make a living selling real estate.

We had already shipped our belongings back to Alaska for our return, without a clear idea of what I would do there, when I received a phone call from a stranger in Washington with a federal job offer. The conduit from Harvard to the Kennedy administration was strong, and it was trying to suck me to Washington. I turned down the job flat. But when the caller insisted and said the feds would pay my way just to talk with him, I agreed to fly down from Boston and meet him in Washington. That would allow me to see Bob Bartlett.

The proffered job was director of program evaluation for the US Housing and Home Finance Agency. In my state housing authority job, I had spent four years interacting with this agency, the HHFA, which oversaw urban renewal and housing funding, as well as planning, public transit, and other grants. Examining these programs from within a massive bureaucracy held no interest for me whatsoever.

Seeing my steadfast refusal and my insistence that I was going back to Alaska, my host—HHFA Assistant Administrator for Policy Morton J. Schussheim— held out a much more interesting carrot. He and HHFA Administrator Robert C. Weaver asked me to come for just a couple of months during the summer to write a report on a fascinating question: How could the federal government, and HHFA specifically, solve the puzzle of planning for the complex and overlapping local governments of the nation's metropolitan areas?

I protested that I was from the one state in the United States without a single metropolitan area. But Weaver responded, "Then you won't come up with any damn foolish notions that don't work anyway."

They wanted me as the resident consultant of a three-person task force. The others, already committed, were MIT political science professor Robert Wood and University of Illinois planning professor Louis Wetmore, both of whom I knew and respected. I was intrigued, but still quite reluctant.

Over lunch in the senate dining room, Bob Bartlett convinced me to take the job. He argued that exposure to the operations of the federal government would be useful to my future in Alaska. He also thought the proposed work was too important and interesting to pass up, and that Weaver would be a fascinating person to work with.

Gloria and the kids went along with the short-term assignment. Our old friends from Madison, Bob and Martha Lewis, gave us their Cleveland Park house while they spent the summer on their Wisconsin farm. While I worked, my family escaped Washington's summertime heat with trips to Manch.

I found myself in the middle of one of the most exciting periods in American history. Our study would explore the purpose and operation of the agency most closely involved with the Kennedy and Johnson administrations' social agenda, which became the Great Society.

HHFA managed a portfolio of programs that had developed through the 1950s beyond its original housing mission. Although organizationally below the level of the president's cabinet, the agency addressed the cutting edge of the era's rapid growth and urban sprawl, including community facilities, sewer and water funding, slum clearance, open space purchase, planning assistance, mass transit, public housing, and home finance.

Our inspiring leader, Bob Weaver, brought me in as part of a team that would use the tools of social science and intellectual discourse, for the first time, in redesigning how the federal government addressed urban regional issues. He became head of the cabinet-level Department of Housing and Urban Development (HUD), which grew out of HHFA in 1965, a move that made him the nation's first black cabinet member. (Today, HUD's building in DC is named for Weaver.)

Besides my basic research, I spent hours that summer in a large, well-decorated office, where Bob Wood, an MIT urbanist and future successor to Weaver as HUD secretary, would sometimes lie on the couch and talk about federal policy and politics and how to get things done in Washington.

Top officials from the Bureau of the Budget in the White House, now the Office of Management and Budget, concerned about effective use of federal dollars within the growing complexity of urban regions, pitched in with their ideas. Others provided additional insights, information, and suggestions. For me, the stimulation of new learning and creative thinking was thrilling. Having left behind the limited stage of Alaska politics, I felt a real part of Kennedy's "new generation," taking part in the hopeful changes in national life.

The optimism of those days may be difficult to imagine in these more cynical times. The power and wealth of the United States were unprecedented in the postwar years. Now a young, dynamic new leader and his beautiful, brilliant wife had taken charge to use that power to solve the nation's longstanding problems. The arts and humanities came to the fore. The president and first lady elevated beauty and ideas. We believed we could address poverty and other urban issues. The agency could make a critical difference.

We needed to solve the same problem nationally that we had addressed when writing the local government article of the Alaska Constitution. Individual local government entities were too small and fractured to address major metropolitan problems. There was need for coordinated federal, state, and local action to carry out federal objectives in line with local wishes in urban areas spanning many local governments. Communities deserved a say—this had been proved many times when controversies exploded over construction of the interstate highways in the 1950s—but could not go it alone.

Alaska's solution of creating a single local government for an entire urban region was not feasible in existing metropolitan areas across the country. Instead, regional planning agencies and metropolitan councils of government could align federal actions with their own goals and objectives, coordinating federal projects at the local level. Federal law already required highway projects, transit, and other facilities to conform to areawide planning. There was a clear need to make these mandates work in practice. For that, metropolitan regions would have to create appropriate intergovernmental institutions and plans.

The task force report offered a series of policy and strategic recommendations and called for a new assistant administrator position under Weaver to help carry them out. This new person would promote regional planning and cooperation among local governments in metropolitan areas, bringing HHFA and other federal agencies to work with them at the same table.

When we finally finished the report in late summer, Weaver offered me that new job. The official title was Assistant Administrator for the Office of Metropolitan Development, which would be created at the same time. I turned him down. I had put off the return to Alaska long enough. Our belongings were there, and it was time for the kids to get back to school.

But once again, Bob Bartlett influenced Gloria and me. He argued that the appointment would be the highest of any Alaskan in Washington, a great opportunity for me to benefit the state, both through HHFA programs and as an ambassador to the federal administration. We relented, agreeing to stay for one year. We rented a house and enrolled the kids in Rosemary Elementary in Chevy Chase, Maryland.

Politics had nothing to do with getting the job—my qualifications and hiring were strictly professional—but the high level of the appointment called for a political blessing from the White House. The White House in turn wanted an endorsement from one of Alaska's Democratic members of Congress. That seemed easy enough, as Bartlett was Alaska's senior senator.

Bob wrote a letter of support to be cosigned by himself, Senator Ernest Gruening, and Representative Rivers. Gruening was out of town, and his assistant, George Sundborg, said the senator would sign it upon his return (George was another old friend from the constitutional convention). Rivers signed the letter in the meantime.

When Gruening saw the letter awaiting his signature, he exploded—as Bob Bartlett told me later. Ernest called Bob and said that if any Alaskan were to get such a plum job, many others were far more worthy, and he named several party stalwarts. Bob explained that the job was professional and would not be offered to just any Alaskan. But Ernest responded that he wouldn't sign anyway. I wasn't an obedient party member, or, as he emphatically put it, "Fischer's a maverick."

So the endorsement letter came only from Bartlett and Rivers. After praising my qualifications, it said, "In addition to everything else, he is our kind of a Democrat." Upon receiving White House clearance, I was sworn in by Bob Weaver, with Gloria and Bartlett at my side. I enjoyed the stir created by the presence of a real US senator at HHFA on that day.

Bob related the story months later, over lunch, when he was complaining once more of his difficult relationship with Gruening, whose imperious style and media showboating were so opposite to his own way of doing things. My relations with Ernest had always been cordial and remained so in the future. My only theory to explain his reaction to my appointment was that he remembered that five years earlier, while in the Alaska territorial legislature, I had upset Alex Miller and the Democratic machine with my highway bill, with its unintentional impact on the liquor control board. He may also have remembered my request for a bribery investigation.

Another incident sheds light on these machinations. In June 1962, shortly after I accepted the temporary assignment at HHFA, Bill Egan was in Washington and asked me to meet him. After all the urging from my friends and me, the state had finally created the Department of Economic Development and Planning. The governor offered me the job of deputy commissioner of the new department.

I turned him down, both because I had just taken a responsible job at the national level, and because I felt that the offer should have been for commissioner, not deputy. The commissionership went to a former Anchorage port director, who made little of the job. And the department had a short life.

Years later, I learned that Bill had wanted to appoint me commissioner but could not. After a conflict with Alex Miller and the state's labor unions, he had agreed to submit his high-level appointments to the state Democratic Central Committee. The committee turned me down for commissioner, which may have put in doubt confirmation by the legislative majority. Maybe Gruening knew about that. I never learned the basic cause of the party's hostility.

My work at HHFA was fascinating and all-consuming. I went to work early in the morning, stayed late at night, and traveled constantly. The Office of Metropolitan Development consisted, at the start, of me and my secretary. My objective was to establish metropolitan planning organizations for the nation's cities and suburbs. My main tools were persuasion and the lure of the agency's grants.

For example, a delegation of Dallas civic leaders called on Weaver to obtain money for a new bus system. He was sympathetic but left it to me to explain that, under federal law, they would not qualify due to lack of a planning program for the Dallas–Fort Worth metropolitan area. They insisted such areawide coordination was impossible in their region, and asked me to come to Texas and give my message directly to the city.

I spent a day in Dallas at the Petroleum Club, at the top of a tall office tower, with what was clearly the power elite. I told them they needed to meet federal guidelines or else transit grant money wouldn't come. While they were intransigent at first, arguing that collaboration with Fort Worth was out of the picture, they soon came around, mentioning that they were already planning a huge shared airport. By the afternoon, everything was sunshine. The mayor of Fort Worth had agreed to create an areawide planning organization, and the powers-that-be were quite satisfied with the results. As was I.

Our purpose was nothing less than to change the development patterns of the entire country: to fight the disorder we now call suburban sprawl. At HHFA, we couldn't plan communities or even implement programs. Everything we did went through grants to state and local governments. But we could use the leverage of federal funds to push regions to examine their own problems.

I explained the issues to Bartlett in a letter when I started the job: "Billions and billions are spent every year on providing facilities for urban areas, but little understanding exists of what the effects of these programs are. Particularly in the suburban fringes, the helter-skelter patterns are certainly not likely to add much to our future urban environment or the way of life."

Tom Morehouse, a brilliant PhD candidate from the University of Minnesota, came into my office as an intern in June 1963. I was leaving on a two-week business trip when he arrived and had time only to give him a sketchy idea of a report I needed for the Bureau of the Budget on HHFA's open space program that provided grants for cities to obtain land for parks. When I returned, I found a magnificently researched, clearly organized, and well-thought-out paper on my desk.

I realized Tom would be an invaluable asset and made him my partner, with as much independence as I could offer to take advantage of his agile and productive mind. Later, I recruited him to Alaska, where he finished his career. He remains today a good friend.

Tom's initial impression of me—as he recently told my co-author—was of extreme self-confidence and ease in handling important people, a task at the center of my responsibilities. He first encountered this ability when we went to talk to Baltimore County Executive Spiro Agnew, who later became vice president, and others in the area who were resistant to our metropolitan planning initiatives. Although the setting was formal and everyone polished in their positions, by the end, the local officials had agreed to comply with our guidelines.

I don't recall strategizing before going into meetings or contriving a way of manipulating people. I naturally enjoy connecting, a characteristic I shared, in different ways, with each of my parents. My confidence was real. Tom witnessed it soon after he came to work for me, when we called on the Bureau of the Budget, which had considerable power over our work. As he told Wohlforth:

> We were talking along and Vic decides to take off his shoes, put his stocking feet up on the table, and lean back in the chair and continue talking, without any kind of interruption or hitch. And I immediately thought, "This guy really, really has chutzpah." I mean he used the occasion and he used that gesture to indicate how comfortable and how much in control he felt...Making that explicit, it was fairly clear. And he was. He was in control.

The work changed me. I took confidence from my office, my training, and my belief in the benefits of what we were doing. The spirit of the Kennedy administration lifted us. The Kennedys had brightened the look and cultural life of Washington and inspired federal employees with a sense that we could make government work to accomplish great things. I had been given an enormous office with a flag, denoting my federal rank. Although my real power was merely persuasive, I naturally bluffed whenever necessary to do the good we intended to do.

The experience of politics in Alaska probably made the adjustment to Washington much easier for me than for many others. During the statehood movement I had been, comparatively, a larger fish in a very small pond. Now, in the biggest pond of all, I wasn't intimidated by US senators and the like. I had worked by the side of each of Alaska's senators and governors and knew them personally.

The exhilaration of the Kennedy years reached a peak one Wednesday in August 1963. Gloria and the children were spending the summer at Manch—I saw little of them even when they were in Washington, with my travel and work schedule. I was in my office on K Street when I heard singing in the street outside and realized that Martin Luther King's March on Washington was passing by. I went down and let the crowd sweep me along toward the Lincoln Memorial.

I found a place near the corner of the National Mall's reflecting pool, close enough to the memorial to see and hear the speakers clearly. I was surrounded by strangers, which was best, for everyone bonded together in a wonderful sense of harmony. We were vibrating with the inspiration and brotherhood of the moment, an indescribably positive sense of togetherness. And when King spoke, repeating the phrase "I have a dream," his transcendence of time and space was instantly recognizable. No one could question we were present at a great event in American history.

The next day, still high from the event, I wrote a letter to my friend Bob Bartlett, who sat on the Senate Commerce Committee, where a vote would be held on public accommodations legislation, with provisions that would ultimately be included in the Civil Rights Act. Publicly, he had remained on the fence.

I described the march and tried to capture the feelings it created: "One thing I kept realizing all along was that not since the statehood fight had I experienced such democracy in its purest form. It was like the pouring out of 'the little men for statehood'—neither organized nor disorganized—a whole mass of individuals come together with a common belief, for a common purpose."

I compared the comments of Senator Strom Thurmond, who denied the existence of racism in America, to those of former Secretary of the Interior Douglas McKay, who had told Alaskans to come "hat in hand" to Congress for statehood. I felt Bartlett, as an Alaskan, needed to stand clearly on the side of civil rights.

> We received statehood primarily because enough people
> throughout the country and in Congress believed that we

should enjoy equal rights status with residents of the other states. The very people who would today deny equal rights and opportunities to Negroes are generally the same ones who opposed our admission. And they opposed Alaska's statehood just because they feared that you would today be able to cast a vote in favor of equality. And I believe that is exactly what you should do.

Bartlett wrote back that he would vote the bill out of committee. A month earlier, told that he was the swing vote, he had committed privately to support it, although he made no public announcement until after the march. Now he joked that he would have to vote for the bill or his wife, Vide—who had also attended the march—wouldn't let him back in the house.

I was part of another public moment, but a far darker one, that fall when President John F. Kennedy was assassinated. I stood for hours in the cold rain to pay respects in the Capitol rotunda, grieving by the side of thousands of other Americans who suddenly shared intense sorrow like family members. Wrapped in that terrible moment, we feared our hopes for creating a better nation had died with the president. Lyndon Johnson was hardly the inspiring figure Kennedy had been, and his swearing in on a flight from Texas back to Washington lent him no grandeur.

But in the months that followed, Johnson's commitment to equality and the poor proved at least equal to Kennedy's, and his prodigious legislative skill began to produce rapid results. A speech Johnson made in Detroit highlighted housing and the work of our agency as a key to the Great Society programs he wanted to build. There was no question we would remain at the center of exciting work.

When the promised year had expired, I elected to remain in the HHFA job. I was already deeply hooked and didn't seriously consider returning to Alaska. At times I expressed frustration with government bureaucracy and the frenetic activity of my days, which made substantive work painfully difficult. But I believed my efforts were important and that I had a unique opportunity to make a difference on the national stage and in urban regions across the United States.

I still wanted to go back to Alaska. But not yet.

———•———

While pursuing my principal work in Washington, I also worked for two years behind the scenes with the federal Bureau of the Budget and with Burke Riley and Hugh Gellert in the Alaska Governor's Office to set up a joint state–federal economic development and planning commission for Alaska. Agencies from each government would be assigned to work together based on a joint executive order from President Johnson and Governor Egan.

At times, Bill was more difficult to get on board than the federal government. During this trial, I snapped in my frustration at my friend Burke, who was still working for Egan. He responded:

> Vic, if anyone is in a position to know Bill Egan's distrust for the product of planners, it must be you. Don't push it. Surely you know he is not about to be hurried. Perhaps we can agree that he's a deep, complex guy, usually underestimated, and equipped as most of us with his own peculiar biases.

I wrote back, "I do know exactly how he feels; I think he knows how I feel. And no matter what I think needs done about planning, development and the like, I like the guy as ever, have a very warm personal feeling towards him."

Ultimately, the commission we were working on was created. But it took a truly earth-shattering event to make it happen.

⊰ 17 ⊱

Earthquake

Late on March 27, 1964, Gloria and I were cleaning up after a dinner party at our house in Chevy Chase when the phone rang. Our dinner guests, listening to the radio on their way home, had heard a report of a massive earthquake in Alaska. It struck at 5:36 p.m. Alaska time, 10:36 p.m. Washington time, and lasted more than five minutes.

We rushed to turn on the radio. I spent the night listening to the news. Communications from Alaska were down. Some few reports that managed to make it across the airwaves were apocalyptic. Anchorage had been "flattened" or "swallowed up." My mind kept going to our house on F Street, rented out to tenants found for us by Cliff Groh. A huge beam supporting the main open part of the house ran directly over the dining table. I couldn't help imagining it falling on a family sitting down to their Friday evening dinner.

After unsuccessfully trying to sleep, I called Bob Bartlett at home in the early morning. His wife, Vide, said he had already gone to his senate office. I went to meet him there. People had congregated in the outer office. We shared our feelings and waited for Bob to emerge from the inner office. When he came out he said, "Vic, we're getting ready to fly to Alaska. Do you want to come with us?"

I had an hour to get home and pack proper clothes for Alaska. I woke Bob Weaver when I called and told him I was going off with Senator Bartlett. Knowing my weakness for Alaska, he said, "OK. Just don't promise them anything!"

At Andrews Air Force Base, our party had grown, adding Senator Gruening, several administration officials and military brass, reporters, and a couple of network TV news crews. We strapped into the tightly packed, rear-facing canvas seats of a windowless KC-135 tanker jet and heard the plane begin to roar. Then it stopped. After a short wait, another try, and another. Then air force personnel put us off the plane. Mechanical problems canceled the flight.

Walking back to the terminal with Bartlett and Ed McDermott, director of the White House Office of Emergency Planning (today's FEMA), we noticed Air Force One on the tarmac. McDermott approached the pilot and asked if he would fly us to Alaska. The plane had just returned from taking the president to Texas for the weekend. The pilot said the plane would need fuel and food, and he would need President Johnson's permission. But a flight to Alaska would be fine with him.

McDermott called Johnson, who agreed to lend the plane on condition he would be picked up in time to get back to Washington on Monday. In the terminal, air force officers sorted us out according to protocol, and I learned that my high civil service rating was equivalent to a general.

The ride to Alaska combined extreme luxury with extreme worry. I was with McDermott, Bartlett, Gruening, and the head of the Alaska command in the sumptuous president's quarters in the rear of the plane. An air force sergeant in full dress uniform came around to ask our preferences of gourmet meals. Staff manned a bank of advanced communications equipment, bringing in frequent updates from Alaska. One report said that seen from Elmendorf Air Force Base, downtown Anchorage was a "sea of flames."

When I could not keep my eyes open any longer, I took a nap in the presidential compartment that had been used by Eisenhower, Kennedy, and Johnson. The plane was the same Boeing 707 on which Johnson had taken the oath of office after Kennedy's death four months earlier.

As we neared Anchorage late Saturday afternoon, the only signs of the earthquake on the wilderness below were the cracks of shattered lake ice, which showed dark across the snowy, flat surfaces. The second-largest earthquake ever recorded had shifted and tipped a region measuring 600 miles by 250 miles, but that movement of the landscape was so huge we couldn't see it, even from an overflying jet.

With relief we saw that Anchorage had neither been completely flattened nor swept by large fires. Major slides sliced away parts of the downtown area and demolished some major buildings there, and the area of the well-to-do Turnagain neighborhood nearest the water had been transformed into a chaotic jumble of cracks and chunks, with houses upended, crushed, and sunk. A school in Government Hill had fallen into a hole, and there were various other signs of damage.

We took in the view from the windows of Air Force One on a low flyover, but the pilot announced he would abort a second run after receiving a radio call that the vibrations from the plane were creating a danger of bringing down damaged buildings. Instead, we landed at Elmendorf, and the VIPs and media were ushered into a military briefing. The military was playing a critical part in responding to the emergency.

Burke Riley met me at the plane. He had become the Alaska coordinator for the Department of the Interior, the top civilian federal official in the state. We skipped out on the military briefing and slipped away to get a look at the town. At the public safety building at Sixth Avenue and C Street—which contained the police and fire departments—we found a meeting of all the local officials dealing with the earthquake emergency. I knew most of them. A friendly shout went up from the police chief: "Vic, I knew you would be here!"

Since leaving for Harvard, I hadn't set foot back in Alaska—a period approaching three years—although I talked about returning so much that I had developed a strong reputation for it among my colleagues in Washington. Now, coming back in the midst of a disaster, I feared I would find grief and devastation. Instead, the mood was energized and elevated. Survivors felt an adrenaline high and knew they were living through days they would never forget.

Here was the spirit, once again, that I had missed after the success of the statehood fight. Everyone dove enthusiastically into the work of disaster response and, later, recovery and rebuilding. Alaskans showed their best when facing a challenge. They pulled together magnificently, dealing with one problem after another in a situation in which most normal civil functions of the region had been disabled or destroyed.

Anchorage was black. Phones and utilities in parts of the city were out. One hospital was structurally unsound, and staff had to evacuate patients to the other hospital, which lacked clean water. But it had an emergency generator, so people congregated there to get away from the dark and cold.

Houses destroyed or uninhabitable numbered in the hundreds. Rail and highway links between towns and out of Alaska were gone. The control tower at the airport had collapsed. Television, newspaper, and radio outlets were incapacitated.

Alaskans solved each problem, one by one, in rapid succession. A typically heroic effort was contributed by Genie Chance, then a KENI radio station reporter. When the quake hit, she was on her way downtown. She drove directly to the Public Safety Building. Other radio station employees had gone to the transmitter to get the station back on the air. Genie called them on her car radio, and they put her on the air. Her voice, and her judgment, brought the news and a sense of calm to the city from her car and later from a phone inside the police department.

Many others similarly responded by finding whatever they could do to help. Ham radio operators worked around the clock to relay messages to the outside world. Military personnel delivered water, served meals, set up generators, and made flights to assess damage. Volunteers were deputized to protect damaged buildings and keep the peace (no looting or disorder occurred). Service clubs and the Salvation Army set up shelters and accounted for missing people. Neighbors whose houses were intact invited in the newly homeless.

On that Saturday evening, the day after the quake, I walked from the Public Safety Building to our house on F Street, hoping to settle my worry over our tenants. I found the blinds drawn and the family huddled inside, physically unharmed but terror-stricken by the continuing aftershocks. The house that I had built was completely undamaged. I went next door to check on the Crittendens and then walked a dozen blocks to the Trycks' house to visit and get some sleep.

I rose at about 5 a.m. on Sunday morning, Easter, to see more of the city. A patrol car enforcing the curfew stopped me almost as soon as I started walking, and the officer asked what I was doing out on the street. I explained that I had come from Washington to survey results of the quake. A sergeant in the passenger seat said, "Aren't you Vic Fischer?" They offered to take me around to see the damage.

We covered downtown, where a theater and businesses on the main street, Fourth Avenue, had disappeared below street level. On Government Hill we saw the destroyed elementary school and other wreckage. We climbed amid the chaos of wrecked homes in the upscale Turnagain area. On the Park Strip, the floors of an apartment building that had been under construction had pancaked down to the ground, one on top of the other; fortunately, the workers had gone for the day.

An area of more than twenty blocks on the west end of town broke away from the rest of downtown and slid laterally westward, leaving a gap of between five and twenty feet. While streets and utilities along this gap were destroyed, miraculously, most apartments and homes in the area that moved remained undamaged.

Later, I rejoined our Washington group for a flight to see tsunami damage in Seward, Valdez, and Kodiak. Seward had been swept by a tsunami wave; ruptured fuel tanks burned and much of the Alaska Railroad yard was wiped out. A wave demolished the waterfront in Valdez. In Kodiak, the tsunami had lifted fishing boats from the harbor and cast them around the downtown area, vessels battering down buildings. All the cities had lost their docks.

One hundred and fifteen Alaskans died in the earthquake, as well as sixteen people in Oregon and California. Most were killed by the waves. We could scarcely believe the relatively low casualty numbers when looking at the severity of the devastation. The largest loss of life was in Valdez, the closest town to the earthquake epicenter. Townspeople had been sitting on the dock and along the bank watching the unloading of a cargo ship. When the quake hit, the ground disappeared from under them into the sea, and massive waves followed. Thirty-one people, mostly children, were lost. The Native villages of Chenega and Afognak were completely destroyed by the tsunami.

Generally, Alaska's thin population meant hardly anyone lived in most of the heavily shaken region. Luck helped, too, as our flexible, low-rise wooden buildings were well suited to withstand shaking, and the earthquake came late on the afternoon of Good Friday, when schools and downtown areas were quiet.

But the quake did overwhelming damage to infrastructure, public buildings, businesses, and housing. Without massive intervention, the area would not survive economically. It was clear that we needed to rebuild on a huge scale, far beyond what the affected communities and the state could afford, and we had to do it quickly, before residents were forced to leave to find jobs and housing elsewhere.

———

Air Force One carried us back to Washington on Sunday night, arriving very early Monday. After spending a few hours in bed, I was awakened by a phone call from Bob Weaver, my boss. He would pick me up in his limousine in ten minutes to go to the White House, where the president wanted to meet with all of his cabinet secretaries for reports on handling earthquake relief and reconstruction. I was dressed by the time he arrived and managed to give Weaver a report in the car on the situation in Alaska.

The president was first shown amazingly detailed photos of the destruction in Alaska taken by U-2 spy planes, followed by a preliminary analysis of the earthquake and tsunamis by the US Geological Survey. The various cabinet secretaries then reported to the president, in the order of when their agencies were created, on what assistance they could provide Alaska.

Our agency, HHFA, was second to last. But thanks to my trip, Weaver was able to shine, with the latest on-scene information and steps already taken to activate our housing and lending branches to provide immediate help. And he announced then and there that he had appointed me as the HHFA coordinator of Alaska recovery and reconstruction operations, both in Alaska and in Washington.

Johnson's response to the disaster was brilliant. He was in the midst of the fight for the Civil Rights Act, the escalation of the Vietnam War, and the approaching presidential election that fall. But he recognized the importance of the earthquake and the opportunity to show the effectiveness of the federal government through energetic coordination from the top. He gave the cabinet marching orders to get involved personally and in concert, to throw everything at the problem and to get the job done without delay.

Johnson didn't wait for paperwork or process. He declared a federal disaster the day after the quake, as soon as he heard from Governor Egan. Freed of usual bureaucratic requirements by the emergency and by the president's directive, agencies that I was accustomed to seeing move at a glacial pace suddenly became nimble and powerfully effective.

The Army Corps of Engineers stood out. At normal times it would grind through endless procedures at an inexorable and unalterably gradual speed. I had many friends there. They normally lacked the ability to do anything quickly. Now the corps' officers seemed to bring their enormous capabilities to bear at a moment's notice. They dispatched heavy equipment to deal with broken roads or utilities on a word and issued contracts for work in a flash, as expeditiously and effectively as the most aggressive of private entrepreneurs.

For two years, we had labored futilely to create a joint state–federal economic development and planning commission for Alaska. Barriers appeared on the state's side, then on the federal side, then back on the state's side. The carefully negotiated presidential executive order to create the commission seemed to have died, lying dormant in the president's and governor's offices. But within days after the earthquake, the White House picked up the document, adapted it, and changed the name to the Federal Reconstruction and Development Planning Commission for Alaska, and the president signed it.

The commission became the critical nexus of coordination for the federal response that President Johnson wanted but could not personally oversee. The order appointed the heads of the relevant departments as commission members, including Weaver. For chairman, Johnson picked Senator Clinton Anderson of New Mexico, his close friend and a tough, well-respected legislator who would be able to get needed legislation through Congress. For his executive director, Senator Anderson chose Dwight Ink, an Atomic Energy Commission administrator, who proved to be a gifted manager of the many moving parts.

Within thirty-six hours of the White House meeting, I was back in Alaska. Before leaving Washington, I met with our top people in community facilities, public housing, housing finance, planning and urban renewal, and other programs, to ask what help they could render Alaska in both the short and long terms. Our agency could not provide immediate disaster assistance, which could best be handled by the Army Corps of Engineers, Red Cross, and such. We would focus on restoring communities and giving financial help to those whose homes and businesses were lost or damaged.

For the next four-plus months, I labored endless hours to coordinate our various programs, commuting between Alaska and Washington. I worked with state and local officials to figure out how we could assist them. I informed the regional and field staffs of our constituent agencies of the high priority the president and Weaver had set for getting Alaska back in shape. And in DC, I was involved in relief legislation, budgets, and more coordination.

Communities returned to basic functioning relatively quickly, but huge issues kept developing. We knew the earth had moved, but not how much. The quake had caused a massive chunk of the earth's crust to shift laterally and to seesaw, with the Kenai Peninsula sinking and eastern Prince William Sound rising. Everyone waited nervously to see how high the big tides of April would roll into towns such as Portage, Hope, Seldovia, and Homer—for only at high tide would we know how much of the town would survive.

The earthquake also had exposed our lack of knowledge about the stability of soils in southcentral Alaska. No one had expected Turnagain to liquefy or Fourth Avenue, the main street in downtown Anchorage, to sink. Before we could rebuild, we would need scientific and engineering investigations of what lay under these communities, and how we could make new buildings safer.

Federal officials would have to decide whether and to what extent towns should be rebuilt; how to handle the finances of hundreds of families whose homes had been destroyed, usually with mortgages still owing; and whether to rebuild the federally owned Alaska Railroad at all, a bad investment financially but a critical part of the state's economy. Likewise, coastal towns could not get back on their feet without rapid reconstruction of port facilities used by the fishing industry.

It took time for people to adjust mentally as well. The prevailing emotions were of optimism and energy, but fear lay just below the surface, as I found out exactly a week after the earthquake at lunch in the Westward Hotel, one of Anchorage's tallest buildings.

The restaurant was packed full of people, many of whom I knew. I sat at a big round table with, among others, Lidia Selkregg, a geologist and fellow progressive involved in local issues. The place had reopened for the first time since the quake, and it was like a big, impromptu celebration for the renewal of normal life.

Earthquake survivors traded stories that day, as they would do for years to come. Bob Atwood's log house had stood at water's edge in Turnagain and had been among the first to tumble down in the slide. Like everyone else in the neighborhood, Bob grabbed what he could and ran—in this case, his trumpet. He fell, and his trumpet and hand went into a crack in the earth that closed around them. To survive, he let go of the trumpet and ran on.

Bob Reeve's birthday party had been in progress on the afternoon of the quake on the top floor of the hotel where we were now dining. The building had swung fifteen feet, slamming the adjacent, eight-story hotel structure. People fled down blacked-out stairwells as the building whipped back and forth. The survival of the hotel had remained in doubt for days as the hill it stood on kept sliding by inches.

At lunch that Friday, I became aware of a sound akin to a New York subway train approaching the hotel underground. A few seconds later, the shock hit hard. Another earthquake. I had been through lots of earthquakes but hadn't lived through the big one. I just sat still and waited, with uncertainty rather than fear my strongest emotion.

But for most others, the raw terror of a week earlier returned. The room exploded into panic. Someone shouted, "Go, go, go…Get out!" and people stampeded for the doors. Selkregg shouted, "No, stay where you are," knowing that was safest. The shaking stopped without anyone being hurt. It had been the strongest aftershock from the quake. For me, it was a window on the psychic impact of what had happened.

I knew many of the people we were trying to help. On my frequent trips to earthquake-impacted cities for public meetings, I always saw old friends. I had worked with their local officials on projects in my earlier jobs. The meetings made clear that, of the many challenges we faced, financing of the rebuilding process would be among our most difficult. The Federal Housing Administration, which set me up in an office in the Federal Building, was already talking to the banks about the complex issue of mortgage relief for homeowners of damaged housing.

Federal agencies worked hard to help. For the most part, they only needed to be asked to set aside their regulations and work quickly. Procedures were cut to a fraction of their usual length. But sometimes I ran into resistance.

A career regional official in San Francisco was dragging his feet and wouldn't waive the rules. At my request, he came to Anchorage to explain his resistance. He pointed out that his boss in Washington and I were political appointees and that we would be long gone when federal investigators came around later and held him responsible for any problems that arose from shortcutting the established procedures. Sympathizing with his concern, I contacted his boss. With a direct written order from the commissioner, he had the cover he wanted and was most cooperative thereafter.

As I managed the process, I became the Alaska ambassador to the federal government that Bob Bartlett had suggested I could be when he convinced me to take the HHFA job. I had to explain Alaska prices to Senator Anderson, who as the president's surrogate frequently questioned cost estimates for reconstruction in Alaska. All prices were higher in Alaska, and construction costs were radically higher, a point I made more than once in testimony to the Federal Reconstruction Commission.

What to do about Valdez was one of the big issues before us. The quake had not only taken the two docks and destroyed many buildings and oil tanks, but the ground had subsided. During high tide, much of the town was flooded. When I visited, I had to wear rubber boots to get to Bill Egan's grocery store on the main street.

Mayor John Kelsey, whose dock company had lost all its facilities, drove me several miles to a site on solid ground with an excellent port location. As a planner, I immediately saw this as the perfect site for relocating Valdez.

Dwight Ink, the top federal coordinator, spent a lot of time in Alaska, too. In an essay about that time, he described an early trip he made with Governor Egan to Valdez in April, flying into the airport in a snowstorm without lights, amid the mountains of the fjord where the town lies. Alaska National Guard Major General Thomas Carroll was on board. After leaving the passengers, the general ordered the plane to depart again without turning off its engines to avoid becoming snowbound in Valdez, as it was needed to continue carrying rescue supplies. The plane crashed minutes later, killing all on board.

In spite of the tragedy, Ink was able to pull together the city council for a meeting and ask them for a decision on whether to move Valdez to a new site. Geologists had officially determined that the old location was unsuitable because of poor soils and was too vulnerable to future tsunamis. In light of the risk, Ink said the commission would not pay to rebuild there. Discussion lasted all night and into the morning. Finally, with Ink's assurance that the federal government would pay the cost, the townspeople voted to move Valdez four miles away to higher ground.

Ink's problem was that the federal government had little history of paying for reconstruction of private facilities after a disaster. I argued repeatedly that urban renewal was the only federal program that would work with both the old and the new Valdez townsites.

Existing urban renewal law would allow for buying up properties in the existing city; acquiring land for a new town; installing the roads, utilities, and other infrastructure; and disposing of the improved land for private development and public facilities. The law could be similarly used to deal with damaged land and property in other cities hit by the earthquake.

In Alaska, the redevelopment process could proceed expeditiously because the Alaska State Housing Authority, where I had worked for years, was the sole urban renewal agency for all cities (unlike other states, where each city dealt directly with the federal government). ASHA had ten years of experience working on this program with HHFA, the federal funding agency. I knew most of the staff, and our agencies meshed well.

As a side benefit, the program could help make Alaskans financially whole. We could buy their damaged property based on values prior to the earthquake.

Ink initially rejected using urban renewal because of how long it could take. The legal and regulatory complexity of these projects meant they sometimes required a legendary amount of time to complete, often extending across a decade or more. But as we worked through the issues, Ink and the commission came to understand that urban renewal was the key to building a new town for Valdez and for other recovery projects. There simply was no other federal program that could do the job.

Along the way, I had to explain to the parsimonious Senator Anderson why, as part of the Valdez relocation, we needed to buy and demolish perfectly good buildings in the old Valdez townsite. Otherwise, some residents and businesses would not move, and the new Valdez would lack a critical mass to become viable.

The urban renewal program did have one complicating aspect. Local communities had to contribute a significant portion of the cost. Alaska couldn't afford to pay much. I asked the commission to increase the federal share of urban renewal costs, even if that meant reducing the overall size of the program. Initially, Senator Anderson believed a reduced local match would encourage wasteful projects, but in later earthquake recovery legislation, he and the commission raised the federal share to 75 percent.

In the end, Alaska's Senator Gruening made a floor amendment increasing the federal share to almost 95 percent, a great help for cities in need of reconstruction. In passing that bill, Congress also provided $80.5 million for Alaska assistance, including $25 million in additional funds for urban renewal and $25 million for capital improvements. These were substantial sums in those days, sufficient for the tasks at hand.

Congress also created a program to help ruined homeowners with their mortgages. It was an alternative to the slow process of urban renewal. But the mortgage program required new laws and regulations, which inevitably led to litigation. That took years. Urban renewal won the race, getting compensation for property owners and rebuilding relatively rapidly.

With high-level effort focused on the problem, we made urban renewal work at light speed. The initial stage, of reaching state and federal decisions on a redevelopment plan, took two months rather than the normal two to three years. Subsequent stages were similarly compressed in time. It was clear that the bureaucrats responsible for the programs had never wanted to be slow or inefficient—it was the federal rules to prevent fraud and the complexity of land transfers that usually slowed them down. Freed of restrictions and in the urgency of the moment, action came fast and money transfers moved quickly.

All in all, the response to the 1964 earthquake was outstanding. The response was immediate and relief came quickly, with services restored with minimal delay. The federal government took on major relief and reconstruction responsibilities and discharged them in a more effective manner than in any disaster before or since.

Not everything, of course, turns out quite as well as one might have hoped.

A lot of wonderful development plans were dreamed up for Alaska's devastated towns. Some of the nation's top architects and planners looked at the problems, rapidly creating town layouts to take advantage of the clearing of old buildings to make better communities. My friends were in the middle of this work, including Ed Crittenden, whose firm came up with a great plan for Anchorage's downtown area. However, city bankers and town fathers preferred a property-by-property approach, so creative opportunities were often lost.

Other plans ran into the twin barriers of Senator Anderson's frugality and the conservatism of small-town city councils and businessmen. Some projects simply were abandoned due to cost. Others amounted to lost opportunities, amended through local politics in ways that led to poor results, as in Kodiak and Seldovia, which lost significant parts of their communities' unique character.

In Valdez, good ideas were poorly carried out. The design of the new town of Valdez used some good contemporary planning concepts but did not adequately take into account winter conditions, particularly the enormous snowfalls in the area. The town was too spread out, lacking appropriate housing density and concentration of businesses.

We never imagined at the time that Alaskans would forget the terror of the earthquake and begin building in the most hazardous areas. Yet that happened before the final reports about the disaster had even been printed. Especially in Anchorage, city fathers simply ignored the risks, allowing construction along the L Street slide and in Turnagain that puts lives at risk when the next major earthquake comes.

In part, the success of the rebuilding allowed Alaskans to forget the earthquake. In less than a decade, Valdez became the southern terminus of the trans-Alaska oil pipeline. Kodiak grew to be one of the nation's largest fishing ports. In Seward, the site of massive destruction was turned into land and businesses for a thriving tourism industry. Through urban renewal, Anchorage's downtown was stabilized by a buttress area of about five square blocks that allowed low-rise construction on the north side of Fourth Avenue and provided extensive land for downtown off-street parking, parts of which are used for fairs and weekend markets. And so it went with other towns.

Most of that happened after I had moved back to my regular, metropolitan development work. I had spent less than five months as HHFA's earthquake coordinator, but it was a tremendously intensive period, an experience that was a major element in my professional career.

The work involved everything from broad policymaking down to the most practical details, from negotiating federal legislation to dealing with the problems of individuals and businesses. It honed my entrepreneurial and negotiating skills, my ability to come up with ideas, and my knack for bringing people together to make plans. And it further reinforced my feeling of self-confidence, always critical to my future endeavors.

———

For our family, the earthquake had the effect of calling us back to Alaska. Returning reminded us of how long we had been gone. When school let out in Washington in early summer 1964, Gloria and the three kids joined me in Anchorage. Our fearful renters having returned to Texas, we moved into our old house, the one we had built.

We rejoiced being back among our old friends and neighbors. Alaska artist Alex Combs made a painting of our family astride a merry-go-round horse. He brought the canvas, the paint still wet, to a party at the Crittendens' to celebrate our wedding anniversary.

Late that summer I wrote to my father:

> It truly is great being home. We are in our own house, which is infinitely more "us" than anything in Washington could be. Kids truly enjoying selves; Glo too, limitlessly. No one wants to return, but that we will. While parting will be hard, we do know for sure that future is in Alaska, only question when.

In the meantime, I was off to the opposite end of the earth. Literally.

⇥ 18 ⇤

Return to Russia, and Alaska

I broke away from Alaska earthquake work to attend a United Nations symposium on new towns in Moscow, a hot topic during those years, when urban migration was occurring around the world and soulless suburban development was spreading across farmland around US cities.

This would be the first such UN meeting held in the Soviet Union. Sessions would convene in the Hall of Columns, the grand space near the Kremlin where the Great Purge trials of 1936–1938 had been held. It was also where Stalin's body had lain in state after his death in 1953, mourned by millions.

I would see Russia again for the first time in twenty-five years. I had left Moscow as a kid, not yet fifteen, knowing no English, eager to get to New York. Now I was totally American, coming back as part of the American delegation.

The visit felt like an awakening, beginning with my long cab ride into Moscow. The conversation with the driver brought my Russian flooding back from the deep recesses of my mind. I connected with several old friends, including my parents' closest friends from the 1920s and 1930s, the Galperins, who now were supplemented with additional generations.

I was paranoid of the secret police, worried that my presence would cause troubles for friends. To visit the Galperin apartment, I slinked through the streets by a circuitous route, peering back around corners to check for spies who might be following me. The Galperins weren't afraid of talking to me, but their son, Yevgeni, being a party member, did stay away so as not to be exposed to a foreigner.

We had a wonderful evening of catching up and reminiscing, drinking and eating. Afterward, the Galperins' son-in-law, Vladimir Bychkov, a medical doctor, walked me back to the Moskva Hotel right past the dreaded Lubyanka Prison, talking loudly all the way, in highly accented English, about his life and desire to come to America. I realized times had changed.

This was the era of Nikita Khrushchev, who finally laid out the horrors of Stalin's repression in a secret speech to the Communist Party, the news of which spread quickly. Thousands of innocent victims were "rehabilitated," many posthumously. Although the Soviet Union remained a top-down police state, and some of the slave labor camps of the Gulag still existed, Stalin was gone and Russians no longer lived in constant fear of arrest.

I spent a week in Moscow, hearing about the issues and problems of building new communities, and also what was being done and contemplated in different countries. Most had but a few examples, although several had plans for the future. The outstanding developments in the United States were Reston, Virginia, and Columbia, Maryland, both in the Washington, DC, area, with diverse housing, business, and employment centers. Russia had by far the most experience in this arena, having built complete new towns in remote areas and satellite cities around urban cores.

I repeatedly asked conference organizers to let me and a couple of other American delegates go to one of the satellites near Moscow of which they were so proud. They kept putting me off with delays and lame excuses. Finally I got a confidential explanation: the few satellite cities that had been built beyond Moscow were for secret defense-related work and access was strictly controlled.

The freer spirit I saw with the Galperins was evident at the new towns symposium, too. Russian participants, including several cabinet ministers, were quite relaxed relating to those of us from Western nations. With some of them I debated American and Soviet ways. From others, I heard complaints and prognostications about international politics.

I met with the chief architect and planner of the city of Moscow and questioned his designs of new residential districts, which did not include parking. He explained no one would have a car. But I pointed out to him that car ownership was the dream every Russian told me about. Today, Russians are fulfilling that dream. As a result, Moscow traffic is impossible.

When I could get away from meetings, I wandered the old, familiar streets of downtown Moscow. I visited my old Arbat neighborhood, looked up at the windows of our apartment, and reminisced, feeling rather sentimental about my early years with my troika buddies Lothar Wloch and Koni Wolf, both now in Berlin. Finding any of my classmates proved impossible because Moscow had no phone books.

I found our longtime maid Nyura in a tiny, neat basement apartment, just a few doors down the street from where she had lived with us. She cried in my arms when she recognized me. I had always been her favorite. While we were having tea, Nyura remembered how I as a kid had loved the cherry preserves her mother would send from the village (our earlier maid, Frossya, had obtained similar gifts of vegetables and preserves from her country relatives).

To my good fortune, Nyura produced a jar of preserves she had recently received. Like a boy, I delighted in their sweetness, transported back in time. The visit also pleased me by showing how Nyura was totally satisfied with her life. She had a good income as maintenance manager in her building, was talking of retiring before long, and had no anxiety about her future.

I played hooky from the conference one afternoon and took a train to Peredelkino, the writers' village where we spent so many summers and skied in winter. I walked several miles from the railroad station, full of memories of my early years, recognizing the embankment where we sat as kids counting the cars of freight trains as they passed. There was the same old bridge, and the cemetery on the hill. I found the Wolfs' dacha, the place our friends and families visited so often. Other houses looked familiar, Boris Pasternak's among them. Some were new, as were the more elaborate fences.

When I came to Korney Chukovsky's house, I couldn't resist and knocked on the door. Chukovsky was Russia's most popular children's poet, and a beloved friend of our family. By now he would have been in his eighties. A woman opened the door, his daughter Lydia. She firmly said Korney Ivanovich was recovering from a heart attack and was under doctor's orders to see no one.

A loud voice called out from another room, asking who was there. When she told him it was Vitya Fischer, George's brother and Louis's son (both had visited Chukovsky in the 1950s), the voice bellowed: "Let him in! Let him in!"

We chatted over tea and cookies about life, my work and family, Alaska, and politics. Korney recounted the pleasure of having George and Louis visit. The political situation in Russia disgusted him. He was outspoken about the persecution of writers and other intellectuals, which he had hoped would end after Stalin's death. I asked how he could be so frank, knowing the authorities could muzzle him. He shrugged his shoulders and said, "What can they do to an old man like me?"

I walked back to the railroad station in the dark, thinking about this giant of a man and what a privilege it was to know him. And about how fortunate my life had become. If we had not been able to leave in 1939, would I even have survived the war and the years of repression that killed so many millions? Despite the familiar people and places, I was acutely conscious now of being a stranger in this land.

The conference sessions in Moscow droned on for a week. I was tense as I worked to elevate my childhood Russian to the professional language of the speeches and presentations. Success came at a price: I began smoking again, after having kicked the habit for several years.

The vice was too easy. The hall filled with smoke, as most delegates puffed away. A ribbon of bottles of mineral water, bowls of chocolates, and cups of cigarettes ran along the conference tables spanning the hall in a giant U. At some point, I weakened and took a cigarette from in front of me, just one, and that was it. I was hooked for another long spell before I would be able, by pure will-power, to quit again.

After covering the week's agenda, the conference adjourned for a week so the staff could put together a final report for adoption by the delegates. A group of about thirty foreign delegates accompanied by Soviet officials set out on a tour to learn more about Russia's new towns.

Among other stops, we flew far south to the oil center of Baku on the Caspian Sea in Azerbaijan, where my father had focused his first book, *Oil Imperialism*. As we approached, I could see Baku's port and the offshore oil fields. I commented to my fellow passenger, a deputy minister of construction, that it was too bad I couldn't take any pictures from the plane. He asked who had such a silly rule, and I told him that the US State Department warned that travelers who photographed bridges, harbors, and other infrastructure could be arrested. My neighbor said that this was nonsense, so I delighted in flaunting these "rules," chalking up the experience as another example of the more relaxed attitude created by the new regime.

Baku was both an old Muslim town and busy industrial city. We went by boat to see the oil field out in the Caspian Sea. Derelict wooden structures extended in all directions as far as one could see. Pumps were rocking up and down, and oil was flowing through a vast network of pipes, but not all of it ended up in onshore storage tanks, judging by the extensive slicks on the water. The air was polluted too. The scene was atrocious.

But our Baku hosts were fun and hospitable. At a banquet in a recreation center I broke away from the foreign guests and their interpreters to use my Russian. My new group, much livelier than the official party, included local professionals, a jolly buxom soprano, and a gorgeous dancer. We had a wonderful time in conversation and friendship and almost continuous toasts on behalf of anything. Each toast required drinking your vodka in one gulp, bottoms up. Feeling that America's honor was at stake, I kept up with the Russians, drink by drink. I survived, though barely.

We saw a new town, Sumgayit, a chemicals center about twenty miles north of Baku. Although a greenbelt separated the industrial and residential areas, foul air covered the whole town, irritating breathing and raising complaints that the children were being poisoned. Flying west, we visited Yerevan, Armenia, where the air was cleaner and builders had won permission to use their local reddish rock instead of the Soviets' concrete slabs—another example of increased flexibility by the regime.

Everywhere in the Soviet Union, I encountered overwhelming admiration for our late president, John F. Kennedy. His photo hung in private as well as public places. People spoke with great sadness about the loss of this attractive young leader and of their hopes for what he could have achieved. I wished I had brought more Kennedy memorabilia for all the friendly people I met. After the forty Kennedy half dollars I brought ran out, I managed to extract several large Kennedy commemorative picture books from the US embassy as gifts for our Russian conference hosts, who received them with great appreciation.

As much as they liked Kennedy, however, Russians feared Barry Goldwater, the ultraconservative Republican nominee running for president against Lyndon Johnson in 1964. One Russian I met, accustomed to single-candidate elections, couldn't grasp why Goldwater had even been allowed to run. I tried to explain American democracy, while reassuring him that Johnson was sure to win.

My two weeks in Russia were singularly fulfilling, with all the visits to old and new friends, amazing natural places to see, and insights from private conversations in Russian. My language returned almost to fluency.

But after the trip ended, I experienced a strange and surprising burst of emotions. Landing in London on Aeroflot, I felt an urge to get down and kiss the tarmac to celebrate freedom, just as I had seen liberated people do in newsreels. Despite the nostalgia of my visit, departure from the Soviet Union had lifted a sense of oppression that I hadn't realized I was carrying.

The psychology of totalitarianism still permeated Russia. Awareness of it had crept into my muscles as a sort of undercurrent of tension even through the fun and fascination of the trip. No matter the exceptions, this land was not free. And so it proved again in September 1964, just weeks after my departure, when the party conservatives ousted Khrushchev and installed the severe Leonid Brezhnev as total leader.

———

My Soviet journey also included an even deeper reunion with my past, which I've saved to mention till now, even though it happened on the way to Moscow. From the beginning, I planned to stop off briefly in Berlin while headed to the Soviet

Union from Washington so I could see my boyhood friend Lothar Wloch again. The other member of our troika, Koni Wolf, was unavailable on a trip.

Thus began a whole new phase in my life.

I got off the plane in the immense Tempelhof Airport, which had been the center of the Berlin Airlift in 1948–1949 that brought critical supplies during Russia's blockade of the city. Half a lifetime had passed since I had last seen Lothar, and in my mind he was still a skinny young man. Only after I heard my name over the public address system did I find the prosperous German businessman in the prime of life who turned out to be my old friend. At first, I felt little connection with this German burgher, with whom communication stumbled along in a combination of my rusty German and his inexpert English.

I had a further shock riding through the city in his Mercedes and seeing the newly constructed Berlin Wall, with its brutal razor wire and the death zone between the two sides, where East Germans attempting to escape to the West had been gunned down. It was one thing to see pictures and read about the wall, and quite another to be there, to see the memorials and read the inscriptions, and to visualize the horrors perpetrated there. The enormity and inhumanity of it all struck me deeply.

But as we drove on, the mood changed. Lothar and I warmed to each other, as the strangeness evaporated. Our friendship revived in full force. The German expression is *bruederschaft*—brotherhood—the kind of connection to another person that transcends time and circumstances. We had that again.

The last time I had seen Lothar we were boys. The war left him in Berlin, penniless and without connections. He had put in long days as a construction laborer while simultaneously pursing his architecture degree. He had worked all his waking hours. Thanks to that work and his brilliance, he now drove a big car and told me of the apartment blocks and office buildings he had designed in Berlin, West Germany, France, and Switzerland.

Lothar took me to a very expensive restaurant on the Kurfuerstendam where the maitre d' and waiters rushed to us, bowing and leading us to a special table in the back with a "Herr Wloch" this and "Herr Wloch" that. We ate a sumptuous meal, sharing the stories of our lives, until Lothar insisted I should drop my plans and go with him to his vacation home on Lake Lugano in Switzerland, where he was planning to meet his wife and children.

I had scheduled several professional meetings in Warsaw and Minsk on the way to Moscow, but I decided on the spot to cancel them. A waiter brought a phone to the table, and Lothar called an assistant to make plane and rail reservations. Shortly, we were driving back to the airport, flying to Milan, Italy, and riding a train up through the Swiss Alps to Lake Lugano.

At the far end of the spectacular lake, an apartment building stepped up the slope of a mountain, ascending through a series of elevators to a magnificent penthouse, Lothar's vacation home. The view of the area spread out like an incredible diorama. Lothar had designed this complex in collaboration with a Swiss architect, who occupied the adjacent penthouse. I was deeply impressed by Lothar's skill as an architect—even more than I was impressed by the effort that had raised him from the abject poverty of a bricklayer's apprentice to this apparent height of wealth.

Lothar and his family—his wife, Eva, and sons Lothar Jr. and Holgar— seemed happy and vigorous, a match to my own family. We talked about Alaska. He was interested, and we again began toying with the idea of Lothar coming to Alaska. He shared my boyhood fascination with the Arctic. We got so far as to look into architectural licensing. I later talked to Ed Crittenden, the dean of Alaska architects, and suggested Lothar as a potential partner.

While that move didn't happen, I never lost contact with Lothar again. After those three days, we were as close as ever, and remained so until his death. To this day, the friendship remains in my heart, and I've made several visits to his family in Berlin.

The discussion of bringing Lothar to Alaska reminds me of how focused I was on getting back there myself. Our time in Anchorage after the earthquake had made the entire family eager to return and nervous about becoming too deeply ensconced in Washington to ever make a break. But I was torn. My professional role continued to grow and I was being seduced by the power and the importance of the work.

My job became more hectic and overwhelming. America's cities grew explosively in those years. All over the country, regions recognized the need for metropolitan coordination and were requesting help from my office. Our family witnessed these changes on our weekend camping trips into the countryside beyond Washington. In a few years' time, our favorite spots in Virginia and West Virginia were overrun by development and recreationists.

In 1965, Congress finally upgraded my agency, the Housing and Home Finance Agency, or HHFA, to a full cabinet department, Housing and Urban Development or HUD. This change had been a goal for years, pursued by both Presidents Kennedy and Johnson.

My boss Bob Weaver was appointed HUD Secretary. My friend Bob Wood, who had helped me with the study that first brought me to Washington, became the undersecretary. As a redesign of the agency came into shape, I saw that I would manage more people and have more responsibility, with an increased ability to bring about the improved regional planning the country needed.

I worked long hours and traveled frequently to meetings and conferences. When in town, I would rise early, scan the *Washington Post* over a quick breakfast, read the *New York Times* on the bus to work, and return in the evening after the children were in bed.

One night when I got home, Gloria met me at the door and said, "Go upstairs. Your daughter's very upset." I could hear Yonni sobbing. I tried to hold her, sitting on her bed, and asked her what was wrong, but her bawling redoubled. She choked out, "I can't tell you, Daddy, I just can't tell you."

When I finally got Yonni to calm down enough to talk, she said, "Daddy, I was lying here in bed, and I was thinking about you, and I couldn't see you. I couldn't figure out what you look like." And with that she started crying again.

That moment, when Yonni was ten, hit me hard. I believed my work was robbing my children of their father during critical years. I needed to make a change.

Ironically, Yonni today remembers nothing about the incident. She insists that I was a better dad than her friends had at the time, as my boys Greg and Joe have also said. We camped on many summer weekends and skated on the canals in the winter. When I was present, I played with the kids. Despite my guilt, we have plenty of good memories from that time.

But as long as we remained in Washington, our lives would not return to the "normal" that we all associated with Alaska. I always expected to go back, but Alaska offered no employment opportunities matching the excitement and importance of what I was doing in Washington. Or so it seemed then. In retrospect, the next phase in my professional life had begun developing soon after I came to DC.

The year was 1962. Paul Ylvisaker asked me to lunch at the Mayflower Hotel. Paul was a fascinating and dynamic man, a mentor to me for years. At the time, he directed national policy programs for the Ford Foundation. He had developed an interest in Alaska through his travels to Japan and a visit to Fairbanks, where University of Alaska President Bill Wood had wooed him for large-scale foundation support. Paul was intrigued by the connection between Alaska's resources and Japan's industrialization, and he wanted to obtain a deeper understanding of the state.

Searching for an Alaska expert, Paul heard about me from John Bebout. I had known John since the early 1950s, when he was assistant director of the National Municipal League and publisher of a journal to which I contributed. John also had taught at Rutgers University. He worked on the revision of New Jersey's constitution and wrote a book about it. In 1955–1956 in Fairbanks, he was among the most effective consultants to the Alaska Constitutional Convention.

A letter John Bebout wrote to Paul Ylvisaker in July 1962 led to our meeting and the string of events that created my later career in Alaska. His appraisal got Paul's attention:

> Vic is one of the best professionals in Alaska, a city planner who has worked both for the City of Anchorage and the state, and was one of the best members of the Constitutional Convention. I believe direct contact with Vic would be helpful in connection with any future consideration of possible Ford Foundation-financed projects of any kind in Alaska.

Our lunch lasted for hours. Paul was in DC to speak to HHFA interns, and he obviously was very conversant with the Washington world in which I worked. I was quickly attracted to Paul, a warm and superintelligent person, with a knack for drawing people out. He was full of questions about Alaska, its needs and its prospects, and about me and my work and my goals.

We talked about Alaska's planning and economic development needs, and how I still saw the new state in peril for lack of a financial base. Paul thought greater economic ties with Japan could help Alaska. When I responded to a question that I had never been to Japan, he promptly offered to pay my way there to see for myself. While tempted, I had to decline due to lack of time in my new job.

Toward the end of our conversation, Paul asked if I would consider returning to Alaska to manage a multimillion-dollar development fund like the one he and the Ford Foundation had created for North Carolina. I had just made my yearlong commitment to HHFA, so I couldn't even contemplate the idea. In any case, running a fund that merely handed out grants to others did not appeal to me.

But Paul and I connected as individuals, and we became close friends for the rest of Paul's years. I kept seeing him on professional and social occasions, including visits to his home in New Jersey. One time, Paul invited me to New York for a weekend at a posh hotel to evaluate accomplishments of some of his Ford Foundation grant recipients.

The hope to bring Ford Foundation money to Alaska surfaced from time to time. In 1964, John Bebout got intrigued by the idea that the earthquake provided the perfect opportunity for the Ford Foundation to get involved in Alaska. However, I joined Senator Bob Bartlett in squelching the idea, as we were in the midst of marshalling reconstruction resources and simply could not afford any distraction from our efforts of directing massive federal money to the disaster.

Late in 1965, I received a phone call from Bill Wood, the University of Alaska president, who had just met with Paul Ylvisaker in New York. Wood asked me whether I would accept the job of director of an institute of social and economic research with Ford Foundation support. I said no, explaining my position with the new department and commitment to my Washington work.

Since I had no academic background, I had no idea why Wood had offered me the job until Paul explained it a few days later. Wood had come to his office seeking money to help strengthen the social sciences on campus by creating an institute on the model of the other sciences. Paul, who had overseen many millions in grants, explained his funding policy. To make a large grant, he wanted three elements in place: a good idea, an appropriate institution, and confidence in the director who would carry out the program. Paul agreed that Wood had a fine idea, and the university was the proper institution. But who would manage the grant?

President Wood gave Paul several names, explaining who each was, including a dean and some faculty members. Paul responded negatively to all of them. Somewhat exasperated, Wood asked what kind of person he was looking for, to which Paul replied: "An activist and experienced administrator. Someone like Vic Fischer." That's when Wood phoned me.

A few days later, the university's vice president for research, K. M. "Peter" Rae, called to renew the offer, and I once more refused. He then wanted to know whether I would assist the university with a proposal to the Ford Foundation for support of the institute. This I agreed to do, though I could not take the time for travel to Fairbanks. Instead, later in December 1965, the university sent three people to Washington to work with me, including my Juneau friend George Rogers.

George became the key to completing my connection to the university and my return to Alaska. In 1961 he had ushered a bill through the second Alaska legislature to create a research institute at the University of Alaska to study business and economic conditions and public affairs. He recognized from early on that such an institute could grow and form the intellectual basis of Alaska's development, and could do that with outside grants.

With only minimal state funding, the institute over the next several years provided a shell for George and for our mutual friend and colleague Dick Cooley to receive grants and contracts for their work. For a while, the nominal heads of the institute were Hans Jensen and Leo Loll, both university deans, but George performed many functions of a director, besides doing much of the research.

As an economist, George had already played a unique part in Alaska history, influencing policy from the 1940s onward without ever being elected to state office or obtaining much personal recognition. During the constitutional convention, when Tom Stewart collapsed from exhaustion, it was George who quietly took over and, with calm and good humor, kept the complex operation smoothly moving forward. After statehood, his expert advice and behind-the-scenes contacts shaped the establishment of the new state in its formative years.

George's books and other writings defined the issues facing Alaska for half a century. His 1962 book, *The Future of Alaska: Economic Consequences of Statehood*, became required reading in the field, for the first time exploring the implications of a state funded by natural resource production rather than broad-based taxes.

His mark was not always visible to those who didn't know him, but he was the economic advisor to two governors, Ernest Gruening and Frank Heintzleman, and a trusted friend and mentor to generations of leaders passing through Juneau. He presided over the local public policy scene with heartiness and warmth, personified by a bushy mustache and twinkling eyes under unruly eyebrows.

Using the institute and small state appropriations, George landed major foundation support for his work. His emphasis continued on resource development as a way to get Alaska's economy off the ground and to support the state. But he became frustrated. The issues facing Alaska were changing and broadening. Economic development depended on land, but the state could not view the land as its own. Alaska Natives had a claim, their numbers and poverty were increasing, and they could no longer be ignored.

George was among the first to recognize the breakdown of the political and social consensus that had carried Alaska through the statehood movement and the early years of statehood. Alaska began to transform in the 1960s. Natives gained their voice. Big oil arrived. Long-deferred land control issues had to be resolved in order for the state to move forward. No longer did everyone in a position of influence agree that rapid development was the best course.

The new values of the environmental movement grew with the recognition that development sometimes carried costs that outweighed the benefits for those already on the ground. In the 1950s, every significant voice on the political scene had called for local control of resources so we could bring economic development as quickly as possible.

I was no different. I had joined the chorus for preposterous ideas such as the immense Rampart Dam on the Yukon River, which Gruening promoted, and even for a proposed Russian dam across the Bering Strait intended to melt the Arctic Ocean (something I forgot and was horrified to realize I had supported when I recently read an old letter I wrote to Bartlett).

A new Alaska would have to accommodate more varying values: not only for resource development, but also for conservation and preservation of traditional Native ways of life. The year after the earthquake, 1965, George already saw that we needed a program that studied much broader concerns than economics and resources alone. In a letter discussing exactly what Alaska should request from the Ford Foundation, George wrote to me:

> I have become completely out of sympathy with any further studies relating to so-called economic development and have been trying to shed light on problems which are more basic. These have to do with the present general drift of our State as a whole and the need to be conscious of the direction in which it should develop. What I have been trying to put into words is some means for consideration of the future evolution of social and political forms most compatible with the most probable nature and extent of our economic development.

I fully agreed with George when we met at the end of that year to draft the preliminary concept proposal to the Ford Foundation. Consideration of these social and economic issues would form the basis for the Alaska research institute that the Foundation would support.

Our small group sketched out an initial work program, but we didn't have enough time to do a complete and adequate job. The Ford Foundation turned down the university's preliminary proposal. Paul Ylvisaker made clear to Wood that the Ford Foundation would not pursue funding of the institute unless I agreed to be the director. Despite repeated approaches, I was not ready to take that step. But the idea kept percolating in my mind.

To some extent, my ego was involved. Stepping off the Washington ladder wasn't easy. The work I was already doing was becoming more professionally exciting and promising, with the design of the new HUD department shaping up on flow charts with my name in a prominent box. Besides, I was no longer starved for Alaska, as my earthquake work led to further federal involvement in Alaska planning and economic development.

Paul helped me see reality more clearly. With prescience, he recognized that Johnson's increasing commitment to the Vietnam War would drain funding from our network of housing and other social programs. Moreover, Paul predicted that producing results from our new department's larger organization would take years. It would be ever more bureaucratic.

Alaska worked on me, too. That spring, the university invited me and Gloria for an all-expenses-paid Alaska visit to attend the ten-year reunion of constitutional convention delegates. The pleasure of being back in Alaska and seeing our friends again swept us off our feet. I was too ignorant of academia to be impressed by the university's generous job offer—to head the institute as a full professor with tenure—but the freewheeling excitement of the fast-growing Fairbanks campus and the dynamism of the other research institutes was contagious.

After the reunion, I rented a car and we took a leisurely two-day drive to Anchorage. Bright spring sunshine glowed on the snowy Alaska Range. We passed many places we knew well, places where we had camped, including the turnoff toward our cabin at Lake Louise. Despite the familiarity, the staggering, blinding beauty of the place shocked us as if seeing it for the first time. We had forgotten how outright magnificent Alaska could be.

Back in Washington, I was still torn, undecided what to tell Bob Weaver as to whether I would take the new job as a deputy assistant secretary of HUD, a major promotion with a large staff. I made an appointment to see him in the office on a Saturday afternoon to force myself to decide. I went in without knowing my answer. Casting the die on the spot, I said yes, I would stay in Washington. With that, Weaver called Bob Wood into his office, produced a bottle of scotch and three glasses, and we celebrated. I felt instant relief at having made a decision.

The next day, Sunday, I drove the family up to Princeton to visit my father. He was a fellow of the Institute for Advanced Study for two years, then became a Princeton faculty member, lecturing on international politics at the Woodrow Wilson School. I visited him fairly often.

I stewed on the three-hour drive north, wondering if I had made the right decision. Originally, I had come to Washington for three months, then agreed to stay for a year, and now four years had passed. I had turned forty-two. At midlife, my choice now might mean never returning to Alaska. Increasingly, my choice seemed wrong.

On the drive home from Princeton I discussed with Gloria my sense that we were facing a critical choice about the future direction of our lives. She concurred that I should turn down the HUD position and go instead to Fairbanks.

This time, after months of agonizing, the decision was firm. It was clearly the correct one. I called Bob Wood on Monday morning and told him the deal was off, that I was going to Alaska.

If I had stayed, the HUD job would certainly have ended two years later with Richard Nixon's election in 1968. By then, of course, the opportunity to join the University of Alaska and take over the institute would have passed. Certainly, my life forked at that moment.

That fall I worked in Fairbanks preparing, with George Rogers's assistance, the final grant proposal for the Ford Foundation and reached an understanding with various state and federal agencies to function more or less as their research arm.

Life in Fairbanks suited us from the start, living in a large house on campus, being part of the university community, and joining in the fun activity of a small town. The trees were golden in September and the weather delightful. Writing to my sponsors at the Ford Foundation, I said, "Have not an ounce of regret about leaving the Washington scene. An individual can be so much more directly involved here, even if the issues one gets into are not at such a grand national scale."

That December, the grant came through for $550,000, equivalent to roughly $5 million today. The funds would allow me to quickly hire a strong staff. In a few years we would apply for individual research grants and grow the institute to more than seventy members. And we would involve ourselves in all the tumultuous issues of that formative period in Alaska's history. It was a heady beginning.

⇥ 19 ⇤

The Institute of Everything

The institute I helped build at the University of Alaska became my permanent professional base, where I have an office to this day. I loved it from the start. Recruiting creative researchers, being surrounded by bright, young people, and finding grants to fund them suited my penchant for activism and enjoyment of life. The issues we worked on put me into the arena of the biggest decisions Alaska ever made.

The period from the mid-1960s to 1980 brought to a head the changes put in motion by statehood. Alaska Natives demanded their lands because of the pressure created by the state's selection of its land endowment from the federal government. The discovery of North America's largest oil field on state lands on the North Slope created an urgent need to resolve Native claims to permit construction of the Alaska pipeline.

Pipeline construction and the delivery of oil transformed Alaska economically in the 1970s. Meanwhile, the congressional debate about Alaska lands continued through that decade until the final resolution in 1980, when the largest conservation bill in history passed the Congress, the Alaska National Interest Lands Conservation Act.

Our Institute of Social, Economic and Government Research—later shortened to the Institute of Social and Economic Research, or ISER—emerged into prominence as the only economics and public policy research organization in Alaska. As these issues broke over the state like waves, we alone had the brainpower and resources to produce substantive research on the problems and proposals.

I approached the task of launching the new institute with all the vigor I could muster. Our Ford Foundation institutional development grant allowed us to do virtually anything in Alaska's social and economic arena. With this money to recruit people, we vigorously went after research contracts.

Our growth was extremely rapid, and we soon gained the nickname "The Institute of Everything." Most research institutes at universities focused more narrowly, but we took on the entire span of Alaska as examined through any of the social sciences. That approach came naturally, as Alaska was too small for multiple social science institutes. It also brought the opportunity to apply our findings to real issues with less concern for the disciplinary strictures of academia.

In time, we did work on mining, transportation, fisheries, agriculture, forestry, oil and gas, education, community planning and development, conservation, reindeer herding, energy, Native land claims, politics, leadership and manpower development, state and local government, tourism and recreation, regional strategy, and other topics. We did research and analysis, we did program evaluation, we prepared plans, and we advised policy and decision makers. We did everything.

A 1967 study I worked on with Don Foote and George Rogers on the island community of St. Paul is an example of how we brought research to real problems. The village, in the middle of the Bering Sea, was created by Russian fur traders who, in the eighteenth century, installed Aleut hunters and their families as virtual slaves to harvest the fur seals.

After the Americans took over, our government continued the arrangement, keeping the villagers like indentured servants to provide furs for the luxury market at a profit to the government. To revise the management of the fur seal industry, Senator Bartlett authored the Fur Seal Act of 1966, which among other provisions called for a study of self-government for St. Paul.

The US Department of Commerce asked us to do this study. George Rogers and I were ready, but we needed a specialist who could analyze large amounts of scientific data. At a meeting in Montreal, I met just the right person, Don Foote, a geographer at McGill University who had lived and worked in Alaska. Back in Fairbanks, I asked university president Bill Wood to approve an immediate hire. But when I gave Wood the hire's name, his face froze. He slowly said, "Over my dead body!"

Bill Wood had been an enthusiastic supporter, along with most of the state's political and business establishment, of Project Chariot, the US Atomic Energy Commission's plan to use nuclear explosions to blast a harbor at Cape

Thompson, along Alaska's northwest arctic coast. Don Foote was one of the scientists who demonstrated the folly of this idea for the region's environment and Iñupiat Eskimos. The AEC killed the project in 1962 after these findings and the bad publicity they generated. Wood vowed that none of the scientists involved would ever work for the university.

I knew all that. Wood's response didn't surprise me. But I had learned how to work with him. We negotiated and I got my way. We would hire Foote for a year and "see if he caused any trouble." He proved to be a skilled and tireless worker. The report on St. Paul was excellent. Unfortunately, before the year was up, Don was killed in a car collision with a state trooper on an icy winter road. A terrible loss.

St. Paul was a typically collaborative project for the institute. Foote analyzed past employment and social conditions of the Native population, documenting the repressive aspects of the federal management. George looked at the economics of the fur seal industry and economic prospects for the future, including tourism development. I studied the community's infrastructure, operations, and finances to determine St. Paul's ability to incorporate as a city and take over operations from the federal government. We showed that the islanders were capable of governing themselves and had the resources to succeed if given the chance.

Projects like this took me deep into Alaska. I spent weeks with the people in their environment: Eddie Merculief, who strove for community independence; the men out on the seal killing grounds; and the women who processed the pelts and made the community tick. I saw clouds of migratory birds swarming their nesting areas on the island's towering cliffs.

In its early years, the institute often grew from my connections and ideas. On a trip to Washington, I asked my former HUD colleagues, Bob Weaver and Bob Wood, to fund a study on the borough government concept I had helped write into Alaska's constitution and its relevance to metropolitan governance in America. Working with me on the project would be Tom Morehouse, my brilliant young intern in Washington whom I wanted to get to Alaska. I lured Tom with an offer to help pay for finishing his doctoral thesis at the University of Minnesota in exchange for a year at the University of Alaska.

The deal worked. Tom did a terrific report, fell in love with the state, became an indispensable faculty member of the institute, and retired from the university decades later after a highly productive career in Alaska. And HUD paid for our study.

I grabbed for every available grant and hired all the staff we could manage. As a new organization, we needed to fly high in order to get noticed. Not every hire worked out as well as Tom—we had to prune after the first years—but the strategy as a whole succeeded. The institute's name spread as the go-to source for social and economic knowledge about Alaska.

To make a difference in the major debates of the day, we needed a staff of self-directed researchers who could dig deeply and rapidly into big questions and produce timely, provocative, and applicable work for policy makers. We knocked down walls between academic disciplines, so economists, anthropologists, and political scientists could work together on common research projects. And we would have a point of view.

My own values and perspective imprinted on the organization in its early years. Much of our social agenda grew out of the War on Poverty and Great Society programs, with a belief that well-designed government programs could guide development in ways that would conserve Alaska's best qualities while alleviating the poverty and the lack of educational and health services that afflicted our rural, largely Native, population.

As George Rogers had originally envisioned and, as our 1966 Ford Foundation grant proposal explained, our research would identify the social structures needed to support Alaska's positive growth. The most important and complex aspects were in the Native community. First, Native leaders needed their own voice. As our proposal said,

> With a few notable exceptions, the Native population of Alaska has been quiet, humble and undemanding. The traditional lack of political organization, formal government or leadership, particularly among Eskimos, has given little experience for the demands of a representative democracy. Recently, however, there has been a growing awareness among the Natives of the realities of political life in Alaska and the need for unity. They are coming to learn that they can have a voice in identifying their own problems and seeking solutions only if they are organized.

The Johnson administration had a program supporting this kind of Native activism. The Office of Economic Opportunity (OEO) made grants for local community organizing. A statewide nonprofit organization called Alaska State Community Action Program (ASCAP, today known as RuralCAP) received the grants and channeled them directly to Native groups, as well as supporting job training, leadership development, and a variety of other social programs for rural Alaska. Anchorage and Fairbanks set up their own community action programs to access the OEO money.

The regional Native associations that ASCAP helped create were a critical element to Alaska Natives winning control of their land. As the state made selections under the statehood land grant, Natives were alarmed by the potential loss of traditionally important hunting grounds and sites such as cemeteries. The new associations began filing protests against state selections and making their own land claims with the Department of the Interior. Those claims eventually forced a solution of the Native land issue.

When I returned from Washington to Alaska in 1966, Governor Bill Egan was openly battling OEO and ASCAP. His concern didn't focus on the land issue. He opposed the federal government giving money directly to local entities and bypassing the governor and the legislature. He expected me, as a constitutional convention delegate, to back him in protecting state prerogatives.

I did not. I argued strenuously in support of federal grants that supported grassroots action rather than top-down state control and urged him to accept this reality and drop his opposition to ASCAP and local independence. Although we maintained our friendship, the conflict was serious, the first of many in that era as our views diverged. From my perspective, Bill needed more flexibility to deal with the changing times.

The governor stubbornly held on to his position of state control of funding to community action programs. He was also slow to pick up on the importance of Natives getting control of their land in the face of state land selections. Both issues spilled over into that fall's gubernatorial election campaign and cost him critical support in Native rural Alaska.

In early fall of 1966, I was in Anchorage for the first meeting of representatives of all of Alaska's Native peoples, hosted by the Cook Inlet village of Tyonek, which had been enriched by oil leases on its land. The meeting was fascinating to watch. Alaska's young leaders—Eskimo, Indian, and Aleut—most of them strangers from different regions, sized up one another and began to recognize the benefits of working together.

My acquaintance with some of these men now extends to fifty years, but I remain in awe that such a large crop of gifted individuals emerged in that one generation from Alaska's villages. They moved with astonishing facility from the world of hunting and gathering in the nation's most remote places to Washington's marble halls of power. Public-interest attorneys and other non-Native professionals also helped Native peoples press their case.

In part, Native empowerment came about because of education. Schools built in Alaska in the immediate postwar years and boarding schools Outside allowed young people to get enough of a start to attend college or get into training programs. Some of those students had just come of age in the 1960s.

Among them, Willie Hensley of Kotzebue wrote a paper for a graduate law class at the University of Alaska taught by Supreme Court Justice Jay Rabinowitz. The paper traced Native rights to land from the United States' purchase of Alaska from Russia in 1867 to the present, and argued that these rights had never been extinguished by war or treaty. It established the legal and moral arguments for the Native land claims movement that emerged in the mid-1960s.

In addition to the influence of education, the wartime work of Muktuk Marston carried through to the land claims era in an unexpected way. After he organized the Eskimo Scouts in western Alaska during World War II, service in the National Guard took hold firmly as a tradition in rural Alaska. Men who served in the Guard traveled, received technical training, and adapted to the ways of the dominant culture. Some Native leaders served in Vietnam. When they returned, they were swept into joining the land claims fight.

Young Emil Notti became the first director of the Alaska Federation of Natives, the statewide organization that began forming at the meeting I attended in 1966. I kept in touch to help AFN stay afloat through its financially precarious early years. At one point, ISER hired AFN to conduct a survey of Native leaders. We didn't really need the organization's help, but the contract income helped keep their phones connected a while longer.

Soon after, during one of my regular visits to the Ford Foundation in New York, I was asked to name Alaska's biggest unmet need. I named AFN, explaining that it was critical to the Native land claims movement. Although the conversation took place during a casual lunch with staffers, it was one of those "right place at the right time" moments. Ford had recently decided to establish a new emphasis on Native American issues.

The Ford Foundation allowed us to use our grant to help AFN. With that support, I hired a consultant who worked with Emil Notti to request AFN's own grant from Ford. That proposal brought an initial $100,000 grant for the AFN Charitable Trust, the federation's nonprofit arm for research and education, which shared its officers and expenses.

The arrangement lasted only until federal tax law changes forced AFN to sever the connection and to found a completely independent Alaska Native Foundation to receive foundation funding. Ford continued contributing to ANF, paying to develop the factual basis for Native claims legislation.

Our institute focused research on Native issues, but political and cultural sensitivities sometimes created difficulties. Judy Kleinfeld, hired straight out of Harvard's doctoral program, became one of our stars, specializing in education.

She published excellent books and articles on Native education. But Judy offended sensibilities and ran into harassment when she focused on under-achievement in village schools and unpreparedness for college—issues that remain too prevalent today.

Anthropologist Art Hippler got in deeper trouble. We hired him from California to work on Native issues. An antiwar radical from Berkeley, where he was a leader in the "Free Speech" movement, Art contributed right away to the leftist image of our institute staff. He organized an anti-Vietnam war demon-stration through downtown Fairbanks, upsetting the city's establishment.

University President Wood urged me to cool down my young colleagues, but I told him they should be free to exercise their constitutional rights. On another occasion, Wood asked me to clamp down on rumored staff drug use. I said I had no knowledge of drug abuse and was not going to get involved in the faculty's personal habits so long as their work held up.

Hippler was brilliant, but he became increasingly eccentric and outrageous in his views, publishing a Freudian analysis of the impact of child sexual abuse in village Alaska that offended many Natives. After a trip to Australia he took to wearing a wide-brimmed Aussie hat and veered into extreme conservative views, seen by many as racist.

I faced a difficult decision when it came time to consider him for tenure and was influenced too heavily in my recommendation by my sympathy for Art, whose fiancée had recently fallen down the stairs in his home and died of her injuries. In later years, I believed he was a liability for the institute, with shrill pronouncements and what I viewed as inability or unwillingness to obtain ade-quate research money to cover his professorial salary.

Such problems resulted in part from my philosophy of gathering the best minds and letting them run free. Some of the successes of the strategy produced the most impressive careers in Alaska public policy, among them Arlon Tussing, Tom Morehouse, Gordon Harrison, Gregg Erickson, and Scott Goldsmith. But we also ran into political shoals. I got mixed up in complicated situations myself, on occasion.

In fall 1966, I appeared on television in Fairbanks, urging Democrat Bill Egan's reelection. The program was rebroadcast several times. Local Republicans wanted me fired as institute director. Then Egan lost the election to Wally Hickel. Besides losing Native support, Bill made many voters unhappy with his attempt to stay in office for a third term. The constitution allowed only two consecutive terms, but his first term had not been a full term due to the timing of statehood, and so his reelection attempt was legally proper.

Over the next year, under Governor Hickel, state agencies stopped working with ISER. It took some time for me to realize this was happening. I saw Wally Hickel at a social function in Anchorage and asked him why he had blackballed us, since our function of doing research to further the development of Alaska matched his own mission. He invited me to meet him in his capitol office in Juneau.

After we sat down for a good, friendly talk, Wally called in his chief of staff and told him state departments were clear to work with ISER. I responded in kind, pledging to stay out of state politics for the good of the institute.

I had known Wally Hickel for many years. We worked together on statehood, hospital fund-raising, and other causes. But this was the point when we became friends, and we remained closer from then on.

As a political leader, Wally expressed an inspiring vision and constantly spun off grand and exciting ideas. He fit very much in the mold of the strong governor we had contemplated at the constitutional convention. But in office, his impact was muted because the people he installed around him couldn't keep up with him. In that first term in office, Wally was often like a general who charged ahead on his horse while the troops were left far behind.

I later learned who had been behind the state's ISER freeze-out. Wally's chief of staff, Carl McMurray, who had come to Alaska for work on the gubernatorial election, had advanced a conspiracy theory that I was a plant from the Johnson administration to take Alaska back for the Democrats. Given our shared history dating to before statehood, Wally wouldn't have believed that, and I doubt he was even aware of the notion.

In fact, most members of my group at the institute were well to the left of the state's establishment Democrats. In 1968, my younger colleagues on campus joined a push to take over the Democratic precinct caucuses. They were slapped down at the district level by the old guard, led by Alex Miller, who shut them out of any positions in the party. However, in deference to my status as a founder and territorial legislator, Alex made a special exception for me, and I became an alternate delegate to the Democratic National Convention in Chicago.

The trip to Chicago was memorable, not only because of the national scandal of the police attacking demonstrators, who were protesting the Vietnam War in the streets outside the convention hall. Bob Bartlett's heart was giving out. He had spent long stints in the hospital. His assistants had begun responding to my letters by saying he was too ill to read them. In Chicago that week, Bartlett often did not feel up to going out and would lend me his credentials so I could be on the convention floor and experience the tumult of the occasion.

Bob Atwood was there, too. He got credentials in an odd way. As publisher of the *Anchorage Times,* he could have attended as a journalist, but he wanted to get into the action on the floor, so he took a position as a page for the Alaska Democratic delegation, putting Alaska's most prominent nonelected Republican in the position of being our flunky, running messages. As I conversed with Atwood on the bus between our hotel and the convention and at other venues, we deepened our long friendship.

Bob confided that he still felt the letdown that had come after the thrill of the statehood fight, a cause to which he had been totally dedicated. His next crusade had been to move Alaska's capital from Juneau to Anchorage. He intended this to take the place of his statehood cause. But after two failed initiative campaigns, pushed hard by his newspaper, the capital seemed safe in Juneau.

Atwood and his wife, Evangeline, were unsatisfied and needed new challenges. They traveled the world looking for an interesting place to settle, but ultimately realized only Alaska would suit them. Bob then began inviting famous writers and intellectuals to visit the Far North as a form of mental stimulation. Despite our political differences and his many editorial positions that were not to my liking, we remained close.

That December of 1968, Bob Bartlett died. In anticipation of his death, Ted Stevens, a member of the state House, had pushed a bill through the Alaska legislature allowing the governor to appoint a replacement from either party, rather than requiring a Democrat for a Democrat as under the previous law. Governor Hickel appointed Stevens, a decision that added to my deep distress over the loss of my friend, because the role Bartlett had served so nobly since 1945 went to a person with contrary views. Shortly thereafter, President-Elect Richard Nixon appointed Wally Hickel to be secretary of the interior.

We were living the most eventful days of Alaska's history. In July 1968, the world learned of an enormous oil find on the North Slope, at Prudhoe Bay. Along with everyone else, we at the institute were impressed by the discovery's size. But we recognized its true significance only when our phones began ringing with a flood of requests from outside Alaska for information and for requests to visit.

The Fairbanks university campus, with its faculties of geophysics, arctic biology, engineering, and ISER's social scientists, represented the primary source of knowledge on issues pertinent to future development of Alaska's oil, including its transportation to the Lower Forty-eight. Before the oil rush came an information rush.

Each major oil company showed up with a different attitude. Atlantic Richfield, later ARCO, had a long presence in Alaska and was sensitive to local opinions. British Petroleum was civilized and polite. Exxon was arrogant and aggressive.

A minor incident a year later dramatized the fear of many Alaskans at big oil's arrival. The state's earth-shaking $900 million North Slope oil lease sale had just occurred, and a mob of people packed into a reception at the Petroleum Club atop the Westward Hotel in Anchorage. I was standing with several friends, including Iñupiat leader Charlie Edwardson, who had come from Barrow to Anchorage to protest the state sale, when a big Texas oilman carrying drinks rudely shoved through our group.

Charlie said, "Hey, you can't treat people that way."

The Exxon guy dismissively responded, "Well...things are going change around here now!"

ISER's founding principles made our role clear. We facilitated Alaska's transformation with research to help get the oil to market, but we also offered intellectual leadership to conserve the state's good qualities, including protecting Alaska's environment and encouraging the social and political structures to keep Alaskans in charge.

The first flood of interest about the oil discovery brought bankers, financiers, and consultants of all sorts to Fairbanks to learn about Alaska. I met many of them, trying to explain more about the state than the statistics could reveal. I took a banker from New York, Vince O'Reilly, on a drive from Fairbanks to Nenana to show him the sort of country a pipeline from the North Slope would have to cross. He was a bright, open person, and we immediately hit it off.

We stopped at an overlook along the highway with a magnificent view, gazing out over the Tanana Valley, the tremendous peaks of the Alaska Range, and the top of Mount McKinley in the distance. It was a moment of epiphany for Vince. He turned to me and said, "You know, Vic, I think this is the first time in my life I've been somewhere where there is no sound." A couple of years later, he moved his family to the Kenai Peninsula, where his daughter still lives.

On other occasions, I simply sat in on briefings offered by our faculty, marveling at their brilliance and range of knowledge as they educated visiting VIPs. One of our brightest and most important economists was Arlon Tussing, who had been hired a year before I arrived at the university. A graduate of the University of Chicago, Arlon combined incisive economic analysis with a radical political perspective—he had worked for the Socialist Party of the United States and in the Free Speech Movement at Berkeley—making him, in the words of a friend, a mix of Leon Trotsky and Milton Friedman.

Arlon became indispensible to our client agencies. We loaned him to the Federal Field Committee for Development and Planning in Alaska, a follow-on organization of the interagency earthquake response commission. Later, he went to work as a top aide to Senator Henry "Scoop" Jackson of Washington, chairman of the Interior Committee, a critical player in Native claims legislation.

Arlon's sense of humor and fearless way of expressing himself combined with his extraordinary intellectual capabilities in an interesting way. While he had a key role in many of the major political issues of the day, he often rubbed important people the wrong way. He never hid his superior intelligence or silenced his unique voice. They put up with it because they respected and needed his skills.

Oil industry executives themselves were far less receptive to learning about Alaska. They thought they already knew it all. The industry arrived with plans to build a pipeline from the North Slope to the Gulf of Alaska the way they did it anywhere else in the world—dig a trench, drop in a pipe, and turn on the tap. In Alaska's permafrost, that kind of construction would be a disaster. The hot pipe would thaw the permanently frozen ground, which would turn into muck, allowing the pipe to float and causing fractures and oil spills.

But the oilmen did show up for our first big event of the oil era. The Alaska chapter of the American Association for the Advancement of Science (AAAS) held an annual conference normally organized by the scientific institutes at the university. In 1969, our institute agreed to run the conference and focus it on the state's biggest current issue. The conference was titled "Change in Alaska: People, Petroleum, and Politics."

Arlon, Tom Morehouse, and I worked on inviting speakers and setting up sessions. Arlon brought in the best oil economists in the country. I rounded up funding from AAAS and organizations such as the Western Oil and Gas Association.

The science conferences typically attracted about 125 registrants, but ours kept getting larger and larger, until we had more than a thousand, including top national resource economists, oil industry executives, and government officials. We invited a number of provocative speakers, among them Robert Engler, whose book *The Politics of Oil* exposed in case studies how the oil industry had repeatedly used its economic power to buy the allegiance of elites and many ordinary citizens until it displaced democracy with its own corporate form of government. Engler wrote:

> Law, the public bureaucracies, the political machinery, foreign policy, and public opinion have been harnessed for the private privileges and the immunity from public accountability of the international brotherhood of oil merchants...Formidable perimeters of defense manned by public relations specialists, lawyers, lobbyists, and obsequious politicians and editors keep the spotlight away from the penetrating powers of oil. Instead the focus is placed on the mystique of petroleum production technology, corporate benevolence, and the possibility of an amenable public to be cut in on "something for nothing."

Many Alaskans were eager to get as close to big oil as possible. The oil industry, in its ignorance, had predicted the pipeline project would be completed in a few years. The business community had gone into a frenzy over the prospect of the wealth coming our way with this immense construction project.

In Fairbanks, with gold-rush vigor and optimism, investors were building warehouses and buying equipment they hoped to put to work on the line. The economy overheated to the point the phones stopped working. Getting a long-distance line could take all day, if you were lucky to get through at all, and even local calls often didn't work.

A segment of Alaskans hoped to manage growth for the benefit of the population, rather than the multinational companies that were on their way to the state. The invitation of Bob Engler was a shot across the bow for the oil industry. When the Western Oil and Gas Association learned that he was coming, they recruited a large cadre of top pro-oil industry people to attend. The conference, held two weeks before the $900 million oil lease sale, crackled with energy and controversy. Each day's events produced front-page headlines across the state.

I moderated the panel that included Engler and several oil industry representatives and supporters. Engler came out shooting, imploring Alaskans to prepare for the coming private government that would try to take over the state for its own ends.

"With whom do you wish to identify?" he asked, implying that the wrong answer would give away the state.

The session lasted three and a half hours, an epic of fiery rhetoric. The strongest of Engler's opponents on the panel was British Petroleum's Alaska manager, F. G. "Geoff" Larminie, who counterattacked with cutting wit and derision. He called Engler a cynic and pessimist whose analysis amounted to "a catalog of original sin." Popular sentiment was with Larminie, for he was saying what people were eager to hear: that the industry would work with the people and that oil was good for Alaska.

Forty years later, Engler's warnings seem prescient. Oil did take over Alaska's cultural and political life, bringing corruption and environmental disaster—as well as vast economic benefits. At times, the legislature danced to the oil industry's tune without question. The personality of the state undoubtedly changed as well. As Engler foresaw, individualism became less important and corporate power more dominant.

At that moment, at the dawn of Alaska's oil era, many raised their voices for conservation and citizen democracy. But those eager for oil riches called even louder to let the industry loose on the land.

The debate exploded into vituperation on the last day of the conference, when Senator Stevens spoke at the final luncheon. I had asked him to talk about the Law of the Sea Conference and its potential benefit to Alaska fisheries, and he came with a prepared speech on the subject. But he set that aside as he rose to speak and dove into the oil fight instead.

For the first time, we got to see Stevens blow his top. Ted had been in office only eight months and had not yet shown the flares of temper that would become his stock in trade over four decades as a US senator.

"I am fed up to here with people who tell us how to develop our country," Stevens raged, blasting conservationists who wanted to delay oil development. Looking directly at the assistant secretary of the interior, who was sharing the head table, he thundered that proposed departmental regulations for building the pipeline, such as strictures about stream crossings and required mosquito protection, were "stupid, absolutely stupid."

Ted went on like that for twenty minutes, venting his frustration with bureaucrats, conservationists, and other naysayers.

I tried to calm the waters when Ted stopped talking, but conservationist Dick Cooley said, "We heard from a man with a Neanderthal mentality, and even that might be dignified." Even mild George Rogers spoke out in disgust. In later years, few dared talk back to Ted's outbursts against environmental protection. But in those days Alaskans debated more freely on these issues.

Weeks later, when I asked Bill Hopkins, president of the Alaska Oil and Gas Association, what he thought of the conference that he had helped fund, he said it "felt like a condemned man pulling the switch at his own execution."

But the institute did not oppose oil development. In 1971, I received a call from Jack Horton, assistant secretary of the Department of the Interior, asking us to write the socioeconomic portion of the pipeline's Environmental Impact Statement or EIS. He needed it in thirty days.

NEPA, the National Environmental Policy Act, had passed in 1969, and the trans-Alaska pipeline became the first major project subject to its requirements, one of which was to file an EIS. The first draft of the study done by the Department of the Interior was widely criticized as grossly inadequate. It was without serious consideration of environmental impacts and gave no consideration at all to social or economic issues.

When Horton called me in Fairbanks, he had been blasted for those omissions at EIS hearings in Washington, Seattle, and Anchorage. He needed a better analysis without delay.

I talked to Arlon Tussing and George Rogers, and the next day we agreed to do the work, for the right price. We had been so deeply involved in the issues for the last few years that we already had most of the research we needed in our heads and our files. No one else could have tackled such an assignment as could we three.

Rather than a quick-and-dirty report, the study we produced contained innovative and fundamental advances to the debate. Arlon contributed its most important point. He recognized and quantified the enormous role Alaska's state government would have in the economy after oil started flowing through the pipeline. State spending of revenues from oil taxes and royalties, not oil industry jobs per se, would become the primary engine of the economy. That prediction opened many eyes at the time and ultimately proved correct.

———•———

Alaskans needed to decide how to handle our collective new wealth. The dilemma first arose in 1969 after the $900 million lease sale. The shock for the new state of receiving that money in just one day is difficult to convey. The entire state budget in fiscal year 1968 had barely broken $100 million.

State Representative Gene Guess spoke with me about his idea of holding a broad-based conference on the future of Alaska to develop a consensus on how to handle the windfall and to do so in the context of longer term goals. He contacted the Brookings Institution, and that fall I helped John Osman of Brookings convene an extraordinary process of group thinking over four long weekends in Anchorage.

The one hundred attendees of what came to be known as the Brookings Seminars included a wide range of Alaskans: liberals and conservatives, boosters and conservationists, business and labor, Native leaders, and academics. State legislators were there as observers but couldn't speak. National guests provided an infusion of broad futuristic thinking, as well as doses of reality.

Soon-to-be-governor Jay Hammond was on hand to advocate saving the money. But the consensus, reached on the eve of Alaska's transformation into an oil state, called for the windfall to be spent on Alaskans' long-deferred needs, with education and health leading the list of priorities, ahead of transportation and economic development.

The participants' caution about the future manifested itself in a desire to slow population growth—to keep the spoils for Alaskans and avoid too much change. Their optimism was reflected in the belief that problems that had lasted generations could be solved by spending oil dollars.

———•———

The pipeline project remained stalled for several years by environmental concerns and the question of who owned the land. The Natives' claims on Alaska land blanketed the entire state. Before the Johnson administration left office, Secretary of the Interior Stuart Udall froze all federal land transfers to the state of Alaska, or anyone else, until the Native claims were resolved.

When Hickel became nominated as secretary, he was forced to agree in confirmation hearings that he would not lift Udall's freeze until the Native land claims were resolved. Short of an act of Congress or other resolution of the Natives' claims, the freeze effectively blocked the oil pipeline.

The solution required a grand compromise between the oil industry, the Natives, and the environmentalists. Alaska Native land claims blocked the pipeline. Environmentalists could not be pushed aside without an agreement to conserve more of Alaska lands. A series of three major bills that passed through Congress from 1971 to 1980 accomplished all three goals: settling Native claims, building the pipeline, and setting aside conservation lands.

The grand compromise put oil pipeline supporters on the same side as the Natives: both wanted land claims settled. In 1970, with the Native land issue still before Congress, a pipeline executive had the idea of funding Native groups to make them more effective partners. He was Edgar Wellbaum, the vice president for public affairs of Alyeska Pipeline Service Company. He contacted my friend Paul Ylvisaker, who had a national reputation for funding innovative community organizations.

Paul, by then no longer with the Ford Foundation, asked me to work with him to provide an Alaska perspective and help with contacts. His concept was to establish a foundation in each of the four Native regions along the pipeline route, to be endowed by large grants from the major oil companies. The foundations would support leadership and technical training programs. The purpose would be to develop local capacity to negotiate effectively with oil companies and the state for local values and goals. They would be run by the people in the region.

I set up a series of meetings for Ylvisaker with Alaska's Native leaders. But on a flight from Juneau to Anchorage in a corporate jet, I suddenly found I couldn't breathe. This had happened once before, and it was terrifying. My chest constricted and I couldn't make a sound. After landing and being temporarily relieved by an asthma inhaler, I received a doctor's orders to stop my hectic schedule until the problem was diagnosed.

My friend Jack Roderick stepped in and escorted Paul to Barrow. He knew more than I did about the oil industry. Paul received a positive response wherever he went. His report, with only limited participation by me, recommended going ahead. But it never happened, as Wellbaum's oil industry colleagues lacked his vision.

The next year, 1971, the Alaska Native Claims Settlement Act passed Congress, ceding forty-four million acres to corporations owned by all living Alaska Natives and extinguishing their land claims.

The incident on the airplane forced me to face up to the consequences of decades of heavy smoking. After a long spell of total fatigue and a series of tests, ending at Virginia Mason Medical Center in Seattle, I learned I had a beginning stage of emphysema. I would be hospitalized for a couple of weeks.

But I didn't lose time. The steroids the doctors prescribed made me feel great and I had brought work with me. Spreading materials around my large hospital room, I made major progress on my book about the constitutional convention, which had long languished because I was too busy.

I now had been director of ISER for five years, longer than I had held any other job. The institute got along well without me when I was absent. We had excellent people who worked largely without my direction. The institute had gained a strong reputation and was a resounding success.

My work had become more routine, raising money and handling managerial chores, while the rest of the staff did interesting projects. I decided to quit the directorship, build a house in the hills behind the university, and work as a faculty member.

But when I communicated this intention to my immediate boss, Peter Rae, the university's vice president for research, he flatly refused to accept my resignation. Rae pointed out that I had barely finished creating the institute and that it had evolved around my personality. My knowledge and connections with federal and state agencies, foundations, universities, and scientific organizations were indispensible to continued success. If I were to leave now, a new person would take years to get back to where we already were.

I agreed to stay, but with a decreasing sense of enthusiasm. In the 1970s, Alaska exploded with new people, new ideas, and new ways of living and functioning as a society. I wanted to be involved as more than an administrator in an office in Fairbanks. Over the next years, my restlessness developed into dissatisfaction and a search for a new direction.

⚑ 20 ⚑

Fairbanks Years

The house we built in Fairbanks stood on ten acres of rolling hills of birch north of the university campus. I obtained the land by creating a subdivision for the owners of a large tract, and the parcel was my payment. Our friend Ed Crittenden designed a graceful house that integrates magically into the birch forest, which I believe is among the best of his outstanding architectural efforts. We lived happy years in that house, enjoying the warm community and limitless outdoors of Fairbanks.

The subdivision I laid out is laced with cross-country ski trails. Legally set-aside routes lead from virtually every back door to link with trails maintained by the university or local government. I often put on my skis at our house, bound for one of the university trails with my kids.

When we arrived in Fairbanks in 1966 I wasn't much of a skier, but I met with great success in my first race. Not knowing much about how to wax cross-country skis, I ended up with something that stuck to the snow like glue. The conditions were such that others were slipping backward on uphills. I was able to pass much better skiers by walking straight up hills on my sticky skis. At the end of the race, the course descended a big, steep hill. Too scary for me, I squatted down on my skis, finishing in that comical fashion to the delight of spectators and even ahead of the university's athletic director.

My three kids became exceptionally skilled skiers, racing on teams from elementary school on. My skiing improved, too. We skied all through Fairbanks's long winters, even during periods of extreme cold. I would hit the trails after work with the kids whenever possible.

One evening Greg and I did a hard workout in chilly weather. We skied ten kilometers (six miles), sweating hard when we came back despite a −35°F reading on the thermometer, and then found we couldn't talk. The cold air we had been gulping had frozen our throats. Our voices didn't return for several days. After that we had a rule: no hard skiing below −25°F.

Joe became a fearless downhill skier and jumper, with the attendant injuries. He had to quit because he ruined his knees, but he continues to run the Skiland skiing area in Fairbanks to this day. In the summer he is a construction worker.

Joe always showed a remarkable mechanical aptitude from a young age and ultimately seemed able to build, operate, and fix anything. He had no interest in college, but has continued to pursue his passion for working with machines. The house he designed and built on several acres next to our old house in Fairbanks is a technical marvel of energy efficiency. He lives there with his wife, Connie, an artist whose paintings and prints show all around Alaska.

Greg worked on pipeline construction right after high school, earning $1,100 a week as a grease monkey. He decided he didn't want to spend his life that way, but the money gave him wonderful college years. He spent the first half of his freshman year at the University of Alaska in Fairbanks and the second half bumming around the Rockies with his skis. The next summer he went back to the pipeline, followed by a fall semester studying scuba diving in Hawaii and spring skiing in the Alps.

Finally Greg found his way to the University of Alaska Anchorage, where the ski team put him on the slopes all winter and he gained credits at the same time. He got into computer science and has had a successful career in the oil industry and with his own computer consulting business. He lives in Anchorage now with his wife, Teresa Imm, who heads petroleum geology for Arctic Slope Regional Corp. Their son, Grady, works on the North Slope and their daughter, Mackenzie, is studying international relations at Johns Hopkins University.

Yonni's focus was always on music. Her talent blossomed spontaneously and unexpectedly, when she was short of six years old. I was studying at Harvard and we were staying in the massive cottage on the Manch estate. An uproarious thunderstorm rocked the house one night, a new experience for Alaska children. The next day, Yonni sat down at an upright piano and composed a song about the experience, singing as she went, "Wind blows in bad weather, so don't you cry." She had never had a music lesson.

Yonni can still play that song. And any other. From the beginning she could hear a song and pick it out on the piano. Her primary instrument is flute, and she has made that her career while staying in Fairbanks, teaching kids and adults, performing classical music and jazz, composing, and recording. Her *Tundra Swan* CD met with great success. She is married to dentist David Sulkosky. Yonni's kids are Gavin, who is attending the University of Alaska, and Yana, a high schooler; both also show remarkable musical talent.

When we arrived in Fairbanks, Gloria dived into the community just as she had done in Anchorage. Considering her involvement, it was natural that local artists approached her for help when the main gallery in the university area was shutting down. The Artworks was in a log cabin just off campus on College Road. We bought the building and worked together painting it and getting it ready. Ron Senungetuk, the now-famous Native artist, designed her logo and the big sign in front (he also designed the logo for ISER and executed it in wood carvings).

The gallery did well and became a center for the artistic community in Fairbanks, with big crowds at the openings of shows. She continued the business for four decades before recently shutting it down. In 2010, she won special recognition from the Interior Alaska Mayors' Awards for the Arts.

Fairbanks is known for long, cold winters, but the summers are warm, dry, and bright, and the city's location near the vast rivers that cross Alaska make it a hub for exploration. I bought a twenty-four-foot flat-bottomed riverboat with an outboard motor and got lessons in handling it from Terry Brady, the river captain husband of our institute editor, Judy Brady. He taught me how to "read" rivers, avoid dead-end sloughs, and jump over logs with the prop pulled out of the water.

On a hot summer day in Fairbanks—and it could get into the nineties—we would load the family on the boat and shoot down the Chena to the Tanana River, where we could run limitless miles in any direction. We might stop on a sandbar for a picnic or, if that proved too hot, just keep the boat running and let the passing air cool us.

We took multiday trips on the Tanana and up and down the Yukon, with our family and with friends. Along the shore, we would stop to explore abandoned cabins or to meet people living along the river. We could camp almost anywhere.

One of my best trips on the riverboat was for business. Toward the end of my time at ISER, I had grown frustrated with being trapped on campus with administrative duties, while staff were off on field trips. Jack Kruse, one of our professors, needed to go to Chalkyitsik, a tiny Athabaskan village on the Black River, forty-five miles northeast of Fort Yukon. I offered to take him. The son of my old friend Dave Loeks and his girlfriend came along for the ride.

We drove 150 miles to the town of Circle with the boat on a trailer and launched into the Yukon, traveling downriver to Fort Yukon, where we ran into Representative Don Young on the beach, on recess from Congress for a fall hunting trip. I had known Don for many years. He gave us instructions to go up the Porcupine River and then up a tributary to a certain spot, where he guaranteed we would catch dinner. We followed his advice and, sure enough, caught a large pike on the first cast.

For a week we traveled, camped along the river, and ate fish three meals a day. The pike were so big you could avoid the plethora of bones. The weather stayed hot and sunny and the swimming was delicious. Jack still laughs at the vision of me standing and steering the boat, stripped to my boxer shorts. The trip was perfect, except that we were ready for hamburgers when we got back to Fort Yukon after all that pike.

I had taken field trips in my earlier years at ISER, too. In 1968, after the Prudhoe Bay oil discovery, Governor Hickel sent a train of bulldozers over the snow to create an ice road from the end of the road system through Bettles at the foot of the Brooks Range and over to the North Slope. I borrowed a couple of university pickup trucks for an ISER field trip, and we went up the "Hickel Highway" to see it for ourselves.

The road was nothing but a bulldozed trail and the going was rough, to say the least. Having two trucks allowed us to winch one back on the road after it slipped off. We experienced the worst of the fiasco Hickel had created as the road began to melt (the environmental damage of creating the ice road became a lasting political liability for him). Coming over the top of a ridge into a valley, we saw that the road had turned into a morass. A line of huge trucks had stopped. At the bottom of the valley, dozers were dragging the trucks one at a time across the quagmire. A giant Caterpillar bulldozer pulled us across, too.

We stopped in Bettles for the night. The place was mobbed with truck drivers. We bedded down in the pickups and drove back the next day.

———

The institute grew through the 1960s on the Ford Foundation grant and individual projects. In the 1970s, we needed to find new base funding. Not long after I tried to resign and was stopped by Peter Rae, an opportunity opened that carried us onward, and proved that he had been right in his judgment that I had to stay to finish what I started.

George Llano, a biologist in the National Science Foundation's Office of Polar Programs, phoned me for advice on social research needs in the Arctic. The NSF, then as now, concentrated its polar funding on Antarctica, for reasons more geopolitical than scientific. Llano was quite aware that people lived in the circumpolar north and that study of human beings had been neglected in NSF's polar programs.

Llano's office had retained consultants to design an arctic social research program, but NSF wasn't satisfied with the results. He contacted me in hopes that we would come up with something better. When I asked him exactly what they were looking for, he said they didn't really know. We were left with a vague "We'll know it when they see it."

The NSF gave us a planning grant, and our institute ran a series of seminars and consultations with other university faculties, Native and community leaders, federal and state agencies, nonprofit organizations, and anyone else who might contribute. Within a couple of months we laid out a multiyear, multidisciplinary, multimillion-dollar research effort that we called the Man in the Arctic Program, or MAP for short. NSF liked it.

Then ensued almost a year of working out details of program substance, process, and budget, necessitating monthly trips by me to Washington. When everything was agreed, Tom Morehouse, George Rogers, and I flew to DC for a formal presentation to the National Science Foundation.

We were on stage in an auditorium with a standing-room-only audience of several hundred scientists and administrators. I was introduced and had just started to speak, ready to begin our MAP slideshow, when I stopped in midsentence. There was a commotion in the rear of the hall, and I saw several people were leaning over someone. A scientist was down with a heart attack, and everyone had to clear the auditorium.

George, Tom, and I wondered when we would be able to reschedule our presentation. Instead of being delayed, we were crowded with a group of the key people into a small conference room and told to go ahead. Although I was concerned for the well-being of the fallen scientist, I felt deflated after weeks of preparing for a grand performance before a star audience, and it was clear that the NSF people in the room who had a stake in our project were equally disappointed. We quickly ran through the program and called it a day.

Despite the setback, however, formal grant approval of MAP followed shortly.

We had taken a big bite. MAP funding would provide several years of major support for work by our staff and affiliates in ethnography, economics, community development, public policy, and other fields. The Ford Foundation grant had covered the full gamut of socioeconomic issues in Alaska. MAP would be just as broad, but on a more integrated, interdisciplinary basis and with a concentrated effort to coordinate individual researchers.

When the time arrived for a one-year progress report to NSF, Tom reviewed what we had done and realized that, rather than pursue our promise of a coordinated attack on big questions, we had allowed researchers to do their own thing. The best we could honestly say was that these projects would become coordinated in the future.

The NSF reviewers of our report confirmed that we weren't doing what had been promised and said that if we didn't get on track the grant would be withdrawn. The crisis got my serious attention.

Regrouping, we realized that the most valuable research we had done was in the economic area. The best way to integrate our work would be with an effective econometric model of Alaska's economy and demography to provide a tool for analyzing where Alaska stood and projecting future conditions.

I went to New York to get advice on economic modeling from John Meyer, president of the National Bureau of Economic Research, whom I knew. Among his suggestions was that we engage economist David T. Kresge to consult with us in Alaska.

I met Dave when he arrived in Anchorage, and together we flew to Fairbanks. It was midwinter, and he seemed in shock as we walked from the plane to the terminal in a temperature of –45°F. Four days later, after intensive work with our staff, Dave and I walked to the plane on which he was leaving. His coat was open, and he commented: "It's gotten warmer. I can actually tell the difference!" And he was right: the temperature had risen to –20°F.

Dave came back to head up design of a regional economic model for Alaska. We called it the MAP Model, after the NSF program that funded it. Dave stayed with the institute for over four years, using the model to analyze what made Alaska's economy function. He went on to be a senior vice president and chief economist of the Dun & Bradstreet Corporation.

The model itself became the baby of Scott Goldsmith, who had been recruited by George Rogers in 1975. Scott said the model was a quantified version of George's decades of economic knowledge: George contained in a computer. George didn't particularly appreciate that.

Besides becoming the core of the MAP project, the model helped set the institute on a new course. Rather than primarily being a breeding ground for ideas, we took on a longer-term role. Scott and a new crop of top-flight younger researchers studied Alaska to provide an intellectual grounding to its ongoing development.

The econometric model, which is still in use on Scott's computer, allowed him to project the path of the state's fiscal health as oil prices and North Slope production varied over time. The institute's perspective became one of tempering Alaskans' often unrealistic ideas about how to spend oil money on economic diversification and various government-driven development schemes.

The purpose of ISER was changing, and I was ready to place the institute in the hands of another manager for that role.

My desire to resign had been thwarted while the organization was reaching maturity. In its formative stages, the institute had generated ideas like a popcorn machine. I had set it on a path to grow fast and develop any kind of research. Now the institute had become a steady producer with less need of my talents as an initiator. I had been the right man to get the institute started and grow its profile. But now my approach was probably too laissez-faire about what our staff was doing.

Besides, as the university became ever more bureaucratized, the fun of running the institute lost its appeal for me. I was very ready for a change. When I canvassed our faculty, none wanted to become institute director. However, several agreed on a candidate.

I met the person whom we wanted to take over while serving as a board member of the Alaska Native Foundation. He was working with Emil Notti, ANF president, on Native claims. Critics of a large Native claims settlement said the Natives would dissipate the wealth they received. McGeorge Bundy, then head of the Ford Foundation, funded a study by Robert R. Nathan & Associates, an international consulting firm, to delineate the economic sustainability of a settlement.

But by the time the details on how to do the study had been worked out, Native claims legislation had already passed Congress. The study would be irrelevant. Instead, the Alaska Native Foundation reoriented the grant to help set up the corporations that would receive the land and to identify the land they should select. The bright young planner assigned for a year to the original study ended up staying for four to help implement the law. He was Lee Gorsuch.

So when I was ready to leave, I asked Lee to come take my place. He had already learned the ropes in Alaska and Congress and was perfectly suited to the job. After he agreed, we set up a selection committee that I felt confident would recognize him as the best candidate, which it did.

Lee wanted to move the institute to Anchorage, and we had started that already. Dave Kresge, Scott Goldsmith, Tom Morehouse, and other staff were already based there, and I kept an office there. Anchorage was where the action was, the center of Alaska's social and economic life, not Fairbanks.

The Fairbanks campus and community bitterly opposed any departure of funds or programs, which partially explains why the School of Fisheries and Ocean Sciences is still located there, in the middle of the state. Even for Lee, with great political gifts, moving the institute was a test of skill and determination. Over a transitional period of time, part of which required him to work in both cities, Lee got the institute officially moved to Anchorage. He dropped "Government" from the institute's name and molded the now-named ISER into an institution with a life transcending any particular director.

I resigned as director in 1976 but retained my position as a professor of political science. By that time, my life had transformed in other ways, too.

———•———

I fully understood Lee's decision to move ISER to Anchorage because I had
been spending much of my time there for several years. As the director of a
well-established research institute and perceived senior statesman, I might reasonably be looking forward to a comfortable retirement in Fairbanks, where I
saw my contemporaries settling into the respectable habits of middle age. But I
could not. I was still hungry for more life and new connections.

In the 1950s, a misdirected love letter had informed Gloria of my first affair.
After that painful incident, I intended to remain completely faithful. But life
happened. There were fun dalliances here and there, and just a few special loves,
but I remained committed to our marriage. Until I fell in love in Anchorage in
the 1970s.

Gloria remained the bright and interesting woman she had always been. In
many ways, I continued to love her. But her interests stayed closer to home: in the
social set with friends our own age, operating the art gallery she owned, seeing
the future with a more conventional, less active view than I had in mind. While I
charged ahead into a new life, she was ready to settle down.

I didn't quite know it yet, but everything about my life was about to change.

⊰ 21 ⊱

Troika Redux

In 1968, my father rented a spectacular, castlelike villa on a cliff above a beach in Tuscany for a joint vacation to bring together George's family and mine. This was the Louis Fischer of his warmer, later years, when he wanted to reconnect with his sons and grandchildren. If the trip had happened as planned, we would have had as much of his undivided attention as at any time in our lives. But Louis had a heart attack shortly before our departure, and the doctor vetoed his travel. I assumed we would cancel the trip, but Louis insisted we go without him.

Our family flew into Copenhagen. We rented a van and on the way to Italy spent two weeks sightseeing our way through Denmark, Germany, Holland, Belgium, and France. All this was new to the family: the castles and palaces, the variety of languages, countrysides so different from anything they'd known. Yonni, Greg, and Joe, all preteens, were particularly fascinated by the Dutch windmills, canals, and ubiquitous bicycles.

We spent an unforgettable month with George, Nell, and their children Mark and Sara at Torre San Biagio, a stone tower located on a promontory in Ansedonia, a small town halfway between Florence and Rome. It was built in the eleventh century as a lookout over the Mediterranean and for many centuries served as part of the region's coastal defense system.

There was plenty to do. We frequently climbed down the steep cliff to swim in the Mediterranean. The kids dove from the rocks and we all swam into grottos. The water was clear and deep and always welcoming.

Lothar Wloch and his family visited us for a week at the Torre. Our three families were together for the first time. Gloria, Nell, and Eva Wloch got along famously. The kids were constantly on the go. The Wloch boys, Lothar Jr. and Holgar, had grown into handsome teens since I had seen them in Lake Lugano, Switzerland.

Young Lothar became my daughter Yonni's first crush at age thirteen. They didn't share a language. His only English phrase was "Yonni, what are you doing?" He never understood her response, but that didn't stop them from walking around holding hands and staring into each other's eyes.

Since I had seen him a few years earlier, Lothar's career had continued on the same upward path. He had become yet more successful economically. The notion of Lothar's family moving to Alaska had evaporated. His driven personality kept him working extremely long hours, as I was doing in those days as well.

We both suffered health consequences from overwork and bad habits, although my hospitalization for emphysema at least put me on notice that I needed to stop smoking, as I eventually did. Lothar smoked and drank too much and didn't watch his weight. At the time, however, we enjoyed the prime of life and success, each in our own fields, and our friendship continued to grow and blossom.

After our Italian month was up, we Fairbanks Fischers flew to Berlin to spend a few more days with the Wlochs. They lived in a spacious home in the southwest suburbs of the city. A swimming pool adjacent to the house was accessible from the basement. Lothar was the king of the manor, the boys totally responsive to him.

I hoped to finally see Koni Wolf and reconstitute our troika. But again, as in 1964, Koni was out of the country. Since I couldn't see him, I decided to talk to his mother, Else, my mother's old friend. She lived in East Germany, and one couldn't telephone there from West Berlin where the Wlochs lived.

Late one afternoon, Lothar drove me to Checkpoint Charlie, where Americans could cross into the Soviet zone. I told him I'd find a phone to call Else and be right back, to which he just laughed and said he'd be waiting. The American GIs at the checkpoint window asked about my purpose and waved me through.

At the other side of the checkpoint, an East German policeman asked me the same question and I gave the same response. At his next request, I counted out my dollars and deutschmarks. He then asked me for my wallet and looked at its contents. With an "Aha!" he pulled out a folded hundred-dollar bill that I had long ago hidden in a side pocket for just-in-case.

An officer escorted me into a back room, where he searched through my jacket and made me turn my pants pockets inside out. He sat down and demanded to know to whom in East Berlin I was bringing contraband money. I told him it was simply an oversight, and that the money would have been hidden better if I had planned an illegal act. The officer kept interrogating me as if I were a criminal. The longer it lasted, the angrier I got. He acted like a KGB agent, which was frightening, but I never thought myself in any real danger. After a while, I was allowed to go on.

Berlin beyond the Wall was a wasteland. For several blocks, not a building was standing. Not a single person or vehicle was in sight. A phone booth stood starkly at the corner of a vacant block. I tried repeatedly to reach the number I had for Else Wolf, but couldn't get through. As my frustration built, I noted that a black sedan with two men drove by several times, one of them glancing in my direction each time. They certainly would know I was trying to make a call.

A bar was across the street. In broken German, I explained my mission. The bartender said that I would have to go to the post office in the main railroad station to make my long distance call. As I was leaving, one of the men at the bar asked where I was from. I said "Alaska" and was immediately surrounded by curious Germans.

The station was about ten long blocks farther. The walk seemed endless as the sky grew dusky. A light rain fell. The sidewalk and street grew busier as I walked. My friends watching from the sedan kept cruising by. I didn't care about them anymore. I was getting ever angrier about the wasted time, particularly with Lothar waiting for me.

Two Soviet soldiers in uniform came out of a doorway and walked toward me on my side of the sidewalk as if they owned the place. While others moved out of their way, I went forward, eyes straight ahead, as though they didn't exist. My satisfaction was total when they parted to let me pass. The American had won!

The pleasure was short-lived. After more bother and waiting, my call finally went through. Else was away, visiting relatives. By then it was pitch dark, and I went back as fast as I could, not caring whether the sedan followed. The tall American flag over the checkpoint was a welcome sight, as was my patient friend Lothar.

Our family connection with the Wlochs continued. A few years later, Lothar brought his family to Fairbanks for a summertime visit. They joined in the rhythm of our active lives, so different from how they lived in Berlin.

Louis never joined us on a vacation nor visited us in Fairbanks. After missing the Italian trip, he went back to his work on a planned three-volume history of Soviet foreign policy, aided by his young research assistant in Princeton, Deirdre Randall.

In early January 1970, Louis was visiting friends in the Bahamas, swimming and playing tennis, when he suffered a third heart attack. A medevac flight took him back to New Jersey, but because of traffic congestion his ambulance diverted from its intended destination—a hospital in Princeton—and he instead ended up at the hospital in Hackensack, sixty miles away. Soon after, I found him there, in intensive care, with George.

Louis was intermittently semiconscious and able to respond, after a fashion, but he clearly was dying. We were allowed in for only brief visits to say hello and offer encouragement. I had been on my way to a conference in Montreal when I got the news to come to his side. Seeing little to accomplish at the hospital, after two days I went on to the conference. George reached me there with the news that Louis had died.

The service in Princeton was huge. George Kennan, former diplomat and architect of American foreign policy during the Cold War, spoke about Louis and his work. Many famous intellectuals were among the hundreds who filled the modern Greek temple of the Woodrow Wilson School of Public Policy, with its tapered white columns. Kennan credited Louis as an early inspiration and mentor, and recalled how his unique personality had put him on the stage of history:

> For him the history he wrote was largely a matter of his own experience. Historical evidence and personal experience were for him inseparable. He saw history in terms of great people and great events. He knew most of the people. He had experienced, in one way or another, most of the events.

After the service, George and I released Louis's ashes in a small stream in Princeton that led, we reasoned, to the Atlantic, the medium of so many of our father's globe-spanning travels.

George took on the job of handling Louis's papers, an enormous task that ultimately required the professional assistance of Princeton University's Mudd Library to catalog hundreds of boxes of letters, manuscripts, photographs, and notes accumulated in the process of authoring twenty-five books and innumerable articles.

After the organization was done, George immersed himself in this material for many years. He understood the quality of Louis's work, but felt Louis had been a fraud for attaining the reputation of a great man while being an inadequate husband and father. Likewise, George came to resent our mother, who he believed had misrepresented herself with her outwardly joyful and nurturing nature, yet hid her true, deep pain.

I never felt such anger against either of my parents. Until writing this book, I rarely bothered to investigate my feelings about my family and relationships, nor analyzed why I made the choices I did or how my parents influenced me. I simply never cared greatly about these matters. When I critiqued George's repeated attempts at autobiography, I probably responded more forthrightly than I should have. He destroyed many of his papers, including several early, angry drafts of his life story.

For me, Louis's death simply came as an event to be acknowledged and dealt with. I knew he was proud of me, and I had enjoyed our usually brief meetings as adults. But without receiving warmth from him, I developed little to give him in return. His death, then, brought me no great trauma.

Yet I have wished many times that I had tried to break through to a more personal, loving relationship with my father while he still lived. Only in retrospect, relatively recently, have I realized that he did change and was probably trying to change more—to be more of a family man, even in his final years.

In 1974, Gloria and I traveled with Joe and Greg to the Soviet Union with a plan to stop in Berlin on our return to meet Lothar and Koni. Yonni, now a young adult, chose not to go with us.

Walking in the streets of Moscow, I saw a book in a store window with its cover dominated by the face of a hearty, bearded man. I would not have recognized him but for the title that jumped out at me—КОНРАД ВОЛЬФ, or *Konrad Wolf*. The book was about Koni, who had become one of the most important film directors and artistic voices of the Eastern Bloc.

Koni's films remain in circulation, resonating with emotional power and deep insight. Before others, he sought to cope with German guilt for World War II. His film *Stars* (*Sterne*), which in 1959 won the Cannes Film Festival's Special Jury Prize, told the story of a German soldier falling in love with a Jewish teacher as she traveled to the concentration camp. *I Was Nineteen* (*Ich war neunzehn*) in 1968 told Koni's own story of advancing with the Red Army and being put in command of a conquered German town amid the chaos of the ragged surrender.

The book cover I saw in Moscow allowed me to recognize my childhood friend when we got off the plane in Berlin. As a contrast to my previous visit to East Germany, Koni's status allowed us to walk through passport control and customs with barely a break to our stride. Besides being president of East Germany's Academy of Arts, Koni was a member of the Central Committee of the Communist Party, with a red card that put him virtually above the law, accountable to but few.

Lothar had put me in touch with Koni. Despite their vastly different lives on opposite sides of the Berlin Wall, they had kept very close over the years. Koni's position allowed him to travel at will and to issue invitations that allowed

Lothar to visit him in East Berlin. When the political situation became too tense, they would meet in Amsterdam or other cities.

Lothar never missed the openings of Koni's films, even if Koni gave him the word too late and he had to change his plans to be there. They treated each other like family. But I had not seen Koni in thirty-five years, not since the day in 1939 when my train pulled away from the platform in Moscow at the start of my first trip to America.

Koni drove me in his sporty little two-seat convertible, while Gloria and the boys rode behind us in a black government limousine with a driver, who also took care of the luggage. Seated at Koni's side and unburdened by the need to translate for the family, I was able to concentrate on him alone. As we sped to his apartment on Alexanderplatz, friendship immersed us in shared emotions and memories. As I'd felt with Lothar, a warmth and closeness beyond brotherhood tied me to Koni. In no time, we were completely connected.

Koni's apartment in a big, imposing building had been created by combining two regular apartments. It was full of fashionable, modern furniture. We arrived and met Koni's beautiful, young wife, Christel, a film actress. Koni set to work cooking a feast.

Koni was an expert chef, with a large kitchen equipped with every conceivable tool and gadget, and with cookbooks from around the world. He had used cooking to dramatize the emotions in his films, including in *I Was Nineteen,* when victorious Russian soldiers made hundreds of *pelmeni* (Russian dumplings similar to Polish pierogi or Italian ravioli) in homage to their humanity and thoughts of home. In our relationship, food stood for a human connection: the love that allowed our friendship to live on despite the barriers of time, space, and politics.

Lothar and Eva came over from West Berlin for the dinner. At last, the troika of our youth was reconstituted. Language somewhat complicated our conversation, but it created no real barrier. Lothar's English was strong, but not Koni's. My German was rusty, but my Russian had come back beautifully. So we mostly spoke Russian, with excursions into German and English as necessary, able to follow each other easily, although I doubt anyone else could understand us.

We talked mostly of happy times, our adventures as children, and the powerful feelings of nostalgia for those years. In some ways, we were the same friends we had been as three boys. But now, at around fifty years of age, a lifetime of experience colored our stories.

Lothar had been the strong, pragmatic boy. He remained a caring friend and father, and in our conversations he contributed with cheer. But his life had been the toughest of the three, and the historical trauma he had survived had marked him. I could feel some of the painful contradictions coiled in his personality.

Raised on our parents' dreams of a better world, Lothar remained a believer in some internal compartment of himself, but he lived as a hard-driving capitalist and voted conservatively. Materially, Lothar had achieved everything he could have hoped for in life, but he did not seem healthy. His striving couldn't hide his rage, and may even have driven it.

The Soviets' senseless execution of his father forced the teenage Lothar into the role of the male protector of his mother, Erna, and sister, Margot. Returning to Germany, they had been imprisoned and, after release, Erna was constantly harassed by the Gestapo, unable to work, forced to move frequently, a broken woman whose health declined. Lothar fought for her by joining the German military, hoping to lighten her oppression by being a patriot. He worked his way up as a soldier and a pilot until his capture, then spent three months in a British prison camp at the end of the war.

After the fighting, when George found Lothar, Erna, and Margot in Berlin, they were scratching to stay alive. He helped get them fed and housed. Lothar worked all day as a construction worker, carrying bricks, and at night studied to become a construction engineer, with George's assistance to pay the tuition. Through his extraordinary will and perseverance, within four years he had become a journeyman bricklayer and a civil engineer, and then began working as an architect. By 1954, he had his own architecture firm, designing and overseeing construction of hundreds of large-scale, middle-income housing projects as well as private homes.

Lothar met Eva, the sister-in-law of a war buddy, right after the war, and they were married in 1947. Erna remained sickly and died shortly after the war, tended by Koni's father, who was a doctor.

Koni and Margot fell in love and had a fiery relationship soon after the war. It was the first of many times Koni's heart would be broken. In 1949, he left for the College of Film in Moscow and started a new stage in his life.

When Koni returned to Germany, he joined the state-owned film production company, rapidly gaining the opportunity to direct. He was known as a darkly serious young man, given to wearing a long, black leather coat. His first film, intended as a comedy, wasn't particularly funny, according to a film historian, but when he turned his eye to portraying the lives of ordinary people in the setting of Germany's recent history and politics, he quickly gained recognition.

Koni's sensitivity and artistic ability as a boy shows through in films of profound emotional impact. But he didn't remain a disengaged dreamer. As a man, he moved through the world with verve and a hearty appetite for experiences. His life was full of glamorous women and disastrous affairs. Associates knew him as a reserved artistic genius. But at the dinner in Berlin, his humor and boyishness flashed brightly. We could also see the joy and intensity of his relationship with his young wife, Christel, although she too would later split with him.

Koni rose as fast in cinema as Lothar had in construction, but the political and social system of East Germany channeled Koni's life differently than West Germany's had for Lothar's. Communism destroyed the Wloch family, but uplifted the Wolfs. Koni's father, Friedrich, had avoided the Great Purge in a French prison camp during the Spanish Civil War, and after his return to Russia, both Friedrich and Mischa, Koni's older brother, accommodated Stalinism and worked their way up through its ranks.

While Koni earned his fame through his talent, his status in East Germany certainly benefited from Mischa, who became one of the most powerful men in Europe. During the war, the Soviets had groomed Mischa to help take over Germany, and by 1952 he had taken command of the new foreign intelligence service of the Stasi, the East German secret police.

When I visited Berlin in 1974, we knew only that Mischa held an important Stasi position, but later his career would be the subject of many books and endless articles and speculation. He was a master in the Cold War duel of spies, infiltrating Western governments, and even bringing down the career of West German Chancellor Willy Brandt. Yet his identity remained a mystery.

That evening with Lothar and Koni was not the time to talk of such things. Politics didn't come up. We three reunited as we had been as boys, full of cheer and warmth, enjoying that moment in the glow of friendship. Each of us had succeeded to an exceptional degree. There was no question of comparing our lives or of analyzing our psyches. Instead, we looked in wonderment on how politics and great events had separated us physically, but had failed to diminish our link to one another.

———•———

As we had done as boys, we began scheming. Instead of planning a journey to the Siberian Arctic or to Arizona, as we had done in Paul Massing's hotel room in Moscow, we now talked about a trip to Alaska, where I could show Koni and Lothar the North and the West of which we had always dreamed. Koni could screen his films at the University of Alaska, giving the trip an official purpose.

We parted that evening with a plan to meet the following year. Our family departed with Lothar and Eva, and we traveled on to Fairbanks.

Our university president easily agreed to issue Koni a formal invitation to Alaska. George arranged a similar invitation from the City University of New York. Lothar tackled red tape and paid for Koni's ticket. The trip occurred in April 1975.

Koni and Lothar flew across the Atlantic together, draining a bottle of Stolichnaya vodka on the way, supposedly to calm their excitement. When George met them in New York, they were already soused.

George had arranged to meet a friend who would take a photograph recreating the image from Berlin in 1945, in which the three of them stood arm in arm, the skinny Russian officer, the beefy American officer, and the emaciated former German soldier in the middle. Now they were all well fed, Lothar most of all. George and Koni wore beards and looked like the middle-aged leftist intellectuals they were. Lothar, thoroughly defeated in the 1945 picture, now projected the self-confidence of a German burgher.

George took them on a tour and for a big meal in his haunts in Greenwich Village. He was the host of the 1945 troika, in which he had taken my place from the original threesome. But his path was quite different. His involvement in the political foment of the 1960s had derailed his illustrious academic career.

George's work on the Soviet Union had carried him into the Ivy League with a tenured professorship at Cornell University. But he became dissatisfied with the study of a subject that seemed irrelevant to the great social changes sweeping America during the years of the Kennedys, Martin Luther King, and the Vietnam War. He wanted to get closer to the center of the action. He quit his safe position in Ithaca, New York, and took a prestigious new job in sociology at Columbia University.

When students seized Columbia's administration building in 1968, protesting the university's support of the US Department of Defense, George spoke out in their support. The university did not renew his contract. Looking for any job, he landed on academia's outermost planet, teaching at a community college on Staten Island that was part of the City University of New York.

George was humiliated by his fall. But, to his credit, he made the best of it, entering into the working-class world of his community, starting an underground newspaper, and becoming a real activist at the street level, rather than only a theorist. Over the next few years, George worked his way up through the City University of New York system and ended up teaching and mentoring working-class PhD students at the CUNY graduate school in Manhattan. Years later, as he lay on his deathbed, many of those students would write moving testimonials to him about his life-changing influence on them.

After touring and dining in Greenwich Village, Koni, Lothar, and George continued drinking in a back room at the White Horse Tavern, the famous bohemian hangout. Lothar and Koni were shocked to see the hippie and radical kids with whom George surrounded himself. Koni knew their clothing wouldn't even be allowed at home in East Germany, much less their lifestyles and ideas. Lothar disapproved, thinking of his own boys and how drugs and radicalism could affect them.

The setting and the times highlighted their differences rather than their connection as friends. An era was ending. While they met, the South Vietnamese military was collapsing and the communists were closing in on Saigon.

Koni remained a communist, even if his films added a humanizing element to his politics. George was an anti-communist, but identified fully with the radical youth movement in America, dressing the part and wearing his hair long. Besides giving up his career by opposing the war in Vietnam, he had been arrested while protesting in the street. But Lothar hated communism and dreaded its advance as Saigon fell.

The conversation grew hotter as the men grew more intoxicated. Susan Heuman, George's friend who had come to take the picture, remained to listen. Later that evening, Lothar told her he had been thinking of his father, executed by the communists, as his temper rose. He more than anyone could identify with the conquered South Vietnamese fleeing in panic on American TV screens.

Lothar grew red in the face and exploded. George and Koni fought back. Lothar said the United States should drop nuclear weapons on North Vietnam. George and Koni were horrified. They thought he sounded like a raving lunatic. The three separated that night in anger.

The incident carried great weight in Koni's mind. To him, it seemed to encapsulate in three friends the political divisions that had split the world.

I viewed it differently. Three strong-willed men got drunk in a bar and argued about politics. Nothing unusual had happened, and certainly nothing that could have undermined my friendship with Koni and Lothar.

George called me in Fairbanks and told me about their heated argument, still with a self-righteous tone in his voice. And when I met Koni and Lothar at the airport, they remained reserved and downcast over the fight. I ignored that, determined to have a great time with my friends.

We drove up the hill from the Fairbanks airport past the university and into the birch forest where our house stood. At the house, the three of us set to work making a vast quantity of pelmeni for the many friends I had invited for dinner. We took over the kitchen, cooked the meat, rolled out the dough, cut it in circles, and placed a dollop of meat on each circle. Then we wrapped them up and dropped them in boiling water. When we had finished cooking, our bodies were white with the dusting of flour and our voices boomed with our Russian-German-English conversation and laughter.

I set aside all my work and commitments while Koni and Lothar were in Alaska. Koni was seeing this scenery for the first time. The big, bright spaces seized his imagination as if he were a boy again. He even praised our Alaska architecture, with the placement of practical modern structures in otherwise natural settings, admiring the capitalists' ability to develop and create monuments in the North.

A big sign advertised three of Koni's films in front the Goldstream movie theater on Airport Way. He also had film showings, talks, and class appearances on the University of Alaska campus. In 1975, the coming of an important East German film director to Fairbanks was a big deal.

Besides attending Koni's films and lectures, the three of us took a flight to Prudhoe Bay so Koni and Lothar could see the true Arctic. The trans-Alaska oil pipeline was still under construction, and I only needed to make a quick phone call to arrange a flight to the oil field and a tour of the facilities.

Flying over the Brooks Range, Koni commented on how akin the land looked to Kamchatka, in the Russian Far East, where he had vacationed. The division between two such similar and spectacular countries brought up the phrase "divided heaven," the title of one of his films, which told the story of two lovers separated by the Berlin Wall and by their aspirations for different ways of life on each side.

We talked about how absurd it was for an invisible wall to stand in the narrow Bering Strait between Alaska and Russia, the first of many times we discussed building bridges between East and West. Reunited personally, the Cold War that had divided us and the world now seemed even more arbitrary and indefensible. Erasing the split inspired me and would develop into a major theme of the next stage of my life, as well as being a recurring topic of conversation and thought for Koni and me and for his work as an artist.

At Prudhoe, my friends caught the excitement surrounding the new technology that allowed work and comfortable living in the impossibly remote and rugged environment. For the three of us, the visit fulfilled a childhood dream. We had finally made it, together, to the northern edge of land where tundra gave way to sea stretching to the North Pole. We walked out on the frozen ice of the Arctic Ocean and had our picture taken.

———·———

Koni and Lothar stayed at our house while visiting Fairbanks, and my focus was strictly on them. But one night, after all had gone to bed, everything suddenly changed.

Gloria confronted me with reports of a sexual affair in Anchorage. I couldn't deny it. In fact, I had assumed she had known of it and had held back because she didn't want us to break up. But I was wrong. Gloria's shock and anger filled the air. I remember exactly the phrases she used: about my dishonesty, her embarrassment, and bitter regrets over the years that had elapsed since she learned of an earlier affair in the 1950s. "Like father, like son," she said.

In my mind, I had prepared for this moment for a long time. I never would have chosen that particular moment for the confrontation, but for some years I had been losing my faith in the future of our relationship. I had waited for the children to grow up. Now I told Gloria I wanted to end our marriage. Gloria said she had always expected us to stay together for the rest of our lives. Our loud, anguished voices carried through the house.

We talked through the night. In the morning, I discussed the situation with my friends, knowing they must have heard everything. They said they had been able to sense the tension since they arrived. I apologized for burdening their visit with my personal problems, and told them about the two lives I had been living: the staid life of a married senior academic in Fairbanks, and a freer and more satisfying existence, both sexually and intellectually, in Anchorage.

Lothar calmly counseled me to take it slow and not to make any sudden decisions. He and Eva had remained together through marital difficulties. I followed his advice for a while, but I never sincerely believed the marriage could continue from that day on.

Our troika traveled on to Anchorage to visit Ed Crittenden and drive along Turnagain Arm, south of town, seeing more outstanding scenery that deeply affected Koni. We took Lothar to the airport, where he was pleased to meet the German-speaking flight crew of a Lufthansa airplane bound for home. Before we parted, the three of us agreed to meet next time in Moscow or Siberia.

Koni and I still had hours left to wait for his plane to depart for Los Angeles. Sitting in the airport, we had our deepest heart-to-heart talk. Both of us were concerned about Lothar. He had restrained his drinking while in Alaska, but we knew of his unhealthy habits. Though sharing joyous times with us, we could sense how troubled he was inside. A grayness impinged on his friendly, open personality.

We also shared our feelings about the importance of our early friendship over decades on our different paths through life. We spoke of our parents, the absent fathers and the caring mothers. Koni was still in deep grief over his mother's death two years before. In both our cases, we were more akin to our mothers than were our older brothers, who were more like the fathers. Long ago, when I was age five, George had explained that to me: "You were born by Mama and I was born by Papa."

Koni wrote in his diary that I reminded him of the young Vitya in Moscow: calm, concentrated, self-confident, always open dealing with other people.

It was during this talk that Koni broached the idea of making a dramatic film about our troika. The thought began as one of our schemes, an exciting notion that would give us an excuse to be together again soon.

When the film idea grew into a real project, we had more serious letter exchanges. I told him I wasn't interested in being any part of an anti-American propaganda film. Koni assured me that he planned a truthful, personal story, not a political vehicle, and I agreed to participate.

But Koni had a hard time bringing the film to the screen. An early version ran into trouble with censors, and he struggled for many years to resolve the dramatic problems of the complex story. The work, although never produced as Koni contemplated, became a powerful strand connecting our lives, even beyond death.

Within weeks of Koni's and Lothar's departures, I planned another get-together for 1975. I would be in Paris for a May UNESCO meeting and would travel to Germany to see Paul Massing. I wrote to Lothar:

> Koni must have told you about our warm and intimate con-
> versation at the Anchorage airport. We particularly noted
> that the important bond between us still exists, and that was,
> as Kon wrote, a highlight of the visit. I'm very sorry we could
> not establish this level of relationship from the very begin-
> ning, but maybe we simply needed more time or needed to be
> alone more. In any case, it is very important to continue our
> friendship, to keep it alive. I am very excited at the prospect
> of seeing you both again and also Ev and young Lothar and
> Holgar and Koni's children. See you soon.

I didn't get to Berlin to see Koni and Lothar on that trip, but I did see Paul. His life was ending and the visit was deeply sorrowful for me. The man who had given a strong, fatherly presence to my life had now withered away. I knew I would not see him again.

Paul had left Hede Massing years earlier. Hede had made a name for herself in the 1950s as a key witness against Alger Hiss in the century's most celebrated spy trial. She testified that a fellow spy had implicated Hiss during a cocktail party conversation while she was still a Soviet courier. She then recounted the tale in a popular book.

I don't know if her testimony was true; her book has many self-serving elements. But for Paul and our liberal friends, her betrayal was unforgiveable. I saw

her only in a chance meeting many years later while walking across Union Square in New York. My feelings for her were cold, and I merely said hello and walked on. It was the last time we saw each other. My love for Paul had never wavered.

My mother died during these years, in 1977. I had been prepared for the event by seeing her age and gradually weaken on our visits to New York, and by a prolonged period she spent in the hospital at the end. Nonetheless, I was devastated when it happened.

George and his son Mark were in Alaska on vacation when she was taken to St. Vincent's Hospital. I flew to New York to be at her bedside, since my brother had looked after her for years. But George couldn't stay away and joined me, leaving Mark in Alaska.

Markoosha lingered without regaining consciousness. George and I made plans for her convalescence, but the doctor said there was no point, that she had massive organ failure and would not survive. After more than a week at her bedside while she was unconscious, I went back to Alaska for a long-planned wilderness trip. After I returned to civilization I received word she was gone.

I still haven't recovered. Talking about Markoosha's death is difficult for me. We had a special connection. I basked in her warmth and knew her pain. In the terrible days of the purge in Moscow, I had sensed her fear and despair. When she wrote in her autobiography that she would have stepped in front of a truck at the Soviet secret service offices but for my suggestion that we buy tickets for the circus, I knew exactly the moment she was recalling. I had known then, too, even as a child, that she needed help and what I needed to say to help her. No one taught me that skill but she herself, in the help she constantly rendered to me and to everyone around her.

The troika met one more time after our reunion in Alaska. In August 1975 we gathered for a meal in Berlin at the end of a trip I took to the Russian North with Ed Crittenden. The visit was fun, as always, but brief and not intimate. The three of us were never alone.

Lothar died of a heart attack in the summer of 1976. It seemed he had finally succumbed to the struggles imposed upon him by Stalin, Hitler, and his father's hopeless commitment to communism. Lothar's great success as an architect and builder came with incessant work, and he drove himself hard to the very end. The striving of his existence, together with stress and alcohol, eroded his health until his body could no longer sustain the burden.

I wrote to Koni as soon as I received the word from George:

> I feel as if a very, very important part of me, of my life, has died with Lothar. Seeing Lotka and you these recent years had helped not only to reestablish an old bond of friendship,

but it had also helped provide continuity for living, relating the early days, the past, to the present and the present to the past…In my mind, today, the images of you and Lothar as last I saw you meld and interchange with vision of our boyhood days…

I guess, Kon, my friend, I'm writing to you in order not only to share my feelings but to also understand them myself. I am overwhelmed, as I have been before, by the depth of bond and love that has overcome the years and the expanse of the world. It may be a matter of the stages of one's life, or one's personal needs for relating to others or for anchors in one's existence, the need to belong, to have, to care. As one gets older, particularly at our age when one has matured and achieved, it becomes evident that so little really matters. So many relationships and glories are transitory or meaningless, or both…

My grief for my friend seemed to encompass much of my world. Besides the deaths of people I loved, I saw the passing away both of my marriage and of the career I had developed for so many years, which now held little interest for me. While the sprouts of my new life were just rising, my first life had already withered.

⊰ 22 ⊱

Starting a New Life

When I first met Jane Angvik, I infuriated her.

It was spring 1974, and she had organized a major meeting at a downtown hotel as part of a long-range planning program for the Greater Anchorage Area Borough. A grant brought interesting national intellects to participate in a series of community forums on the future of Anchorage. A luncheon preceded each forum to brief the visitors on forum procedures, particularly the order of the speakers, a ticklish process with self-important men.

I had been corresponding with one of these experts, Alfred Heller, who headed a citizens' coalition that drafted a statewide plan for California, and I wanted to meet him in person. I asked the mayor's assistant Susan Ruddy, whom I knew, how I could visit with Heller before his scheduled talk. She agreed to squeeze me in for an hour after he took a helicopter ride to see the city, so long as I would pick him up at Merrill Field and get him to the hotel by noon.

I met Heller as planned. We went to a coffee shop and got into an engrossing conversation about California and Alaska. I totally lost track of time, so we got to the hotel more than a half hour late. I introduced Heller to Borough Mayor Jack Roderick, my old friend, and he affably invited me to take an open chair next to him.

A little later, Susan and a young woman strode into the room. It turned out they were concerned that shortly there would be a ballroom full of people, and the principal speaker hadn't shown up for the preforum briefing. The two had left the room to call the police for an all-points search for us, by the mayor's authority. And while they were gone, Jack had unintentionally given me Jane's seat at the table.

Susan briefly introduced us, and I hastily obtained another chair. When we sat down, Jane expressed her fury succinctly, demanding, "In twenty words or less, who are you and why did you steal my speaker?"

It didn't take me twenty words. My planning background impressed her immediately. But as the afternoon forum proceeded, she impressed me even more. Besides being young and beautiful, Jane possessed an extraordinary command of the room and grace in managing the meeting.

The session could easily have gone the wrong way, with the tendency of experts and politicians to monopolize the floor, but Jane played the room like Jascha Heifetz playing the violin. She kept the discussion moving forward, involving the ordinary citizens as well as the invited VIPs, and leading us toward consensus and conclusions.

Who was this woman who had developed such remarkable skill at such a young age? While I was entering middle age in the 1960s, Jane was growing up in a warm and energetic family in St. Paul, Minnesota. Her specific ambition was to be the president of the United States. Although her name and strong cheekbones would often get her mistaken for an Alaska Native, her heritage was Norwegian and Irish. Her parents were a combination of a conservative Lutheran father and a Roman Catholic mother, who had worked for Democrat Hubert Humphrey when he was mayor of Minneapolis and later a congressman.

Jane grew alongside her identical twin, Judy, with whom she shared a telepathic link and a private language. Both became high-achieving students and athletes, competitive swimmers and basketball players. Among her early post-college jobs, Jane worked in Minneapolis in a Great Society program called Model Cities, organizing and empowering disadvantaged communities. When President Nixon's administration ended that work, she came to Anchorage to visit her older sister Peggy and found a much better paying job as a planner in local government there.

Our arrivals in Alaska, separated by two decades, followed a similar pattern. As when I arrived in 1950, young people in 1973 again seemed to be running everything in a fast-growing and changing community. Like me, Jane quickly got a job at the center of the action, writing the borough's comprehensive plan and introducing neighborhood community meetings as its foundation. Despite being a recent college graduate, she quickly took on a role of innovation and leadership. She helped invent Anchorage's system of community councils and then worked for the Alaska Federation of Natives, providing technical assistance to villages and helping implement the land claims settlement.

I tagged along with Jane and her group for the rest of the day, talking with her through a big dinner put on for the visiting dignitaries and then over drinks late into the evening. She got over being angry and seemed interested in my history as Alaska's first city planner. I had preceded her on the path she was following. My interest was equally strong, but different, as I was captivated not only by her work but also by her liveliness, intelligence, and her loveliness.

By 2 a.m., we were alone at the hotel bar. I had postponed my flight back to Fairbanks and rented a room in the hotel. Jane wouldn't accompany me there that night. She thought of me as a fascinating older man, not a potential lover.

During the following months, the relationship grew and developed. While Jane might have been a compelling reason for me to travel to Anchorage, I was constantly there anyway for professional reasons, as the city was the center of the changes sweeping Alaska.

Alaska's Democratic Party had remained, since statehood, the party of Bill Egan, whose pro-growth perspective had changed little since territorial days. But the coming of oil had shifted the issues for many Alaskans away from a desire for rapid development to a recognition that many of our state's best qualities could only survive with controlled growth and conservation. The political environment also changed with the influx of young people, like Jane, with new values reflecting the social changes of the 1960s.

Young Democrats in Fairbanks had tried to take over the party from Egan's old guard in 1968, when Alex Miller quashed their efforts but helped me to the national convention. A statewide effort in 1972 was successful, as the so-called Ad Hoc Democrats flooded the party's caucuses and took over control of its mechanisms—realizing only after the fact, as my friend Bill Parker recalls, that the party was an empty shell without any real power.

In 1974, Alaska politics turned even more to the left. Nationally, Watergate invigorated young reformers and crippled the Republicans. In Alaska, Egan resisted the long-haired, pot-smoking crowd that controlled the Democratic Party's offices. He and his reelection campaign team, including Helen Fischer, our fellow constitutional delegate, refused even to cross the threshold of the party headquarters in Anchorage where the Ad Hoc group held sway.

Meanwhile, the Republicans, surprisingly, nominated for governor the folksy state legislator Jay Hammond, a champion of conservation and managed growth. Hammond advocated buying back oil leases that Egan's administration had issued in fish-rich Kachemak Bay, a move Egan stubbornly defended. When Egan held off the environmentalists and reforming Democrats with a stiff arm, they switched to supporting Hammond—including the new party hierarchy itself.

I talked to Egan in his office not long before the general election and urged him to recognize the new political landscape. He should come out and say he was a true environmentalist, too, as he loved nature and our beautiful land and would always defend it. Bill refused. He said the people should already know him after his decades of service and he wouldn't pander to followers of a new political fad.

Although I liked the policies Hammond advocated, I ended up voting for my old friend Bill. Egan lost reelection and ended his political career. I'm sure he later realized that the outcome might have been different if he hadn't allowed himself to be seen as an enemy of the environmentalists.

With the 1974 election, Jay Hammond became governor and the Democrats took huge majorities in both the state House and Senate. With Jane often as my companion, I became close to the enthusiastic young crowd in Anchorage, with its fun, excess, and thought-provoking, leftist agenda. My age didn't go unnoticed. Bill Parker told my co-author that he felt my arrival on their scene was like having a figure from Mount Rushmore show up at the party and behave just like the kids.

My dalliances in those days were fun and nonexclusive, but slowly Jane and I became more serious, and I often arranged my schedule around opportunities to see her. I agreed to teach a graduate planning course at the University of Alaska Anchorage, which would give me a weekly reason to travel to Anchorage, where we could meet.

Around the same time, I learned from the Anchorage city manager of the need to recruit strong candidates for a charter commission that would write a constitution to unify Anchorage's city and borough governments. I thought of Jane, and when we next met at the bar in the Hilton I encouraged her to run. She was twenty-seven and had lived in Alaska only two years, but I said her natural expertise would more than make up for that.

Jane countered that she didn't have money for an election campaign. Whereupon I got up from the table and walked her around the room, introducing her to each of my friends in the bar and touching them for campaign contributions. I particularly remember my friend Cliff Groh, a Republican Party stalwart and veteran of Operation Statehood, who handed Jane a fifty-dollar bill. At the end of the evening, she had $2,000 and was on her way to a successful campaign.

Only later did I learn that one plan had foiled another. Jane was elected to the Anchorage Charter Commission. At its first session the commission scheduled regular meetings for the same nights as my planning classes. Jane seldom made it to class.

The problem facing the charter commission grew from roots in the local government article of the Alaska Constitution, as did the solution. Anchorage was organized as a borough, a regional government intended to contain towns and cities within its boundaries. But the time had come for Anchorage to be a single entity.

The city of Anchorage overwhelmed the other constituent parts of the borough in size and contributed half the members of the borough assembly from its city council. For years, assembly meetings were pitched battles between the city and the borough. The relationship deteriorated into litigation and even a tragic incident in which Anchorage city firefighters refused to bring their trucks across Northern Lights Boulevard, the boundary between city and borough, to douse a hotel fire that killed five people.

State law allowed a city to unify with a borough that surrounded it to create a home-rule municipality with powers limited only by its own charter and specific prohibitions in state law. Unifying required drafting a charter, like a constitution, that voters in both the borough and city would approve. Jane became one of Anchorage's founding mothers as a charter commission member.

The commission resembled the Alaska Constitutional Convention in a variety of ways. The body was diverse in age, gender, and geography, and included old-timers and newcomers, all elected on a nonpartisan basis. It also comprised a bright and politically savvy group able to work through differences at a high intellectual level and to prepare the public to pass the resulting document. In 1975, the charter was approved and, in 1979, Jane was elected to the municipal assembly, still short of her thirtieth birthday.

Those were exciting years, when I felt myself again at the dawn of a new era for Alaska, as the oil pipeline was being completed and major decisions facing the state's future came in quick succession. Jane worked at the Alaska Federation of Natives and then in the policy-rich environment of the Hammond administration, where she coordinated the Alaska Public Forum, holding town meetings across the state.

My extracurricular life with her and my other friends in Anchorage kept me in constant motion. Jane and I even met during a trip to Europe. Jane had a conference in Frankfurt and I had one in Paris. We met in Germany and visited Jane's twin, Judy, who was teaching there for the Department of Defense. We ended up in Paris, soaking in the romantic atmosphere of the Left Bank.

But our lives and times together were anything but smooth. Jane hated the deceit implicit in our relationship and felt guilty about what we were doing to Gloria. We fought and broke up many times over the years, only to drift back together when our professional lives overlapped and we remembered anew the affection and interests we shared.

The blowup with Gloria during Koni and Lothar's 1975 visit to Fairbanks forced things into the open. I agreed to work on reviving our marriage. I was unrealistic and misguided, but I wasn't malicious in stringing out the breakup with Gloria while continuing to pursue Jane. For Gloria and the children—who were devastated far beyond my expectation—I somehow believed that easing out of the marriage would be better than a sudden break. Now I see I prolonged the pain. I still cared about Gloria and my home in Fairbanks, but I simply didn't see a future there.

Many things ended in a short time. The last of my children finished high school. My marriage collapsed. I quit as director of ISER. Lothar died.

For Thanksgiving of 1976, I had accepted an invitation to dinner with Jane and other friends in Anchorage, where I needed to be on Thursday to make an early flight on Friday for meetings in Kodiak. Gloria was furious. The grown children all had other plans, and now my announcement suddenly meant she would be alone on Thanksgiving Day. I agreed to take her along to Anchorage, where we dined with the Trycks.

I stood up Jane. She broke up with me once again. When I came back from Kodiak, she wouldn't see me.

I finally realized that I could not continue to live two lives. The day after Christmas, I loaded my International Scout with some basic things and left Gloria, our home, and Fairbanks. I drove the snowy Richardson and Glenn highways to Lake Louise, crossing the frozen water to the cabin we had built so many years before on the far shore. I spent the next week there in isolation, just thinking.

Our marriage hadn't worked in years, but deeply hurting Gloria as I did was terrible for me. We still shared values and interests and enjoyed each other's company. We had grown up together. Gloria said she thought we would be together through our old age, to death, and for most of our years I thought so, too.

Gloria was alone for many years in Fairbanks. The split divided our friends and weighed on our children. I carried my sadness over what I had done to her for many years, until she found a companion of her own. However, I never felt ashamed. The decision I made was, for me, unavoidable, and it made possible the next decades of my new life.

On New Year's Eve, I drove from Lake Louise to the airport in Anchorage and met Jane, who was arriving from a Christmas holiday visit with family. She

In New York City in 1975, George Fischer, Lothar Wloch, and
Koni Wolf joined to recreate the "troika" picture they had taken
at the end of the war in Berlin, thirty years earlier. —SUSAN HEUMAN

Vic Fischer, Koni Wolf, and Lothar Wloch stand on the frozen
Arctic Ocean near Alaska's new Prudhoe Bay oil field. The 1975 trip
fulfilled a lifelong dream of seeing the Arctic together.

The author and Jane Angvik were married in Anchorage in 1981. Both were elected to represent downtown Anchorage, Jane on the Anchorage Municipal Assembly, Vic in the state senate.

Vic and Jane adopted Ruthie Fischer in 1983. Kayaking in the ice at Aialik Glacier in Kenai Fjords National Park, 1985. —CLAY MCDOWALL

The Fischer-Angvik family traveled often to Russia, including living in Moscow for a year in 1994–1995. Here, Ruthie visits a statue of Lenin in Magadan, 1992. —JANE ANGVIK

Vic served in the Alaska State Senate 1981–1986. With staff in 1982, from left, Ira Winograd, Laura Fleming, Nancy Groszek, Ginger Baim, and Bob Williams.

A 1985 trip to the first high school graduation on Little Diomede Island. From left, Bob Rubadeau, daughter Ruth Fischer, and Jane Angvik. Russia's snow-covered Big Diomede Island can be seen behind the plane across the Bering Strait.

Alaska Native businessman Perry Eaton led the first business delegation to Magadan in 1989. Upon arrival, a steam bath broke the ice. From left, Gennadi Zavolok, Alaska Commercial Co. CEO Sam Salkin, local business executive Zelim Khan Tamirov, interpreter Steve Zelner, Perry Eaton, Vic, and a KGB overseer.

Doug Drum, left, and Andrew Crow, foreground, worked across the Russian Arctic to improve reindeer enterprises, 1992. —ANDREW CROW

Close friend and colleague Alexander Granberg, a world-class economist. In his Kremlin office while President Boris Yeltsin's economic advisor, 1992. —JANE ANGVIK

The author "claimed" Wrangel Island, in the Arctic Ocean north of Chukotka by raising the flag there in 1992. In foreground left Asylbek Aidaraliev and right Arkady Maximov, both colleagues in cross-border scientific and academic ventures. —JOHN TICHOTSKY

Vic met his half-brother, Vanya Leshchenko, in 1992, after one of their father's lovers wrote a memoir revealing his existence; here, in Kremlin garden, Moscow, 2008.
—JANE ANGVIK

A letter from Vadya Popov, left, reunited the author with his 1930s Moscow classmates in 1991. At center is Maya Turovskaya, also a student at the Nansen school Number 110, shown here in 1993.

The author's childhood friends Zilya Selvinskaya and Anarik Eisenberger, Moscow, 1995. After a life apart, including Anarik's decades in labor camps and exile, they rekindled a teenage love in their old age. —JANE ANGVIK

Markus Wolf, former East German spy chief and STASI general, with Vic in Zilya's apartment, 1998. Their conversation over vodka, bread, and cheese was filmed for a documentary about Zilya and Anarik, "The Late Dating." —EVGENI GOLYNKIN

University of Alaska Board of Regents chair Brian Rogers served on the Northern International University Board of Trustees with Magadan university's President Evgeni Kokorev, 1996. —JOHN TICHOTSKY

The Mask of Sorrow monument commemorates the millions of Gulag prisoners who passed through Magadan. It was designed by Russian sculptor Ernst Neizvestny and built by Magadan architect Kamil Kazayev, on right with Vic, 1996. —GUNNAR KNAPP

Russian billionaire Roman Abramovich visited the author at home in Anchorage in 2000 to discuss a proposal to draft Vic to run for governor of Chukotka. Abramovich ultimately took the job himself, and used his wealth to transform the region.
—JANE ANGVIK

All eight living Alaska governors joined to celebrate the fiftieth anniversary of statehood in Anchorage, 2008. From left to right, latest to earliest, are Sarah Palin, Frank Murkowski, Tony Knowles, Steve Cowper, Bill Sheffield, Keith Miller, Wally Hickel, and Mike Stepovich. —CLARK JAMES MISHLER

The author with his 1965 Ford Mustang convertible, Anchorage, 2010. Vic's first car was a 1936 Ford roadster with a rumble seat. —CADY LISTER

Jane Angvik received the 2011 Athena Award for outstanding professional accomplishments, community service, and advocacy for women leadership development. Shown on the Matanuska Glacier, 2008. —KATYA NEKRASOVA

Yonni Fischer's family. From left: son Gavin Hage, daughter Yana Fischer, Yonni, a musician, and husband David Sulkoski, a dentist. —NIKO SULKOSKI

Ruthie and Jonathan Dinkins with son Aiden, born January 2011. Jonathan, a US Army sergeant, has been twice in Afghanistan. Ruthie gave up a job as a Head Start director to become a full-time mom.
— TIFFANY HESS

Connie and Joe Fischer, 1990s. Joe runs a ski lift and Connie is an artist. They built a phenomenally energy efficient house in Fairbanks. —JANE ANGVIK

Greg Fischer's family at son Grady's 2006 high school graduation in Anchorage. From left: Grady, his mother Teresa Imm, girlfriend and fellow graduate Kayla Shepherd, father Greg, sister Mackenzie. —JANE ANGVIK

Vic began to paint in oils in 2004 at age eighty, never having studied or done art before. —JANE ANGVIK

Poppies, 24x12 in, oil on canvas by Vic Fischer. —CLARK JAMES MISHLER

Red Salmon, 48x24 inches, oil on canvas, by Vic Fischer. —CLARK JAMES MISHLER

"Susitna van Gogh" 48x24 inches, oil on canvas, by Vic Fischer. —CLARK JAMES MISHLER

Mischa (Markus) Wolf's best-selling book, *Die Troika*, told the story of the three troika friends and their families, subtly critiquing the communist system he had served as a spy chief for East Germany. This 1991 edition cover shows the original troika from Moscow days: Lothar, Vic, and Koni.

The Russian translation of *Die Troika* was entitled *Трое из 30-х*, meaning "Three from the thirties" and has Arbat Square on its cover. Issued by Progress Publishers in 1990, this book played an important role in Vic's autobiography.

hadn't spoken to me since Thanksgiving and was shocked by my appearance at the gate, even more so when I gave her the news I had left Gloria. We went to a New Year's party at our friend Lidia Selkregg's house. When the party was over we left together. I started living with Jane during the dawning hours of 1977.

That fall, I took a sabbatical from the university and went to Harvard for an academic year as a visiting faculty member in the Graduate School of Education, of which Paul Ylvisaker was the dean. Jane came and studied in the graduate school of education and at the Kennedy School of Government, and was the first in an Alaska underground railroad of friends we helped send there for one-year master's degrees for midcareer public servants. I worked in a bedroom of the faculty apartment we shared on a research project about Alaska Native regional corporations, funded by the Ford Foundation.

For me, the break from Alaska and return to the cultural and intellectual environment of Harvard effectuated an energizing restart of my life. I sat in on seminars during the day, joined colleagues for wine and cheese at the end of the day, and in the evening met old friends or attended films or lectures with Jane. Paul's office formed a base for our active social life. The year flew by in stimulation and renewal.

Koni visited me for a week in Cambridge to work on his troika film, bringing a producer, a scriptwriter and his wife, a cameraman, and a translator. He had in mind a dramatic film, not a documentary, and intended to consolidate characters and events to help the story. But the history it would portray was our own, and he wanted to use reality to fully develop the concept and a script.

Our interviews lasted many hours, in fact days, as we recalled the scenes and incidents of our childhood together—the fun at Peredelkino outside of Moscow, the dark months of the Great Purge, and my departure in 1939. No detail was too small. We recalled, for example, how for a period Koni and I wore hairnets to force our big manes to lie backward on our heads, something that Lothar didn't have to do. We covered my whole transformation into an American and life in Alaska. Koni collected Fischer family photographs and interviewed George in New York on that trip as well.

When the camera was off, we enjoyed a glorious week of socializing and celebration. Koni's colleagues were fascinating people. The interviews were in Russian, because both my German and Koni's English were too weak for a sophisticated conversation. The rest of the group was German, except the scriptwriter and his wife, who were Bulgarian. The language barrier didn't dampen the conversation. As Jane recalls, when someone told a joke, you could hear it progress around the circle, passing like a wave through translation from one language to the next, with a new laugh at the punch line every few moments.

We saw the group again briefly in Washington, DC, during a lavish reception given by the East German embassy for Koni, the famous filmmaker and president of their academy of art. He returned home and worked for years more on the script.

When our year ended at Harvard, I realized that I had no interest in returning to the life of an academic at the University of Alaska. I no longer enjoyed teaching and needed more involvement than producing research reports. After a final year at ISER, I retired from the university in 1979, planning to work as an independent consultant, but with no clear direction for my professional life.

The most interesting work of that period brought me back to the Alaska Constitution. The document includes a provision that requires a referendum every ten years on the question "Shall there be a constitutional convention?" Alaskans would need to answer soon.

The question had been a lively one at the first ten-year birthday of the state in 1970, because the ballot language was drafted in a way that suggested that the constitution required that a new convention be held: "In accordance with the constitution, shall there be a constitutional convention?" Litigation corrected the ballot language, and the proposition was soundly defeated at a revote two years later.

With the second decennial vote approaching in 1982, the state legislature set up a committee to study whether a convention was needed. Co-chair Rep. Brian Rogers asked me to examine constitutional amendments proposed over the previous twenty years and potential revisions that might be considered if a new convention were held. I also studied what lessons Alaska could learn from Hawaii, where a similar decennial question had actually led to a convention that revised their constitution in 1978.

In Hawaii, I interviewed Native leader John Waihee about his accomplishments in the convention, as well as other leaders and delegates. Despite the convening of various interest groups to rework the constitution, Waihee and his allies won the day, with significant changes benefitting indigenous Hawaiians, including creation of the Office of Hawaiian Affairs and making Hawaiian an official state language. Waihee later was elected governor.

Working on this study was interesting, plus it gave me an opportunity to spend time with my friend Tom Dinnel and his family in Honolulu. Tom had been director of Hawaii's legislative research service and then joined the University of Hawaii faculty, heading planning and environmental programs. We had first connected in 1967, when the Ford Foundation advised him to use our ISER grant application as a model for requesting funding. We had over the years become close professional and personal friends.

The constitutional studies convinced me that a convention presents far more risk than potential benefit. Never again could there be a process and assembly of people akin to those that created the constitution prior to statehood. Furthermore, a new convention opens the entire constitution to revision, including such exemplary provisions as the merit process of selecting judges. Opportunities for powerful interests to do mischief for their own benefit would be plentiful in a new convention, while the alternative method of change by amendment without a convention had worked reasonably well.

In our constitution, amendments are proposed by the legislature by a two-thirds vote and decided by a public vote. For the most part, the changes made by amendment have addressed the constitution's deficiencies and adapted it to new circumstances. The legislature also proposed some clumsy or ill-considered provisions that made it into the constitution, but there have been no wholesale revisions and few significant errors.

Since that project, Alaskans have never again given serious consideration to holding a new convention, although we have voted on the matter every ten years.

After Jane and I returned from Harvard we broke up again. Although we had lived together in Cambridge and shared a place in Anchorage, I still had not divorced Gloria. Yet at times I became possessive, questioning Jane about her whereabouts or meetings with other men, while her professional life kept her busy with collegial meetings and gatherings. She understandably kicked back, saying that I needed to straighten out my own life before telling her how to live hers. Because I also felt tied down at times, we agreed to split up permanently rather than ruin our friendship and affection for each other.

Being unattached allowed me to deal with my unfinished emotional business with Gloria. Now on my own, I could see that clinging to a dead marriage made no sense. We divorced in 1980.

For the first time since I entered the army at eighteen, I was without a job or a steady relationship. My parents were dead, as well as my surrogate father, Paul Massing. I was disconnected. And I was rather happy with the situation. Without reflection, I simply pursued the enthusiasms of the hour, having plenty of consulting work and enjoying my social circle in Anchorage, which included both the aged pillars of the community and younger friends. I was in this uncommitted frame of mind when I encountered a new problem I might help solve.

Republican State Senator Bill Sumner was coming up for reelection in 1980. He was widely considered to be corrupt. Senator Ed Dankworth, himself a conservative Republican, had publicly accused Sumner of taking a thousand-dollar campaign contribution in return for intervening to delay revoking a hunting guide's license. Sumner had also pushed legislation that would benefit his own business.

Sumner played the toughest form of politics, having won the downtown senate seat by beating liberal favorite Senator Genie Chance with innuendos about her husband, a state representative from Ketchikan. He seemed solidly entrenched and supposedly had strong support from senior, minority, and religious groups.

Getting Sumner out of the Senate became a cause for many in the community. None of the obvious Democratic prospects were planning to take him on. Before the spring filing deadline, a breakfast meeting was scheduled at the Sheraton Hotel among potential candidates and leaders, including my friend Arliss Sturgulewski, a Republican senator concerned about Sumner's behavior, and Jane Angvik and Joe Josephson, both strong potential candidates. No one had volunteered to run. All were holding back, as if waiting to see who would pull the short straw.

Anticipating the meeting, I realized it was important for me to know my own mind, so my path wouldn't be decided by others. Would I be the strongest candidate to defeat Bill Sumner? My assets against a politician with a dirty reputation were my status as a senior statesman and my clean record of public service. I fit the bill and was free to do battle, so I was the one to get rid of Sumner. I did not then think seriously of another consequence of winning—the necessity of serving in the legislature.

At the meeting, I said I would be willing to run, and that made the decision for the group.

I was unopposed in the Democratic primary. My first priority was drafting position papers, for which I convened a variety of experts. My experience from the personal politics of territorial Alaska and from a decade as an academic gave me all the wrong instincts, such as an interest in substance. I am told my first campaign speeches sounded like academic lectures. In retrospect, such naiveté is laughable. The big-money televised politics of the oil era ran on sound bites and images.

Yet my own memory tells me we ran a really good primary campaign. We did use all available media, and I spent much time going door to door meeting voters. We didn't receive much attention from political insiders, who figured I didn't have a chance. That is, until the election results showed that my vote count in the Democratic primary far exceeded Sumner's in his Republican primary. Seeing the opportunity to knock off the incumbent, supporters began contributing money and expertise for the general election contest.

One of my key supporters was Jane Angvik, who took over running the campaign. She now says she took charge because I desperately needed the help, and she was the only one I would listen to. Jane had been elected to the Anchorage Assembly the previous year. Although we remained friendly, we led different lives. Only in the process of redrafting my campaign biography did she learn that I had divorced Gloria, when I told her to edit out the line that said I was married.

Although working closely through the campaign, we remained strictly colleagues. We had no intention of becoming romantically entangled again. We had hooked up and broken up so many times that it seemed we had already hurt each other in every possible way. We were better off apart.

Today, Jane remembers me as a hapless candidate who needed constant oversight, though I was confident all along that I would win. No doubt her help was essential to building our campaign machinery and revving it up to the speed needed to take on a brutal opponent such as Sumner.

I never really enjoyed running. Although I got better at boiling down complex issues into superficial slogans, I never believed in that. But I had a great team helping me with that, particularly media expert Tim McGinnis, who had helped elect Jay Hammond governor a few years earlier.

Our message was simple. We said Sumner was corrupt and must be removed for the good of Alaska. A reporter had asked me when I filed for the Senate why I was running, and I blurted out, "Integrity is the issue." That became our campaign theme.

After Sumner saw the primary results in my favor he came after me, seeking to destroy my reputation for honesty. He attacked the work I had done on the constitution in Hawaii to suggest I had used state funds to go on vacation there. His smear campaign was funny and effective: postcards with hula girls that purportedly came from me on my state-funded Hawaiian junket, and a matching TV commercial. In fact, I had paid my own way to Hawaii, doing state business there and never even submitting a bill for the travel.

We were invited to debate before high school students at Steller Secondary School. The anger and nastiness of the campaign degenerated into shouting and personal insults. Former students still remember the bad taste from the event thirty years later.

The election of 1980 marked a turning point both nationally and in Alaska, as Ronald Reagan and the Republican Party swept into power. With Frank Murkowski's election to the US Senate, Alaska wouldn't have a Democrat in Washington for another twenty-eight years. But in downtown Anchorage, we beat Bill Sumner.

After the election, my son Joe and I went to Hawaii for some rest and recreation. I was totally exhausted and planned to stay with Tom Dinnel for the six weeks before the legislative session began. Tom had a house overlooking Honolulu on Wilhelmina Hill and also had access to a house on Oahu's North Shore that Joe and I were able to use for extended visits full of swimming and long walks and talks.

I was in a funk. Quickly recovering from the physical toll of the campaign, I came face-to-face with my fate. Now I would have to serve in the legislature. My upcoming senate term loomed over me like a four-year prison sentence.

If any reader has doubted my statements that I tend to live in the moment and rarely reflect upon myself, this is proof—when running for the state senate, I had never even considered how I would feel about actually being a senator. I had disliked the job of territorial legislator in 1957, and that lasted only for a single sixty-day session. Now I would be trapped in Juneau for four sessions, each lasting as long as half a year.

The loss of freedom rankled. For the first time, at fifty-six, jobless and unattached, I had carved all structure away from my life. I was liberated. Like a young person just starting out in life, I could greet every day as an opportunity, free to do almost anything. Now I would be stuck in the state capitol in the daily grind of floor sessions and committee meetings, following schedules set by others, with all the political and constituent meetings that fill the days of a legislator with urgency, largely without consequence.

For a time I moped around in self-pity. But on my long beach walks, I gradually adopted a more realistic perspective. I had taken on this responsibility and was now obliged to fulfill it. So I posed a question to myself: to what ends would I work in Juneau? The quiet and the lack of pressure allowed me to strip the question down to the basics. I surveyed my values and considered how the power of a state senator could be used to advance them.

As I walked, I decided to do what I could for the poor and underprivileged. To advance women's rights, improve women's economic status, and protect women from domestic violence. I would pursue equity, equality, and individual rights and freedoms. I would help protect Alaska's environment during the mad rush for resource development.

Having seen how the legislature works over the years, I also resolved to recruit a really good staff, without which a legislator cannot be effective.

To clarify and focus my ideas, I sat down to write them out in the form of a letter to Jane. My long letter contained no romance. I simply unloaded the thoughts that I had gathered on those long walks. By writing, I hoped to refine my purpose, connecting my work ahead to the lessons I had learned and the values I had absorbed over the course of my life.

But for Jane, these turned out to be words of love. With her dedication to public service and social justice, nothing I could have written would have moved her more deeply. She saw one more time that we shared common values.

Tom Dinnel's eight children were arrayed around the table for Christmas dinner when the phone rang. Jane was calling to say she had read my letter and that she loved me more than ever. I responded that she should come and join me in Hawaii. She said she already had a ticket and would arrive the next day.

I felt as if an on switch had been thrown in my mind and heart. From my gloomy ruminations, I now found myself in a euphoric new connection with Jane.

In January, I went to Juneau for the interminable 1981 legislative session, the longest in Alaska history, while Jane went on an extended consulting trip to Malaysia with a male colleague. Now she was doing her own thinking about the future. She wanted to have a child. She weighed whom she wanted as the father.

On Memorial Day weekend, I was home for a legislative break and picked up Jane at the Anchorage airport. Riding downtown in my Mustang convertible in the sunshine, she told me about her deliberations, and her decision that, of all the people she knew, I was the one with whom she would like to have and raise a kid.

We kept driving and talking all the way to Wasilla, where we dropped in on my old friend Katie Hurley, who happened to be visited by our mutual friends Malcolm and Cindy Roberts. They were the first to know that we had decided to marry.

Full Circle

≼ 23 ≽

State Senate

With my arrival in Juneau as a senator in January 1981, I began another of my fascinating encounters with Alaska history. The 1981 legislative session proved to be the longest and highest-spending ever. The session dragged on past mid-June, when a surprise coup in the state house of representatives switched the leadership and started things over. A flood of oil money washed through the capitol, making anything possible.

Good luck put me in a position to spend with the best of them. During the campaign, I had formed an unlikely alliance with Senator Ed Dankworth, a former director of Alaska State Troopers with a Texas drawl. Few politicians could have been more different than we were, except for the one thing we had in common: we had both wanted Bill Sumner out. Dankworth had publicly exposed his fellow Republican for accepting campaign money in exchange for intervening on behalf of a law-breaking hunting guide.

We met during the campaign in a coffee shop. He said it would be difficult to support me because he always thought I was a communist. I responded that I always thought he was a fascist. After that, we got along just fine. When the legislature convened, we were both in the bipartisan senate majority. Though a freshman, I became chair of the State Affairs Committee and vice-chair of Resources.

The amount of money coursing through the legislature is hard to grasp. The trans-Alaska pipeline pumped two million barrels per day while oil prices spiked to unprecedented highs. Legislative spending exceeded $30,000 per capita in today's dollars. The finance committee had to be equipped with new calculators because the old ones didn't have enough zeros to handle the figures we were dealing with.

Doing significant good was absurdly easy in this environment. On a flight to Juneau during this period, I coincidentally sat next to Kit Evans, who said she was going to lobby for an abused women's shelter in Anchorage. I responded that I would support the idea, but why build a shelter only in Anchorage? Why not build shelters all over the state? I easily added the funding for six shelters to the budget. We paid cash for new women's shelters in Anchorage, Fairbanks, Juneau, Bethel, Dillingham, and Kotzebue.

On another occasion, Molly Tryck asked me to help get space for a children's service organization in which she was involved. The result was state money for a family resource center that housed a gamut of children's and family services programs.

Aside from individual items we could add to the state capital budget, each senator had $11 million to spend any way he or she wished. Requests came from constituents, and long lists of projects were submitted by the city. Among other items, I obtained money to build a new soup kitchen for homeless people in downtown Anchorage, known as Bean's Cafe, and to expand a health center and a recreation center for the low-income Fairview neighborhood.

Resources seemed available to solve any problem. Don Clocksin, who represented downtown Anchorage in the state house, worried that Mayor Tony Knowles wanted to take funds allocated for a coastal bike trail and apply them to cost overruns on the city's new convention center. I made sure that the Senate kept the trail extension in the budget, and it became an icon of the city, with Tony Knowles's name attached to it. At the same time, I saw to it that the mayor also got enough money to finish the convention center, subsequently named for Bill Egan.

I knew at the time this high level of spending was unsustainable and called attention to the issue in the Senate. ISER's Scott Goldsmith wrote a paper in 1981 that pointed out the impossibility of continually expanding the Alaska economy with state spending. The bubble couldn't grow forever. In fact, it burst when oil prices dropped in 1985, causing a bust that crashed the Alaska economy.

Scott described our Prudhoe Bay oil as a finite savings account that could be spent only once and for which we had no reasonable expectation of a replacement. Using that framework, he calculated how much money Alaska could spend annually without touching our principal, living only on the income from our assets. The amount was generous: we could spend $1.4 billion. In other words, by saving and investing the balance of our annual oil revenue, the state could live perpetually on $1.4 billion in annual investment income, allowing increases for inflation.

I read from Scott's paper on the senate floor in 1982, calling for the legislature to spend only $1.4 billion and deposit any income over that amount in our new Alaska Permanent Fund. Nineteen pairs of senatorial ears seemed to be listening, but when I finished talking, my speech fell as if on an empty room.

Two or three years previously the state had gotten by on roughly the amount Scott prescribed, but in 1981 we had more than tripled the amount spent. We saved, too, but not enough. The Alaska Permanent Fund had been created by constitutional amendment in 1976 to divert a portion of the state's nonrenewable resource income into long-term savings. We made substantial deposits above the amount required by the constitution. But most of the money that came in from our oil bonanza went right out again in a frenzy of new spending.

So long as the money would keep flowing, I did my best to get a share of that funding for the poor and disadvantaged and to address the problems faced by women.

As during my ten years as a university institute director, I knew the key to success in my new job would depend on the quality of the staff I could recruit. The cadre of liberals I brought together, most of them young women, was the smartest and hardest working group in the building. And we had far more fun than any other legislative office.

I had met Nancy Groszek during the campaign at a get-acquainted event in a supporter's home. She asked rapid-fire questions about a series of women's issues, including the Equal Rights Amendment to the US Constitution, a hot topic at the time, and daycare for children of working mothers. I gave the right answers, and Nancy volunteered to work on my election campaign. When we won, Nancy became my key legislative aide and forever a close friend.

Nancy played a critical role in my legislation addressing the fairness of the Alaska Permanent Fund Dividend.

We arrived in Juneau as Jay Hammond was finishing his time as governor, focused on the dividend as his single fixed idea. Although voters had established the fund in 1976, its purpose and function as an inviolate savings account was not established until after a five-year series of legislative battles to invest the money prudently and insulate it from inflation. In 1981, the expenditure of the fund's earnings still had not been resolved.

Hammond began thinking about a fund in the late 1960s with the hope of creating a dividend to distribute shares of the state's wealth through an annual payment to every Alaskan. He later added another purpose for the dividend: to create a constituency to protect the permanency of the fund's principal. The dividend's deepest impact, however, and the aspect that has received attention internationally, is that it provides basic income that significantly reduces economic inequality.

Hammond's original dividend program passed in 1980. It distributed money based on citizens' length of Alaska residency. That concept was successfully challenged by two courageous young attorneys, Ron and Penny Zobel, for violating the equal protection clauses of both the United States and the Alaska constitutions. In 1982, the US Supreme Court appeared likely to strike down the dividend. A backup dividend bill, in case the Supreme Court ruled against Hammond's dividend, would instead treat everyone equally. It rushed through the legislature.

The new dividend concept would pay the same amount to each resident after living in Alaska for one year. This fairness gives Alaska our remarkable income equality. The payments function like a highly progressive tax. They make a big difference to low-income families, both rural and urban, while being relatively insignificant to the wealthy.

But this almost didn't happen. Nancy Groszek and Ginger Baim, who came to work for me in 1982, deserve major credit for making sure that it did.

They became aware that the proposed dividend could actually hurt the poorest of the poor: women on welfare. The annual payment could increase their income above the federal eligibility level for the particular month in which it was received, and that would bump them off the welfare rolls. Regaining eligibility could take three to six months, more than erasing the benefit of a permanent fund dividend check.

Nancy and Ginger developed an amendment for me to propose on the floor, a so-called hold-harmless clause. It would guarantee that welfare recipients would get as much from the dividend as other Alaskans.

When the dividend bill came up before the Senate, I offered the hold-harmless amendment on the floor. It was rather complex, and Senator Tim Kelly rose to ask for an explanation. I did my best, but I had not paid much attention to the mechanics of using permanent fund revenues to make the proposal work. That did not, however, stop me from talking on and on about its intricacies, trying to extricate myself from my ignorance of the details. Finally, in apparent exasperation and eagerness to move on, one of the senators asked that we proceed to vote.

Meanwhile, Nancy and Ginger were in the gallery cringing. They fumed. They despaired. They thought I had killed our chances of passing the bill. But I had either clarified everything or had so utterly confused my colleagues that the amendment was approved by unanimous consent.

The hold-harmless provision became law and allowed welfare mothers to receive the full amount of the first $1,000 dividend paid later that year, a major benefit for families with multiple children. The balance of my time in the Senate was spent fighting to keep the law from being repealed. It still exists today as an established part of Alaska's peculiar dividend tradition. Partly as a result, the disparity between rich and poor in Alaska has not changed much in thirty years, unlike other states in the Union.

———

The work of a state senator can touch an extraordinary array of issues and problems in rapid succession. Effectiveness requires quick study, willingness to grab opportunities, and, if the work is to mean anything, a clear sense of values to bring direction to the chaotic environment of choices.

I followed through on my resolution to address social issues. I fought for the life of the state's women's commission, for strengthening child support enforcement, to require that state statutes be written in sex-neutral pronouns rather than using *he* for either gender, and to establish Martin Luther King Jr. Day as a state holiday. My bill to require car seats for children under six has saved untold lives. Pediatricians called it the single most effective measure to protect children in Alaska.

Social advances we take for granted today resulted from much effort and compromise. Reining in Alaska's wild bars came about thanks to long and difficult negotiations I managed between Mothers Against Drunk Driving and lobbyists for the liquor industry. The resulting law prohibited "happy hour," drinking contests, and other sales techniques that encourage bar and restaurant patrons to drink too much too fast.

Other opportunities brought change in different arenas, connected only by my underlying beliefs. For my first four years in the state senate I chaired the State Affairs Committee, dealing with state operations: personnel, contracting, elections, campaign finance reform, ethics, public information, and veterans' issues, among others. I pushed to reduce the influence of big money in the election process, including closing a loophole that allowed a legislator to give a vote or official action in exchange for a campaign contribution.

As chairman I could also kill bills. Some that got lost in my bottom drawer were the perennial proposals to bring back the death penalty and a constitutional amendment to elect the state attorney general.

For two years, I served on the powerful Senate Finance Committee, but my six years of service on the Resources Committee provided the most interesting work of my senate service. Here we dealt with the lifeblood of state government, oil taxation (as I will discuss in the next chapter), as well as oil and gas development, land, mining, agriculture, and other resource issues.

The bulging treasury helped breed many unwise resource development projects in those years. With Senator Arliss Sturgulewski, I strongly opposed the

Hammond administration's disastrous agriculture development program. As we predicted, the projects wasted millions in public money and ruined small farmers. State funds bought a failed barley project south of Fairbanks, abandoned dairy farms on Point MacKenzie near Anchorage, unused railroad cars and grain silos, and a bankrupt state-owned creamery.

Even larger boondoggles died after great waste, but before consuming as much money as they threatened to squander. The state abandoned the oversized Susitna hydro project after years of fieldwork, studies, and designs, accompanied by endless promotion. A similar level of ballyhoo accompanied a private-public petrochemical extravaganza that proved so uneconomical, it just faded away.

As a resources member, I enjoyed learning about new topics, such as mining. The legislature was considering support for the massive Red Dog zinc and lead mine in northwest Alaska. To learn more, I joined an Alaska Miners Association tour of Canadian mines and saw various kinds of operations in remote areas. In Yellowknife, several of us went one mile down the shaft of a gold mine (more than five thousand feet) and crawled through several drifts to see the miners at work. (Never again.) On Little Cornwallis Island in Canada's high Arctic we saw a mine with integrated office and residential facilities similar to those at Prudhoe Bay.

My brother, George, joined a field trip to prospective mining sites in northwest Alaska. We met friends in Kotzebue and Nome and he got a first taste of Iñupiaq culture, stories, and life. We stayed with my old friends Charlie and Brenda Johnson, who served us a dinner of wild foods, capped by *Akutuk*, Eskimo ice cream.

One of my proudest legacies from my years working on resources was to establish a series of marine parks in some of the loveliest coves on Alaska's coast. Working with State Parks Director Neil Johannsen, I sponsored legislation that created a new system of state marine parks and designated thirteen of them, five in Southeast Alaska and the rest in Prince William Sound; more have been designated since. Most of these places I've never seen; those I did visit year later brought a surge of gladness when I realized that I had participated in their preservation.

Among my legislative contributions of which I am most proud is personal-use fishing. Alaska's Board of Fisheries formerly divided the salmon catch among commercial, sport, and subsistence. My bill added the personal-use category to allow even urban Alaskans to fill their freezers with salmon using nets, not only rod and reel.

The idea was brought to me by Larry Smith of Homer while the Senate Resources Committee was working on a new subsistence law to replace one struck down by the Alaska Supreme Court. The Alaska Constitution's requirement that all Alaskans receive equal access to fish and game created a conflict with federal law—and with justice—when times of scarcity put rural Alaska Natives' subsistence at risk.

The legislature never did satisfactorily resolve the subsistence dilemma, but I took the opportunity when the issue was on the table to give all residents access to fish for family consumption. The busy dipnet fisheries on the Kenai and Copper rivers continue today under this law. In upper Cook Inlet, twenty-five thousand residents received setnet and dipnet permits in 2010 and harvested half a million wild salmon, while the Chitina fishery attracted eight thousand people who caught a hundred thousand fish. The law also gives families priority for hunting moose, deer, elk, and caribou for meat before nonresident sport hunters.

The life of our legislative office gave me the warmest memories of my years in the Senate, memories that have endured more persistently than thoughts of political accomplishments. Our team worked hard but related like a family. In the morning, we had coffee and sweet rolls during staff meetings. On my birthday, it was strawberries and champagne. At the end of the day, we would bring out a bottle or box of red wine, talk about work, and enjoy one another's company.

One of my best and most enjoyable colleagues the first year was Sumner Putman. He had sought me out during the election campaign, coming to my apartment door to give me a contribution from a roll of hundred-dollar bills, money he earned as a pilot flying fish in Bristol Bay. He also brought into our circle his partner, Ginger Baim, who later became a loyal staffer and longtime friend.

Sumner was a gentle and wise six-foot-three-inch giant, full of energy and cheer. One sunny June day, when we streamed down from my office to sit by Juneau's waterfront and enjoy lunch, he and another huge man, newsman Bob Roark, also on my staff, picked up Nancy Groszek and swung her by her arms and legs, surprising and delighting everyone when they let her go flying, fully dressed—*kerplop!*—into Gastineau Channel. Nancy came up sputtering, but even she joined in the laughter after getting back up on the float.

The young women working for me were aware of common rumors in the capitol that they were part of Fischer's "harem." The truth is that in those wild years in Juneau my personal life was more conventional than many legislators'. I didn't do drugs, which were endemic to the legislative partying that commonly started as soon as the workday ended in the capitol and continued until late into the night. During the 1970s and until scandals quieted Juneau later in the 1980s, many legislators and aides would arrive at the Juneau airport and go straight to whatever Franklin Street bar functioned as the current "animal house."

One weekend during that first session, in 1981, Sumner invited me to fly with him and Ginger in his floatplane to White Sulfur Hot Springs on the west side of Chichagof Island. The hot springs faced out to the Pacific Ocean and were exquisitely remote.

The weather sparkled, and the views of Southeast Alaska's scattering of wooded islands were spectacular. We landed on a lake above the springs. Sumner lugged my foldable Klepper kayak down the mountain. Seeing a whale swimming just offshore past the islands, I hurriedly assembled my boat while my friends went off to soak in the hot springs.

Sea otters surrounded me as I paddled toward the whale. They bobbed next to the kayak with curiosity, the first time I'd encountered them so closely. (Their population was still recovering in those days and they were not as common as today.) Passing the islands, I entered the open ocean among four feeding humpback whales. Amid warm sunshine on gently undulating swells, they paid me no mind, but allowed me to follow as they slowly moved southward, gently surfacing and submerging.

The whales split up and I followed one pair, realizing only after I'd gone some distance from the hot springs that I had rushed off without a life jacket and the spray skirt designed to keep water out of the kayak. But I was too fascinated to turn back. I had to follow these huge beasts that were gliding with me through the smooth water. It occurred to me that I must seem like a toothpick to the whales, each forty to fifty feet long and weighing hundreds of times more than my boat, with me in it, but I was sure they wouldn't harm me intentionally. I figured that if a whale accidentally flipped my boat, I could hang on to the unsinkable kayak, and sooner or later Sumner would come looking for me and pick me up in his floatplane.

Finally, only one whale remained. I would follow until it disappeared under the water. Then I would wait patiently until I heard the *whoosh* of the exhaling whale and paddle hurriedly in its direction. This went on for a while. And then, while I was sitting quietly in the kayak, I felt a slight surge of water right next to the boat.

The whale surfaced, rising straight up, slowly, water pouring off its back as from the deck of a surfacing submarine. As if sensing my vulnerability, it came up with perfect gentleness, simply floating upward. The whale broke the surface about ten feet from me and lay still. We stared at each other for a long moment, me from my tiny boat, dwarfed, inspected, and somehow linked through the big, liquid eye of the whale.

And then the whale submerged, as gently as it had risen, next surfacing far away. I paddled back, deeply affected by one of the most indelible moments of my life.

Later that summer, my wonderful pilot, Sumner Putman, died tragically in a mid-air collision over the Bristol Bay fishing grounds. Ginger, who had worked for Representative Brian Rogers, came to work for us the next session, and she stayed with me for the rest of my legislative service.

Jane and I became engaged toward the end of my first legislative session. Our wedding on September 5, 1981, brought together a wonderful cross-section of friends from Alaska and Outside, people from the broad span of our active lives.

A symposium on the future of Alaska, with funding from the Alaska Humanities Forum, more than coincidentally brought in old friends such as Paul Ylvisaker and Tom Dinnel to Anchorage just before the wedding.

In the total equality of our relationship, Jane and I had two ministers manage the vows, one male and one female. Both were public policy experts, and good friends: Don Mitchell and Esther Wunnicke. Don at one point in the ceremony asked if anyone in the congregation wanted to say anything. The voice of our friend Jim Murphy came from the balcony, prearranged, making a brief comment and finishing by saying, "And I'm so glad Vic and Jane are getting married."

Without missing a beat, the sardonic voice of assembly member Heather Flynn shot back: "It's about time!" That brought the house down, as most everyone present had seen the travails of Jane's and my seven-year relationship.

With the exception of my brother, George, family representation at the wedding was from Jane's side. My children didn't attend out of respect for Gloria, and some of our old friends from the early days didn't either. So my heart leapt on that sunny day at a mountainside restaurant high above Anchorage when I saw through a window Ed and Kit Crittenden approaching across the parking lot. (My children came to know and love Jane.)

Jane's parents, Margaret and Arthur, were there, as well as her sisters Judy, Patty, and Peggy, and brother, Bill; her nieces Monica and Erika; aunt Ruth; and a couple of brothers-in-law. Beyond these, I married into an extended family that included literally dozens of first cousins and a myriad of other relatives, who all seemed to love and get along with one another.

The many women in my life had not, however, allowed me to marry without a proper send-off. They secretly organized a "doe party" (rather than a stag party), to which I was driven blindfolded by three gorgeous women in a Cadillac convertible. I was taken to an unfamiliar place, led down steep stairs, and stripped bare. When the blindfold was removed I was astonished to see twenty women sitting on a long wraparound couch, their feet toward me, none wearing any clothes.

It was a situation from any man's fantasy, but the women, ranging up to sixty years old, were there as friends and as feminists who saw me as a champion of their causes. After a couple of hours, Jane, who had not been told what was planned and was not allowed to be there, was called to come and pick me up.

Our unconventional marriage united two political careers and two cities. As a senator, I was gone half the year, although our generous legislative budgets allowed me to fly back and forth frequently between Anchorage and Juneau. Jane's membership on the Anchorage Assembly and her work as president of the Alaska Native Foundation kept her equally busy. When at the end of 1982 we took a postwedding trip to visit our friend Steve Reeve and his family in Africa and receive his gift of a hot air balloon ride over the Serengeti, Jane twice had to backtrack all the way to Anchorage to provide the deciding vote Mayor Knowles needed for the assembly to pass his budget.

After I won the 1980 election, I had been sincerely reluctant to become a legislator. Two years later, I had adapted emotionally and thought I couldn't be anything else. When reapportionment unexpectedly required me to run again in 1982, I didn't consider quitting, although my original purpose of eliminating Bill Sumner had been achieved. I was reelected without difficulty to a full four-year term.

⇥ 24 ⇤

Transitions

In 1983, Jane was at work when she found her assistant, Geraldine Squartsoff, crying at her desk. Geri was nineteen, working and attending college, and had a new husband. A troubled younger sister, Irene, unable to care for her baby, had dropped the newborn on Geri, who felt overwhelmed and asked Jane if she knew anyone who wanted a baby.

Jane had suffered two miscarriages since our wedding. She called me in Fairbanks, where I was having dinner with my three grown children, and asked if I still wanted a child. I said, "Sure. Are you pregnant?" Jane said no, but there might be a baby to adopt, to which I responded, "Don't do anything till I get back."

We met our daughter, a beautiful six-week-old, at Jane's office the next day. She was an Alaska Native from Kodiak, and there was a problem. Under federal law, prior right for adoption rested with a child's tribe. Fortunately for us, we found that a recent court case had established that the mother could direct who could adopt her child, even over the wishes of the tribe. Jane met the birth mother, Irene, to see if she would agree to a similar arrangement through our attorney, John Reese.

Jane came back from that meeting wishing we could adopt Irene as well. The girl came from a family of six children, who had been scattered after the death of their parents in a car accident. Irene's sad and chaotic childhood had left her with a disrupted education and not much hope for the future. She told Jane that what she wanted for her daughter was a family that would be kind to her, provide a good education with plenty of opportunities, and a pretty dress.

When they shopped together, Jane was always on the lookout for pretty dresses for our daughter Ruthie. She knows well that was what her birth mother wanted for her. Today Ruthie has graduated from college, married, and become a mother.

Ruthie met Irene along with her birth mother's other siblings at a reunion thirty years after her grandparents' death. Ruthie said she enjoyed seeing a group of relatives who all looked like her. But Irene's life remained tragic. She died in Los Angeles at a young age. Ruthie laid her to rest at her Kodiak home village of Port Lions in 2007.

On her first night with us, in September 1983, Ruthie slept in a bureau drawer so we could keep her at our bedside.

I was delighted to be a father again and relished having a baby to care for. I had time and maturity that I had lacked twenty-five years earlier when Greg, Yonni, and Joe had come into my life.

Jane and I both had busy careers, and Ruthie would come along with whoever could best manage her each day. She had been ours only a few days when I took her along to a legislative hearing in Anchorage that I chaired, and put her up on a counter in the middle of the proceedings to change her diaper.

When it was time to go to Juneau for the next legislative session, I wanted to take our baby with me, but Jane would have none of that. So Ruthie became a commuter—one week in Anchorage with Jane, next week in Juneau with me. Since I usually had business in Anchorage during weekends, I would often transport her. If Jane had business in Juneau, she would do the honors. If neither of us was able to travel, Ruthie would go with a friend. We knew so many people going between Anchorage and Juneau, it was easy to find a lap for her to sit on. The powerful lobbyist Sam Kito did the duty a couple of times, taking Ruthie from me at the gate in Juneau and handing her over to Jane in Anchorage. The flight attendants got to know Ruthie, too. She was something of a favorite on the planes.

During her Juneau week, Ruthie would lie on a pad in my office or swing in her Johnny Jump Up during the day, interacting with everyone who stopped by. She rode around the capitol on my back, smiling down from her perch on anyone we encountered. My capable staff often stepped in as babysitters in the office, too. After hours, Ruthie and I might drop by a reception, where she would reach down from her backpack perch to grab a cracker or a carrot.

In 1984 a trip to China revived my thoughts of Russia. Rick Mystrom, chair of the Anchorage Assembly, and Jane, incoming assembly chair, were traveling to Harbin, China, to establish sister-city relations, and Rick's wife, Mary, and I got to go along. During the first part of the twentieth century, Harbin had served as the administrative center of the Chinese portion of Russia's Trans-Siberian Railway, with most of the town's population Russian. The architectural style of the city's downtown reminded me very much of St. Petersburg. It had a population of millions.

Russian turned out to be my principal means of communication. Most formal discussion with our hosts and conversations with others had to go through Chinese-English interpreters. But one of the key Chinese officials with whom we dealt had been born in Irkutsk, Russia. He and I paired off and enjoyed using the common Russian language of our youth.

In 1984 China's transition to capitalism and modernization had hardly begun. The Communist Party imposed total uniformity and conformity. Roads and bridges were built by hand labor, with shovels and wheelbarrows. Long rows of peasants in coolie hats worked the fields with scythes. Bicycles dominated the streets of Beijing and Shanghai, with few autos in evidence.

Yet, the stirrings of change were also evident. Deng Xiaoping was instituting economic reforms, and that was evident in establishment of private enterprises and cooperatives. Tourism was being actively promoted, as we saw during excursions to the Great Wall and Xian, site of the excavated terra cotta soldiers commissioned by China's first emperor.

Later in 1984, I lost most of my power in the legislature. Jane, Ruthie, and I had gone to Hawaii to visit the Dinnels and partake of sun and sand. I wasn't up for reelection and didn't come home for the senate's organizational maneuvering. I had assumed that Senator Jalmar Kertulla, who was managing committee assignments for the Democratic side, would take care of my interests in the inevitable coalition that would form, since I had been a loyal Democrat and majority member for four years.

But when I returned, I found I had been excluded, without provocation. The senate minority, stripped of power, contained only four members, all Democrats, including my old friend Joe Josephson of Anchorage, Bill Ray of Juneau, and Bob Ziegler of Ketchikan. Minority members can always find ways to fill the days, but after four exciting years of accomplishment there seemed little of great import for me to do.

My wings had been clipped professionally, but personally the time I gained with Ruthie more than made up for the loss. During those two sessions, I picked her up at daycare at five or earlier. We would go for long walks, rain or shine, and spent lots of time reading, playing, bathing, and bonding.

In May 1985, I took several days' leave from the legislature to be the guest speaker at the high school graduation in Diomede. The Iñupiaq village lies on an island of high, rocky cliffs in the middle of the Bering Strait, only three miles from Russian territory. Jane and Ruthie accompanied me. The single-engine plane that brought us had to circle over Soviet air space to land on the runway cut from the sea ice. (Without ice, only helicopters can land in Diomede.)

This was the first high school graduation in Diomede, a big day in the village. The gym in the brand-new school was festooned with welcoming and congratulatory banners. Three twelfth-graders were graduating from high school and two eighth-graders from middle school. The entire population of 150 villagers turned out for the occasion, which was followed by a potluck feast and Iñupiaq dancing, in which Jane and two-year-old Ruthie participated, to the joy of the onlookers.

That happy day brought me as close as I had been to the Ice Curtain, our arctic version of communism's Iron Curtain dividing Europe. The narrow span of the Bering Strait to the Soviet-controlled island of Big Diomede allowed us to watch sentries guarding Russia as they moved about. The villagers' relatives used to live there, but at the start of the Cold War the Soviets had evacuated the Eskimo village from the island on their side and resettled them to the mainland. Diomede families had been decades without seeing those relatives.

Despite such diversions, my exile for two years in the senate minority drained my work life of fun and interest. But I had been sucked into the belief, common among elected leaders, that I was needed to do good. I thought I had become indispensible. As the 1986 election approached, I prepared for a tough fight to hold onto my seat as if my life depended on it. The oil industry had other ideas.

In 1926, my father predicted in his book *Oil Imperialism* that "the history of the next generation or two will be read in the light of the struggle for oil." In fact, five generations have passed since that was written, and oil wars continue, with our nation deep in economic and social turmoil as a result. The dreadful consequences of this struggle even affected my dear Ruthie, as her husband, Jonathan Dinkins, an airborne infantryman, was deployed to the Middle East in 2009 and 2011.

Bob Engler predicted at the 1969 science conference that big oil would reach tentacles of control into Alaska's culture and government, as well. But it took a while before a large part of the state's political elite came to see the world through oil's lens rather than through the demands of the constitution to use, conserve, and develop its natural resources "for the maximum benefit of its people." Through the 1970s most members of the legislature shared the Alaska-centered perspective they had held before the industry arrived.

Governor Egan had advanced the idea of the state itself building the Trans-Alaska Pipeline. Governor Hammond and a group of legislators created the Alaska Permanent Fund, gave it a prudent investment philosophy, allocated a dividend to every resident, and socked away enormous deposits of oil revenue.

The most important debate of the 1970s, which continues today, centered on how much the industry should pay for Alaska's oil. The $900 million lease sale in 1969, which had seemed so enormous, in fact represented a fire-sale bargain for access to America's largest oil field, at Prudhoe Bay. With tens of billions of barrels of oil to be removed, Alaska was selling a one-time asset, by far its largest, and needed to reap "maximum benefit" for all future generations.

As the pipeline reached completion in 1977, the legislature considered a tax and royalty system to recover the state's share of the profits. The oil industry cried foul with a series of bogus claims that it continues to use, despite the continuing failure of its repeated predictions that Alaska's taxes would stop investment and kill the golden goose.

I was still an ISER faculty member when I testified to the state House Finance Committee in April 1977, pulling apart each of the industry arguments and calling them "gibberish." The points I made could be recycled verbatim for the oil tax debate gripping Alaska today. Most important among them was a simple formula for applying the constitution's dictum of "maximum benefit."

The challenge for the legislature was not, as oil executives maintained, to find a fair level of taxation for the oil industry, nor to treat industries equally, nor to set a tax rate in line with other states. None of those goals is mentioned in the Alaska Constitution. Instead, through our tax and royalty system, we were obliged to maximize the price at which we would sell a barrel of oil on behalf of the people of Alaska.

We were engaged in a commercial transaction with the world's richest companies. We needed to find the highest price the market would bear. I argued that Alaska should extract every cent up to the amount that would stop the oil from flowing.

Alaskans often don't appreciate our excellent bargaining position in this negotiation with big oil. Two strategies would allow us to maximize the value we receive for our oil at any particular time. One strategy is to sell the oil for its true current value, which is simply the maximum a willing buyer will pay. The other strategy is not to sell it at all. Over time, oil left in the ground has appreciated rapidly in value, as I predicted would continue. Oil we didn't produce turned out to be our best investment by far, rising from as low as $9 a barrel in the 1980s to more than $100 a barrel today. As I noted in legislative testimony in 1977:

> In working toward establishing a fair value for Alaska's
> resources, we must keep moving toward the point at which
> we have tangible evidence that the industry is "walking away."
> Only at that point are we at the critical point. Until we reach it,
> we are giving away resources or values that belong to Alaskans
> of the present and the future.

In 1977 I emphasized my point about the future. Even then, with oil not yet flowing through the pipeline, we realized that it would eventually run out—we expected it to stop in 2000—and that our only chance of making those finite resources last for generations was to save the money in the Permanent Fund. Alaska's taxes and royalties were not high enough to turn our oil resources into financial assets providing long-term support for public services.

In 1978 the legislature adopted a system of taxation for Alaska's oil called "separate accounting," which, with other measures, gave us the highest oil taxes in the nation. But that didn't last long. When the oil started flowing, the influence of the oil industry grew. In the 1980s, the industry became more sophisticated in how it worked on the legislature.

Bill Allen, a former oil field welder, became the industry's face in Juneau as head of Veco, an oil field services firm. He was soon exposed for making illegal campaign contributions, but still lasted three decades more as Alaska's top power broker, until in 2006 he was caught on video by the FBI bribing Republican legislators with cash in return for lower taxes. Six members—a tenth of the legislature—ultimately pled guilty or were convicted in the investigation, along with lobbyists, the bribers, and Governor Murkowski's chief of staff, Jim Clark.

The first big rollback in oil taxes came at the height of pipeline flow, in 1981, after I entered the legislature. The battle for maximum benefit for the people became my personal crusade as a member of the Resources Committee, which often meant opposing giveaways to the oil industry. A tax cut given to big oil with nothing produced in return is simply an abdication of the responsibility entrusted by the state's founders.

It took a lot of work to learn the complexities of oil taxation and challenge the industry's self-serving arguments. In 1985, as a minority member, I introduced legislation for tax credits to reward particular industry actions that would increase production or achieve other state goals. But many legislators understood neither the technical issues nor their role as advocates for the state. They developed concern for "fairness" for the industry, whose lobbyists became their friends, information sources, and campaign supporters.

A note I wrote to myself in May 1984, while still a majority member of the state Senate Finance Committee, brings back the level of my frustration and disgust with Alaska's changed politics:

> Much of the time, I am ashamed to be a part of the legislature as it exists and functions today. Compared with a current batch of legislators, those of years ago appear composed of giants... It is horrible to contemplate, particularly in the context of all the lofty ideas expressed today, the tremendous difference between the idealistic and moral heights reached at the Constitutional Convention and the depths in which this legislature wallows. I feel dirty, slimy, just being part of this.

When I faced reelection in 1986, the oil industry had realized how cheaply legislative seats could be bought compared to the billions to be saved in taxes. I became a prime target in its effort to keep the legislature obedient. Allen led the way, unburdened as he was by scruples for campaign finance legalities.

My Republican opponent was Rick Uehling, an inoffensive and ineffective member of the state house who had focused on constituent relations and was a tireless door-to-door campaigner. Besides large oil industry contributions, he put $50,000 of his own money into his campaign and received money from some business supporters who had been by my side in less partisan days. I was angry to see some of my friends turn coat, but I also knew how to raise money and brought in as much as Uehling from my liberal sources. Our race became the most expensive of the election.

At the same time, Jane had political ambitions of her own, which could only be put on hold for so long. Democratic Governor Bill Sheffield had been politically damaged by a corruption investigation that led to impeachment hearings. Representative Steve Cowper challenged him in the primary. It seemed logical that incumbent Lieutenant Governor Steve McAlpine would have trouble because of his relationship to Sheffield, although in Alaska the elections for the two offices are separate in the primary. Jane challenged McAlpine in the Democratic primary for lieutenant governor.

Our household now contained a three-year-old, a statewide election campaign, and the toughest legislative campaign of the season. We were stretched thin, as were our friends and contributors. Our friend and childcare professional Kalen Saxton became Ruthie's primary caregiver. But there simply wasn't enough energy for both campaigns to flourish.

Jane's twin, Judy, came to help. The two still looked so similar that at our wedding the congregation had stood up when Judy walked into the hall, thinking she was the bride. Now Judy styled her hair like Jane's, allowing the candidate to appear in two parades on the Fourth of July. Jane marched in one city, while Judy marched in another.

Jane came close to winning the primary but couldn't upset the incumbent, despite strong support in southwest Native villages. Cowper and McAlpine ran together and won the general election.

My own election race came down to a virtual tie. The postelection period produced even more stress and effort than the campaign, as we worked with volunteers in recounts and ballot challenges. As often happens, the count went to court, where Uehling ultimately won by twenty-one votes. So there we were, both lost.

The outcome left our family exhausted and broke with campaign debts. Jane and I were both out of work and without income except for a small pension I had earned as a legislator.

Our losses came at a bad time. A 1985 fall in oil prices and attendant state budget cuts had abruptly cooled the overheated economy and popped the real estate bubble. Job prospects were dreadful, especially in the kind of high-level government and nonprofit work Jane and I had done. Highly qualified employees laid off by the oil industry also swamped the job market.

We owned a beautiful penthouse condo on Sixth Avenue in downtown Anchorage, but it wasn't a proper place for Ruthie, without outdoor space to play or ride a tricycle, so we moved back to Jane's house. However, in the devastated economy of the post-1985 oil crash, we couldn't find a steady renter for the condo, and when finally a buyer was found, we had to put in cash to get out of the mortgage.

Christmas approached with an impending visit from Jane's parents. We didn't have the wherewithal to even put on a show of prosperity. We couldn't afford gifts. But friends rallied around. John Hale and Nan Elliot gave us $500 to put on a proper Christmas for Ruthie and Jane's family. (In our undying gratitude, we have since paid it forward to other families in need.)

We weren't alone in our troubles with the condo. Foreclosed properties glutted the market as tens of thousands of residents abandoned the state. Before the recession ended, ten of Alaska's state-chartered banks had collapsed as well.

Our financial salvation came, improbably, from within this same economic despair. Conservative Republican Tom Fink won election as mayor of

Anchorage in 1987 by promising to "blast money out of Juneau" for economic recovery spending. ISER produced a report poking holes in such ideas and predicting that the economy would soon recover on its own. Fink, whom I had known for many years, contacted me to produce an analysis he hoped would counter the ISER study.

My position as a well-known liberal and former ISER director made me an attractive candidate to do the study for this very conservative mayor. I accepted without being dictated any predetermined outcome by Fink. His staff gave me a list of one-line topics to address, but I went off on my own, enlisting economist-planner Kevin Waring to help with the analyses.

In fact, I did not believe the economy was coming back very soon. Although I disagreed with Fink's idea to use state money mainly to prop up the real estate market, I did think we needed a comprehensive attack on unemployment and the gluts in housing and real estate markets to jumpstart economic activity.

My report made headlines and brought a $26,000 payment from the city, a personal stimulus that got our family back on its feet. I don't know if I had much impact on the outcome of the debate, but I was right about the direction of the economy. The legislature approved some modest spending for capital projects to boost economic activity, but no broad package such as we proposed. In the absence of such a boost, the recovery didn't come until two years later, after the 1989 *Exxon Valdez* oil spill brought an enormous burst of spending for cleanup work.

Jane also put us back on track financially when the Alaska State Chamber of Commerce hired her to manage the Alaska pavilion at Expo 88 in Brisbane, Australia. She would construct the exhibit and operate it daily from May through October 1988, with the help of a staff of Alaskan employees and volunteers, including many prominent people and old friends (Bob Atwood was the exhibit's nominal chairman). Jane went to Australia in February of 1988, and Ruthie and I followed in mid-May, when my work schedule allowed.

My role in Australia was to scope out the best beaches to take Jane to when she could get away, entertain our many visiting friends, look after Ruthie, who was then five, and provide backup for Jane in any way I could, including as a typist. We made good friends in our neighborhood and with families from Ruthie's kindergarten. The father of her best friend was a marine biologist, who took us snorkeling with sharks and rays from an island on the Great Barrier Reef, one of our many adventures exploring the country.

As part of the Alaska operation, we had access to all other expo venues. One of particular interest to me was the Russian pavilion, where I sharpened my Russian language skills and dined several times at a great restaurant called Troika. It was colorfully decorated in a traditional folk motif, its symbol the troika of old: three powerful horses pulling a sleigh through a winter landscape, a fur-clad figure at the reins.

Russia was on my mind as new connections between Alaska and the Soviet Far East were developing, even while we were in Australia. As I thought about my next step in life, my attention began to turn in that direction, rather than simply taking up more consulting work on our return to Anchorage. But I didn't yet know what form that next step to Russia might take.

The new openings between Russia and Alaska grew from Mikhail Gorbachev's programs of Perestroika and Glasnost (meaning, respectively, "restructuring" and "openness"). The Communist Party relaxed controls over life and the economy and invited more international exchanges. I wanted to be part of the changes, but I wasn't sure how. Fortunately, I only had to wait for opportunities, as human connections between Alaska and Russia began to blossom.

Dixie Belcher, a member of a group of Juneau singers, had since 1986 organized a series of trips to the Soviet Union for Alaska performers. Her amazing drive brought about trips that spanned Russia with as many as sixty-seven participants, including members of several rural Alaska Native groups.

Russian audiences went crazy for the Alaskan Performing Artists for Peace, even breaking down the door of one hall to get more people inside. Dixie formed a relationship with Gennadi Gerasimov, Gorbachev's foreign affairs spokesman, who followed her back to Juneau to meet Governor Cowper. She had campaigned to reunite Eskimo families living almost within sight of each other on opposite sides of the Bering Strait. Gerasimov and Cowper started talking about a flight to reconnect them.

It was Gerasimov who coined the term *Ice Curtain* for the political barrier between the Russian East and Alaska. He charmed us Alaskans with a lively personality and perfect colloquial English and showed real interest in creating links across the Bering Strait. These contacts planted the idea of a friendship flight, as I have been told by those involved.

The approval process for the flight went on out of sight in the black box of the Soviet government. One day, out of the blue, Cowper picked up the phone in the governor's mansion to hear a Russian voice from the Soviet embassy in Washington advising him that the flight had been approved. A plane would go from Nome, Alaska, to Provideniya, Russia, with the governor, a few other Alaskan leaders, media representatives, and many Alaska Natives to meet their counterparts in the Russian Far East in the spring of 1988. I was to be one of the interpreters.

The departure kept being postponed, and I became unsure the flight would really occur. It was hard to believe that an Alaska Airlines jet could fly directly from Anchorage to a town built as a military outpost during the years when Soviet forces had massed on their eastern coast in opposition to our own military in Alaska. Only five years earlier, the Soviet air force had shot down a Korean Air 747 full of passengers that strayed from its course from Anchorage to Seoul and entered Soviet air space. Americans would have to install new equipment at the Provideniya airport for a US airliner even to operate there.

Ruthie and I had joined Jane in Australia by the time the flight happened on June 7, 1988, symbolically melting the Ice Curtain. As Cowper aide David Ramseur recalls, the weather was clear and bright. The plane landed and, after the speeches and proclamations were done, Native people linked up with families and melted into the community. The English-Russian barrier didn't exist for them because they shared their Native languages.

The experience was extraordinary for the politicians and reporters as well. After a lifetime of thinking of the USSR as an inscrutable enemy, they now joined in friendship with people from deep within its most forbidden recesses, which turned out to be much like Alaska. The warmth and human connection put everyone involved on an emotional high, with many tears and smiles, and demands that the exchanges continue.

I was deeply disappointed to have missed the Friendship Flight and the opportunity to reconnect. I felt I had lost out on something important that would never be repeated. But after we moved back to Alaska from Australia at the end of 1988, I got another chance. I was asked to coordinate the February 1989 return visit of Soviet citizens to Anchorage.

The request from the sponsoring group, the Alaska State Chamber of Commerce, came just days before the Russians' arrival. The chamber was overwhelmed by the logistics of running the event. It had already organized most elements of the visit, including lodging, meals, transportation, interpreting, and venues.

My role as operations coordinator was mainly to keep everything on track once the Russians arrived, working with an army of volunteers from our headquarters in the Egan Convention Center. Not an easy task. Crisis followed crisis from early morning until late at night. There were special requests to deal with, meetings to arrange, and missed connections to remake. My Russian was constantly in play, and I personally met almost every one of the visitors during that week.

To truly manage such a crazy explosion of humanity was quite impossible. The planeload of more than a hundred Russians arrived knowing almost nothing about Alaska and we knew little about them. There were high federal and regional officials, businesspeople, artists and entertainers, journalists, indigenous leaders, and Russian and foreign media.

Some details that had been completely overlooked included clearing US Customs on tons of goods they brought to sell and trade, a problem that was resolved only with days of frantic work with high-level politicians. The Russians didn't know what Alaskans would want to buy: a reporter described some of the Russian stuff as "discount store grade." Alaska businessman Perry Eaton bought all the leftover goods for distribution through Alaska Commercial stores in rural Alaska. He also promised to make a return trade visit to Magadan, Russia.

At that point we didn't know if the Russian connection offered real business or political opportunities, but the human link was exhilarating and overwhelming. Russians took Anchorage by storm, and the community responded with enthusiasm.

Russian folk singers and dancers performed on the city's main stages and entertained at elementary schools. The top Soviet rock group Stas Namin captivated a sold-out crowd at the city's sports arena and partied at local nightclubs. Interpreters were in short supply as the visitors fanned out across the city in as many as fifty delegations at once, but people managed to get along just fine.

A fleet of volunteer drivers provided transportation. Most of the visitors stayed in private homes and learned how rich, casual, and generous Alaskans really were. More than once—many times over the years—I accompanied Russian visitors to Anchorage grocery stores and saw them break down in tears when they saw the abundance and quality of the goods for sale. They often had no money, so we would buy things for them.

The visit was a chaotic mess. And it was an exalting triumph. The week left everyone exhausted, happy, and with minds spinning with the possibilities of these new friendships.

I bade farewell to each of the Russian visitors as they went through the gate to the Soviet charter plane, with many Russian-style hugs and kisses, telling them *do skorovo svidaniya,* or "till we meet again soon." I got home after midnight, totally exhausted and relieved that it was over.

A few hours later, I was rousted out of bed and told that the plane was returning to Anchorage within the hour. It couldn't land on the Russian side due to bad weather. More crisis management.

Jane called Larry Baker, a fellow Anchorage Assembly member and owner of the local Burger King franchise, and asked, "Can you feed a hundred and fifty stranded people?" He fed the entire Russian delegation, gratis.

That evening, as they got back on the plane, I chose a different farewell phrase. Loosely translated, it was, "Till we meet again, but not so soon!"

After the Russians' visit, travel to the Russian Far East began to open up. Scientists at the University of Alaska wanted to get involved with their counterparts. The Soviets' arctic science endeavors were far beyond ours in ambition and facilities. I began coordinating Soviet relations for the university from ISER's offices in Anchorage. For most of the next two decades I served as a node in the expanding web of links between Alaska and Russia.

This work would open an extraordinary new chapter for me, one of my richest and most eventful. I had to thank Rick Uehling for that.

I happened to see the state senator in a funky Juneau restaurant where I went to meet a friend. He was alone, waiting for someone. I plopped myself down at his table, and he shrank back, as if fearing I would attack him. Instead, I shook his hand and extended my sincere gratitude for getting me out of politics. Without his election victory, I might have been stuck in Juneau for years more and missed out on some of the most exciting and rewarding events of my life.

⊰ 25 ⊱

Russian Reconnection

My interest in reconnecting with Russia had never died. As director of a social science research institute in Fairbanks, I knew Alaska had a lot to learn from the Soviets. Economist George Rogers and I discussed as early as the mid-1960s the need to develop relationships with other circumpolar regions to find out how they were addressing northern development issues. Russia occupied far more of the Arctic than any other country and had made a particular point of settling the North.

I reached out directly to Russian academics in 1969. The top non-Soviet expert on the Soviet North, Terence Armstrong of Cambridge University's Scott Polar Research Institute, who spent a semester at ISER, provided a number of invaluable contacts. My brother, George, gave me a book that listed all of the Soviet scientific institutes, and I wrote official letters to the twenty that seemed to have some relation to economic and social issues in northern regions. Eight responded, and we began corresponding and exchanging materials, developing collegial relationships and friendships that lasted for decades.

I first met some of these new friends in 1974 when I went to Russia with Gloria and my two sons, Greg and Joe (the same trip that included a stop in Berlin and the first reunion of the original troika). My contact with the Soviet Institute of Geography was with professor Grigori Agranat, Terence Armstrong's counterpart as the top Russian expert on the non-Soviet north. He hosted us in Moscow at the Prague Restaurant with an elaborate banquet of champagne, beluga caviar, and seemingly endless courses of delicious Russian food.

At this event I also met ethnographer Svetlana Fedorova, a specialist on Russian America. Although Agranat never came to the United States, Fedorova was in Alaska several times and taught a semester at the University of Alaska Fairbanks and became a close family friend.

Officials of the various institutes I visited offered utmost deference and high-level connections, despite ISER's small size relative to most of their organizations. I had a staff of about fifty, focusing mainly on Alaska, while Arganat's geography institute had five thousand people and studied the entire globe.

The science city outside Novosibirsk housed the Siberian branch of the academy of sciences, where I met Abel Aganbegyan, director of the Institute of Economics, the top-rated organization in its field. I talked for several days with his staff of interesting and deeply involved professionals. As everywhere, people wanted to hear about Alaska, and I was glad to lecture and answer all their questions. My visit proved fortuitous for their work, as members of their group were studying alternative models for northern development.

The slave labor camps of the Gulags were gone, and the Soviets were embarking on a strategy of populating northern regions by building cities and filling them with workers and their families, to be attracted there by high wages. Remote jobs also paid well in arctic Alaska and Canada, but rather than shipping families to the North we housed workers in camps, as at the Prudhoe Bay oil fields. A driller there might work twelve-hour days for two weeks and then have two weeks off at home with family.

Ultimately, most of the northern cities the Soviets built with enormous effort were an economic disaster. The communities survived only through huge government subsidies to provide wage differentials and the necessities of life for those who were attracted to move there. With closure of a nearby mine or other big projects, the towns became useless outposts full of residents without any reason or desire to remain.

When the collapse of the Soviet Union ended subsidies for these towns, most of those who could afford to leave the North did so. Some new cities were abandoned entirely. Others were left with residents who had nowhere to go. Their hardships and poverty in the post-Soviet era were horrendous and became a target of our work from Alaska in the 1990s.

In the 1970s, when Gloria and I visited, those high-arctic towns were still being dreamed up and built. On the other hand, some of their large-scale regional development plans were more balanced and creative, with less of the megalomania of the earlier decades. I found those involved to be bright, well informed, and relatively flexible in their thinking. Spending time with them, as well as visiting spectacular places such as Lake Baikal near Irkutsk, rekindled my youthful fascination with Siberia.

Joe and Greg found our institute visits wretchedly boring, but on one occasion our host stepped out and came back with two bottles of Pepsi—an indescribable treat after weeks when the most exciting drink was mineral water. Russians and Americans had exchanged Pepsi bottling in Russia for Stolichnaya vodka imports to the United States, perhaps the only time our negotiators ever got the better of theirs.

The next year, 1975, after Koni and Lothar came to Alaska, I received another invitation to travel to the Russian Far East, this time to go much farther north. A small delegation of architects and planners would exchange knowledge about design for northern regions, a subject about which the Russians had extensive experience. Ed Crittenden had become one of America's top experts on northern design, so we had the pleasure of traveling together.

Even in that period of détente, the Soviet Union remained strictly controlled. With our official focus on building construction and cold climate design, we were taken to places few outsiders had ever visited. Thanks to my language ability, I could have candid conversations about politics when I found myself alone with a Russian.

On a multiday train ride from Murmansk to Leningrad I enjoyed a fascinating debate over chess with a Red Army colonel who believed that controls on information were necessary because of the masses' lack of political sophistication. I pointed out that my father's books in Moscow's Lenin Library were restricted. He countered that party cadres who were educated to understand the material could read them. The truth, of course, was that while Communist Party members were an elite, they were totally subservient to top-down control and had to conform their ideas to the official party line.

Our trip took Ed and me far to the east and north. Western visitors were so rare that the hospitality of our reception grew to absurd proportions. In Yakutsk, on the Lena River in northern Siberia, we endured a marathon of drinking and eating that even decades of official travel in Russia could never equal.

This trial by vodka began at the airport, where the deputy mayor and other city officials ushered us into a VIP lounge for sandwiches and a series of toasts. Each toast, whether to peace, to mutual understanding, to success in our work, or whatever, required enthusiastically throwing back another shot of vodka, lest reticence suggest a lack of support for the sentiments expressed.

After the bout of drinking at the airport, we finally got to the hotel and into our rooms well past midnight, exhausted. But before we could get to sleep, our State Department minder beat on the door and said Ed's and my presence was required to join our hosts for tea, and that the gathering could not proceed without us.

It turned out our hosts had prepared a full reception in a hotel dining room, where a table was heavily laden with various kinds of caviar, sturgeon and other fish, and various meats and vegetables, as well as copious bottles of champagne, vodka, and cognac. Politeness required heavy eating and drinking till around two to three o'clock in the morning.

We were up the next morning bright and early and again presented with a feast, although breakfast mercifully did not require drinking more vodka. However, during that morning's tour of a factory that manufactured large concrete panels for building construction, the director pulled us into his office, locked the door, and brought out vodka and cognac for a series of friendly toasts.

It never let up. Big, heavy-drinking lunch. Visit to a club for drinking in the late afternoon. Back to the hotel for another banquet with a lot of drinking. The next day, a cruise on the great Lena River, with a huge banquet on board and a lot of drinking.

When the hydrofoil stopped and the crew built a fire on shore to cook fish soup in a cauldron, Ed and I wandered along the river to clear our heads and found ourselves next to a herd of small, shaggy horses. A biologist later told me that these wild horses survive through the winter in temperatures below −40°F and that they could do as well in the Tanana Valley region around Fairbanks.

In general, Yakutsk and Fairbanks were very much alike. They were alike in continental location and extreme climate, in each having a university, and in the attitude of free thinking that comes from being remote from the centers of power. They became sister cities twenty years later, when the political situation allowed cooperative relations.

After two informative days in Yakutsk we realized that our hosts were tag-teaming us. While they spelled one another in the banquets and drinking bouts, we had to imbibe without relief. We felt a sense of relief when they drove us directly to the plane that would take us south to Irkutsk without a stop at another banquet. But instead of putting us on board, our hosts piled everyone into a Volga sedan, where they produced a bottle of vodka and hunks of cheese and salami for toasts to peace and friendship, to success, to collaboration, and on and on.

I thought I was finally safe on the airplane and prepared to detoxify. But partway through the long series of flights, in the early hours of the morning, I was seated next to an older rural couple who offered me a drink. I tried to turn it down, saying I had just finished forty-eight hours of hard drinking, but the man said he was traveling back to Ukraine to bury his father and wanted to toast to the departed. How could I say no?

Too groggy to pay much attention, I threw back the shot and immediately felt like the top of my head would blow off. This wasn't vodka, it was pure alcohol, 200 proof. Subsequent conversation brought on toasts to peace and friendship between our nations, to family—and then I passed out.

On our return from that trip, Ed and I stopped in Berlin to see Koni and Lothar in Koni's apartment. The visit was brief and light, just long enough for a meal and to enjoy each other's company for an evening. I did not see Lothar again; he died the following year.

As I've already described, Koni came to America in 1977 to interview me for his film about the troika. He also made a trip to Moscow in 1981 with a photographer to record the places of his youth. East German censors interfered with the work, but the project itself was the greater difficulty. The troika was an emotional and artistic puzzle of storytelling. Koni's need for honesty in capturing these rich memories kept him from perfecting the concept in his notebooks.

He continued to direct during the period, the waning years of the Cold War, modernizing his work with his final film, *Solo Sunny*, about a female pop singer struggling for independence in a male-dominated world. He fell ill during a public appearance in January 1982 and died of cancer two months later, with his notebooks for the troika film at his bedside, where he had worked on them to the end.

Only after Koni's death did I come to realize the true political might of his brother, Markus Wolf, our Mischa, in the East German government. I already knew about his identity as the head of espionage for the Stasi, the security agency. But when I traveled to Berlin for a commemoration of Koni's life and saw him in full command, I was much more impressed.

Western spymasters had for years been unable to get a picture of Mischa and knew him only as "the man without a face." A surreptitious photograph taken in 1979 in Sweden ended this mysterious nom de guerre. He later used the phrase as the title of his autobiography.

Mischa was the product of the system that created him, which he came to recognize had conditioned him with blinders to ignore the humanity of those outside of his elite circle. He explained in his autobiography the process that eventually made him feel exempt from moral norms. It began with the same premise that influenced my father: opposition to fascism. Trained to see the world as a struggle of extremes, the West later filled the role of the fascist enemy in Mischa's mind.

Mischa described some of the terrible events that he was able to minimize or ignore, including his discovery of a torture chamber in the basement of the building where he lived.

> I did of course know of many of the terrible crimes of the Stalin era even while they were under way; anyone who says he

knew nothing is a liar. These are not things I look back on with pride...I can only remind the reader again how my character was formed in the struggle against fascism; we came to feel that against such tyrannical opponents, almost anything goes.

Western officials later charged that as a Stasi head Mischa funded terrorists, but he always denied that. He maintained that he played the spy game by the same rules as his Western opponents and that he had no part in the internal repression of East Germany's people.

After Koni died, Mischa ushered through the production of a one-hour documentary on his life. The story of the troika played an important part, and the film crew came to Alaska. I took them to the places Koni, Lothar, and I had visited together, and did various interviews, while driving on Turnagain Arm and in our Barrow Street condo (I was still in the state senate at the time).

When the film premiered in 1985, Mischa orchestrated a grand weeklong celebration in Berlin to mark the sixtieth anniversary of Koni's birth, managed by the East German Academy of Art, of which Koni had been president. George and I rendezvoused in Amsterdam and flew to East Berlin together.

We were treated as if rules did not apply to us. Officials called us off the plane while the other passengers waited. They put us in a special lounge where we waited briefly, without customs checks and other border-crossing formalities, before being driven in a limousine to the hotel to meet Mischa.

The dinners and ceremonies were lavish. George gave a long speech and I made a few remarks at a banquet premiering the Koni Wolf documentary, *Die Zeit, Die Bleibt* (The Times, They Remain). A major road was named in Koni's honor. Mischa took us to his luxurious apartment in Berlin and to his country home, a classic German hunting lodge. He didn't wear his general's uniform, but the authority he carried and the great deference of everyone around him showed that he held enormous power.

Mischa later wrote in his autobiography that he already had serious qualms about the future of East German communism at that time, worries dating to the rise of the Solidarity trade union movement in Poland in the early 1980s. He talked with friends about the failure of his nation's rigid old-guard rulers to adapt. He subtly reported in his intelligence analyses about the downward spiral of East Germany compared to the West. But he took no overt action on these feelings, at least not until it was too late.

In 1986, he won a fight to retire, leaving a declining system and work that no longer held its former excitement. When protesters seized the streets of East Berlin in their peaceful revolution of 1989, he identified somewhat with their aims, and was invited to speak to a rally of half a million people. He took the stage to call for the reform, but not the overthrow, of East German socialism. The crowd booed and hissed.

Mischa claimed he heard little of the booing, but others report he was driven from the stage. Events rapidly ran forward that year, 1989, until the Berlin Wall fell that autumn and German reunification began.

Subsequent looting of the Stasi's secret files exposed Mischa's name in daily media denunciation for various crimes by the East German regime. Before reunification, he left for Moscow, avoiding prosecution and receiving protection from the Soviet government.

I saw Mischa in Moscow during the early 1990s. On one occasion, we agreed to meet at a popular spot on Pushkin Square. I waited by the Pushkin statue, watching cars splashing through a light rain. A big black sedan with tinted windows pulled up to the curb.

Out stepped a tall man wearing a trench coat and fedora, looking exactly like the Hollywood image of a communist spy. It was Mischa. We shook hands and I joined him in the backseat, with the driver closing the door behind us. I felt like I was in a movie. And we did drive to a movie studio, where we viewed a film of Koni's that I had not seen before.

During that period, we essentially initiated our friendship, which was lasting. I've always taken people as they come. Shorn of his power and the ideology that justified his position, he lost the distance that had separated him from us since our parting as boys in Moscow. We now were simply two older men who shared memories and the events of the day.

Mischa never did overcome his past. After the collapse of the Soviet Union, he returned to Germany to face trial, was convicted of treason, then had his conviction overturned by the Supreme Court, on the ground he could not have been a traitor for doing work with the approval of the state that had existed at the time. A subsequent trial for particular crimes brought a suspended sentence. Ultimately, he spent three days in jail for refusing to testify against a colleague. But he never was rehabilitated and never was allowed to visit the United States.

Mischa's love for his brother formed a key link in the chain that reclaimed my earlier life in Russia. As Koni lay dying in the hospital, Mischa saw his continued struggle with the concept for a film on the troika. Afterward, he picked up that trove of material—Koni's notebooks, documents, and interviews—and decided to write a book of his own.

As described in Koni's notes, the film would have indirectly criticized communism by showing how politics and the arbitrary brutality of Stalinism had divided our lives, but it also would have shown the strength of human connections as we bridged those differences to reunite as adults. It was the same subject Koni and I had discussed on our flight to Prudhoe Bay in 1975, when he noticed the similarity of Alaska and Kamchatka and we discussed *Divided Heaven*.

Mischa became fascinated with the story and the political message. He worked on it while still functioning as East Germany's spymaster, a situation his politburo boss knew about and disapproved of but allowed to continue.

Mischa wrote in his diary,

> Amazing how alive Koni now seems to me again... Many people seem to expect me quite naturally to take up where he left off. There are many hopes and human contacts to be kept alive. It seems so important to so many people who knew him. For the first time in my life, I am aware that the clock is ticking. It is time to get on with things.

The Troika: Story of an Unmade Film was published in both halves of Germany in March 1989 and a year later in Russian translation under the title *Three from the Thirties* (avoiding the word *troika*, which carried the negative connotation of Stalin's tribunals). The book was a sensation with its frank history of communist wrongs coming from a former insider. East Germany, unlike the Soviet Union under Gorbachev, had never acknowledged the flaws of Stalinism. If the book had come earlier, perhaps it would have done more to rehabilitate Mischa.

The Troika narrates the Fischers', Wolfs', and Wlochs' arrival in Moscow and the beginning of the Vitya-Koni-Lothar friendship, tracking the three lives to the final meetings of the troika in America more than forty years later. It covers Koni's artistic life and political activities and includes his plan for a dramatic film, in which he intended to conflate the characters of me and my brother George to make the complex story more manageable. The one thing that struck me negatively in the narrative is a statement that Lothar took his own life, which I don't believe is true. The book and its 150-page appendix are rich with photographs and facsimiles of old letters and diaries that form a core record of the three families and our friendships and loves. The book profoundly affected the course of my life.

On a spring day in 1991, in Anchorage, I received a letter in Russian at my office in Anchorage. On the envelope were only my name and the University of Alaska's. That had been enough to bring me the letter from Moscow. In the first paragraph, the writer addressed me with the formal tense of his Russian verbs, as in proper business correspondence. He began, "You will be extremely amazed when you receive this letter."

He was correct. The letter had traveled as if from another world. Suddenly, I was back in Moscow in the 1930s, hearing from my old classmate at the elite Fridtjof Nansen School, number 110. The writer was Vadim (Vadya) Popov, my friend from the class that had lived together through Stalin's Great Purge.

By that time, my travels to Russia had become too frequent to remember each trip clearly, as I was coordinating the university's Russian work and working on many other Russia–Alaska links as well. But in all those trips, I never had been able to find my old classmates. Still, no simple way existed for an ordinary citizen to track someone down in Moscow.

Vadya had been browsing in a sidewalk stall when a book caught his eye with a cover picture of our childhood haunts in Moscow's Arbat district. Inside the book, *Three from the Thirties,* he found a picture of me as a kid, and elsewhere reference to my career at the University of Alaska.

In his letter, he inquired whether I, Victor Fischer, had been a boy named Vitya, whom he knew at School Number 110 in the Arbat, but who had left for America in 1939: "If one is to believe the caption under this photograph, then you and he are one and the same person."

In the second paragraph, the letter switched to the familiar verb form, *ty,* the casual form of address we would have used as children and intimate adults. He gave me news of our classmates and teachers. One former student, a close friend of my early years, had recently died. Others had perished in the Red Army, fighting Germany in World War II. And he gave news of himself, Professor Popov, now a renowned physicist. At the end of the letter, in a postscript, he wrote, "Prof. Fischer, you are not offended that I allowed myself to switch to *ty,* mentally plunging into the 1930s?"

I called Vadya on the telephone and told him that I would be in Moscow within two weeks on an academic trip and would meet him there.

Vadya and I walked around Moscow all day looking at the places where we had been young together and telling the vastly different stories of our lives since. We walked by my family's old apartment in the Arbat, where Vadya remembered being amazed by the luxury of our surroundings after the hardships of his family's communal flat. He remembered Markoosha filling him with food and me giving him an American-style flashlight, which he treasured for years, despite the impossibility of obtaining the round batteries it used.

We walked by the Nansen school, where a famous statue stood on the corner showing figures of five young men who had died in the war. One of our classmates, Daniel Metlyanski, had created it (we later held a big, joyous party in his large Moscow studio). The faces of the soldiers were plainly recognizable as students from our class.

Vadya suffered through the war years operating a lathe in a defense factory in Siberia, years of extreme cold and hunger so severe he lost all his teeth and considered suicide. News came of desperate defeats and retreats before the advancing Germans, unexplained and bewildering, until the first hope, the report of the American declaration of war after Pearl Harbor.

Vadya remembered hearing the announcement on a very dark, very cold morning from a loudspeaker outside the factory. Somehow, his knowledge that he knew an American—me—brightened that dawning. In 1943, Vadya and his mother harvested their own potatoes and ended their period of starvation.

Telling me about his father's fate came with extreme difficulty for Vadya. Years after we reinstituted our friendship, he handed me a pile of documents and asked me to read it so we could discuss it later.

Vadya did not know what had happened to his father all through the war or in the years later when he resumed his studies, working toward a career as a physicist. His father had been a hero of the Revolution, imprisoned by the tsar's government in 1908, and had won a lifetime pension in the civil war waged after the 1917 Bolshevik revolution. Stalin's agents arrested him in February 1938.

Vadya remembered the night clearly. After taking his father away in the small hours of the morning, agents came back to the apartment and rifled through his books and papers. Before leaving, they told Vadya that if he revealed the fact of his father's arrest to anyone, his mother would be taken away as well.

The rest of us supported our many other classmates whose parents disappeared. Three-quarters of our class lost at least one parent in the purge. But we knew nothing about Vadya's father. Even with his closest friends, he couldn't share the deep misery of his life.

Vadya and his mother believed his father was still alive. He carried care packages to the prison. He tried, as a teen, to be the man his mother needed, even as he lived in terror for her. It was ten years later that they learned his father, Andrei Sergeyevich Popov, had been condemned and executed within a week of his arrest.

Only in 1989 did Vadya receive the papers that showed his father was shot along with 528 of his associated pensioned civil war veterans and was cast into a mass grave in Butovo that ultimately held twenty thousand of Stalin's victims. Vadya's mother had died long before the truth came out. She cursed the murderers of her beloved husband, but never knew of his fate or his later political rehabilitation by the post-Stalin regime.

The same evening that Vadya and I walked around the Arbat, he hosted five other classmates at his apartment. We enjoyed a wonderful Russian banquet of caviar and sturgeon, champagne and vodka, despite a scarcity of food at the time. Some of my friends looked like older versions of the teenagers I had known. Others had changed unrecognizably.

The bond remained. We picked up where we had left off more than fifty years earlier in the same light and brotherly spirit that had seen us through the purge.

A couple of weeks later, those warm feelings became even stronger and more joyous when I returned to Moscow and my friends gathered at a party that included almost all of our surviving classmates. Fourteen of us celebrated at the apartment of Lena Kostyakova, an astronomy professor. Her infallible memory ultimately allowed her to write a book manuscript that recalled all the tiniest details of years of our adolescence.

We didn't talk of the difficult years. We reunited as if we had never parted. Most of my friends had thrived in the Soviet Union by focusing their talents outside of the political sphere. Typical were Popov and Kostyakova, both scientists, sculptor Metlyanski, and Svetlana Gurvich (Bukharina), who had devoted herself to classic French poetry.

Even Shurik Radionov, a physical chemist who worked for years in a secret city developing the Russian atomic bomb, had managed to remain apolitical and focus only on his technical work. An exception was Boris Smirnov, a physicist involved in Cold War work, who had become an active prodemocracy dissident.

My presence brought them back together. They had kept in touch for years, but time had atrophied their personal connections. My reappearance provided a catalyst for everyone to renew friendships. Only one surviving classmate declined to come. Ira Kuzmina remained a confirmed communist and would not associate with a capitalist pig such as I. The gathering took place only months before the final fall of the Soviet Union.

Then in their late sixties, most of my friends were relatively fit and active. But Svetlana had aged more and seemed tiny, fragile, and worn. She had stayed away from the first gathering at Vadya's out of fear of the painful memories that would resurface in the presence of old friends. Even at Lena's festive party, with lots of vodka and Russian food, she remained quiet and reserved, as if much older than the rest of us.

I knew that Svetlana's father, Nikolai Bukharin, had been condemned at the greatest of the show trials in 1938. In 1991, Svetlana was still caring for her mother, Bukharin's second wife, who had never recovered her health from years in the Gulags, problems now compounded by age. That was all I knew when we met again.

On a later trip, I learned Svetlana's mother had died and she was suffering deeply. When my travel schedule permitted, I arranged to meet at her apartment, a half-basement on the huge Gagarin Square, which has at its center a statue of Yuri Gagarin, the first man in space, and of his spaceship. Svetlana gave me tea and little sandwiches and told me her story, which I recount here from my memory.

After Bukharin's execution, Stalin arrested, tortured, and killed his first wife and her extended family and imprisoned the third and then current wife. Svetlana's mother, Bukharin's second wife, remained free. Unlike many families who were dispossessed and humiliated, Svetlana was allowed to continue in our elite school under the protection of our heroic principal, Ivan Kuzmich, until the war dispersed the school and sent its teenage students to fight.

After the war, however, security agents showed up at Svetlana's apartment one night and took her mother away. Three hours later, they returned and arrested Svetlana herself. Both went to the Gulag in Siberia, but to different camps, with no way of contacting each other or even knowing the fate of mother or daughter.

Communication from the Gulag usually was impossible. Friends have told me of prisoners writing letters and throwing them from the windows of the eastbound prison trains. Their only hope, sometimes fulfilled, was that someone would find the letter on the ground and put it in the mail.

Svetlana was released and returned to Moscow after years of imprisonment but her mother was not. Through someone who had been imprisoned there, she learned the name and location of the camp where the mother was held in Siberia and set out to find her. The journey took Svetlana across the breadth of Russia, often following the railroad tracks on foot. But when she found the camp, she still couldn't contact or even see her mother.

Workers from the camp would emerge in work parties to cut firewood. Svetlana managed to meet some as they worked and they confirmed that her mother was in the camp. They agreed on a plan, and on a certain day Svetlana was standing outside the camp when the side of a truck hauling wood collapsed while going through the prison gate, blocking it open. She then saw her mother on the far side, and they were able to exchange looks. That was all.

Svetlana's mother was released after Stalin died. Svetlana had become an academic, teaching French literature, her primary joy in life. She spent the rest of her years nursing her mother, who never recovered her health. Svetlana never developed other intimate relationships and when I last met her was living alone with her French books.

I kept in touch with most of these friends over the following years, but Vadya Popov remained among the closest. He came to Alaska later in 1991 and was with Jane and me watching the television news on CNN when hard-line communists and generals tried to overthrow Mikhail Gorbachev. Liberals resisted in the Russian White House, then the seat of parliament, including Russian Federation President Boris Yeltsin, who leapt atop a tank in a Moscow street and peacefully seized power for democratic forces, bringing an end to the Soviet Union.

Vadya called his wife, Ira, at home in their apartment in Moscow. She had no idea anything was going on. We watched and described to her what was happening blocks from her home.

Two years later the situation repeated in an odd way. Vadya again was in Alaska, eating dinner at my house with Jane, when they got the news that hard-liners had taken over Russia's White House and Yeltsin had sent tanks to dislodge them. The seat of Russian government went up in flames. Again, Ira didn't know anything: it was morning in Moscow and the news was blacked out.

I was in Norway bound for Moscow, also unaware of what was happening. Jane called and asked me to cancel my trip. I made some noncommittal response and got on the plane the next morning.

I could move around in Moscow with greater ease than most. When I wanted to, I could avoid special attention by passing for a native Russian. But when special attention would help me, I could switch to English and adopt the attitude of an entitled American. That day I got right to the edge of the battle and watched it unfold.

Besides finding my classmates, I also discovered I had family living in Russia. In May 1992, I was visiting family friends in New York who had emigrated from Russia with help from George and me fifteen years earlier. They showed me a full-page interview in a New York Russian-language newspaper that mentioned my father. The interview subject, ninety-year-old Tatiana Leshchenko-Sukhomlina, had written a memoir of her long and eventful life as a beautiful Russian singer, her many lovers, travels, and troubles, and mentioned she had given birth to a son by the famous American journalist Louis Fischer.

I contacted the reporter, who gave me Tatiana's phone number in Moscow and told me where I could find a copy of the book in New York. It described Louis as a great love in Tatiana's life of several great loves. Their son, Ivan, known as Vanya, showed up only sporadically. His childhood had been spent in exile from his mother—she had shipped him off to his grandparents in the Caucasus to keep him from underfoot of her husband at the time. After all my reunions, the prospect of finding this lost brother ignited me.

A month later, in Moscow, I called Tatiana and introduced myself.

She asked, "Is Louis still alive?"

I told her he had died more than twenty years earlier and asked how I could find her son Vanya.

"He lives right here in Moscow."

I asked if she could give me his phone number.

She said, "Yes, but only after you come to visit and talk to me about Louis and yourself."

Her apartment was crowded with photographs and memorabilia from her ninety-year life and the guitars she still used to perform at cultural events and recitals. The fascination of our talk softened my impatience to meet my brother. As we drank tea and later sat in a park, she told me stories and asked endless questions about Louis. Finally, after a couple of hours, she gave me the phone number I was seeking, asking me particularly to tell Vanya she loved him.

Vanya surprised me by taking my call with complete calm, almost as if he had expected to hear from me. I went straight to his apartment. When he opened the door, I saw a face bearing a striking resemblance to my own, and even more so to my father. His brow even wrinkles in the same pattern as mine. We embraced as brothers, both overwhelmed by the emotion of our sudden but very deep connection.

As the evening passed in his small kitchen, over vodka and goodies, we shared the two very different lives that had made us far different men. Vanya had overcome terrible hardships to succeed as a PhD petroleum geologist, keeping his head down and avoiding special attention. His personality became cynical and pessimistic, and he doesn't easily cultivate social connections. Knowing and loving him has helped me realize once more how the fortunate circumstances of my youth developed my positive outlook and outgoing nature.

Our lost family story reemerged from a combination of Vanya's memories, Tatiana's often-inaccurate memoirs, and a 1949 clipping recently found in Louis's papers at Princeton, in which the *Washington Post* described letters the FBI uncovered in a celebrated spy case.

Louis and Tatiana met in the early 1920s in Moscow when he had just started writing for the *Nation*. She was teaching Russian to Americans from Agrojoint, including the American lawyer she married, Benjamin Pepper, who took her back to New York. In her memoir she wrote, "If it were not for my love for Ben, I'd have promptly fallen in love with LF. When he would gaze at me, it was as if a hurricane hit me. I consciously tried to avoid him."

While married, she kept traveling back to Moscow, performing, and carrying on affairs, which wasn't unusual in their free-loving set. Living in Paris, she met a sculptor sent by the Soviets to study there, Dmitri Tsaplin, and had a daughter with him. They moved together to Majorca, an island off Spain's Mediterranean coast.

Vanya always assumed his father was a Spaniard because Tatiana was there when he was conceived. But my father was there, too. Vanya was born in 1935 in Moscow. Tatiana wrote to a friend:

> Vanya is wonderful. His eyes are beautiful, dark brown, such long lashes. He is tall and thin. I feel that I am only grateful to LF for giving me the happiness of such a son. All my resentment to LF for his caddish, scounderly [*sic*] behavior toward me because I became pregnant—melts. I did love him. And the best of him I kept, I have.

But the warm feelings didn't protect Vanya. Tsaplin resented having another man's child in his apartment, and Tatiana sent Vanya away to live with her parents in Ordzhonikidze, in the Caucasus. She later also applied to my mother for food and for medicine for a lung ailment. While Markoosha endured the pressure of the secret police and made do with little money, she also assisted Louis's abandoned mistress, just as Koni and Mischa's mother took in her husband's many odd children.

After the war, Tatiana disappeared for six years into the Gulag, mainly at Vorkuta, for making a mildly critical remark about Stalin. When she emerged she restarted her singing career and went on to greater success than ever.

Meanwhile, Vanya grew up in a two-room communal apartment with a view of the Caucasus Mountains in the tense household of his grandparents. Although the apartment was better than others had, it lacked hot water and he rarely washed or brushed his teeth, which affected his health. During the war, when he was still a child, the Germans came to the edge of the city and Vanya survived terrifying bomb attacks. One air raid killed seven residents of his house and left two holes in the ceiling of the apartment that weren't repaired for many years.

After the war, he returned to Moscow and spent some time with his mother before she was arrested. His hunger was so severe that he sold the chocolate her American friends gave him for more basic food. But his intellectual ability took him far in school and he eventually built a career as a geologist and economist, working across the expanse of Russia, as well as in Libya and Cuba.

When Tatiana published her memoir in 1991, Vanya learned the identity of his father for the first time. He felt humiliated among his colleagues by the negative descriptions she included about his continuing anger and the anger of his sister Elena. In the book, she blamed his resentment on Stalinism, not on the dreadful childhood she had consigned him to.

A typical passage reads: "Vanya came by, skinny and angry. Said tomorrow he will move in with me, as he can't pay rent for his room. He is not working. Elena stopped by...Said you abandoned us...I thought of Vorkuta."

Vanya and his mother remained estranged when I met them. Hence, her request that I tell Vanya that she loved him. Vanya was not impressed. He had made use of her book, however, starting his own search for my brother George and me. After learning his father's name, he found some of Louis's and Markoosha's books in the Lenin Library. Those books gave him our names. Further research turned up the titles of our own books and their publishers.

When I returned to Alaska from meeting my new brother, a letter addressed to the University of Alaska Press was waiting on my desk. In it, Vanya asked the Press for information on how to contact Victor Fischer, author of *Alaska's Constitutional Convention*. Rather than responding, they forwarded the letter to me, which was just as well, as by then Vanya and I had already met.

Vanya and I continued to build our relationship, and I treasure him as a brother and friend. He and his wife Tanya have traveled to Alaska and spent time with our friends and family in New York, Philadelphia, Washington, Wisconsin, Oregon, and Hawaii. They are a well-integrated part of our extended community, and we've spent a lot of time with them in Moscow.

⇥ 26 ⇤

Working Internationally

My new life in Russia grew far beyond the reconnected ties of youth and family. For almost two decades, I worked across a vast swath of the North as it awakened from dark ages of authoritarianism. My colleagues were energetic Alaskans motivated by the excitement of change. I was an ambassador for the University of Alaska and a freelancing world citizen. My portfolio was my belief in the power of humanity, liberalism, and freedom, the values I had learned from my parents and from my decades in Alaska.

Many friends were at my side. John Tichotsky fell into our ad hoc group as a young graduate teaching Russian at the University of Alaska Anchorage, one of a handful of fluent Russian speakers in Anchorage before the Ice Curtain fell. John recruited Andrew Crow, who was at the same early stage in life.

We formed academic and scientific institutions, arranged humanitarian food and medical assistance, installed communications, funneled money from Congress into small business development, helped build political and social service capabilities, worked for indigenous rights, and even got embroiled in the strange postcommunist politics of the eastern regions. Rather than simply making links, we tried to create lasting bridges for relationships in the economic, political, and personal realms.

Because this is an unusual thing to do, we aroused suspicion. A recent Russian magazine article took that theme. After admitting the tangible benefits for the region, the writer speculated on the true and nefarious motivation for an American professor to go to such effort. We must be hiding the faults of America's role in Alaska or planning to exploit new Russian businesses.

John interpreted the article this way: "The Russians have a hard time understanding Vic, Andrew, and John. We're not agents of the US government. And we're actually scarier than that. We really want to internationalize the world. And we can do it. We can speak the language. We understand the culture. We understand the mind-set. And we can offer the tools. And there is nothing more frightening for a fascist or a communist or a totalitarian or a Stalinist than internationalism."

The part of Siberia closest to Alaska, eleven time zones from Moscow, is Magadan, once home of the deepest recesses of the Gulag system. Besides the secrecy of its hellish labor camps, which were built to mine gold, the region was off-limits because of its importance in Soviet military operations. Troops massed there in the early years of the Cold War.

When we began visiting, armored personnel carriers remained a primary means of transportation, and tanks and fighter jets were a common sight. Even tiny Native villages had large staffs of secret police. An underground city near Anadyr supposedly was large enough to house an entire army division.

Even today, John and Andrew encounter suspicion and bureaucracy when entering Magadan or Chukotka, the easternmost province that lies directly across the Bering Strait from Alaska. A Russian woman there explained to Andrew that it was hard to break a habit of suspicion bred for a lifetime. She recalled receiving training as a schoolgirl, when she had won a trip to Moscow, instructing her to tell no one in the nation's capital about infrastructure in Chukotka, because Western spies were everywhere.

American experts on the Soviet Union couldn't believe what was happening when the Ice Curtain suddenly fell in 1989 and interaction opened across the Bering Strait. We in Alaska found extraordinary access that virtually bypassed the national capitals, with direct connections to people like ourselves on the other side. Although Magadan was vastly different in its economics and history, the region's land, climate, and Native cultures did resemble what we knew in Alaska. We were closer to Magadan than Moscow was in other ways than just physical distance.

The first Alaska connections were for business. Soon after Russians initially flooded Anchorage in February 1989, I traveled with my friend Perry Eaton and several others to Magadan to help him make business deals for Alaska Commercial Company, the supplier of rural Alaska whose history dates back to the trading posts of Russian America. The company was then Alaska Native owned. Perry, besides being a successful businessman and banker, now is among the most respected of Alaska Native artists for the Alutiiq masks he creates.

Just before leaving on the trip, I fell off a curb in downtown Anchorage while watching a parade at the Fur Rendezvous winter carnival with Ruthie, breaking my leg. The injury added to the ordeal of flying over the North Pole from Anchorage to London, thence east to Moscow, crossing Moscow by car, and then flying eastward many hours to Magadan—a twenty-six-hour journey all the way around the world to make what should have been a short jump across the Bering Sea from Alaska.

As soon as we arrived, exhausted, our hosts wanted to launch into trade negotiations. Perry knew our fatigue would put us at a disadvantage, so he suggested a *banya* instead. The Russian steam bath is a staple of life in coastal rural Alaska, where it was introduced by the Russians two centuries ago. The negotiators quickly agreed and soon enough I was hobbling into the *banya* without my aluminum crutches or the brace on my leg, as the metal would have rapidly heated to burning.

The Russians decided what I needed to heal was a good beating with *veniki*—birch twigs—to improve my circulation. I took it like a man until they reached the broken leg, when the agony of the blows to my not-yet-healed bone put a quick halt to the treatment. I survived with the help of the subsequent shots of vodka, accompanied by sausage, cheese, pickles, and more vodka.

My official role began in September 1989. After coming back from a week in Magadan, I spoke with ISER director Lee Gorsuch about the rich economic and social promise of collaborating with the Russians. Lee understood immediately. To those working in and familiar with the North, the relationship across the Bering Strait had ultimate logic, with the similar geology and biota on either side. Indigenous settlements and historic migrations were linked. With the melting of the Ice Curtain under Gorbachev, those studying these fields realized they might be able to extend their efforts to the other side.

Lee suggested I go to Washington to explore federal sources for research funding. I got nowhere. Federal officials cared only about direct relations between Washington and Moscow. For the State Department, the fact that the United States and Russia shared a common border amounted to mere esoterica.

In Alaska, however, change was coming rapidly. Research scientists were inundating University of Alaska administrators with requests for help to get to Russia. At the same time, a flood of Soviet scientists inquired about coming to Alaska.

Some collaboration had been going on for a long time. Twenty years earlier, researchers from the university's Institute of Biological Science had visited Magadan and conducted fieldwork in Chukotka. University geophysicists participated in international projects. Ted Mala, director of the University of Alaska Institute for Circumpolar Health Studies, established medical ties in

Novosibirsk and Magadan. But as the Ice Curtain melted, the desire for cross-border cooperation exploded.

The university's staff was overwhelmed. On the recommendation of colleagues in the administration who knew of my Russian background and my university experience, President Donald O'Dowd created a position for me as Director of Soviet Relations to deal with the issues in his office. (With the fall of the Soviet Union in 1991, the name of my office became Russian Affairs.) Lee Gorsuch housed me at ISER in Anchorage.

The new job tied together all the strands of my life with a challenge perfectly matched to my interests and abilities. I would need my knowledge of Alaska and Russia, my experience working in the state and federal governments and the university, and the skills I had developed in both official management and back-channel finagling. The wide-open field of the new Russia resembled my early days in Alaska, when virtually anything had been possible.

Scientific collaboration was the initial focus of my job. Many of our formal links grew from negotiations I carried out at the local, regional, and national levels of the USSR Academy of Sciences, which does most scientific research, unlike the West, where universities are centers of research. After almost a year of groundwork, university President O'Dowd and an entourage went over to consummate the connections. He became a real Russia enthusiast on that grand two-week trip, which spanned the country from one end to the other—St. Petersburg in the northwest to Vladivostok in the southeast—with many stops in between. We visited over a dozen research and academic institutions and signed agreements laying the foundations for lasting relationships.

When O'Dowd left the university his successor, Jerome Komisar, took the job in part because of our Russia connections. He traveled to Russia a number of times and supported me strongly. One year, Komisar, Tichotsky, and I celebrated Thanksgiving in Moscow with a turkey leg and a glass of champagne in the Metropole Hotel bar after a long day of meetings with the Ministry of Education.

My life was one of constant travel. While I didn't need interpreters, finding my way through the labyrinth of Russian science required good guides. I had several. One key partner for making scientific connections was Asylbek Aidaraliev, a fearless operator in overcoming institutional obstacles.

Asylbek and I met in February 1989 when he arrived on the first Russian flight to Anchorage. A native of Kyrgyzstan, he would have been successful wherever he landed, thanks to his intelligence, commanding presence, humor, and a knack for working the system. He had both an academic and a medical doctorate and was director of the Institute for the Study of Biological Problems of the North.

Some Soviets who arrived in Alaska carried a greater air of official weight than Asylbek, but many were unable to shed the bureaucratic mental processes of communism. They expected to be treated with deference and given benefits regardless of their contributions or talents. Asylbek, on the other hand, at first struck some as a wheeler-dealer trying to get away with something, but in reality he was exactly the kind of entrepreneur Russia needed to move forward.

With his central Asian features, Asylbek was easily mistaken for an Alaska Native, and he slipped effortlessly into Native communities with his work on human adaptability to extreme conditions. When he went to the North Slope Borough to meet Iñupiat whalers, he and his new friend Mayor Ben Nageak began telling people they were brothers because they looked so much alike.

Asylbek stayed for weeks at a time in our home. Jane taught him to drive. He got an Alaska drivers license to tool around in her Corolla. He still has the license. I took him to Washington, DC, and showed him how to work the halls of the Capitol and federal agencies to get funding for his work. He was naturally talented, with the ability to turn any meeting to the topic that suited his objectives. After I taught him how to write a grant application to an American foundation, he was unstoppable.

On the Russian side, Asylbek guided me on many trips to meet the top echelons of the Russian scientific establishment, where his connections were superior to mine in the United States. His institute and noted work as a biologist gave him impressive status. He put me in contact with the nation's highest academic authority, the presidium of the Academy of Sciences, the vice president of which was a close friend. We negotiated a broad academy-university cooperation agreement, which O'Dowd signed in Moscow during our cross-country trip.

Asylbek and I also created a new international scientific center on northern issues. Named Arktika, the center was chartered under a special agreement between our university and the academy. We became founding codirectors. Located in Magadan, Arktika continues to operate with academy support.

In 1992, Asylbek and I arranged a joint meeting of the US Arctic Research Commission and its counterpart in Russia. After three days of discussions in Magadan, we went by chartered plane to the North, stopping in several places. The next morning we boarded a large helicopter for the hour's flight to Wrangel Island, eighty-five miles north of Chukotka in the Arctic Ocean, the waters of which remained ice-choked and forbidding in July.

The island is a spectacular wildlife sanctuary, the largest polar bear denning area in the world, and the place where the last mammoths still survived four thousand years ago. It was closed and difficult to access. In the 1920s, Wrangel Island had been the subject of ill-fated western expeditions and attempts to claim it for Canada or the United States, although it is naturally in Russian territory and already belonged to Russia. Some American right-wing conspiracy theorists still allege it is our island.

Up on the mountain in the middle of the island, where we dropped in on a lone biologist studying birds, I decided to make a joke. Surrounded by our international dignitaries, I set up a pole in an empty barrel and held a mock ceremony raising an American flag, which I had brought from home, and claimed the island on behalf of Alaska. Thereupon John Tichotsky proclaimed me governor of the new land. The Alaska members of the commission were totally amused, some of the Russians hardly, while our State Department minder seemed to want to sink into the frozen tundra with embarrassment. But Asylbek loved it.

The collapse of the Soviet Union made Asylbek Aidaraliev's homeland of Kyrgyzstan an independent nation. The former head of the academy of science became president of the new country. Asylbek decided to move back home. Applying his new American experience and the contacts he had made, and using money from the Ford Foundation, he created the Kyrgyzstan International University, which unified several former Soviet institutes and colleges. He said it was modeled on the University of Alaska.

<hr />

Another lifelong friend dating from these years was Alexander (Sasha) Granberg. We met in 1989, when I was crossing the country to contact Russian scientific centers. Granberg was director of the Institute of Economics of the Siberian branch of the science academy, where I had met Abel Aganbegyan during my 1974 visit.

At the end of our business day, Granberg and I spent a long evening talking over dinner. It turned out he had grown up in the Arbat area just a half block from the Russian school I attended. The principal my classmates and I so admired would not admit Sasha because his apartment building had the reputation of housing delinquents. Nonetheless, he went on to become a professor and Russia's leading regional economist.

Granberg came to Alaska several times to give lectures and speeches, and on one trip we both went on to Hawaii for a scientific meeting and to brief high military brass about Pacific economic issues. During that era of liberalization brought about by Mikhail Gorbachev, he moved up rapidly in Russian government.

Granberg was elected to the Russian Federation's legislative body, the Supreme Soviet, later called "duma" as in prerevolutionary Russia. During the heady reform days following the Soviet Union's breakup, President Yeltsin appointed Granberg as economic advisor.

On a couple of occasions I called on Granberg at Yeltin's headquarters, sweeping past the Kremlin tourists with whom I formerly would have trouped along, to enter the inner sanctum surrounded by armed guards. Sasha's office was near the president's. On one visit he used the proximity to my great benefit: he helped me become a Russian citizen.

As the son of an American father and Russian mother, I was born with dual citizenship, but I became strictly American when I joined the US military during the war. In the 1990s, as I traveled back and forth many times a year, I often ran into hassles with getting visas and dealing with Russian bureaucracy. I was with Granberg in the Kremlin during one of of these frantic episodes, when he suggested I simply get a Russian passport.

He walked me down the corridor to meet with the chairman of the Commission on Citizenship, who said he would go along with the idea to support my work for Russian-American collaboration. I next asked the consul at the US embassy for advice. He highlighted two concerns. First, I could be called up for service in the Russian military and forced to renounce my US citizenship. Smiling, he opined that it should not be a problem—I was seventy at the time. Second, I might be subject to Russian taxes. Also not an issue, because I wasn't earning any money there.

Thereupon, with amazing speed, Yeltsin signed an executive order granting me full Russian citizenship. Since then, I have been able to enter either of my home countries easily, presenting my Russian passport when going to Russia and using my US passport when coming home or going to another country. As immediate family of a Russian citizen, Jane and Ruthie also received Russian passports, allowing for almost effortless side trips from Russia to Finland or southern Europe and then back to Russia.

Despite such access to power, Granberg grew frustrated with the economic turmoil of Yeltsin's early years and he resigned from government. He became head of the Council for the Study of Productive Forces, or SOPS after its Russian name, a prestigious organization affiliated with both the Academy of Sciences and the Ministry of Economic Development.

SOPS was an exciting place to visit as well. His office there was always piled high with books and scientific papers to review. People discussed esoteric economic science, practical issues of industry locations, and broad concepts such as opening the northern sea route to commercial traffic or building a tunnel to connect Chukotka and Alaska by road, rail, and pipeline. After our meetings we would dine downstairs in a private room and steam in the sauna, all in the SOPS building.

Granberg also took me to events at the Academy of Sciences, where he had the rank of "academician" and was a member of the presidium. Along with Asylbek and my brother Vanya, he attended the ceremony and reception when the Russian Academy of Economics (known as the Plekhanov Academy) awarded me an honorary doctorate of science for working to connect Russian and American higher education and science.

The University of Alaska became a national leader in connecting with the Soviet Union and Russia. Besides our many research partnerships, we gave technical assistance, established training programs, and educated Russians. Our offer of in-state tuition brought close to two thousand Russian students to the University of Alaska, more than at any other university in the United States at one time.

In Magadan, we worked to improve college instruction. The project grew from the first 1989 Russian exchange trip to Anchorage. With blessings from the Ministry of Education, the Magadan Pedagogical Institute added trustees from the University of Alaska and from Japan's Hokkaido University of Education, forming the Northeastern International University. University of Alaska presidents O'Dowd and Komisar served on the board, as did Brian Rogers, the president of the board of regents. I did too.

It is impossible to omit the names of many people crucial to connecting Russia and Alaska. Many were in my home, and I in theirs. They include Miron Markovich Atlis, a Gulag survivor, one of the most intelligent people I ever met, who once in Moscow taught me how to pack twice as much into a suitcase; Governor Vyacheslav Kobets, totally committed to every possible connection with Alaska, who treated me to banyas on many visits; Evgeni Kokorev, Lyudmila Biryukova, Roman Romanovich Chaikovsky, Larry Rockhill, and many others with whom we marched to strengthen educational ties across the ocean.

Those who managed the American Russian Center that organized aid included: Charles Neff, the first director in 1993, and Russ Howell, who followed in 1997, and the directors in Magadan, Tiffany Markey, Molly Davenport, and Sergei Talanov. Nor can I leave out Gretchen Bersch, University of Alaska professor and my wonderful friend, who has kept connections alive, traveling to Magadan annually, teaching, and giving students awards for excellence—all with her own money.

Rarely did projects come easy. Doing anything in Magadan required a lot of work. At first, communications were tortuous. Arranging a trip required many steps, but phone calls to Magadan were scarcely possible and the mails took a long time. Sending money was a bad gamble, as it often didn't arrive. At times we could only get funds for our projects into the country by stuffing our pockets with enormous bundles of currency.

I took the first nongovernment fax machine and first copier to Magadan to equip my counterpart there. The event had the feeling of a giant step, as if we had installed a communications outpost on another planet.

We achieved good voice communications thanks to an Alaska telecommunications company, Alascom, which agreed in January 1990 to install a satellite ground station in Magadan. The decision was a symptom of Russia fever: only enthusiasm at ending the Cold War and optimism about future trade explain the company's willingness to overcome the obstacles of installing US high technology to a remote corner of the Soviet Union. The expertise of telecommunications pioneer Alex Hills made enthusiasm into reality.

I could find no flights from Anchorage capable of carrying the dish to Magadan, but about that time the Khabarovsk Red Army hockey team arrived in Fairbanks in a large military cargo jet to play the Gold Kings. The two teams planned to fly back to Khabarovsk for a return game. The pilot agreed to drop our equipment and technicians off in Anadyr, a stop on the way to Khabarovsk. It was left for me to find transport from Anadyr to Magadan.

After further negotiations, we found ourselves in the belly of the huge jet with rows of side-facing seats and a gun turret in the back. Besides the satellite dish, we shared the space with piles of hockey equipment and case after case of beer, many of which the players emptied during the flight.

Flights within Russia got the dish to its connection point in Magadan. Alascom activated the link into the city phone system, carrying calls from there to Alaska. Formerly, connections had gone all the way around the world through Moscow and Novosibirsk, if one could get through at all. The university even established a four-digit Fairbanks campus number that would connect us directly to Magadan. Later, of course, the Internet and e-mail provided the easiest way to communicate across the border.

When direct flights connected Nome to Provideniya and Anchorage to Magadan, the new energy of our international relationship hit a peak. Cab drivers in Nome began accepting rubles for payment. They could exchange them with travelers heading back to the Russian side.

Americans went to Russia for business ventures, to hunt and fish, to find wives, or to help alleviate the poverty in Magadan. Russians came to Alaska for education, to learn about business and find investors, and to acquire goods that weren't available in their country, the most important of which were computers.

We found places to stay for visiting Russians and often gave them money, as they had little and their currency was next to worthless for purchasing American goods. Over and over we saw Russians weep over the abundance of Alaska's stores. Often, at a certain point, they would ask not to be exposed to such places anymore. They didn't want to see the kind of wealth that they could not afford.

I became so enmeshed in the business of our cross-border enterprises that I began issuing official invitations for Americans to visit Magadan using letterhead and validating stamps for Arktika and the Northeastern International University. I kept the materials in my office in Anchorage and used them at will, as if I were a proper Russian bureaucrat.

When I traveled in Russia, I was sometimes besieged by people requesting help. Early one morning in 1992, Jane and I found a line outside our door extending down the hall in the VIP Communist Party hotel in Magadan. The hotel lacked heat, and at 7 a.m. the people waiting were wrapped in blankets.

Their requests were mostly personal and difficult to fulfill: Could I find a missing relative, provide a food package, get someone into school? Would I find a company to manufacture an invention? Could I get an American operation for a sick child? And so on. I talked to each supplicant and wrote down the requests, but I couldn't help most except to pass on their request to someone who might.

After the Soviet Union collapsed in 1991, the economy lay in shambles. Pensions and government salaries were unpaid. President Yeltsin decreed that anyone could sell anything anywhere. Streets in Moscow and other cities were lined on both sides with residents trying to sell whatever they could turn into cash. One person might be trying to hawk a bottle of shampoo, the next a pack of cigarettes, and a third grandma's wine decanter. A guy outside a metro station might be holding up a piece of meat or a bunch of bananas. In the Far East, where subsidies suddenly disappeared, the situation was even worse. Food and heat ran out.

We knew of these problems and believed we could help. Our ally was US Senator Ted Stevens, Alaska's legendary appropriator of federal funds.

I had known Stevens since his days as US attorney in Fairbanks in the 1950s. Later he moved to Anchorage and practiced law with my friend Jack Roderick. Alaska's political world was so small in those days, and the partisan divide so unimportant in personal relationships, that it would have been odd if we had not known each other. Although Ted and I never became close friends, we were always friendly and worked together well.

Ted shared Alaskans' general enthusiasm when the Ice Curtain fell. In his position for many years on the Defense Appropriations Subcommittee, he believed some of the money that had been poured into the Cold War should now be diverted to secure the peace. He focused particularly on providing funds to secure and decommission the Soviet nuclear arsenal.

I approached Stevens a year after I took the job in the university president's office in 1989. I had seen how the Russian Far East struggled due to a lack of technical know-how, a problem far beyond our ability to address. He readily agreed to fund our work to provide assistance. The idea united his priority on the national level with his constant desire to send support home to Alaskans. A Stevens grant of $2 million came through the State Department's US Information Agency.

We also asked Stevens to help alleviate human suffering in the Russian Far East. Funds from USAID, the American foreign aid agency, channeled through Moscow, with little making it to the east of the country. At Stevens's insistence the situation was rectified, and eventually another $24 million went to the university to help build local economies in the region.

The president's office, where I worked, did not operate programs. Instead, we created the American Russian Center, the ARC, on the Anchorage campus to manage the Stevens-funded aid work. Capable Alaskan and Russian staff made it work.

Stevens and I maintained a frequent correspondence. I kept him updated on what was happening with our efforts and in Russia in general. The CIA contacted me a couple of times, too, and I would tell their agents the same information and general impressions I might cover at Rotary Club and World Affairs Council luncheons. I knew no secrets.

In March 1991, while the Soviet Union was still intact, Alexander Granberg invited me to a regional economic conference in Murmansk, the northern port city. The mayor arranged for him to see the naval base that housed Russia's northern fleet. I asked to go along, but the navy refused permission for me, a foreigner, to visit a secret base. It took some doing—I pointed out the American satellites could already record anything I might see—but the military finally relented and allowed me in.

I rode on the naval base in a limousine between two admirals. At one point I saw a large warship in the distance and asked if it was a Kirov class cruiser. The admirals turned to me with amazement and one said I was correct, asking how I knew. I pulled out a publication Stevens had sent me, a slick Pentagon production titled *Soviet Military Power*, with pictures of ships, aircraft, descriptions of Red Army strength, and so on.

I gave the publication to the admirals and told them where I got it, explaining that I assumed the Pentagon produced it to impress Congress with Soviet might in order to get more money for their own armaments. The Soviet admirals nodded knowingly, saying they did the same thing to get money from the Kremlin.

Besides the educational and humanitarian work by our Alaska group, Stevens funded us to help former Russian communists learn to be effective free market capitalists. Russians had grown up in a state-run economy and even the brightest frequently didn't understand how businesses and markets work.

I came to understand the need for this work one night during the chaotic early post-Soviet period, when my brilliant young Russian friend Ivan Bogdanov and I rode around Khabarovsk in a car with a driver trying to find sausage, cheese, and vodka. A little shop in an apartment basement had none. Another store had a line of people outside with buckets and jars. They were waiting to get a share of a beer shipment, but the store had no vodka. Typically, Soviet citizens would line up to buy whatever suddenly became available, whether they needed it or not, in order to be able to trade for something they did need.

Finally we found an indoor market of private stalls, some of which had salami for sale, but for much more than the prices posted in the government stores with empty shelves. Ivan was outraged and refused to pay.

I said, "Okay, here you have a market economy. You have the choice of buying salami at the price that it is available for, and you have the choice of going to a government store and not buying any salami."

"The Soviets would never have allowed such price gouging," Ivan said.

I responded, "Okay, fine. Soviets would not have allowed it. And at their official price there would have been no salami available. And now, you have salami."

I paid the market price, but Ivan remained indignant.

Using Stevens's grants, the ARC set up small business development centers in Magadan, Yakutsk, Khabarovsk, Yuzhno-Sakhalinsk, and several other cities under partnerships with local authorities. Russians received training to create and manage businesses. Those who showed promise would often come to Alaska for internships to learn more and get practical experience.

At the time, it was hard to know how much benefit we provided, but in hindsight this educational work seems to have shown some of the greatest long-term impact of our work.

Often, the most important learning happened when Russians saw new ways of doing things in Alaska and then applied them to their very different circumstances. A man from Yakutsk started a business delivering water cooler jugs to offices, as he had seen in Alaska. A woman from Yakutsk noticed that American convenience stores charged more than large grocery stores and realized she could do the same if she set up shop near where people lived. In her city, a shopping trip could require a long walk in −40°F temperatures. Likewise, no one in that part of Russia had ever thought of delivering pizza.

A woman from the far north community of Cherskiy came to Alaska to learn about domestic violence prevention. We suggested she visit Kotzebue, an arctic Alaska town somewhat similar to her home. When she returned to Russia, we heard nothing more and assumed that the exchange had been one more opportunity that might never have a tangible result. But five years later we got word: she had established a complete regional network to deal with domestic violence, including police, doctors, courts, and safe houses. She had replicated what she learned, on a big scale.

Alaskans received less long-term benefit from the melting of the Ice Curtain, despite our best efforts. ISER's experts had early predicted how the opening of the Soviet Union could affect Anchorage economically. In a report to Anchorage airport officials, Professor Gunnar Knapp wrote that when Russian airspace opened, the many international flights that routed through Anchorage—giving us the nickname "Air Crossroads of the World"—would no longer need to land there for fuel. His clients at the airport laughed at the prediction, saying Soviet airspace would never open. Three years later, the only international carrier coming to Anchorage was Aeroflot, and that only because of a requirement enacted by Stevens.

Direct flights from Anchorage to Magadan, primarily operated by Alaska Airlines, opened up opportunities for ordinary people to trade internationally. Anchorage became a hub, although never in the large-scale way we hoped. Russians would come to shop at Costco, filling large suitcases with goods they could sell back home. Costco noticed: when the Russians came, sales spiked and the store had to restock.

Direct attempts to help Alaskans do business in Russia generally met with less success. Russia never established the basic protections businesses need: contracts couldn't be enforced, dishonesty carried no penalty, the banking system didn't work, and Russian money had little value.

Some Alaskans made money for a time selling American goods by demanding cash up front for everything. Few successful ventures lasted, and most supply contacts migrated to centers in the Lower Forty-eight with lower prices and better freight connections than Alaska's.

The potential and pitfalls showed most dramatically in the saga of Alaska sausage-maker Doug Drum. Doug's Russian fever dated from the February 1989 flight, when Magadan Governor Kobets visited his Indian Valley Meats plant on Turnagain Arm south of Anchorage. Doug's equipment and skill processing reindeer and wild game were of obvious value to a region with huge reindeer herds but a primitive and wasteful system of preserving and distributing the meat.

Doug is an avid hunter and a warm and enthusiastic man. It was easy to convince him to go to Magadan. I saw him there the next month on my first visit with Perry Eaton.

All across the Russian North, not only in Magadan, indigenous people cared for large reindeer herds, but state enterprises responsible for getting the meat to market were so poorly run that they often let carcasses rot and bulldozed them into ditches. A housewife buying meat would have to find a truck on the side of the road with uncut sides and haunches of reindeer. Meat for her dinner would be hacked off on the spot, complete with hair and broken bones. Naturally, the prices were low.

We took Doug to villages to demonstrate proper butchering of reindeer meat. Audiences fell silent and looked on with rapt attention. After one demonstration, conflict erupted among villagers over who would get to take home the neat filets and roasts Doug had cut up. Although the villagers ate reindeer just about every day of their lives, they were used to crudely cut hunks boiled in stew. They'd never had it looking like our supermarket beef, the way Doug cut it.

With Andrew Crows's help, Doug developed a joint venture to make the most use of the reindeer resource and get hard currency out of it. Reindeer antler could be sold for high prices in Korea, where it was used for traditional medicine, particularly as an aphrodisiac. Koreans would pay Doug dollars for the antler, and Doug would in turn provide the Russians with sausage plants and training to operate them.

At first the joint venture worked. A couple of plants were installed and operated. The antler made it to Korea. Money came back to an account in Anchorage. Doug and Andrew had extraordinary adventures as celebrities in far-flung communities across the remote Russian north.

But the venture couldn't survive the Wild West practices of post-Soviet capitalism. The Russian partners began trading their antler directly with the Koreans, for bribes or for consumer electronics that were like gold in the barter market. Ignoring their contracts with Doug, they abandoned their deal and the long-term benefit of making better use of the meat. In a banking crisis that followed the fall of the Soviet Union, Doug and his investors lost more than half a million dollars.

We later salvaged some of the work by setting up a training program for Russians at Doug's Anchorage plant using a USAID program. Doug stayed involved, although not at the same high level. Andrew later brought him to an arctic village in Chukotka to figure out how to can walrus meat (it reportedly was delicious).

Andrew felt a sense of failure. The work surrounding the sausage business seemed to have yielded few benefits other than great stories. But recently he saw reindeer for sale in a store in Yakutsk. It had been cut up and packaged as in an American grocery store, just as Doug Drum had taught. At least some of the lessons had taken hold.

All of our efforts were worthwhile if they could help heal the wounds history inflicted in Magadan. Millions of Stalin's prisoners had been brought here on one-way trains and ships to be sent on to camps where inmates were systematically worked to death. Except for some memorials and museums, most evidence of the Gulag system had disappeared. The guards fled. But some inmates remained: the strongest, those who had survived.

One such survivor was Yevgeni Bogdanov. I stayed in his apartments in Leningrad and in Khabarovsk, where he kept one empty room for exercise. He would race around the room, rising up on the walls, jumping up and down as he spun in circles. At that time, he was director of the Institute of Mining of the Academy of Sciences, an old man who had risen to the top of his profession, a man of marvelous life and energy, a unique survivor.

Yevgeni was studying in Leningrad in 1934 when the assassination of Kirov set off the first fury of Stalin's purges. Agents swept him up along with some classmates and sent him to a prisoner shipment point, the port of Vanino. He was loaded like a slave on a ship, with rows of men packed so tightly they could only move in unison. The voyage took seven days and when he arrived, the men on either side of him were dead of exposure or disease.

Yevgeni took me to the Gulag museum in Khabarovsk and told me about the horrors of the camps—the cold, the lack of food, and the sadistic punishments, such as prisoners being tied to trees to be devoured by mosquitoes and left to die. As winter approached in the gold placer mining camp where he was imprisoned, Yevgeni realized he probably wouldn't survive without a miracle.

Gold mining would stop in the winter when the ground froze. Pushing a wheelbarrow, Yevgeni thought about the problem as a way to escape. He approached a guard to say he knew how work could continue into the winter.

With his two years of university training as an engineer, Yevgeni theorized that water, even if only barely above freezing, could be pumped into the ground to thaw it for mining. After checking with a camp engineer, the authorities gave Yevgeni two weeks to flesh out the idea. If he failed, he would be executed.

His idea worked. The authorities sent him back to Leningrad to finish his university studies. A device used in the Russian north to mine the permafrost still bears Bogdanov's name. He remained an inventor through his career, holding some seventy patents. He became a giant figure in Russian mining, head of the school of mining and a figure of interest even to Alaska geologists and miners, presenting papers at conferences in Fairbanks and Anchorage. When John Tichotsky embarked on a research project using the archives of gold mining in Magadan, he learned that all of Yevgeni's stories were true.

Bogdanov was my elder by a decade and is no longer living, but his son Ivan Bogdanov, whom everyone called by his Russian nickname Vanya, the same as my Russian brother, also became a close friend. It was he who, besides Asylbek Aidaraliev, served as guide and escort as I was connecting with Russia's scientific establishment.

With his bushy black hair and enthusiasm for his work as a soil scientist, Ivan exuded an irresistible love for life that energized everyone around him. One time, I spent a day at his side as he dug up soil samples on the taiga. He convinced me, despite my better judgment, to illegally smuggle the material back to Alaska for his botanist colleagues at the University of Alaska.

Ivan's sense of humor was legendary. On a ten-hour car trip, he told John Tichotsky ten hours worth of jokes. He memorized the entire classic Russian comic novel the *Twelve Chairs*. On his many trips to Alaska, he entertained everyone around him, and his energy never flagged. At midnight, he went out on the tundra around Barrow to find soil samples, and then to pee into the holes left behind. I'm not sure why or where he learned that custom.

Young Bogdanov had a magnificent attitude in facing down the authorities in the many situations in which our work came under their scrutiny. Before the first Russian flight to Alaska, in February 1989, sponsors had to provide the secret police with a minute-by-minute schedule of how the visitors would spend their time in Anchorage. On returning they were expected to explain any deviations from the schedule. Of course, deviation from schedule was constant—the visit was ad hoc and chaotic.

Ivan was the perfect person to provide the explanations. He knew how to blow off border guards and secret police with an attitude that told them he couldn't care less what they thought, with bluster so effective it could intimidate those who were thoroughly used to intimidating others. His prestige and that of his father surely helped, but he also explained his attitude by saying, "What are they going to do to me? I was born outside of a Gulag concentration camp."

Ivan died recently, much too young.

In the Bogdanovs, father and son, I always sensed the human spirit overcoming the immense horror of Stalinism and the camps. But the past never disappeared. Today, on a hill high above Magadan, stands a giant memorial to the millions of Stalin's victims who passed through this gateway on the way to the prison camps, most never to return. Its designer was sculptor Ernst Neizvestny, whose parents were victims of the 1930s purge and who in the 1970s moved to the United States. I had a small part in bringing it to reality and continued to stay in touch with the artist.

Neizvestny shipped his model of the monument from his New York studio to me in Anchorage in fall 1990. I put it on an Aeroflot flight to Magadan for exhibit there. The following year, he stayed with Jane and me while working on the project, meeting with Alaska business and labor leaders to learn about best arctic construction practices, before traveling on to Magadan. The memorial was completed under the direction of Magadan architect Kamil Kazayev in 1996.

The monument, "The Mask of Sorrow," is a monstrous concrete hulk looming more than five stories high, a grotesque head thrusting from the earth, strewing boulders in all directions. One side of the head appears raw and rough, reflecting Gulag life. The other side sheds stone tears for endless victims, each tear a human mask. There are more masks within the masks, faces within faces, dozens of them: large, small, and tiny; men, women, children; a grandmother; a Japanese war prisoner.

I've stood before this stark creation on several occasions, overwhelmed by its intensity, pulled back into its aura of epic suffering, forced to contemplate the horrors perpetrated by Stalin's regime. Winding through the darkness of the monument's interior, one steps into the past, into a tiny prison cell, into the life of a single individual.

Overhead a six-foot bronze body is twisted and wracked in agony, reaching to the sky. Below it, in an alcove, a girl of smooth bronze kneels, head buried in her hands.

Her gentleness contrasts with the rough surroundings, the personification of the children of the repressed. She was of my generation. As I stood before her, she rekindled memories of my Moscow years, my friends and classmates.

But generally, Stalin's ghosts did not haunt my return and reconnection to Russia. That era had receded to a distant memory. In our period of hope and enthusiasm, when communism and the Soviet Union collapsed and any experiment seemed possible, a return to heavy-handed dictatorship was nearly unthinkable.

But I was to live to see authoritarianism fall over the country once again.

⇥ 27 ⇤

Russian Endings

After five years managing Russian Affairs for the University of Alaska, I retired again in 1994, but not because I wanted to reduce my involvement with Russia. Jane, Ruthie, and I moved to Moscow for a year and made good use of our citizenship. Despite the chaos and crime of the new freebooting capitalist economy, we lived in a brief golden period of Russian freedom.

The three of us had visited Magadan, St. Petersburg, and Moscow two years earlier. Then, in 1994, Jane finished her work founding the Alaska Native Heritage Center in Anchorage. Ruthie at eleven seemed a good age for an adventure. And I could continue Alaska–Russia work as a freelancer in Moscow, compensated whenever I did university work.

Jane had made friends with many of the Russian visitors who had stayed with us in Anchorage. Although she spoke little Russian, she shared my eagerness to return those visits and enter into the rich social scene that was awaiting us. Besides the friends made during five years of citizen diplomacy, my old circle of classmates and childhood friends would surround us.

We were invited to stay with the prettiest girl among my early Peredelkino playmates, Zilya, the first love of Lothar Wloch. She had inherited a huge apartment in the House of Writers from her father, the poet Ilya Selvinski. It occupies half a floor with windows on three sides and has three bedrooms, more than enough space to add our family.

Zilya had not changed. She was still beautiful after seventy years and still as dramatic as if spending every moment of her life on stage. In the morning, she wouldn't show her face until she had spent an hour or more in the kitchen applying layers of makeup, a private process that always delayed breakfast until after 10 a.m.

Zilya had ended her acting career because of difficulties with her voice (which was hard to imagine, given the strength with which she projected in everyday conversation), but worked with the Moscow Circus, teaching performers and announcers how to hold the audience with their presence and dramatic gestures.

Her talents were in full use when we went to take Ruthie to the neighborhood school, the same school that Zilya and her daughter Oksana had attended. Zilya swept imperiously into the principal's office and declared that Ruthie was her granddaughter and must be admitted. The principal said there was no room, objected that Ruthie wasn't from the area, and insisted her attendance was impossible. But she crumpled before the force of this magnificent woman.

We were naturally worried about how Ruthie would fare in an all-Russian school, but on her first day a group of girls ran to meet us, eager to try out their English. Being American made her a school celebrity with an entourage of friends. Although she couldn't follow math or science, she did well with cross-county skiing, sewing, and other skills that didn't require fluent Russian.

One day, a new friend handed Ruthie a note inviting her to attend the ballet with her family. She brought the note home. Ruthie was reluctant to go with a strange family by herself, so I wrote on the note and sent it back: Could her parents come, too? In that way we met friends with whom we became close: Ruthie's friend Olya, her younger sister Alyona, and their parents, Larissa and Vladimir "Volodya" Polyakov.

In many ways the Polyakovs were a typical Russian family. Volodya was an economist and Larissa a music teacher. They lived in two rooms, the girls sleeping in the bedroom and the parents in the common room. The place was full of books, they recited Pushkin for entertainment, and Larissa would play the piano while Volodya sang folk songs and opera and the girls danced.

Volodya found employment doing financial work for large enterprises that were exploding across Russia at the time. While our other professional friends scraped by on subsistence government salaries of $15 or $20 a month from their institutes or, even worse, on tiny pensions, he made $200 a month and began taking the family on wonderful vacations. We accompanied them to the Black Sea and to many performances and cultural events.

The Polyakovs were like friends we could have made through Ruthie's school in Anchorage, but their future wasn't much like our Anchorage friends'. A few years ago, Volodya was killed on a work trip when the plane he was on was blown up by Chechen terrorists. The family was left destitute.

Russia's traumas continued to shape my old school friends' lives as well. After the initial reunions, our gatherings became more routine, simply get-togethers of a group of seventy-year-olds with affection for one another. Jane couldn't always follow the conversation but paid attention. She noticed that most of my friends seemed much older than I.

Physically, Russian life had always been hard, and it still was. Even a top scientist such as my friend Vadya Popov kept his small apartment stacked with sacks of staples: flour, sugar, salt, cereals. Russians knew real scarcity and would stockpile anything that suddenly became available.

The passing seasons came in Moscow with the harvest. Urban dwellers had to put up food whenever it became available, as we did decades ago when Anchorage was still a remote outpost. Even fashionable Zilya pickled cucumbers, beets, and other vegetables. When cherries were ripe, she spent days putting up preserves. In the fall, she spread potatoes across the kitchen floor to dry so they would keep through the winter. In winter, the only affordable food was bread and mystery meat.

But the difference in the apparent age between my friends and me went deeper than the difference in our physical circumstances. The fun and freedom in which I had grown left me an optimist, still active with a myriad of opportunities. My friends' lives had been hemmed in by communism and need. The stereotype of Russian fatalism is often accurate. Russians have had good reason to be fatalistic.

Patience with Russia's experiment in chaotic capitalism had worn thin by the mid-1990s. Basic government functions did not work. Salaries went unpaid for months and pensions didn't arrive. Hustlers were getting rich while ordinary workers went hungry. Street crime and brutal organized crime bloomed along with corruption, bringing new fear to daily life.

Zilya's daughter, a PhD chemist working in a research institute, had gone six months without being paid, as had her husband, also a scientist. To survive he drove the family car around Moscow as an unofficial taxi cab.

At our gatherings, my friends discussed Russia's problems, which were the routine difficulties of daily life. I once took a poll among my classmates, asking who would be willing to go back to the communist authoritarian system that had at least provided order and security. Not one preferred that option. All said they preferred the present situation, with the freedoms it offered.

But Jane understood something quite different in their answers. Only recently did we talk about her impression of that same moment. By watching their emotions and listening to their voices without understanding all the Russian words, she concluded they had said the opposite. She believed that in their advancing age and weariness from so much hardship, they were ready to return to the stability of an all-powerful state.

I prefer to think my friends' words expressed their true feelings. But history shows that most Russians soon reached the decision that Jane saw in their body language. They lost faith in the dream of a free Russia. A livable form of democracy had not come into existence.

The past was inescapable in Moscow. Zilya still lived in the apartment where she said goodbye to Lothar as he left for Germany when she was sixteen years old. She had built a personal mythos around that moment.

Through a full and eventful life that brief teenage affair had remained her one true love, an anchor. Above her daybed, she kept a sort of shrine to Lothar, a collection of pictures and memorabilia dating back to the summer of 1940, when they fell in love at Peredelkino.

Whether Lothar ever fully reciprocated Zilya's feelings will never be known. Certainly, he moved on and had a wonderful lifelong relationship with his wife, Eva, without many backward glances, so far as I could ever see.

Zilya married, too, and raised her family, but she and her husband came to detest each other. They divorced, but he stayed in the apartment, because the authorities would not assign him new quarters when Zilya already had so much floor space. For fifteen years they lived within the same walls without speaking to each other. Jane called it the husband-from-hell lifestyle.

The husband had been dead several years when we arrived in 1994, but his things still filled the closet in the room where Jane and I slept, and his old medicines were still in a bedroom cabinet. Zilya wouldn't touch anything that had belonged to him. We cleared it out so we could settle in.

But the operatic story of Zilya's love life had not ended. Two years earlier, in 1992, we had been staying with her for a week when it began an extraordinary coda. Lothar's old friend from Peredelkino, Anarik Eisenberger, had suddenly reemerged via a letter from Ukraine.

Back in the 1930s, Anarik's communist German father was liquidated in the purge and his family expelled from the Lux Hotel, like Lothar's. He had stayed for a while with Lothar's family in the Wolf's apartment. He was with us during those years when, as teens, we simultaneously endured the Great Terror and joyfully reveled in the energy of youth at the Peredelkino dachas of the Wolf family and of Zilya's father.

During the summer of 1940, Anarik and Lothar both fell in love with Zilya. Lothar spoke to her first, and Anarik kept quiet out of respect for his best friend. In Moscow, he carried notes between the lovers without saying a word.

In 1942, after Lothar had left for Germany and Hitler had invaded Russia, Anarik received a draft notice. He was overjoyed. He had been working in Moscow's Stalin Automobile Factory and wanted to fight the fascists on the front line, although realizing he would be fighting on the opposite side from his friend. He left for the war carrying a photograph of Zilya.

But, as I mentioned in Chapter 7, Anarik and other German-speaking Russian recruits were segregated to the last car of the troop train. That car didn't go west to the fighting but was unhitched and taken east. The thirty-three young Russians were arrested as traitors because of the German nationality of their parents.

Anarik disappeared into a nightmare. Without winter clothing, the young men traveled across the frigid taiga by rail, stranded in bitterly cold buildings, and trudging through the snow and ice for many miles with sledges. Some collapsed and many had frozen hands, feet, and faces.

Without explanation or outside contact, they were deposited in a logging barracks built for summer use and left to freeze and starve. The men gathered wood to burn and appointed one of their number to be a cook, but at times they could find no food for days. At one point, the group discussed suicide as the best escape.

One night, one of Anarik's comrades became hysterical, shaking and sobbing. Anarik couldn't calm the man but tried to change the subject. After the war they would all be released and get married. To whom? The men described their sweethearts and their hopes. The mood changed. But Anarik always kept his love for Zilya secret, because he had promised Lothar when they parted that he would help her wait for him.

Anarik was a huge, powerful man. He survived through his own strength and his ability to lead others. He got help from local peasants and learned to hunt, snaring rabbits while working in the forest. He learned to fight to protect himself. He and his friends remained patriots, believing that their dangerous work as loggers, cutting down large trees with primitive hand tools, would help defeat the Nazis.

The men assumed they would be released when the end of the war arrived. But after the victory celebrations ended, their commandant announced that their exile had been made permanent. Anarik saved himself from disillusionment with dreams of Zilya. He hid her small picture in a crack in a tree where he could retrieve it while working. He wrote hundreds of letters and poems for her and buried them in bottles in the woods and along the bank of a river.

As the years passed, Anarik learned the skills of a machinist to fix equipment in the camp. He met a Ukrainian woman who lived nearby. Part of their relationship consisted of Anarik telling her about his now-mythic love for Zilya.

When his release finally came, they married and moved to Ukraine, where he ran a large machine shop and raised a family.

Fifty years had passed when Anarik picked up a copy of *The Troika* in its Russian edition, titled *Three from the Thirties,* and read that Lothar had died and that Zilya was alive and well in Moscow. He wrote to her and she responded, eventually inviting him to visit Moscow. Their first letters were just friendly, but shortly before Anarik came he wrote again, to declare his love. He told Zilya about the decades he had dreamed of her and how her image had helped him survive his years in the camps. He wrote, "If I don't tell all, I'll suffocate."

Jane and I were there when he arrived in 1992. Anarik was in love, but Zilya was not. The reunion was friendly, like the other reconnections of old friends in those days. When we came back in 1994, however, their relationship had developed into one of total mutual devotion. After a lifetime of waiting for Lothar, Zilya had finally found someone who fulfilled her fantasies and was totally present for her.

Besides being tall and handsome, with piercing eyes, Anarik is the kindest and gentlest of men. He gave his wife the pension and apartment in Moscow that he had received as a victim of Stalin's repression and survivor of the camps. His children accepted Zilya into their family. When we lived in Zilya's apartment, Anarik was living there, too. Ruthie commented on how the seventy-year-olds were like teenagers in love.

One day, Anarik came home sad and upset. He was shaking. He had been attacked in the street by three young men who tried to mug him and probably thought a man his age would be an easy mark.

But the attack wasn't what disturbed him. He had come away unscathed, breaking the nose of one of the muggers with his knee and knocking out another with a hard punch before the third ran away. Anarik was upset by his own capacity for violence.

He said, "I was back in the camp fighting for my life. It happened so fast, and I didn't know that was still in me."

His skill for making do also survived from the camps. Anarik fixed everything, even a broken mirror. He melted down torn nylons to repair Zilya's worn high heels. The mattresses in the apartment were unbearably hard and lumpy. They weren't replaced: they were repaired with new horsehair and springs retied.

Jane thought she was doing Zilya a favor when she replaced a worn-out potato peeler with a new one. Zilya was outraged that Jane had thrown away the broken peeler, which could have been repaired. The wastefulness of Americans astounded her. She persistently turned off the lights to save energy while we were reading.

One day, I heard Jane and Zilya yelling at each other in the kitchen, each in her own language. Jane was on her knees, washing the floor with a rag. She was saying to Zilya, "I don't mind doing it. I want to help. Let me clean the floor." But Zilya, in Russian, was screaming, "That's my dish towel! You must not use it on the floor!"

In retrospect we laughed, but at the time the incident was embarrassing. We enjoyed living with Zilya and Anarik and had many more good times, but we decided to get our own apartment after six months of sharing space with Zilya in Moscow.

Later, with Zilya's help, Anarik published a book about his experiences as a prisoner and his relationship with Zilya, which was made into a documentary film. They traveled together widely to publicize the book, including a stop in Berlin organized by Mischa Wolf. We invited them to Anchorage, where they told their story on stage for an evening at Cyrano's Theater.

Zilya died a few years ago, but Anarik still lives in her apartment with care from her family, which has adopted him as a grandfather.

When we moved out of Zilya's apartment, Ruthie transferred to a new school where she could study in English as well as Russian as a second language. She met American kids who had never been on the Moscow metro, which she managed almost daily. Our apartment was on the fourteenth floor of a building about half an hour from the center of Moscow by the subway.

We shopped for food at a local store a short walk from the building. Going farther we could buy many Western products—except decent lettuce. The Russian economy provided goods to those who had money, but few ordinary Russians could afford the prices.

We felt safe in the streets and let Ruthie make her own way riding the metro and walking to the store. She became competent in Russian. On return visits, she has been able to drop into Moscow life much like I can. We had arrived in Moscow with pepper spray and lots of trepidation about the crime problem, but learned that getting along was similar to being in any large American city. You simply behaved like everyone else and avoided sticking out as a foreigner.

On one of our walks we made a startling discovery that led to a job for Jane. We stopped in the office of a prodemocracy group, the National Democratic Institute for International Development, and asked what Russian-language materials they had to assist newly empowered regional governments, as I was doing in the Far East. Yes, they had a model American city charter and gave me Los Angeles's charter in Russian translation. And they had a model state constitution and handed it to me. It was the Alaska Constitution, translated into Russian.

Jane said, "He wrote it."

The group's representative was duly impressed, and asked if I would help train local elected officials. I suggested Jane do it, as she had drafted a municipal charter and had been a local elected official. She was hired to travel with translators from town to town to teach newly elected as well as existing mayors and council members how to set up municipal governments and manage budgets in an open society. She also trained candidates, especially women, how to run election campaigns in a democracy.

The cultural life of Moscow also kept us constantly engaged, with the ballet, chamber music, museums, the circus, and our round of friends, my old classmates, our new friends, and a number of visiting Alaskans and other Americans. We also used our location and special passport status to make several trips to the rest of Europe.

One of our most memorable trips came when we accepted Asylbek Aidaraliev's invitation to visit him at his new university in Kyrgyzstan. All the time we had spent with Asylbek traveling and at our home in Anchorage had made him among our dearest friends. He felt the need to pay back our hospitality, and he did it in a big way. On our visit to Bishkek and Lake Issikul, we were VIP guests of the highest order.

For two and a half months around the middle of the school year we traveled around Europe. (That was when Jane and Ruthie became US–Russian dual citizens to simplify visa requirements.) We flew to Berlin to visit the Wlochs and Mischa, who lent us a car for our wanderings. I once flew back to Alaska to coordinate a study tour by Magadan's university trustees and top administrators.

On this trip, we visited Austria, Italy, Greece (including Rhodes and Crete), France, Spain, Portugal, Gibraltar, and Morocco. The Christmas holidays were spent on Spain's Mediterranean coast with John Tichotsky and his wife, Mary Core, and daughter, Hannah, who joined us from England, where John was working toward his doctorate at Cambridge University.

Driving back to Berlin, we went through Switzerland, where Jane and Ruthie went skiing, and then back into Germany to fly to Moscow. Most of the time, we traveled spontaneously, going wherever we fancied and staying in cheap lodgings, without advance planning. But we punctuated those weeks with weeks relaxing in prearranged time-share condos.

When our overseas year ended, I rejoined ISER and Jane was appointed state director of land in the Alaska Department of Natural Resources.

At ISER I continued to work on Alaska–Russia connections, which became more sophisticated, especially a project with a bright, young Russian economist, Alexander Pelyasov. Known as Sasha, he was originally from St. Petersburg and was working in Magadan at the time. He had spent a residency at the institute to learn about Alaska, expand his knowledge of research methods, and perfect his English. He later was recruited by Alexander Granberg to work at SOPS as a senior regional economist on issues of northern development.

At the time, Sasha led a three-year collaboration to examine Alaska's experiences in resource development, government, and indigenous self-governance and their applicability to the Russian Far East. The outcomes were books that Sasha authored and conferences we organized in Magadan and Moscow covering the three topics. They influenced thinking and action in the region for years to come.

These joint conferences epitomized the close relationship that had evolved in education, business training, science, and many other areas. But one part of the Russian Far East increasingly fell outside our sphere of collaboration: Chukotka, the area that lies closest to Alaska, directly across the Bering Strait, and that seemed to need our help the most. When the Ice Curtain melted in 1988, the first Friendship Flight landed at Provideniya in Chukotka. People-to-people and business connections blossomed quickly, especially between Nome and Provideniya. But Chukotka's governor, Alexander Nazarov, began choking off connections within a few years.

Nazarov transformed his remote region into a personal fiefdom, in the style of Stalin's dictatorship. To maintain control he cut off outside links, limited travel, and even hindered entry to the region by other Russians. Regional officials threw up barriers to our work and harassed those who cooperated with us.

Chukotka was a desperately poor, sparsely populated arctic province on the Bering Strait and fell far outside the consciousness of any outsiders but our group of Alaskans who cared about our counterparts in Alaska's closest Russian neighbor. The national government didn't care what happened there. Nazarov, a former Soviet functionary, had parlayed an appointment from Yeltsin to his personal profit. He diverted revenues from Moscow into American real estate holdings and to import expensive vehicles. Nazarov and his cronies not only held tightly to political power but also squeezed the region economically for total control.

Poverty in Chukotka was horrendous. Collapsed arctic industries stranded unemployed Russians who wanted to leave but couldn't afford the trip. Food and fuel were unavailable. Indigenous people lived in subsistence villages without health facilities or adequate food sources. Chukchi people commonly ate seal meat three meals a day.

Like the Eskimos of Alaska's arctic coast, the Chukchis' traditional culture and diet relied on harvesting whales. The Soviets had outlawed Native whaling while slaughtering whales in large numbers from factory ships that supplied meat to industrial fur farms. After the fall of the Soviet Union, village elders still remembered how to hunt whale, but they lacked proper equipment.

Villagers could harpoon a whale and bring it near their small boats, but they couldn't kill it. In the old days they would have used Yankee whaling devices that could shoot powder-filled brass tubes into a whale that would explode and cause death. But those guns were all in museums. They tried Soviet antitank grenades, which required two men to fire. The projectiles tended to pass right through the whale and blow up on the other side. Rifles weren't effective either.

Iñupiat whalers of Alaska's northern coast offered to help. They had never lost their whaling tradition and had the tools, including the unique whale guns. North Slope oil revenues, flowing through the borough government, provided the Iñupiat the wherewithal to offer their Chukchi cousins equipment, training, and help with scientific research.

Under Mayor George Ahmaogak, the North Slope Borough Department of Wildlife Management paid Chukchi whalers to gather data about whale numbers and migration patterns. Borough scientists analyzed the information for presentation to the International Whaling Commission. Based on the studies, the commission allocated a quota for the Chukchi to harvest whales. As a side benefit, the money the Russian whalers received for the work helped them organize politically.

Ahmaogak hired John Tichotsky to work out travel arrangements and resolve red tape for the groups. Governor Nazarov's hostility transformed ordinary bureaucratic recalcitrance into outright resistance, but John is a master of the wiles, patience, and combativeness necessary to force Russian officials to do their jobs. Getting the weapons from Alaska to Chukotka was a tour de force effort. He even had to become a registered arms merchant!

Exceptional Native leaders emerged on the Russian side. Vladimir Yetylin grew up a nomadic reindeer hunter in his parents' tent. He rose to a high governmental level during communist times. When I first met him, before the Soviet Union fell, I assumed he was just another placeholder, but when the situation became desperate in Chukotka, he proved an indefatigable foe to Nazarov. He ran against him for governor despite the hopeless odds of being a minority Native without funding against Nazarov's corrupt and all-powerful regime.

Yetylin united the sometimes conflicting Chukchi and Yup'ik people into a single Chukotka Association of Marine Mammal Hunters, which managed the exchanges with Alaska's Iñupiat. They met annually in Barrow or Anchorage. With its outside funding and success in restarting the whaling tradition, the group became the only opposition to Nazarov. The whalers alone could inform the outside world about what was happening in his miserable little realm.

The governor focused on stamping out the association. He reported Yetylin and the other leaders to Moscow as enemies of the Russian state. He even sent a group of imposters to one of the annual meetings in Alaska, apparently to seize control of the money and assistance going to his foes.

To the astonishment of the Iñupiat, two groups appeared claiming to be the Chukotka Association of Marine Mammal Hunters. Nazarov had chartered an organization with the same name and registered its founding on the same day, although in a different year. The fake whaling group presented papers to Mayor Ahmaogak to prove they were the real association.

Ahmaogak knew with whom he had worked before and didn't care about the papers. He threw out Nazarov's group. Yetylin's group reorganized under a new name, the Chukotka Traditional Marine Mammal Hunters Association.

Despite winning that skirmish, the struggle against Nazarov was unsustainable. The leaders were afraid of arrest. Chukotka had become unlivable. Nazarov would be up for reelection in December 2000 and no one in Chukotka could take him on. Yetylin didn't think the hunters could make it through another term.

In January 2000, John Tichotsky and Vladimir Yetylin schemed for a solution while attending a whalers' meeting in Barrow. Someone from outside the region would have to run, because no one who lived in Chukotka could stand up to Nazarov. Russian law required only that the governor be a Russian citizen, not a resident. They decided I was the one.

When I got Tichotsky and Yetylin's phone call, I could only laugh. They believed my role as a founder of Alaska statehood would allow me to project a vision of Chukotka's possibilities. But the idea of leaving Alaska to run for the governorship of a Russian province struck me as absurd.

I didn't even like Chukotka much. The people were good, but the land was stark and the largest town, Anadyr, had only twelve thousand people, mostly living in cold concrete apartment blocks. I had enjoyed living in Moscow, but there I was on home ground. Anadyr would be nothing like that. Besides, I had long retired from politics and my life was as I wanted it.

I had greatly reduced my involvement in Russian work. When I counted up my time traveling, I realized I had been making eight trips a year to Russia, taking me away from my family for a combined three months out of twelve. At seventy-five, I preferred to spend more time at home, with Jane and Ruthie and my other children.

But Tichotsky and Yetylin persisted. John Tichotsky's wife, my good friend Mary Core, lobbied me as well, describing the desperate conditions in Chukotka. I reluctantly agreed to talk when they came to Anchorage.

We met around our dining room table in Anchorage: John Tichotksy, Mary Core, and Vladimir Yetylin, and with them Jane, whom I wanted at my side to help defend me, since I knew she would never agree to the scheme and would strengthen my resolve. Our guests related how families in frigid apartments in Anadyr were keeping warm by wrapping their bodies together in layers of blankets and staying put all day. Children were dropping from hunger on the way to school. People in villages and towns were dying from starvation and scurvy. When Nazarov came to Provideniya to make a speech, he told the people their poverty was due to their own lack of initiative.

My friends believed I could end this nightmare or at least alleviate the suffering. Maybe I could if I were governor. But I didn't think their scheme would work. The Native vote would simply not be enough.

Jane's career working in the Alaska Bush made her particularly sympathetic to the stories of poverty. To my dismay, her resistance evaporated and she agreed that I should try for it, so long as I would have plenty of bodyguards to protect me.

I never really relented. But to end the discussion I added two conditions to Jane's bodyguards, stipulations I was sure could not be fulfilled and would thus kill the scheme. Yet, they were reasonable conditions, because without them I couldn't win, and with them I might have a chance. First, I required a million dollars for the campaign and, second, they would have to bring me an endorsement by Roman Abramovich.

We all knew that Roman Abramovich was the only person who could possibly give a million dollars to such a campaign and that his power could sweep aside Nazarov and any other opposition. But it seemed totally improbable that he would even consider doing that.

Abramovich was among the richest men in Russia. He remains on the list of the richest men in the world, regularly making headlines for his Chelsea football club or his yacht, which is the size of a cruise ship and has its own submarine. I couldn't imagine any reason why he would want me to be governor of Chukotka.

Abramovich had no natural connection to the region. In 1999, he had won Chukotka's seat in the Russian Duma, the parliament, although before initially running he had never visited and knew little about the region. Oligarchs were buying Duma seats as insurance against prosecution, which was presumably his original motivation as well.

Why would oligarchs need shelter from prosecution? Many people assumed that their wealth was ill-gotten. Abramovich rose from a tough childhood, an orphan, starting in business on the level of a street vendor, and by his thirties owned huge oil and aluminum concerns. Yeltsin's corrupt privatization program helped make him rich.

In the lawless world of Russian capitalism, the oligarchs had as much to fear from the arbitrary use of government power as they did from justice. Rich men who opposed President Vladimir Putin ended up in jail or had to leave the country. Abramovich reportedly got along well with Putin, but being in the Duma also made him immune from arrest.

My friends negotiated a meeting. After being assured that Abramovich would accept, Governor Tony Knowles issued an invitation for him to come to Alaska, with Yetylin acting as a go-between. That summer Abramovich and his entourage arrived in a chartered Boeing 707 to meet various important people. As arrangements were being made, he said that he wanted to meet the American who was planning to run for governor of Chukotka.

The day before he was scheduled to come to my house, I decided to attend a legislative committee meeting organized in his honor. I wanted to see what he was like. At the Anchorage legislative offices on Fourth Avenue, I boarded the elevator with a group of unshaven young people in jeans. When I got to the meeting, I realized I had ridden up with Abramovich and his retinue. Except for his Russian speech and the obsequious treatment he received from the legislators, this billionaire could have been any American thirty-something.

The next day he sat alone with me in my living room. Abramovich addressed me respectfully, as appropriate when speaking to an elder, with the formal Russian verb tense for *you* and using my patronymic name, Victor L'vovich (essentially, "Victor son of Louis"). I, in turn, as an elder and informal American, simply called him Roman.

He asked why people were advising him that I, as an Alaskan, would make a good governor of Chukotka. I briefly summarized my background: childhood in Moscow during the Stalin years, constitutional convention delegate and state senator, and a decade as a citizen ambassador helping rebuild Russia. I explained that my friends believed my history in Alaska political and social development could be translated to Chukotka. But I also assured him that I had no desire for the job and, in fact, still thought it was a crazy idea.

The conversation turned to conditions in Chukotka. A very reserved person, Roman talked with emotion about the appalling conditions and how he had been moved by the people's hardships, which reminded him of his own child-hood. Just as I had been besieged by petitioners in my hotel room years earlier, he faced long lines of people asking for help—but longer ones. To campaign for the Duma, he had sent each resident a box of food.

"It brings you to tears, listening to the misery of the people," Roman said. "And it is frustrating that you cannot solve everybody's problem, no matter what your position or your wealth."

Certainly he could do far more than I could. He had already formed a char-ity called Pole of Hope to ease the suffering in Chukotka. One of his charity's programs, inspired by Roman's childhood memories, was sending children from Chukotka on vacations to the Black Sea, where they could receive special medical attention.

Nazarov had initially invited Abramovich to run for the Duma, but Roman was quite aware of the governor's fault in Chukotka's problems. Nazarov's peo-ple were even shaking down the parents of children Pole of Hope wanted to send to the Black Sea, demanding bribes in exchange for allowing them to go.

Abramovich made no effort to convince me to run. From my end, I suggested he assign one of his bright lieutenants to run against Nazarov. Half a dozen of his young colleagues, including Ida Ruchina, who was running the Pole of Hope foundation, joined us after our meeting around the dining table, where Jane served pizza and a big tossed salad for lunch. They loved it and we had a jolly meal together.

Toward the end of the Russians' stay, Roman called and asked me to sit with him at a banquet hosted for their group by the Native-owned Arctic Slope Regional Corporation. He spoke no English and probably enjoyed my company and ability to converse without a translator.

The visit had made an important impact on Abramovich. He had been busy, meeting many leaders in business, industry, and politics, and traveling to the Prudhoe Bay oil fields and to Barrow, the seat of the North Slope Borough where the Iñupiat self-government had brought the benefits of oil wealth to tra-ditional indigenous communities. His conclusion: Chukotka should develop on the Alaska model, a phrase he would repeat in years to come.

I took the opportunity to assure him once more that despite my strong sym-pathy for the people in Chukotka, I had no intention of seeking political office there. Our relationship has remained friendly over the years, but I've never cul-tivated it, because our worlds are so different and I have never wanted to be a hanger-on.

Some months later, rather than put up one of his friends for election, Abramovich decided to run for governor himself. Shortly afterward, Russia's cen-tral government announced it was investigating Nazarov for tax evasion—surely no coincidence—and he dropped out of the race. As a reward, Nazarov received a promotion into the Russian Federation bureaucracy in Moscow.

Abramovich won the election without opposition and set about the rescue of Chukotka. Besides contributing hundreds of millions of dollars of his own fortune through his charity, he moved his official residence and the domicile of his oil company, Sibneft, so they would be taxed in Chukotka. Those revenues dwarfed the income from all other taxpayers (and the move also yielded nice tax savings for Roman's company, as well).

Some time before Abramovich became governor, I attended a reception in Anchorage with Ted Stevens. As always, Ted asked about the progress of our work in the Russian Far East and listened to my answers with interest. When he asked the region's greatest unmet need, I told him about the tragic poverty in Chukotka. Ted said we should address that and told me to work it out with his staff.

This contact with Stevens yielded $5 million in congressional earmarks for our new Alaska Chukotka Development Program and brought me out of semiretirement once more. Our program came on line around the time Roman took office.

Abramovich and his administration strongly supported our work. He assigned his cousin Ida Ruchina to take over the Chukotka Red Cross offices, which then became the lead partner in our program. Ida proved to be an exceptional leader and brought direction and administrative power to many activities, including the Red Cross.

Our team included Crow and Tichotsky, who had become Abramovich's foreign affairs advisor, and a young Russian-speaking Iñupiaq college graduate, Andrea Greene from Kotzebue, who developed into a gutsy and effective project manager. Our freewheeling operation met needs and opportunities as they arose: food, clothing, materials, and tools for humanitarian relief, and even obtained a fully equipped surplus military field hospital that we shipped to Chukotka after jumping through endless bureaucratic hoops in Washington and Moscow.

We also worked to give Chukotkans the ability to support themselves. Our program offered a competition in business plan preparation; training in building aluminum boats and repairing boats and motors; treatment for alcoholism and drug abuse; construction of a meat processing plant and training in food preservation; and many other efforts. Most involved developing human capital, both by bringing specialists to the Russian side and by bringing Russians for training and internships in Alaska.

As we phased out of direct aid in Chukotka after six years, we saw some of the people we had worked with become key players in Abramovich's transformation of the region. Some of them had been on Nazarov's enemies list, the Native leaders who had resisted him by accepting our whaling aid.

Ludmilla Ainana shone as one of these heroes. A Yup'ik elder, birdlike in build, she could be underestimated by those who hadn't run into her. Those who did know her dubbed her the "silken bulldozer," because no one could stand in her way. The power of her personality, combined with the new money coming into Chukotka, made things happen.

Ainana recalled how the arrival of change dawned for hungry people. Her grandson called her in Anadyr: "Grandma, there's a ship delivering coal, and it's still unloading." The next day, "Grandma, there's a ship with food, and it's still unloading." And then, "Grandma, there's heat in the apartment."

Chukotka is unrecognizable today, with new houses, schools, roads, power plants, health facilities, self-determination for Native groups, and a quality of life that could barely be imagined a decade ago. And a significantly smaller population. The new government and prosperity had finally allowed stranded people to go south.

Abramovich's photograph commonly showed up in families' homes where they normally would have displayed religious icons. He was their savior. I could never have done what he did for Chukotka.

The year Jane, Ruthie, and I left Moscow, 1995, was a turning point for Russia. Yeltsin launched an inept and corrupt rapid privatization of state industries that gave away vast resources, creating a group of superrich oligarchs at the expense of the public (including, perhaps, Roman Abramovich). His erratic leadership culminated in a banking crisis in 1998, when the currency collapsed, investors lost their deposits, and the business relationships we had built from Alaska became problematical.

After a decade of chaos, Russians craved order and stability. Vladimir Putin gave it to them with a strong military response to rebellion in Chechnya, increased competence in managing the government and economy, and good luck, as the price of oil rose and provided his administration with a surge of revenue. Pensioners and teachers began getting paid. Following years of hardship, a livable existence returned for the middle class.

In the 1980s, I had watched Mikhail Gorbachev's reforms with great interest. After I became actively involved in 1989, I saw changes as they happened and Russians' responses to them. Relaxation of restrictions on the press and other media quickly brought out alternative viewpoints. New parties and new leaders emerged. Voters relished the opportunity to choose among candidates rather than facing ballots with a single, party-endorsed name. When an outraged populace squelched the right-wingers' 1991 attempt to overthrow Gorbachev, it was clear that things had changed.

Public interest in the proceedings of the newly elected parliament showed how democracy was dawning. People in Moscow congregated to watch television coverage in stores, clubs, and public places. Across Russia, citizens gave close attention to the discussions.

But the sprouts of democracy didn't keep growing. Interest in parliamentary debate slackened before long. The talking heads went on and on, but life didn't change much. Attempts at economic reform provided few benefits. Inflation and measures to deal with it ate away savings and created hardships. The period of democratization ended as other concerns pushed it from the public arena and most people's lives.

The stage was set for Putin to reestablish a powerful central state in the style of the Soviets and the tsars, reining in press freedom, diluting electoral democracy, and stifling regional autonomy. Putin installed his own governors instead of having them elected, consolidated power, and set up barriers to international collaboration.

Ordinary Russians cheered Putin because he tempered the harsh realities of Yeltsin's crony capitalism. Russia had lurched into a free market without the controls we take for granted in the United States, such as government regulation or a functioning judicial system. The strong and crafty made fortunes while others went hungry. Hunger and fear made the benefits of democracy difficult to appreciate.

Today, a strong hand in the Kremlin provides more security to the people at the expense of democratic reforms, but Russia remains a failed nation when it comes to law and law enforcement. Graft and corruption are endemic in Putin's Russia. Only the names of those who benefit have changed. That's the current reality.

———

As these changes occurred, Alaska's relations with Russia changed. With the banking crisis, Alaska Airlines halted flights connecting us to the Russian Far East. Once again, Alaska travelers seeking to cross the Bering Strait either had to pay for extremely expensive charters or spend a full day flying through Korea or all the way around the world via Moscow.

Business ties withered for other reasons, as well. Stories of early ventures that had gone bad were well known on both sides. More importantly, as Russia opened up to foreign imports, Alaska could hardly compete.

For me and my colleagues, new rules stifled direct relationships across the Bering Strait. Our work had never been easy, but regional officials had cooperated to accept our help. Putin's policies created ever-rising barriers to collaboration.

During the early years of our work, an American with a visa could go anywhere in Russia. But Putin brought back the old suspicion and bureaucracy to control visitors. In addition to getting a visa, an Alaskan traveling to the Russian Far East also had to provide a list of the towns he would visit, asking permission for each. Security officials would check these permissions even in tiny Native villages. Some of their decisions seemed totally irrational, such as freezing old hands Andrew Crow and John Tichotsky out of the country completely for two years.

International nongovernmental organizations and all foreigners became increasingly unwelcome. A dictate of a few years ago barred foreigners from boards of institutions that received any government money, forcing Brian Rogers and me to resign from academic and scientific institutions we helped create.

American policy changes also forced cuts in our university involvement. Diversion of US foreign aid from Russia to Iraq and Afghanistan eliminated funding that had supported our programs under Senator Stevens's earmarks.

My Alaska–Russia work was done. Looking back on it, I see little wasted effort. We worked for people, not dogmas or abstract ideas. We invested in human beings—their minds and experience, as well as their sustenance. Those investments paid off immediately in the currency of the heart. They continue to yield benefits today, in countless ways that will never be directly known.

Early excitement at the melting of the Ice Curtain faded, but ties remain strong. Friendship and shared values endure through individual relationships and organizations such as Rotary International. Alaska and Chukotka whalers still work and meet together. Collaboration continues between managers of marine mammals and other natural resources, scientists, and search and rescue officials.

Although my focus has returned to Alaska, my Russia world remains. As I write this, my links are active with my brother Vanya, classmates from the 1930s, scientists from the 1990s, and friends from all over. I see them in Anchorage, Provideniya, St. Petersburg, Krasnodar, and Moscow. And, as I've done on every visit to Moscow, I still wander the streets of my youth, with sadness and joy, and with love of the life I've lived.

————

My parents, Markoosha and Louis, went to the Soviet Union in the 1920s in a euphoria of hope following the Russian revolution. They lived through the heady days of making a new society and the bitter disappointment of Stalinism.

While they turned their backs on the Soviet Union and communism, they never gave up caring for Russia and their belief in a better future for its people.

In my lifetime, this pattern repeated. The Soviet Union collapsed, freedom flourished amid chaos, and then the heavy hand of authority fell over the country once again.

But what a difference remains! I have described the fear and horror of life under Stalin. Despite my criticism of Putin, his Russia is a bastion of freedom compared to the one I lived in as a teen.

Although the history, geography, and psychology of Russia and Russians make hard soil for the seeds of democracy to take root, dissent has always existed: under the tsars, under the Soviets, and now under Putin. Russia now is irrevocably part of the world, and the winds of democracy around the world are inevitably felt there, too.

So it's not the end. My optimism is learned from life and the changes I have seen. I can see the dark side as well as anyone, but the spirit of humanism has never failed. I don't know when Russian freedom will blossom again, but eventually it will grow.

⇥ 28 ⇤
Secrets to a Long Life

I have reached an age that inspires people to ask for the secret to my longevity, although they certainly don't intend to act on any answer I may provide. Usually I evade. I have shrunk six inches in height, and I have plenty of ailments. But age is not a topic that interests me, and I rarely bother thinking about death.

The question is not a serious one. It is like asking a child, "What do you want to be when you grow up?" The questioners remind me of how old I am. Actually quite old. Going through my papers, I found a record of someone asking me about my age and whether I had accomplished my goals in life, seventeen years ago.

In the 1980s I adopted the goal of living to see my daughter Ruthie graduate from high school. Now she is out of college and married with two kids. I haven't bothered to come up with another goal.

But after all this time, I have devised an answer to the insistent longevity question. The secret to my long life is that I avoided getting killed, barely, on many adventures over the years. If I had gotten killed, my life would not have been as long. If I hadn't gone on the adventures, I wouldn't have cared as much how long my life would turn out to be.

That may betray the shallowness of my wisdom and self-examination. I still want to have fun, meet interesting people, go fascinating places, have adventures, stay healthy, and avoid death, if only narrowly. My humanistic values can be boiled down as well: I want everyone else to have my same opportunities.

So herewith is my secret: my adventures, at least a few of them, and how I did not get killed.

———•◦◦•———

In July 1967, near the beginning of my years at ISER, I flew to the middle of the Bering Sea to work on St. Paul Island, where we were studying the capacity of the community for self-government rather than control by the federal government.

Besides the extraordinary wildlife on St. Paul's shoreline, the beaches there are famous for beachcombing. The Pribilofs jut up midocean, catching anything that goes by. The coveted prizes of beachcombers, then as now, were glass fishing floats used and lost by Japanese vessels, orbs of green, blue, or amber, often enmeshed in hemp webbing. In those days, dozens of small balls could sometimes be found in half an hour on the storm-tossed beaches of St. Paul.

I was walking late one evening near the village when I spied a large object floating in a mass of kelp way off the shore. I was intrigued. The next morning I borrowed a pair of binoculars and took another look. It was a giant ball. I wanted it, but I couldn't get to it. No skiff.

Later that day, George Rogers flew in to work with me on the island. A couple of women and I drove out to the airstrip to meet him. One of my companions, Ann Baltzo, was an eager beachcomber. On the way back to town, as we passed by, I pointed out the ball. Ann said it was quite a find—big glass balls didn't show up so often anymore. With that encouragement, I decided on the spot to swim out to get it.

I've always enjoyed long distance swimming. My brother George and I used to make offshore swims together. During the war, we chased a sailboat in the Mediterranean on that memorable leave when we established our lasting brotherly connection. But the Bering Sea was another matter. Ann recorded in an article she wrote ten years later that the water was 38°F. No one swam at St. Paul.

I climbed down the bluff from the road, ducked behind a rock, and stripped down to my underwear and argyle socks, which Gloria had knitted for me. I launched myself from the shore of piled boulders. I had no doubt I could swim the distance to the ball, but the water of the Bering Sea was frigid and long strands of kelp kept wrapping around my arms, legs, and body. Carrying a knife in my teeth, I laboriously untangled myself again and again, while George Rogers shouted encouragement from shore, "Are you OK? Are you OK?"

When I arrived at the ball, I found it attached by a heavy hawser to a huge bamboo pole, thirty feet long. I had suspected as much, and that was why I brought the knife. I could sit on the pole while I cut the rope, but getting up onto it meant disentangling myself from the kelp. In the process, Gloria's handmade socks slipped off my feet with the kelp.

Cutting and sawing through the thick rope took a long time. I was totally numb with cold and increasingly wondered about the wisdom of my adventure. While I worked, the heads of fur seals by the hundreds bobbed up nearby, watching me. George's increasing concern brought him down the rocks, barefoot, to the water's edge, but there was nothing he could do.

By the time I got the ball loose and headed back for shore, I was freezing and grateful the float made my way easier. With success in sight, I felt newly confident I would survive.

Suddenly, nearing the rocks, I heard the roar of a large wave behind me. I had no time to react. The wave broke over me and I went under, holding tight to the ball. As I tumbled, it slammed into my head. A thought flashed through my semiconsciousness, "Oh shit, I won't survive after all." But I held on, and the buoyancy of the ball eventually pulled me back up to the surface.

The next wave was on its way. I swam back offshore to avoid being hit again and to catch my breath. With preparation, I rode a wave back toward shore and, yelling to George to catch it, let go of the ball. Amazingly, he grabbed the ball just as the wave brought it over the edge of the rocks. The following wave carried me to the rocks, and I was able to emerge, bruised, scratched, and very cold, but triumphant. The ladies wrapped me in blankets, poured whiskey into me, and warmed me up in the car.

A day or so later, I saw a couple of tourists walking down the street, a kid with them carrying a large glass ball just like mine. Still sporting a black eye and with a large knot on my head, I caught up and asked where they got it. They had bought the ball from a villager for twenty dollars. Whereupon George and I got into a discussion of the escapade's economics. Would I have made that swim for a twenty-dollar bill? No. A hundred-dollar bill? No, I would not.

The ball still resides with Gloria in the house in Fairbanks. I wish I had it, but I suppose this is a fair exchange for the argyle socks.

Lest readers draw the conclusion that all my adventures were ill-considered, careless, or harebrained, let me assure you that many trips went by without any close scrape with death. My outdoor enthusiasm began during my college years. Usually nothing went wrong.

I met one of my greatest outdoor companions at MIT in 1948. Dave Loeks was a big, kind-hearted guy who was always ready to try something new. I bought my first collapsible kayak while in Boston and used it to paddle across the Charles River to class on the Cambridge side. Dave and I took it out on the ocean, first at a beach in New Hampshire, then on a trip to Maine's Acadia National Park.

After graduation, Dave became a top planner: planning director of St. Paul, Minnesota, president of the American Institute of Planners, in charge of Hudson River Valley regional planning, and in other important jobs. But he always made time to come to Alaska and go on adventures, which we referred to as wilderness bonding.

Dave joined Gloria, our son Greg, and me in July 1973 when we drove to the small town of Circle on the Yukon River, put in my riverboat, and went upriver to meet a raft on its way down that was carrying Keith Tryck, son of our old friends Charlie and Molly Tryck.

Keith and his three buddies were retracing the route of Charlie's father during the Yukon Gold Rush—over the Chilkoot Trail, down to Dawson City by homemade raft, and then floating onward all the way to the Bering Sea. The journey became a *National Geographic* article and TV special and a book by Keith entitled *Yukon Passage*.

We met the raft in my riverboat up above the Canadian border and tied alongside so we could drift down to Eagle, just inside Alaska, where the boys would rendezvous for Independence Day festivities with the Trycks and other parents and friends. They were big, powerful guys, and we enjoyed relaxing with them on their floating home.

We even slept on board until the guy on watch late at night yelled for all to wake up and hold on tight. We were being rapidly pulled by the current toward a steep bank, and the massive log raft was about to smash into the rock wall and crush my aluminum boat, which was tied on that side. I quickly jumped in, started the motor, and got away just in time.

After that incident, we took no chances and traveled separately to the meeting in Eagle, parting only after Charlie and I had cleaned out the boys' pockets in a poker game.

———

In fall 1978, Jane and I kayaked with Arlon Tussing and a friend along the west coast of Chichagof Island Southeast Alaska. To make camp away from bears, we paddled out to some small islands a mile out in the Pacific that, according to our guidebook, were bear free. As we approached, a grizzly rose on its hind legs to check us out. We circled around this one, only to encounter another bear swimming in front of us between two small islands. Apprehensive but undeterred, we made camp on another island, bear spray and guns at the ready... No marauding bears that night.

A few days later, we became the toys of several dozen sea lions. We were traversing narrow channels between a myriad of islands, when a herd of these sleek but enormous mammals decided that their entertainment for the next hour was to scare the hell out of us. There were dozens, maybe hundreds of the half-ton animals.

We hung on to the sides of our boats as the beasts did their best to frighten us. They were very fast and came at us in a stream just below the water surface, swerved around or under the boat, and roared back again. They simply seemed to be roiling, up and down and round, over and under, at a speed that one could hardly fathom.

Our kayaks shuddered and constantly seemed on the verge of capsizing from the wake and from being lifted up when they swam under us.

At one point, the sea lions seemed to have had their fun and, as if by a signal, called off their assault. It was a great experience—after our heart rate went back to normal.

In 1991, Dave Loeks arranged for us to float down the Tatshenshini and Alsek rivers in Canada's Yukon Territory and Southeast Alaska, a trip through ferocious whitewater and spectacular mountain country. We were into the second generation now: Dave's son owned a rafting business in Whitehorse. His guides treated us with the comfort, food, and safety afforded to paying guests. The first evening I met Dave at the riverbank and enjoyed him as much as always.

I wrote to Jane after days of paddling down the river and running rapids:

> Dave and I have had the greatest of sessions. Now, five days later, we are still talking, reminiscing, discussing, bullshitting, doing things together. We are of course tent mates, hike often, wash dishes together, etc. It's great, easy, natural, good.

George Nez graduated from MIT with Dave Loeks and me and was a good friend to both of us. He worked in St. Paul; was Denver planning director; planned post-earthquake reconstruction in Skopje, Macedonia, and Managua, Nicaragua; and designed innovative low-cost roof structures that provided housing for hundreds of thousands of poor families in Afghanistan, Rwanda, Haiti, and two dozen other countries.

George came to Alaska several times while with the US Economic Development Administration. During one of these trips, we hitched a ride to Juneau on a twin-engine plane piloted by Don Jonz. His friend Arlon Tussing, our institute's economist and himself a flier, sat in as copilot, while George and I chatted alone in the large cabin.

We were about an hour and a half out of Anchorage when the plane started descending over the forty-mile-wide Malaspina Glacier, the largest piedmont glacier in the world, consisting of a seemingly endless mass of broken ridges and crevasses. George, who was a navy pilot during the war and safety officer of his squadron, became increasingly agitated and told the pilots to get up to a proper cruising altitude.

They ignored him. Ice sped past the windows, truly breathtakingly frightening, as the plane skimmed at about one hundred feet altitude over the glacier's broken surface. Totally angry by then, George yelled to Don and Arlon to get the plane up immediately or he would report them to the FAA, if we ever did get to Juneau. As the plane rose, he explained to me that flying so low, a pilot would not have even a second's response time if anything went wrong.

Less than a year later, in October 1972, Alaska Representative Nick Begich, his aide Russell Brown, and House Majority Leader Hale Boggs of Louisiana were flying from Anchorage to Juneau for a fundraiser when their plane disappeared. Over many weeks, the US Coast Guard, Navy, and Air Force carried out a massive search. The wreckage of the twin-engine Cessna 310 was never found, nor were the remains of the passengers or pilot Don Jonz.

———

None of my outdoor adventures came closer to disaster than a 1977 float trip on the Telaquana River, in the Alaska Range west of Cook Inlet. The journey included ten men, women, and teens in eight kayaks, two doubles and six singles. We planned to float 180 miles down the Telaquana and Stony rivers in about a week. We made it ten miles.

Our friends who organized the float had been told the route would include nothing worse than class I and II rapids, easy paddling even for the five members of our party who had never been in a kayak. That included Jane. Although she was an experienced canoeist, her first kayaking came when we assembled our kayaks after unloading the floatplanes that dropped us off at Telaquana Lake.

Arlon Tussing and Dick Fischer, the son of my old political colleague, Helen (not related to me), had set up the trip. We were well prepared with food, wine, and equipment and had a great steak dinner and party the first night in camp. The next morning we set off over the lake and down the river in gloriously warm weather.

The river was high and running fast. One of the novices tipped over, but we got her squared away and everything seemed manageable. We didn't even put on spray skirts to keep water out of the kayaks because the day was sunny and we were all convinced the river would be easy.

The first signs of trouble were a series of large standing waves. The first splashes felt delightfully cool on the hot day, but then they filled the heavily laden boats.

Suddenly, the main current turned sharply left, dropped about ten feet, and at the bottom of a chute flowed to the right directly against a tremendous uprooted tree spanning the river. I couldn't avoid it, and in a flash I had flipped and was tumbling through the water clinging to my paddle. The boat came up next to me and I hung on to it as the now wider and shallower river swept me downstream.

Jane had been right behind me, but looking back I couldn't see her. I had lost my glasses and mistook a floating duffle bag for Jane's lifeless body. Then I saw her overturned kayak near the right shore, swam over and righted it, tied the boats together, and continued floating downstream along the steep bank.

After a while, I came across Dick on some flat ground and threw him a line, which he tied to a small tree. But the force of the river was so great that it pulled the tree out, and the kayaks and I floated farther down till I came to an eddy and dragged us to shore.

I hiked overland and stood with Dick wondering where all the others were, when I heard Jane's screams from where I had just come. There she was, hanging on a line extending downriver from the second boat. As I pulled the line in and reached for her, she yelled, "Don't touch me!" and clambered right over me and the kayaks to reach firm ground.

Jane too had come around the bend with no chance of avoiding the tree, which knocked her out of the kayak and left her injured, tumbling down the river, initially unsure which way was up. She was swept down through the icy water for about half an hour before she saw the kayaks. She'd had just enough strength left to grab onto the line.

Each of us thought we were dead at least once. Dick's wife, Terry, got around the tree that had knocked Jane and me from our kayaks. But her kayak got caught upside-down under another giant tree, where the current held her tight, head down. Thinking about her children, she finally pushed herself downward and squeezed out underneath. She popped out the other side covered in bruises, swam to shore, and climbed up a bank so steep that only a desperate mother could have managed it.

When Arlon and our friend Jeannine came through the chute in a double kayak, their boat smashed and wrapped around the log. Jeannine's face hit the tree and she was seriously injured, her nose broken and jaw knocked out of place. Arlon managed to get her onto the nearest dry ground. After more struggles, all ten people were accounted for, and in a few hours we all were in one place. Aside from Jeannine's injuries, we had among us some broken toes and fingers and massive bruising. We were utterly amazed that no one had died, considering what each had experienced.

We had lost most of our gear and supplies. We still had some freeze-dried food, but nothing in which to cook it. We had one tent and three sleeping bags for the ten of us. And we were a week and more than a hundred miles from where the plane would be looking for us. Even if someone did find us, it would be impossible for a plane or helicopter to land where we had ended up.

That week was a wonder of cooperation and good spirits. We made it through with only our metal Sierra cups for cooking, multitudes of blueberries, some fish, and pilot bread. We found a better camping spot and got there with our kayaks, overland. The kids taught the others new dance steps and took turns hanging tent flies in the trees to signal airplanes. We entertained ourselves with the single mystery novel we had, ripping out the pages and passing them around. Unfortunately, we never learned the solution to the mystery, as someone used those pages for toilet paper.

When we got back to Anchorage we gathered to tell the story over drinks and music, reveling in the miracle of our survival. (It was during that party that I received a call informing me that my mother had died in New York, a shock I still feel.)

———

Five years later, Jane and I paddled through Wood-Tikchik State Park with Jim Murphy and Peter Dinnel. A series of lakes is connected by rivers, generally without whitewater. The Telaquana incident remained fresh in Jane's mind, and she didn't want to ride any more wild rivers.

An extraordinary run of red salmon had jammed the lakes and rivers. There were times we could barely fit our paddles among them. But of course, they weren't biting. I usually strictly obey fishing laws, but the presence of so many fish and the inability to catch one by hook and line began to drive me mad.

I tried to shoot a fish with my rifle. It was like shooting a fish in an aquarium, just inches away, but with the refraction of light through the water, I missed every time. Next I made a spear by tying a knife to my paddle. Again, failure. Even when I climbed on a boulder and the others herded a massive school of fish toward me I couldn't stab one. We tried herding them toward our friends as they held a net in waist-deep water. The herding worked, but the mob of fish knocked the men over.

In the chaos, however, one fish got caught, by pure luck. So we had a fresh salmon dinner after all.

The next-to-last day of the trip was a long one. Rain had fallen for days, and we were anxious to get to our pickup point. As dusk was falling, Jane insisted she heard whitewater ahead, but as I paddled onward in the back of our two-seat kayak I pooh-poohed that as her imagination. Not long after, however, we found ourselves at the top of a waterfall with Jane, in her front seat, seeming to hang for moments over the roaring water and rocks.

We tumbled down over and between giant boulders, fighting to stay out of whirlpools, but amazingly got down safely, as did the other kayak. Both boats were totally swamped and darkness had arrived. Once again everything we owned was wet, but we were alive.

Like a mirage, we saw the lights of a lodge across the lagoon at the bottom of the rapids, the first sign of human life in a week. We laboriously paddled our almost-sunken kayaks to the dock below the lodge and slogged up to the door.

We received a notably inhospitable welcome. The owner was not interested in having us make a puddle on his white rug. His first words were, "We're full."

Jane and I looked with thirsty eyes at the bar on the far side of the luxurious room. Wealthy out-of-state guests were seated around a roaring fire. It was time for some Alaska charm.

In answer to a guest's question, "Where did you come from?" we described our plunge over the waterfall and our week paddling in the rain, then moved on to other Alaska adventures and tales of a lifetime in the North.

The tourists were hooked. We got our cocktails. But we still never made it in past the door.

Not all of our adventures and death-defying incidents happened in Alaska. I have stories about Australia, Kenya, Peru, many countries in Europe, and, of course, every corner of Russia. I've experienced the Arctic, the equator, mountains, deserts, and oceans. The only continent where I haven't tested my longevity is Antarctica.

As I've aged, I've necessarily chosen less strenuous ways not to get killed. In the last decade, Jane and I enjoyed many delightful days sailing with Jerry and Nancy Wertzbaugher on the *Escapade* in the Caribbean. These were easy times, gliding through clear, warm water, anchoring in remote coves, diving from the boat, and swimming, swimming, swimming. We'd take the skiff and go to fascinating places or walk the beaches. Nancy always produced marvelous meals, and we had great conversations as night fell.

One time, flying to connect with the *Escapade,* Jane and I found ourselves on the wrong island. The next flight out was two days later. But fortunate our mistake had been. The cottage we found by chance sat on a pale white beach in front of a smooth blue sea, and palm trees bordered the gorgeous half-moon bay. We were in utter paradise.

Jerry and Nancy commonly landed and explored the islands to which we sailed. To keep up my theme of near-death adventures, rather than delving into the marvelous times we had, I will note one of these occasions when we hiked up to an old fortress on Guadeloupe. Along the trail, fruits that looked like crab apples were scattered below the trees, and I began eating them. But I stopped when Jerry pointed out ubiquitous signs in French and English that warned the fruit was deadly poisonous.

We hiked on and were enjoying looking at the fortress when I got faint and passed out. Somehow Jerry and Nancy got me back down the mountain to the village and found a doctor. I don't even remember that part. I survived.

⸻

I could go on with these stories. I keep having adventures as I work on writing the book, a process now in its third year. I keep meeting fascinating young people and learning about the world. I usher at the Alaska Center for the Performing Arts, I drive my red 1965 Mustang convertible, and I accept many invitations—since starting to write, to an art show in Paris, seeing old friends in Berlin, on a boat to Chukotka, to an annual Independence Day celebration on an island in Kachemak Bay, to Moscow and Krasnodar in Russia, and so much more.

The book might never be finished if I don't put a stop to it now. The words can never catch up with the life.

Despite my youthful activity, however, people keep asking me questions that seem designed to make me feel old, like the one about the secret of my longevity. I'm often asked to speak to groups about experiences that happened before most of their members were born. I never know if I'm a sage or a curiosity.

The most awe-filled introductions I receive are when I'm invited to speak as one of the few surviving delegates of the Alaska Constitutional Convention. Someone said my presence at a gathering was similar to having Benjamin Franklin showing up in their midst in 1840, as the railroads were crossing America.

But that's not right, because Franklin was already old in 1787. Alexander Hamilton was about my age, at thirty, when the US Constitution was signed. While I don't fare well in most comparisons with Hamilton, I certainly lived longer. Part of the secret of my longevity is avoiding duels.

Chapter Notes

My primary source for telling my life story is my own memory. Wherever possible, however, my co-author Wohlforth and I have used documents to verify and expand upon what I recall. These notes provide general sources for readers who want to learn more, as well as citations for exact quotes that are found in the text.

Unpublished materials are primarily found in three places. Documents accumulated by my father and mother are in the Louis Fischer Papers, Seeley G. Mudd Manuscript Library, Princeton University. All quotations from the collection are used by permission of the Princeton University Library. Hereafter I will refer to these as Louis Fischer Papers.

My own personal papers are in my possession, in my home or my office at the University of Alaska Institute of Social and Economic Research. Other personal files are in electronic format, including about 130 transcripts of interviews conducted by Wohlforth with me and others, and of lectures and other recordings, such as translations.

Finally, the archives of University of Alaska Anchorage contain many boxes of papers I deposited there years ago. Since these papers are not organized, we have accumulated all the material used in the book into Box 101. Unless otherwise noted, everything cited here as Fischer UAA papers is in that box. After this book is completed, the rest of my papers will be deposited together with an inventory in the UAA archive.

⊣ Chapter 1 Notes: The Reichstag Fire ⊢

The most important single source on my family's early life in Germany and the Soviet Union is my mother's autobiography: Markoosha Fischer, *My Lives in Russia* (New York: Harper & Bros., 1944).

Markoosha's letters found in my father's papers offer an even more frank picture of her hardships. Markoosha Fischer's letter, "Russia is the goal of everything," is to Louis Fischer, October 11, 1929, Louis Fischer Papers, Box 41.

My brother's thoughts and memories are recorded in a pair of autobiographical manuscripts found in my personal papers: George Fischer, *Pink Diaper Baby: A Tale of Russia and America,* two-volume typescript, Philadelphia, January 1982; and George Uri Fischer, *Insatiable: A Story of My Nine Lives,* self-published photocopy, Philadelphia, 2000.

My father's autobiography covering these years contains scant family information, but is excellent for the political conditions of the time and the rise of Nazism. Louis Fischer, *Men and Politics* (New York: Harper & Row, 1941).

For the Berlin years, some details come from Hede Massing, *This Deception: KGB Target America* (New York: Ivy Books, 1951). Since her book is generally self-serving, however, I have not followed her account of some events that do not square with my own family's versions as found in their contemporary letters and their memories, particularly concerning our departure from Germany.

Paul Massing's novel of his experiences resisting the Nazis, published under a pseudonym, is also a source of details: Karl Billinger, *Fatherland* (New York: Farrar & Rinehart, 1935). The quote by Lincoln Steffens is from the foreword to the novel.

The quotation from Günther Rücker is from a letter to Markus Wolf, May 30, 1988, quoted in Markus Wolf, *Die Troika* (Berlin und Weimar: Aufbau-Verlag, 1989). The translation from the German is mine.

⊣ Chapter 2 Notes: Markoosha and Louis ⊢

When my mother published her autobiography, two finished chapters on her early life were excised. I can only speculate on the reasons. An editor may have feared her depiction of the radical personal freedom of her youth would alienate readers in the mid-twentieth century. In any event, the material was a revelation and unexpected gift for me. Extensive background and three direct quotes are from this document: Markoosha Fischer, manuscript for *My Lives in Russia*, Louis Fischer Papers, Box 39.

Details on my father's early life come from a variety of sources, with his autobiography, *Men and Politics,* beginning at age twenty-two. More is found in his papers at the Mudd Library at Princeton, much of it summarized by my brother, George, in his family writings. The material quoted about the Middle East is Louis Fischer, letter to Schifrah and Ida Fischer, April 24, 1919, Louis Fischer Papers, Box 4.

The incident involving Stalin's daughter, Svetlana Alliluyeva, is retold in "The Saga of Stalin's 'Little Sparrow,'" in *Time,* January 28, 1985. The Gandhi biography that formed the basis of the film is still in print and periodically provides royalties: Louis Fischer, *The Life of Mahatma Gandhi* (New York: HarperCollins, 1997). The other book mentioned is Louis Fischer, *A Week with Gandhi* (New York: Duell, Sloan and Pearce, 1942).

Louis's memories of early days in the Soviet Union, including the quotations here, are found in his *Men and Politics.* Markoosha's are mainly from *My Lives in Russia.* See Chapter 1 notes for both. The oil book is Louis Fischer, *Oil Imperialism: The International Struggle for Petroleum* (New York: International Publishers, 1926). The Stalin book quoted is Louis Fischer, *The Life and Death of Stalin* (New York: Harper & Bros., 1952).

The letters concerning the death of Louis's father are all in my personal papers: Ethel Berman to Louis Fischer, n.d.; Louis Fischer to Ethel Berman, February 26, 1931; Ethel Berman to Louis Fischer, n.d.

⊰ Chapter 3 Notes: Early Soviet Years ⊱

Besides Markoosha's *My Lives in Russia,* we have drawn background about Agrojoint from Yehuda Bauer, *My Brother's Keeper: A History of the American Jewish Joint Distribution Committee, 1929–1939* (Philadelphia: Jewish Publication Society of America, 1974).

I've gathered information about the British ambassador's residence on recent visits, including seeing our old rooms there. The original edition of my father's book, since republished, was Louis Fischer, *The Soviets in World Affairs: A History of the Relations Between the Soviet Union and the Rest of the World,* 2 vols. (London: Jonathan Cape, 1930). The quote about Louis's "wishful thinking" is from a review of *Men and Politics:* "Books: Retreat from Moscow," *Time,* May 12, 1941.

The family story of my mother's hardship and relationship with my father comes from family letters and my brother's autobiographies (see Chapter 1 notes).

Louis's thoughts on Stalin's innovations in human control are in his book *The Life and Death of Stalin.*

⫷ Chapter 4 Notes: The Troika ⫸

Besides my mother's book, several other books include material that was helpful for reviving and expanding upon my memories of childhood with Lothar Wloch and Konrad Wolf and our parents' families, including Markus Wolf's *Die Troika* (see Chapter 1 notes), and Wolfgang Jacobson and Rolf Aurich, *Der Sonnensucher Konrad Wolf* (Berlin: Aufbau-Verlag, 2005).

The anecdote about the Moscow map is found in Wolfgang Leonhard, *Child of the Revolution,* translated by C. M. Woodhouse (London: Collins, 1957). Leonhard was our contemporary and his book is a vivid account of coming of age in Russia during those years.

⫷ Chapter 5 Notes: The Purge ⫸

Our primary source on the purge has been this powerful book: Richard Conquest, *The Great Terror: A Reassessment*, 40th anniversary ed. (Oxford: Oxford University Press, 2008).

My father described his conflict with Berkman and his late conversion to oppose Stalin, his "Kronstadt" moment, in one of his strongest works, an essay in *The God That Failed,* Richard Crossman, ed. (New York: Harper & Brothers, 1949).

Lena Kostyakova's story of the students turning on their teacher for mentioning Trotsky is from her unpublished 1992 Russian typescript, *Our Class: The Real Children of the Arbat,* which I have in my papers. Rosa Aronova's story of her father is from a transcribed interview by Maya Turovskaya in Russian, dated December 28, 1989. At that time Maya was preparing a book on our Russian childhood during the 1930s to be titled "Stalin's Children: Classmates of an Elite Moscow School." The book was never written, but I have eight interview transcripts in my papers.

Bukharin's comments about 1919 and the purge during the First Five-Year Plan are from Conquest's *The Great Terror* (see above).

Stalin's proclamation of a more joyous life is covered in Karen Petrone, *Life Has Become More Joyous, Comrades: Celebrations in the Time of Stalin* (Bloomington: Indiana University Press, 2000). It quotes the letter to the editor by Pavel Postyshev, *Pravda,* December 28, 1935.

My mother's quote about the children at Yalta, and other material and quotes, are from Markoosha Fischer, *My Lives in Russia*. Louis Fischer's quotations about the purge are from his *Men and Politics*. Full citations for both are in Chapter 1 notes. In addition, a number of personal details in the chapter are from my mother's letters, found in the Louis Fischer Papers.

A detailed and vivid recent history contains the story of Louis Fischer in the Spanish Civil War, including the quotation of his letter to Frieda Kirchway, "We need men and women": Paul Preston, *We Saw Spain Die: Foreign Correspondents in the Spanish Civil War* (Bloomington: Indiana University Press, 2008).

The letter in which Eleanor Roosevelt relates the president's refusal to help Spain is to Louis Fischer, February 28, 1938, quoted in Louis Fischer, "Letters from Mrs. Roosevelt," *Journal of Historical Studies* 1, no. 1 (1967).

Some purge details, including the quotation of Yezhov's cable demanding ten thousand victims, are from Tim Tzouliadis, *The Forsaken: An American Tragedy in Stalin's Russia* (New York: Penguin Press, 2008).

⊰ Chapter 6 Notes: Escape to America ⊱

We have reconstructed the final years in Moscow from a combination of sources, including Markoosha's many detailed letters in the Louis Fischer Papers and her *My Lives in Russia*; Markus Wolf's *Die Troika;* Hede Massing's *This Deception;* and my brother George's autobiographies. Full citations for each are in Chapter 1 notes. In addition, I have relied upon numerous private communications from my former classmates.

The dialogue quoted between George Fischer and Paul Massing comes from *This Deception.* George's thoughts about the influence of my parents on his communist indoctrination come from volume 2 of his *Pink Diaper Baby,* which also includes the text of his juvenile letter about Stalin reprinted in the *Nation.*

The quotation of Enya (Evgeni) Levin's mother is in Maya Turovskaya's transcribed Russian interview with Enya, June 17, 1989, in my papers. The quotation of Wilhelm Wloch upon his arrest, "Stalin knows nothing," comes from *Die Troika.*

Details about the Great Purge and the fate of Bukharin and other major victims come from Conquest's *The Great Terror* (see Chapter 5 notes).

The private memoir by my mother, Markoosha, with the quotation "We walked through room after room" is an undated typescript document in which she set down events that had been too sensitive to be included in her book, *My Lives in Russia.* She wrote it more than twenty years later. The document is in my papers.

The quoted letter ending with "Goodbye" is Markoosha Fischer to Louis Fischer, December 7, 1938, Louis Fischer Papers, Box 41. In the same box is the letter ending with "it is the end," Markoosha Fischer to Louis Fischer, January 5, 1939.

Louis Fischer's January 1939 correspondence with Eleanor Roosevelt is in his papers at the Princeton Mudd Library but is more easily accessed in the article cited in the previous chapter notes, "Letters from Mrs. Roosevelt." The story also is told by Roosevelt herself in Eleanor Roosevelt, *This I Remember* (New York: Harper & Brothers, 1949), including the detail about the flight with Oumansky and his remark.

The quotation of my brother, George, about his reaction to the truth about Stalin is from his *Red Diaper Baby*.

⫷ Chapter 7 Notes: The Troika at War ⫸

Besides using numerous family letters and personal communications, we also researched the war years in various books (cited earlier unless otherwise noted). Among the most important is Markus Wolf's *Die Troika*. Its appendices contain many original letters and memoirs, including the quotation from Zilya Selvinskaya about her love for Lothar, which I translate here. Anarik's side of the love triangle is described in his book: Andrei Eisenberg, *Yesli Ne Vyskazhus'—Zadokhnus'! [If I Don't Speak—I'll Choke!]* (Moscow: Vozvrashcheniye, 1994).

War memories also come from Markus Wolf with Anne McElvoy, *Man Without a Face: The Autobiography of Communism's Greatest Spymaster* (New York: Public Affairs, 1997); Wolfgang Leonhard's *Child of the Revolution*; and George Fischer's autobiographies, with all quotes coming from *Pink Diaper Baby*. The story of George's attendance at Churchill's White House visit is also told in Eleanor Roosevelt's *This I Remember*.

⫷ Chapter 8 Notes: Coming of Age ⫸

Family letters were a critical help to augment my memory of the war years and early adulthood, including Gloria Fischer's vivid letters and my letters to her and my parents from the war. They are in my personal files and in the Louis Fischer Papers. Gloria Fischer also consented to an interview with Wohlforth, March 17, 2010.

Numerous details about my unit's war experiences are in a mimeographed booklet produced by the veterans of the 1155th Engineer Combat Group, which is in my papers. The quoted letter from George Fischer to the family describing our meeting in Marseilles is in the Louis Fischer Papers, Box 44.

⫷ Chapter 9 Notes: Alaska Bound ⫸

Numerous family letters verified and expanded memories from this period. The quotation comparing New England to Arizona is from a Gloria Fischer letter to Markoosha Fischer, September 10, 1948, Louis Fischer Papers, Box 48.

Ed and Kit Crittenden gave an interview to Wohlforth, October, 5, 2009, covering their part in the story of my coming to Alaska. In addition, my personal papers contain a complete file about the hiring and the background of the job.

My letter, "tell pap not to be so blue," is to Markoosha Fischer, June 11, 1950, Louis Fischer Papers, Box 48. Gloria's letter, "that vestige of pioneering," is to various family members, July 28, 1950, found in the same box.

⊰ Chapter 10 Notes: Becoming Alaskan ⊱

Again, my family's letter-writing habit allowed us to bring back many details from early days in Anchorage; letters from this period are found in my papers and in the Louis Fischer Papers. Ed Crittenden's comment about the nature of planning in Alaska is found in my personal papers, along with the BLM reports and correspondence concerning my job there.

Early BLM history in Alaska and Harold T. Jorgenson's huge contribution are partly from his paper "Recollections About Early Efforts of Land Management in Alaska; Draft," July 12, 1995, in my files. The same folder contains a number of informative letters accumulated to recommend Jorgy for an honorary doctorate from the University of Alaska, which was approved but sadly had not been awarded when he died in August 1997.

The description of flying through Rainy Pass is from Gloria and Victor Fischer, letter to Markoosha Fischer, August 13, 1950, Louis Fischer Papers, Box 48. My letter "A picnic outdoors" is Victor Fischer to Markoosha Fischer, et al., December 12, 1950, Box 48.

During our frequent travels in the early 1950s Gloria and I kept in touch with long letters, which re-create the times. They are in my papers. Gloria's letter to me about missing Alaska is dated November 20, 1951.

⊰ Chapter 11 Notes: Little Men for Statehood ⊱

My letter "Revolting thought" was to Markoosha Fischer and other family, June 4, 1952, Louis Fischer Papers, Box 48.

Butler's remark about the "little people" is quoted in *The Daily Alaska Empire,* April 3, 1953, according to Claus-M. Naske, *A History of Alaska Statehood* (Lanham, Maryland: University Press of America, 1985).

Some Operation Statehood details are from original documents in my personal papers, including my own notes of the meeting in Washington with Congressman A. L. Miller on May 10, 1954, when he made the remark "there will always be Eskimos," and the appearance in Anchorage of Interior Secretary Douglas McKay, July, 20, 1954, when he made the infamous "act like ladies and gentlemen" remark.

We have relied heavily on Terrence Cole, *Fighting for the Forty-Ninth Star: C. W. Snedden and the Crusade for Alaska Statehood* (Fairbanks: University of Alaska Foundation,

2010). Cole's book contains many new insights into statehood politics and is also our source for the quotations by Margaret Rutledge and by Senator Wayne Morse.

Many Operation Statehood files, including organizational details and arrangements for the 1954 flight of Alaskans to Washington, are in the archives at the Rasmuson Library at the University of Alaska Fairbanks, including Barrie White's letter to delegate Bob Bartlett about the outcome of the flight, June 1, 1954, and Bartlett's quoted response to White, June 7, 1954.

Wohlforth interviewed Charlie and Molly Tryck on April 14, 2010, about this period.

⊰ Chapter 12 Notes: Constitutional Delegate ⊱

Victor Fischer, *Alaska's Constitutional Convention* (Fairbanks: University of Alaska Press, 1975), is the most complete work on the subject.

For material on Ernest Gruening, Wohlforth interviewed Katie Hurley, March 17, 2010, also covering other territorial and Constitutional Convention issues; see also Gruening, *Many Battles: The Autobiography of Ernest Gruening* (New York: Liveright, 1973).

Evangeline Atwood's letter to Gloria Fischer extolling Louis Fischer, January 10, 1952, is in my personal papers.

Wohlforth interviewed Tom Stewart, August 8, 1999, for another project.

Campaign materials and clippings from the delegate election in my personal papers helped fill out details on the election. The quoted campaign letter to "Fellow Alaskan," August 30, 1955, is in those files.

⊰ Chapter 13 Notes: Convening the Convention ⊱

Gloria's long letters about the convention provided many pages of previously unknown contemporary detail on the people and politics. They are Gloria Fischer to family, November 9, 1955, and January 16, 1956, Louis Fischer Papers, Box 48.

A thick bundle of photocopied newspaper clippings is in my files, forming an excellent day-by-day account of the convention. Some material on Egan's decision to run is from Florence Douthit, "Egan Enjoys Non-Political Meet," *Fairbanks Daily News-Miner,* November 18, 1955. Douthit's coverage of the convention is an invaluable historic resource. Egan's decision is also covered in Elizabeth A. Tower, *Alaska's Homegrown Governor: A Biography of William A. Egan* (Anchorage: Publication Consultants, 2003).

The controversy and reaction surrounding the open meetings debate at the convention is covered in my book *Alaska's Constitutional Convention* (see Chapter 12 notes), as are most other issues mentioned here. The quoted *Fairbanks Daily News-Miner* editorial, "Convention 'Censorship,'" was November 11, 1955.

My original minutes from the Local Government Committee are still in my possession in a pair of binders and allow one to trace the development of the article day by day. The list of potential names for what became "boroughs" is from those minutes.

I have written elsewhere about the home rule concept in Victor Fischer, "Home Rule in Alaska," in *Partnership Within the States: Local Self-government in the Federal System* (Urbana: University of Illinois, Institute of Government and Public Affairs, 1976), and a report documenting the failure of the state to implement the article: Thomas A. Morehouse and Victor Fischer, "Borough Government in Alaska: A Study of State-Local Relations," Report No. 29, Institute of Social, Economic and Government Research, University of Alaska, March 1971.

⤙ Chapter 14 Notes: Constitutional Battles ⤚

Convention floor sessions were recorded and later transcribed. Much of this chapter is based on those transcripts, including all quotations of floor speeches, which are published as *Constitutional Convention Minutes of the Daily Proceedings, Alaska Constitutional Convention* (Juneau: Alaska Legislative Council, 1965). The entire document is online at http://www.law.state.ak.us/doclibrary/cc_minutes.html (accessed October 20, 2011).

The story of the preamble is contained in Gloria Fischer's January 16, 1956, letter, cited in Chapter 13 notes, including the reaction of Evangeline Atwood to Barrie White's perceived lack of religiosity.

⤙ Chapter 15 Notes: Fatherhood and Statehood ⤚

The adoption story is told in letters in my papers and a letter from Gloria Fischer to Markoosha Fischer, January 18, 1957, Louis Fischer Papers, Box 48.

Ratification is covered in my book on the Alaska Constitution (see Chapter 12 notes), including the quoted *Washington Daily News* editorial of April 26, 1956. Material on the passage of the Statehood Act in Congress comes from Terrence Cole, *Fighting for the Forty-Ninth Star* (see Chapter 11 notes).

David Postman's extraordinary series on the Spit and Argue Club, "Inside Deal," ran in eight parts in the *Anchorage Daily News* from February 2 to February 11, 1990.

My quoted campaign speech for territorial legislature is in my papers. It is undated.

Bob Kederick's column with the controversial item about rumored bribery was "All Around Alaska," *The Daily Alaska Empire,* February 25, 1957. It is in my papers along with the committee proceedings dated February 27 and my undated minority opinion.

The best record of Warren Taylor's death penalty speech and the subsequent vote are in an Associated Press article, "House Votes to Abolish Alaska Death Penalty," *Anchorage Times,* February 22, 1957.

My letter "Wrings out dirty diapers" is to Markoosha Fischer, May 15, 1957, Louis Fischer Papers, Box 48. Gloria's letter about the statehood celebration is to Markoosha, July 26, 1958, Box 48. My letter to my father about my decision not to run for the legislature is September 29, 1958, Box 48.

⊰ Chapter 16 Notes: Seeking Challenges ⊱

I have a thick folder of letters exchanged with Bob Bartlett from the early 1950s until his death, which almost provides a running commentary of those years, courtesy of Terrence Cole. The letter "The tremendous effort" is October 27, 1959. The letter "Piddling little projects" is January 24, 1961.

Most of the sources in this chapter and the next are held in the Fischer UAA papers. That is the location of the Alaska State Planning Commission report, "State of Alaska Capital Improvement Program 1960–1966," January 28, 1960, and newspaper clippings covering reaction to the report. Also, see my letter "We need something new," Victor Fischer to William Egan, September 14, 1960.

My exchange with Bartlett concerning accepting the Littauer Fellowship and Gloria's views are in my personal files, Bob Bartlett to Victor Fischer, May 4, 1961, and Victor Fischer to Bob Bartlett, June 1, 1961.

A carbon copy of the HHFA report, Bob Weaver, "Task Force Report on Metropolitan Development," September 1962, is in Fischer UAA papers, as is the letter "Our kind of Democrat," E. L. Bartlett and Ralph J. Rivers to Hon. Lawrence F. O'Brien, The White House, September 3, 1962.

The letter "Billions and billions," Victor Fischer to Bob Bartlett, n.d, is in Fischer UAA papers.

The quote from Tom Morehouse is from an interview with Charles Wohlforth via telephone from Salem, Oregon, April 22, 2010.

My letter about King's March on Washington is Victor Fischer to Bob Bartlett, August 29, 1963; his response is September 3, 1963; both are in Fischer UAA papers.

The letter "Don't push it" is Burke Riley to Victor Fischer, February 5, 1963; my response is February 12; both are in Fischer UAA papers.

◅ Chapter 17 Notes: Earthquake ▻

Sources on the earthquake, including letters, reports, proceedings of the commission, and articles, are from the Fischer UAA papers. The legislation funding reconstruction was Public Law 88-451, "1964 Amendments to the Alaska Omnibus Act" (August 19, 1964). My letter, "Great being home," is to Louis Fischer, July 13, 1964, Louis Fischer Papers, Box 48.

◅ Chapter 18 Notes: Return to Russia, and Alaska ▻

My memories of the 1964 trip to the Soviet Union are vivid. In addition, the papers from the trip, including detailed agendas and voluminous notes, are in the Fischer UAA papers.

The letter "Vic is one of the best" is John Bebout to Paul Ylvisaker, July 31, 1962, in my personal papers, along with extensive documentation of the early history of ISER and development of the original Ford Foundation grant.

The dam across the Bering Strait was a serious proposal by P. M. Borisov, studied for years by the Soviets. My endorsement is in the same letter to Bob Bartlett cited in Chapter 16 in which I bemoaned the loss of excitement after statehood, October 27, 1959, in my personal papers.

George Rogers's letter "Completely out of sympathy" is to Victor Fischer, April 5, 1965, in the ISER/Ford material mentioned above, as is my letter "Have not an ounce of regret" to Louis Winnick of the Ford Foundation, September 30, 1966.

◅ Chapter 19 Notes: The Institute of Everything ▻

For this chapter, I made extensive use of the files and library of ISER in Anchorage, where I have an office as director emeritus. Files include lists of our projects and personnel and copies of our reports. In addition, Wohlforth interviewed Arlon Tussing on April 16, 2010, by telephone; Lee Gorsuch November 10, 2011, in Seattle; and Scott Goldsmith April 14, 2010, in Anchorage.

The Pribilofs report is Don C. Foote, Victor Fischer, and George Rogers, "St. Paul Community Study: An Economic Analysis of St. Paul, Pribilof Islands, Alaska,"

Fairbanks, Institute of Social, Economic and Government Research, 1968. It is found in the ISER library. For Project Chariot, see Dan O'Neill, *The Firecracker Boys: H-Bombs, Inupiat Eskimos, and the Roots of the Environmental Movement* (New York: Basic Books, 2007 [1995]).

The story of Hensley's paper for Rabinowitz is in his book, William L. Iggiagruk Hensley, *Fifty Miles from Tomorrow: A Memoir of Alaska and the Real People* (New York: Picador, 2009).

The coming of big oil, including the AAAS conference ISER held in Fairbanks, is covered in Jack Roderick, *Crude Dreams: A Personal History of Oil & Politics in Alaska* (Fairbanks/Seattle: Epicenter Press, 1997). He quotes Engler's book, which is Robert Engler, *The Politics of Oil: A Study of Private Power and Democratic Directions* (Chicago: University of Chicago Press, 1961).

Quotes from the conference come from newspaper clippings found in a scrapbook kept in the ISER library. Engler's quote "With whom do you wish to identify" is from Joe LaRocca, "Engler, Oilmen Trade Shots on Confab Panel," *Fairbanks Daily News-Miner,* August 26, 1969. Ted Stevens's quotes and Dick Cooley's reaction are in "Stevens Levels Blast at Conservationists" and "Excerpts from Stevens' Speech," *Fairbanks Daily News-Miner,* August 28, 1969, and Tom Brown, "Stevens Blasts the Conservationists," *Anchorage Daily News,* August 28, 1969.

The pipeline EIS document is Arlon R. Tussing, George William Rogers, Victor Fischer, "Alaska's Economy, Oil and Gas Industry Development, and the Economic Impact of Building and Operating the Trans-Alaska Pipeline," Fairbanks, Institute of Social, Economic and Government Research, University of Alaska, 1971.

The working papers from the Brookings Conference on the Future of Alaska are in my personal files.

⊰ Chapter 20 Notes: Fairbanks Years ⊱

Wohlforth's interviews with Gorsuch, Tussing, Morehouse, and Goldsmith informed the chapter. He also interviewed my daughter Yonni Fischer on November 5, 2010, and her family memories are in various chapters.

The Man in the Arctic Program is amply documented in my files and in ISER's files and library. ISER's publications during the period include David T. Kresge, Thomas Morehouse, and George W. Rogers, *Issues in Alaska Development* (Seattle: University of Washington Press, 1977).

-̋ᖍ Chapter 21 Notes: Troika Redux ᖘ̏-

On my father's death, see "Louis Fischer, a Correspondent in Soviet Union, Is Dead at 73," *New York Times,* January 17, 1970. George Kennan's eulogy is contained as the foreword in Louis Fischer, *The Road to Yalta: Soviet Foreign Relations 1941–1945* (New York: Harper & Row, 1972).

Two of my brother George's autobiographies are cited in Chapter 1 notes.

Konrad Wolf's films and life are covered in many volumes. A handy brief biography and appraisal of his films in German and English is in my personal papers: Regine Sylvester, *Konrad Wolf Retro* (Munich: Goethe Institute, 1992).

Lothar's biography, like Koni's, is well known to me. In verifying my memories and filling in gaps, I relied on family letters and personal communications with Lothar's wife, Eva.

Our reunion of old friends is covered in depth in Markus Wolf's *Die Troika* (see Chapter 1 notes), which also includes original letters and other documents from the period and the quoted impressions from Koni's diary. My quoted letter to Lothar, "Koni must have told you," May 3, 1975, is reprinted there, as is my letter to Koni about Lothar's death, "A very, very important part of me," July 26, 1976.

Hede Massing's book, *This Deception,* is cited in Chapter 1 notes.

-̋ᖍ Chapter 22 Notes: Starting a New Life ᖘ̏-

Wohlforth interviewed Jane Angvik several times; for the material on her early life, April 18, 2010. We also used a transcribed cassette tape of the story of our meeting, dated September 4, 1995.

Bill Parker provided memories of Alaska politics from the 1960s to 1980s to Wohlforth on April 22, 2010. A letter I wrote to Bill Egan on October 21, 1974, strongly repeats the criticism I made in his office; it is in my personal files.

Extensive material on constitutional revision, decennial constitutional convention votes, and the Hawaii Constitution are in the Fischer UAA papers. My paper is Vic Fischer, "A New Constitutional Convention for Alaska? The Lessons of Hawaii 1978," Interim Committee on the Constitutional Convention, 1980; it is in my personal files.

Clippings on the 1980 race, allegations against Bill Sumner, and extensive campaign material are found in Fischer UAA papers.

⊰ Chapter 23 Notes: State Senate ⊱

Records on my state senate service are in the Fischer UAA papers. Wohlforth interviewed Nancy Groszek and Joe Josephson about this period separately on April 28, 2010.

The paper on sustainability of state spending was Scott Goldsmith, "The Three Basic Policy Questions Concerning the Permanent Fund: Remarks Made Before the Board of Trustees of the Alaska Permanent Fund," Institute of Social and Economic Research, October 22, 1981. It was provided by Goldsmith.

The history of the Alaska Permanent Fund is covered in Dave Rose as told to Charles Wohlforth, *Saving for the Future: My Life and the Alaska Permanent Fund* (Kenmore, Washington: Epicenter Press, 2008).

⊰ Chapter 24 Notes: Transitions ⊱

I have all the material from the Diomede appearance in a folder in the Fischer UAA papers, dated May 14, 1985. My angry note to myself about the legislature, dated May 9, 1984, is in my personal papers. My testimony to the Alaska House Finance Committee, April 14, 1977, is in my personal files.

Besides the voluminous files on the 1986 election in the Fischer UAA papers, a summary of the Fischer-Uehling race and campaign finances is in Larry Makinson, *Open Secrets: The 1986 Alaska Elections* (Anchorage: Rosebud Publishing, 1987).

My report on Alaska's late-1980s economic depression is covered in Don Hunter, "Mayor Gets Grim View of Economy," in *The Anchorage Daily News,* February 24, 1988.

On the Friendship Flight, Wohlforth interviewed David Ramseur, February 25, 2011. Details of Dixie Belcher's involvement are found in clippings and letters in my personal files. The return visit was richly described in Larry Campbell and Stan Jones, "One good time," in *The Anchorage Daily News,* February 26, 1989.

⊰ Chapter 25 Notes: Russian Reconnection ⊱

I produced extremely detailed typed notes of the June–July 1974 visit to the USSR, which are in my personal files, where I also have a report arising from the September 1975 trip, calling for a new program: Victor Fischer and Edwin B. Crittenden, "Proposed Program for US–USSR Cooperation on Community Planning and Construction in the Far North," prepared for US Department of Housing and Urban Development, Washington, DC; Fairbanks, Institute of Social and Economic Research, June/December 1976.

My friend Svetlana Grigor'evna Fedorova wrote a book about Russian America, which was published in English as *The Russian Population in Alaska and California, Late 18th Century to 1867,* translated from the Russian edition of 1971 by Richard A. Pierce and Alton S. Donnelly (Kingston, Ontario: Limestone Press, 1973). The original title was *Русское население Аляски и Калифорнии: конец XVIII века.*

Markus Wolf's autobiography, *Man Without a Face* (see Chapter 7 notes) is readable and complete, and includes the quotation from his diary about writing *Die Troika* (also cited in Chapter 1 notes). Perspective is provided by a review of the autobiography by David Wise, "Spy vs. Spy," *New York Times,* July 13, 1997, and by Mark Landler, "Markus Wolf, 83, Spymaster with the Hidden Face, Dies," *New York Times,* November 10, 2006. The booing of his 1989 speech and bad actions as a spy chief, is from Wolfram Weimer, "Former East German Spy Chief Was a Man on the Run," *German Tribune* (in English), September 29, 1991.

Vadya Popov's letter to me, December 10, 1990, is in my personal papers. It didn't reach me until March 1991. He also provided me with answers to written questions I sent in the process of researching the book, covering his father's death and his wartime experiences.

The experience of reuniting with my classmates and friends in Moscow is indelible in my memory. I also have extensive material on this period, including interviews and talks that I gave during the 1990s, e-mails and other documents, all in my personal papers.

I wrote an essay, "How I Found My New Brother," which is in my papers. The article that alerted me to Tatiana Leshchenko-Sukhomlina's book is by Bella Ezerskaya in *Novoye Russkoye Slovo [Russian Daily],* April 25–26, 1992. Tatiana's book itself is titled *Dolgoye Budushcheye [A Long Future]* (Moscow: Sovetskii Pisatel', 1991). In response to my request, my brother Vanya Leshchenko provided details on his life in a series of e-mails, March 18, 2011. Tatiana's letter to her friend, "Vanya is wonderful," is in Joseph Paull, "Reports on Russian Bare Love Tragedy," *Washington Post,* June 12, 1949.

ᢒ Chapter 26 Notes: Working Internationally ᢓ

Voluminous files covering the last twenty years of my work in Russia are in my personal papers, including letters, e-mails, transcripts of lectures and interviews, articles, clippings, reports, and so on. In addition, Wohlforth conducted four interviews with Andrew Crow and John Tichotsky, individually and together with me and Jane Angvik, December 9, 2010, to February 8, 2011. The article speculating about our nefarious motives was "Chukchi in their Chum wait for an American Dawn" in the magazine *Dalnevostochyi Kapital.* I do not have the date.

Key correspondence with Senator Stevens were Victor Fischer to Ted Stevens, October 29, 1990; Ted Stevens to Vic Fischer, November 16, 1990; and Vic Fischer to Ted Stevens, September 16, 1991. All are in my personal papers.

⊰ Chapter 27 Notes: Russian Endings ⊱

The sources mentioned in the previous chapter were used here, too. Anarik's book *If I Don't Speak,* is cited in Chapter 7 notes.

In all, Abramovich is believed to have spent $2 billion helping Chukotka: Evgeniya Chaykovskaya, "'School before sport' urges Russia's audit chamber boss," at TheMoscowNews.com, July 13, 2011.

⊰ Chapter 28 Notes: Secrets to a Long Life ⊱

All sources for the chapter are in my personal papers, including letters, itineraries, and a recording made immediately after the Telequana adventure.

Ann Baltzo's article about my Pribilof swim was in *Alaska* magazine, January 1977. The quotation about Dave Loeks on the Tatshenshini River is from a long handwritten letter addressed to Jane Angvik, dated August 10, 1991, which was written over a series of days and probably never mailed, in my personal papers.

Acknowledgments

For many years I promised to write the stories of my life. And I would still be saying that, if not for the help of many people, only a few of whom I have room to thank here.

In producing this work, I was assisted by my brilliant book partner, Charles Wohlforth, who so thoroughly immersed himself in the research and writing that he came to know more about me than anyone else, myself included. He captured my stories more vividly than I could do on my own. The work involved months of interviews, documentary research, repeated drafts, and discussion of innumerable details. Eventually my voice was enhanced with his talent and the book emerged as a shared creation. Charles is a gifted tactition and a generous human being. He has been an inspiration and a delight to work with.

Marissa Palmer, who is smart, efficient, and always cheerful, organized my materials and faithfully transcribed hundreds of hours of interviews Charles conducted with me and with others, right through her pregnancy.

The interviews with old friends and intimates renewed my memory and brought perspective to what I believed about my life. My wife, Jane Angvik, not only engaged in this process but generously allowed her private life to be included in my public story. She also made invaluable contributions as a reader of many drafts of the manuscript and painstakingly helped with selection of photographs. My first wife, Gloria Fischer, also consented to an interview and allowed me to share our story in print.

Those whom Wohlforth interviewed also included Ginger Baim, Ed and Kit Crittenden, Andrew Crow, Yonni Fischer, Scott Goldsmith, Lee Gorsuch, Nancy Groszek, Katie Hurley, Joe Josephson, Don Mitchell, Tom Morehouse, Bill Parker, David Ramseur, Malcolm Roberts, John Tichotsky, Charlie and Molly Tryck, and Arlon Tussing. The chapter notes are fuller acknowledgment of those who lent information to the project.

Several generous friends reviewed the manuscript and offered helpful corrections. Nan Elliot, an accomplished author and editor in her own right, not only edited the initial draft but also spent weeks listening to it being read aloud. She posed many insightful questions that affected my thinking about the substance and structure of the book.

Tom Morehouse and Andrew Crow reviewed many sections of the manuscript and provided wise counsel. John Tichotsky filled in critical blanks. Fairbanks friend Terrence Cole dug up material I would never have located. During Jane's and my visit with his family, Bob Rubadeau woke from a dream in the middle of the night with the perfect title for the book. That's what good friends are for.

My brother Vanya Leshchenko devoted endless time channeling information from Russian sources, finding archival materials and photos, and obtaining consent to use them from people and institutions in Russia. Many required hours of painstaking persuasion on his part to engage institutional gatekeepers. The twelve-hour time difference between our homes was navigated thanks to our discovery of the Internet.

Moscow classmates from the 1930s—Lena Kostyakova, Vadya Popov, and Maya Turovskaya—provided me with invaluable information and insights, and I am joyous to have them in my life again. Alexander Pelyasov was helpful as always, particularly with respect to our colleague and friend Alexander Granberg.

Eva Wloch and her sons Lothar and Holgar filled in parts of history unknown to me and, with their families, opened their hearts and hosted us repeatedly in Berlin.

Grants from the University of Alaska Foundation paid for professional assistance to research and draft the book, as well as to gather and organize a vast amount of information collected over a lifetime. UA Presidents Mark Hamilton and Pat Gamble made most of this support happen. University Vice Presidents Karen Perdue and Wendy Redman believed in the book project and helped see to it that the resources became available. Chancellors Brian Rogers, Fran Ulmer, and Tom Case also gave wonderful support and encouragment. Without them, this book would not be.

The same can be said for the Rasmuson Foundation and its president, Diane Kaplan, who took a personal interest in the project and provided critical financial support.

My office at UAA's Institute of Social and Economic Research remains my professional home, with friends and traditions that help anchor me. ISER Business Manager Marcia Trudgen enthusiastically gave me invaluable help, as did ISER Fiscal Manager Linda Grant.

Joan Braddock, James Engelhardt, Sue Mitchell, and Amy Simpson were our faithful guides through the University of Alaska Press's publishing process. My utmost appreciation for making this book a reality.

Librarians and archivists make work such as this possible. Many helped, but I received particular kindness from the staff at Princeton University's Seeley G. Mudd Manuscript Library, especially Amanda Hawk, Daniel Linke, and Helene van Rossum, who organized the voluminous Louis Fischer archive. My thanks also to Arlene Schmuland, Megan Friedel, and Mariecris Gotlabayan, who were wonderfully forthcoming in providing access to the UAA/APU Consortium Library archives.

Katya Nekrasova, Zilya's granddaughter, came from Moscow and helped me copy some of my family's voluminous correspondence at the Princeton library. She also tracked down critical video footage.

While writing the book, I constantly wanted to mention people who were part of my life, who worked with me, and who contributed to the state and institutions I was a part of. However, my coauthor and editors were adamant about not breaking the flow of the narrative with such detail. As a result, it may appear that I give myself more credit than I deserve for many accomplishments, including the book itself.

Here, inadequately, I sincerely thank many, many friends, colleagues, and supporters—named and unnamed—for enriching my life. I am grateful for all the grand schemes, invigorating work, engaging dinners, and the joyful travels and crazy stuff we've engaged in together.

My four children—Yonni, Greg, Joe, and Ruth—as well as their spouses and children, are the inspiration for this book. You now have a more coherent record of my life's stories than my typical ramblings. Thanks for the joy you've given me. I love you all.

Index

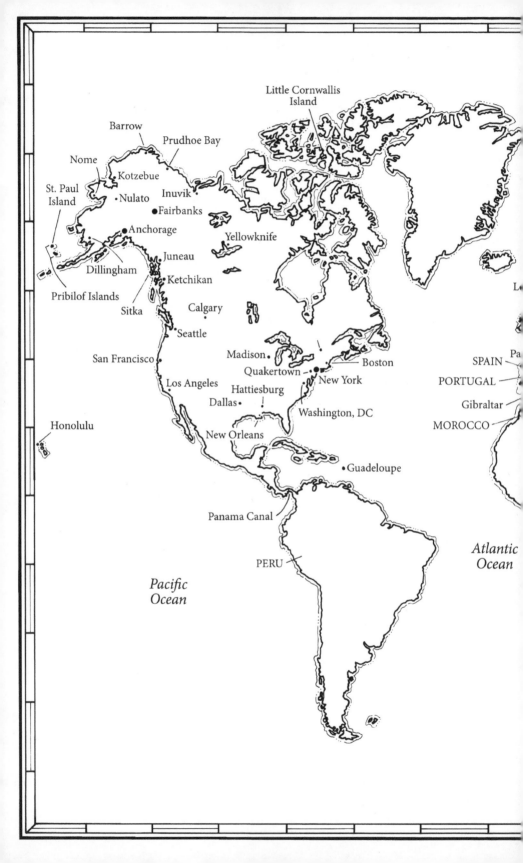

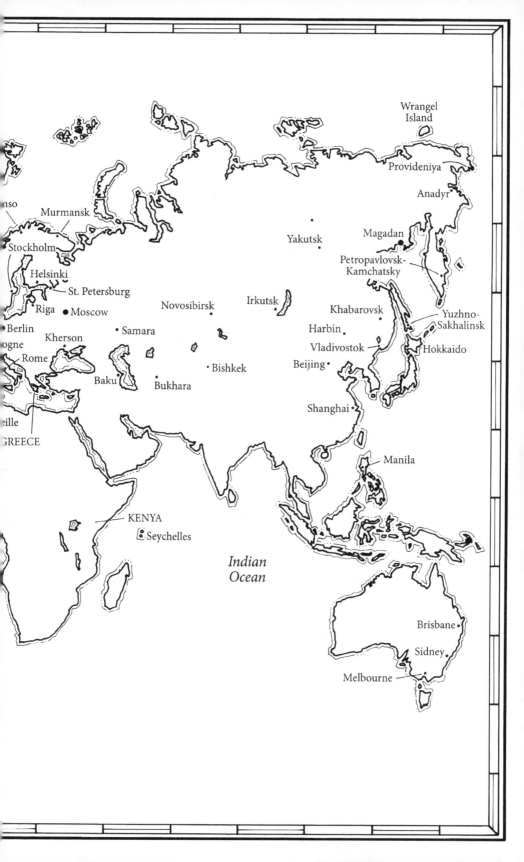